"AND SCRIPTURE CANNOT BE BROKEN"

SUPPLEMENTS TO
NOVUM TESTAMENTUM

VOLUME XCVI

"AND SCRIPTURE CANNOT BE BROKEN"

The Form and Function of the Early Christian
Testimonia *Collections*

BY

MARTIN C. ALBL

BRILL
LEIDEN · BOSTON · KÖLN
1999

This book is printed on acid-free paper.

Library of Congress Cataloging-in-Publication Data

Albl, Martin C.
    And scripture cannot be broken : the form and function of the
early Christian Testimonia collections / by Martin C. Albl.
        p.   cm. — (Supplements to Novum Testamentum, ISSN 0167-9732 ;
v. 96)
    Includes bibliographical references and index.
    ISBN 9004114173 (cloth : alk. paper)
    1. Bible.   O.T.—Quotations in the New Testament.   2. Bible.
O.T.—Quotations, Early.   I. Title.   II. Series.
BS2387.A43   1999
221'.09'015—dc21   99-11377
                                                                                                    CIP

Die Deutsche Bibliothek - CIP-Einheitsaufnahme

Albl, Martin C.:
"And scripture cannot be broken" : the form and function of the early
Christian testimonia collections / by Martin C. Albl. - Leiden ;
Boston ; Köln : Brill, 1999
    (Supplements to Novum testamentum ; Vol. 96)
    ISBN 90–04–11417–3
[Novum testamentum / Supplements]
Supplements to Novum testamentum. - Leiden ; Boston ; Köln : Brill
Früher Schriftenreihe
    Fortlaufende Beiheftreihe zu: Novum testamentum
Vol. 96. Albl, Martin C.: "And scripture cannot be broken" - 1999

ISSN   0167-9732
ISBN   90 04 11417 3

Meinen Eltern

CONTENTS

PREFACE

This book has its origins in my interest in early Christian use of the Jewish scriptures. A primary focus of this interest has long been the twin references to scripture in the tradition related by Paul "that Christ died for our sins according to the scriptures, that he was buried, and that he rose again on the third day according to the scriptures" (1 Cor 15:3–4). Do these phrases refer to scripture as a whole or to particular passages? If particular passages, which ones? What is the rhetorical force of "according to the scripture"? How did these references to scripture become part of an authoritative tradition accepted by Paul? The answers to these questions, it seemed, would take one back to the very beginnings of Christianity.

As I began research into early Christian exegesis, my attention was quickly drawn to the so-called *testimonia* hypothesis—the proposition that the earliest Christians collected, edited, and gave authoritative interpretations to a select group of scriptural quotations which served as proof-texts for basic Christian beliefs. This theory, popular earlier in this century but little discussed today, attracted me as the most plausible explanation for common early Christian scriptural traditions. In this book, I wish to recover the insights of the great *testimonia* scholars such as Rendel Harris and C.H. Dodd; at the same time, however, I wish to update their theories by engaging them with recent work on scriptural collections at Qumran and in the patristic era. The result, I hope, is to shed some light on an intensive and sophisticated exegetical activity which began prior to the writing of the New Testament documents.

A few remarks on style are in order here. Abbreviations follow the standards of the 1994 *SBL Membership Directory and Handbook*, with the following exceptions: EC=extract collection and TC=*testimonia* collection. In tables, A=allusion, Q=(direct) quotation, and UQ= unknown quotation. I cite Psalms by their Masoretic numbering with the Septuagint numbering in parentheses; in tables only the Masoretic numbering is given for sake of space. All scriptural quotations are NRSV unless otherwise noted.

This book is a lightly revised version of my dissertation, accepted at Marquette University in August 1997. My work therefore interacts very little with scholarship published since that time.

A book is never written in a vacuum, and I have been most fortunate to be a part of a true scholarly community of fellow graduate students and faculty at Marquette University over the past five years. Among my many excellent teachers at Marquette, I wish to acknowledge in particular the members of my dissertation board: Carol Stockhausen, who guided my first steps into the study of early Christian exegesis; William Kurz, S.J., who served as an expert on Luke-Acts and issues of method; Michel Barnes, who helped me remain engaged with patristic studies; and Deirdre Dempsey, who was a patient instructor of Hebrew. My greatest debt is due my director, Julian Hills, who went far beyond the call of duty in his meticulous editing and careful written and verbal responses to my work; at the same time he entrusted me with a great amount of freedom in pursuing my own vision of this project.

The Marquette University Department of Theology awarded me a dissertation fellowship for 1995–96, and the President's Council of Marquette funded the Reverend John P. Raynor, S.J. Fellowship, which I received for 1996–97. Their generous financial support allowed me the luxury of devoting my full attention to this project; without this support the work would have been much the poorer.

I am grateful to Professor David P. Moessner for accepting my manuscript in *Supplements to Novum Testamentum*, and to Mr. Theo Joppe and the rest of the editorial staff at Brill for their unfailing courtesy and professionalism in the process of turning the manuscript into a book.

I wish also to thank my wife Judy, my daughter Maddie, and my son Daniel, who was born as this book reached its final stages. They have constantly supported my work, while at the same time reminding me that there is more to life than academic pursuits! Finally, I wish to recognize my father and mother: it is to them that I dedicate this work.

Martin C. Albl
Presentation College
Aberdeen SD

INTRODUCTION

The influence of the Hebrew scriptures (Old Testament) on New Testament and other early Christian thought and literature is hard to overestimate. Early Christian writers often used quotations from the Hebrew scriptures to demonstrate the continuity between these sacred writings and their faith centered on Jesus Christ. The Gospel of Matthew, for example, has fifty-four scriptural quotations, while Paul has sixty quotations in his letter to the Romans alone.[1] More subtly, early Christians used scripture allusively and implicitly: scripture provided models and patterns which were used to describe and reveal the significance of Jesus and the emerging Christian church. In these early writings, Jesus was often portrayed as the suffering righteous one who would be vindicated (a portrait drawn from patterns in Psalms and Isaiah) and the Christian church was understood as the new Israel (Hosea and Jeremiah 31 provided the models for these claims). Scripture provided the basic categories of Christian thought: covenant, salvation, messiah. Early Christian use of scripture can rightly be called the "sub-structure" of NT theology.[2]

Scripture was not read as an undifferentiated whole, however. From the beginning, Christians quoted or alluded to certain passages or sections of scripture more than others. Psalm 110:1, for example, is quoted eight times in the NT and alluded to another ten times; the Song of Solomon, on the other hand, is neither quoted nor, apparently, even alluded to in the NT. Similarly, the models of Abraham's faith and the endurance of the suffering righteous one in Psalms were far more important than stories in the book of Judges.

Nevertheless, identifying precisely which scriptural passages and patterns were central for early Christians, and asking just how and why these passages and patterns were chosen, is a complex task. One proposal, which came to be called the *testimonia* hypothesis, held that early Christians gathered, edited, and gave authoritative status to collections of scriptural excerpts. The term *testimonia* refers to the

---

[1] Quotation and allusion statistics are taken from the indices of the UBSGNT 4th ed.

[2] This is the apt phrase of C.H. Dodd (*According to the Scriptures: The Sub-structure of New Testament Theology* [London: Nisbet, 1952]).

proposed legal or forensic function of these supposed collections: they were used as "witnesses" to, or "proofs" of, Christian beliefs.

The discussion of *testimonia* in twentieth-century scriptural research has been dominated by three scholars: J. Rendel Harris, C.H. Dodd, and Barnabas Lindars. Harris proposed that prior to the NT writings a *Testimony Book* was compiled under the authority of the apostle Matthew.[3] This *Book* consisted of topically arranged scriptural proof-texts that fell into two major categories: proofs of christological beliefs (e.g., that Jesus, the messiah, had to suffer) and anti-Jewish proofs (God had rejected the Jews as his people and had instead chosen the Christians). Harris was led to this conjecture by two major pieces of evidence: (1) extant patristic writings in which scriptural *testimonia* are indeed topically arranged (especially Cyprian's *To Quirinus* [248 CE] and Ps.-Gregory of Nyssa's *Against the Jews* [ca. 400 CE]), and (2) peculiarities in early Christian quotations of scripture (use of non-standard [i.e., non-MT and non-LXX] texts, conflated quotations, false attributions, the same series of quotations in independent authors) which suggested that the Christians were not quoting directly from scriptural manuscripts, but rather from collections of proof-texts. Harris held that the Testimony Book was developed and employed in a context of early Christian-Jewish debate and conflict.

C.H. Dodd followed Harris in isolating a central core of scriptural *testimonia* used by NT writers, arguing for the pervasive influence of these select *testimonia* passages on earliest Christian thought.[4] He rejected, however, Harris's proposal of a *Testimony Book* influential in NT times, arguing that written collections were a later development. Dodd attributed this common use to Christian oral tradition in which certain larger sections of scripture were considered *testimonia* blocks. Dodd recognized three major groups of *testimonia*: apocalyptic-eschatological scriptures (e.g., Joel 2–3; Zechariah 9–14); scriptures of the New Israel (Hosea; Jeremiah 31); and scriptures of the Servant of the Lord and the righteous sufferer (Psalm 22; Isaiah 53). The quotation of a single verse from any one of these *testimonia* blocks was enough to evoke the whole passage.

Barnabas Lindars accepted the main lines of Dodd's argument, but filled out in much greater detail the life-setting in which these

---

[3] Harris, *Testimonies* (2 vols.; Cambridge: Cambridge University Press, 1916–20).
[4] Dodd, *According to the Scriptures*.

testimonia were employed.[5] For Lindars, early Christian use of scripture was primarily apologetic, an often highly sophisticated exegetical response to Jewish objections against basic Christian beliefs. Lindars showed the flexibility of this apologetic tradition: the same *testimonium* could be applied to different situations. Isaiah 6:9–10, for example, was used both to explain the Jews' rejection of early Christian proclamation (Acts 28:25–28) and to explain why those "outside" heard but could not understand Jesus' parables (Mark 4:12).

Since Lindars's book, there has been little direct discussion of the *testimonia* hypothesis in scriptural studies.[6] Research in fields outside of NT studies proper, however, has re-opened the debate on the possible use of written *testimonia* and other scriptural excerpt collections in the early church. The Dead Sea Scrolls, especially documents such as 4QTestimonia, offer concrete evidence that a variety of Jewish scriptural collections were employed at a time contemporary with earliest Christianity. In the patristic field, studies of *Barnabas* and Justin's *First Apology* and *Dialogue with Trypho* have established that these second-century works used written Christian *testimonia* collections as authoritative scripture, and that such collections continued to be influential well into the fourth century.[7] Despite some preliminary comments, the full implications of these Jewish and patristic studies for *testimonia* use in the NT and earliest Christianity have not yet been worked out.[8]

The contribution of this study will be to draw out some of these implications with an investigation of the form and function of the earliest Christian *testimonia* and other scriptural excerpt collections. The study of course builds on the work of earlier scholars, but attempts to combine their insights in a comprehensive manner. For

---

[5] Lindars, *New Testament Apologetic: The Doctrinal Significance of the Old Testament Quotations* (Philadelphia: Westminster, 1961).

[6] An exception is Robert Hodgson ("The Testimony Hypothesis," *JBL* 98 [1979] 361–78), who provides an overview of research into NT *testimonia* together with his own proposals.

[7] On *Barnabas*, see Pierre Prigent, *Les Testimonia dans le christianisme primitif: L'Epître de Barnabé 1–16 et ses sources* (EBib; Paris: Gabalda, 1961); on Justin, see Oskar Skarsaune, *The Proof from Prophecy. A Study in Justin Martyr's Proof-Text Tradition: Text-Type, Provenance, Theological Profile* (NovTSup 56; Leiden: Brill, 1987); on the general influence of patristic *testimonia* collections, see Jean Daniélou, *Etudes d'exégèse judéo-chrétienne (Les Testimonia)* (Théologie Historique 5; Paris: Beauschesne, 1966).

[8] A start is made in Joseph A. Fitzmyer, "'4QTestimonia' and the New Testament," *TS* 18 (1957) 513–38; repr. in idem, *Essays on the Semitic Background of the New Testament* (SBLSBS 5; Missoula, MT: Scholars Press, 1974) 59–89.

example, while Harris's view of a single *Testimony Book* has been rightly
abandoned, the criteria with which he and others uncovered scriptural
collections in early Christian literature remain valid. Dodd insight-
fully pointed out Christian use of broad sections of scripture, yet his
underestimation of early Christian use of non-contextual proof-texts
and of evidence for written *testimonia* collections needs correction.
Lindars demonstrated the importance of early Christian apologetical
efforts aimed at Jews, but his proposal should be placed within a
broader framework that shows how Christians also employed *testimonia* (often in written form) for didactic, catechetical, parenetic, and
compositional (i.e., using scripture as a model for composing narratives) functions.

Although this study focuses major attention on evidence for *testimonia* and scriptural collections within the NT, I place this NT phenomenon within the larger context not only of Jewish and patristic
scriptural collections, but also of contemporary Greco-Roman literary customs. Ancient Greco-Roman literature was filled with anthologies and extract collections, used especially for teaching purposes;
this same spirit of the pedagogic collector permeates early Christian
collections of scripture as well. The Jewish background, in particular the Dead Sea Scrolls, is essential for providing analogies of early
written scriptural collections which served a variety of functions:
forensic, didactic, compositional, and liturgical. Beyond these formal
and functional parallels, striking content parallels are also evident:
Christians often drew on messianic and liturgical collections first
compiled by Jews. Finally, the study of the patristic evidence is important not only to show development of, or continuity with, NT traditions, but also to emphasize that scriptural traditions based on written
collections of scripture were transmitted independently of both Jewish
and Christian scriptural manuscripts.

In my first chapter, a review of the scholarly literature, I attempt
both to present the results of previous scholarship and to clarify central issues of terminology and method. Since the *testimonia* discussion
has often been hampered by lack of precise terminology, I argue for
clear distinctions between *testimonia* collections (which serve forensically to "prove" a certain point) and other scriptural groupings (liturgical or didactic collections) and literary genres (e.g., midrash, sermons)
which also collect scriptural quotations. Criteria used to distinguish
between an author's use of a scriptural collection and that author's
direct use of scripture, together with criteria to differentiate written

collections from oral tradition, are synthesized and evaluated. In presenting the various *testimonia* studies, I evaluate the methods that each scholar uses in identifying the form, function, and original life-setting of actual or proposed *testimonia* sources.

In chapter two, I consider the *testimonia* hypothesis against the background of both ancient Greco-Roman and Second Temple Jewish literature. Greco-Roman literature contains a wide variety of collections of extracted material, ranging from the poetic anthology to the philosophical handbook, much of it used in a didactic or "school" setting. This literature offers analogies to Christian *testimonia* collections in content (oracle collections), in form (thematic collections), and in function (use of quotations as witnesses to establish claims). The Jewish material also contains numerous examples of liturgical, didactic, and thematic scriptural collections, both with and without commentary.

In chapter three, I present extant examples of *testimonia* collections from the patristic era. Particular attention is given to the studies of Pierre Prigent on *Barnabas* and Oskar Skarsaune on Justin, which establish the existence of authoritative *testimonia* collections in the first half of the second century. *Testimonia* groupings, often marked by non-standard, conflated or otherwise edited quotations, can be traced in Greek, Latin, and Syriac Christian writings throughout the first three Christian centuries and indeed beyond. This chapter documents the considerable geographic and temporal range of these *testimonia* collections and provides evidence that these collections were transmitted in authoritative, written collections independently of the NT and other early Christian writings.

A great number of these patristic collections are arranged in a creedal pattern, i.e., the topically arranged proof-texts correspond to events in the life and work of Jesus (incarnation, healings, suffering, death, and resurrection) and to other central Christian beliefs. A common core of proof-texts and exegetical traditions is remarkably consistent throughout many of these collections; at the same time, the tradition shows fluidity in local variation of texts and in the application of standard *testimonia* to new situations. The most likely life-setting for this pattern of continuity and flexibility is Christian teaching: the creedal proof-texts may have formed part of catechetical instruction; Christian missionaries and teachers may well have been equipped with small *testimonia* collections designed for ready reference.

Chapters four and five argue that the roots of the patristic *testimonia* tradition are already evident in the NT. Chapter four focuses on the probable use of *testimonia* collections in four sections of the NT: Paul's writings, Matthew's formula ("fulfillment") citations, the speeches in Acts, and Hebrews 1–2. Chapter five has a broader focus, tracing common *testimonia* across a variety of NT writings: the use of Ps 110:1, messianic collections (Gen 49:9–11; Num 24:7; Isa 11:1, 10), "hardening" *testimonia* (using adapted versions of Isa 6:9–10), a reworked version of Zech 12:10, and the "stone" *testimonia* tradition. These examples show reliance both on written collections and on more general oral tradition. Against a current scholarly tendency to attribute this exegetical work to the creativity of NT writers, I argue that authoritative Christian exegetical traditions, often in the form of written *testimonia* collections and exegetical comments, were established even before the earliest NT compositions.

CHAPTER ONE

REVIEW OF THE SCHOLARLY LITERATURE ON THE *TESTIMONIA* HYPOTHESIS

1.1 *Overview of the Chapter*

In this chapter I will review and evaluate the modern scholarly literature on the *testimonia* hypothesis. Rather than presenting each scholar's work discretely, I will attempt to trace the larger contexts and movements within which scholars developed their proposals. This review has two major goals: to clarify terminology and to evaluate the method by which scholars reached their conclusions.

As a step to the first goal, I wish to present each scholar's understanding of the term *testimonia*. While Harris used the term to refer to actual or hypothetical written collections of OT proof-texts, Dodd and Lindars used the same word to refer to common uses of scripture rooted in oral traditions. Again, while most scholars properly associate the term *testimonia* with the forensic function of proving theological assertions, a significant number of others have applied the term more broadly to collections of scriptural passages which serve other functions. To keep this latter distinction clear, I will use the short-hand terms EC (extract collection) for general scriptural collections, and TC (*testimonia* collections) for those collections that function as proofs. In my review of the literature, I will summarize and comment on each author's understanding of the form, genre, life-setting, and function of *testimonia* as far as judgments can be made from his or her statements.[1]

---

[1] This study is first and foremost a *literary* study of the *testimonia* genre and its forms in early Christianity. Although I do address to some extent the social setting in which this literature was produced, space precludes a thorough analysis of this important aspect.

The distinction between "form" and "genre" is often not clear in scholarly use. I use the term "form" for shorter, less complex structures (e.g., a list) which are capable of independent transmission, and "genre" for longer, more complex literary forms (e.g., a gospel). For similar distinctions, see James L. Bailey and Lyle D. Vander Broek, *Literary Forms in the New Testament: A Handbook* (Louisville, KY: Westminster/John Knox, 1992) 13–14. I thus understand *testimonia* as a genre which may take a variety of forms.

My second goal is to discuss the *method* employed by scholars in reaching their conclusions regarding *testimonia*. Since much of the *testimonia* debate has centered on developing sound criteria to establish the use of written TCs in a given document, I will pay special attention to each scholar's treatment of this question. At the same time, I will also consider the steps that scholars have taken to reach conclusions regarding wider issues of the form, function, life-setting, and theological influence of actual and hypothetical ECs and TCs. At the end of this chapter, I will offer a summary in which I list and evaluate what I judge to be the central issues that have been raised in the scholarly discussion.[2]

1.2 Modern Scholarly Investigations of Scriptural Quotations in the New Testament

Quotations of the Old Testament in the New have long occasioned scholarly interest.[3] Early studies presented the OT quotations as messianic prophecies, fulfilled in the life and work of Jesus, which functioned as proofs for the truth of Christianity. A representative statement of this position is found in a 1731 study of the NT quotations by Hermann Samuel Reimarus, who maintained that the truth of Christianity is most strongly supported by the OT prophecies and the miracles of Jesus and the apostles.[4] Already seven years earlier, however, the English Deist Anthony Collins had challenged this posi-

---

[2] Useful summaries of the history of the *testimonia* hypothesis include James Moffatt, *An Introduction to the Literature of the New Testament* (International Theological Library; New York: Scribner, 1911) 24–25; E. Earle Ellis, *Paul's Use of the Old Testament* (Edinburgh: Oliver & Boyd, 1957) 98–107; Prigent, *Testimonia*, 16–28; L.W. Barnard, "The Use of Testimonies in the Early Church and in the Epistle of Barnabas," in idem, *Studies in the Apostolic Fathers and their Background* (New York: Schocken, 1967) 109–13; Krister Stendahl, *The School of St. Matthew and Its Use of the Old Testament* (2d ed.; Philadelphia: Fortress, 1968) 207–17; Joseph A. Fitzmyer, "4Q Testimonia"; Martin Rese, *Alttestamentliche Motive in der Christologie des Lukas* (SNT 1; Gütersloh: Mohn, 1969) 217–23; Hodgson, "Testimony"; Harry Y. Gamble, *Books and Readers in the Early Church: A History of Early Christian Texts* (New Haven/London: Yale University Press, 1995) 25–28.

[3] The earliest list of quotations seems to be that of Robert Stephens, which he prefixed to his edition of the Greek NT (Paris, 1550); so Robert Gough, *The New Testament Quotations Collated with the Scriptures of the Old Testament* (London: Walton and Maberly, 1855) iii.

[4] Reimarus, "Religionis Christianae veritas duobus maxime fulcris nititur, scilicet vaticiniis Veteris Tti et miraculis Jesu Christi atque apostolorum." See Peter Stemmer, ed., Hermann Samuel Reimarus, *Vindicatio dictorum Veteris Testamenti in Novo allegatorum*

tion with his anonymously published *A Discourse of the Grounds and Reasons of the Christian Religion* (London, 1724). Here Collins argued that OT texts cannot be used to "prove" that Jesus was the messiah, indeed the texts do not speak of Jesus at all.[5] Collins's work, and that of the German Johann Lorenz Schmidt, who denied the applicability of the messianic passages in the Pentateuch to Jesus ("Wertheimer Bibel," 1735), provoked immediate reactions.[6] While the hermeneutical controversy over the legitimacy of applying OT quotations to Jesus is not part of modern *testimonia* discussions proper, it is of interest to note that the same apologetic concern that first led to the collection of these passages was also a motivating factor behind many of the first modern studies of OT quotations.

1.3 *Nineteenth Century German Roots of* Testimonia *Hypotheses*

Testimonia hypotheses have long focused on determining which specific OT passages were collected by early Christians for use as proof-texts. In 1829, Johann Christian Karl Döpke referred to the possible existence of scriptural *loci classici* which were used by both Jews and early Christians as proof-texts for their positions.[7] Karl August Credner, attempting to account for the LXX-deviant texts in Matthew and Justin, maintained that the earliest Palestinian Christians "searched the scriptures" to match OT passages to the life and teachings of Jesus in order to prove that Jesus was the messiah. He referred to these passages, which he argued were first drawn from Hebrew and Aramaic sources and then translated into Greek, as the *das alttestamentliche Urevangelium*, a central part of the early Christian oral tradition. Credner pointed to passages such as Zech 12:12 and Dan 7:13 (quoted in Rev 1:7 and Matt 24:30) as original passages of this Ur-Gospel.[8] Both Credner and Döpke, however, said little concerning

---

1731: Text der Pars I und Conspectus der Pars II (Göttingen: Vandenhoeck & Ruprecht, 1983) 38.

[5] See Stemmer, *Vindicatio*, 10.

[6] For the history of these early controversies, see ibid., 10–11, 61–68. On Lorenz Schmidt and the Wertheimer Bibel, see Emanuel Hirsch, *Geschichte der Neuern Evangelischen Theologie im Zusammenhang mit den allgemeinen Bewegungen des europäischen Denkens* (5 vols.; 3d ed.; Münster: Stenderhoff, 1984) 2. 417–38.

[7] Döpke, *Hermeneutik der neutestamentlichen Schriftsteller* (Leipzig: Vogel, 1829) 54.

[8] Credner, *Beiträge zur Einleitung in die biblischen Schriften*, vol. 2: *Das alttestamentliche Urevangelium* (Halle: Waisenhaus, 1838) 318–28.

the precise form and life-settings of these scriptural collections.[9]

Carl Weizsäcker, reflecting on the similarity of Paul's use of the OT in Galatians and Romans, proposed that the apostle had made a collection of scriptural passages which formed an outline of his theology on various topics. Paul used this collection as he had occasion during the composition of his letters.[10] Weizsäcker here anticipated the more sophisticated analyses of Christopher D. Stanley and Dietrich-Alex Koch, who argue for Paul's use of a personal scriptural anthology in the composition of his letters.[11]

1.4   Edwin Hatch's "Excerpta Collections" and German Reaction

Edwin Hatch presented a hypothesis on the use of scriptural extract collections (ECs) which would decisively shape future testimonia discussion. Hatch sketched his ideas briefly and suggestively in the course of his study of OT quotations in Philo, the NT, and the Apostolic Fathers as witnesses for the first-century text of the LXX.[12] He suggested that the literary technique of making collections of OT extracts began in pre-Christian times among the Jews:

> It may naturally be supposed that a race which laid stress on moral progress, whose religious services had variable elements of both prayer and praise, and which was carrying on an active propaganda, would have, among other books, manuals of morals, of devotion, and of controversy. It may also be supposed, if we take into consideration the contemporary habit of making collections of excerpta, and the special authority which the Jews attached to their sacred books, that some of these manuals would consist of extracts from the Old Testament.[13]

Hatch, then, held that these OT extracts appeared in different literary genres ("manuals" of morals, devotion, and controversy), in a variety of life-settings (the worship service; educational or polemical

---

[9] Credner's suggestion that Justin and Matthew use a common non-LXX source for their quotation of Isa 42:1–4 was supported by A. Hilgenfeld in his own study of Justin's OT quotations ("Die alttestamentlichen Citate Justin's in ihrer Bedeutung für die Untersuchung über seine Evangelien," Theologische Jahrbücher 9 [1850] 572).

[10] Weizsäcker, Das apostolische Zeitalter der christlichen Kirche (Freiburg i. B.: Mohr-Siebeck, 1886) 113–14.

[11] See section 4.2.1a below.

[12] Hatch, "On Early Quotations from the Septuagint" and "On Composite Quotations from the Septuagint" in idem, Essays in Biblical Greek (Oxford: Clarendon, 1889) 131–214.

[13] Hatch, "Composite Quotations," 203.

milieus), and served different functions (as religious propaganda or *apologiae*, material for moral instruction, and texts for worship services).[14] The argument is not necessarily for TCs which function as proof-texts, but simply for a general use of ECs. Hatch considered that this Jewish technique of making collections of OT quotations was later taken over by early Christians for their own purposes.

One can distill three basic criteria by which Hatch discerned the use of underlying ECs in a text:

(1) *LXX-deviant readings*: If a quotation deviates from the LXX, Hatch reasoned, this can be explained either by the author's intentional alteration of the text or by the author's quotation from a LXX-deviant source, perhaps "a current manual of Scripture History."[15] The options for an LXX-deviant source, of course, are much more complex than Hatch suggested; I take up this question in my excursus on the LXX (sect. 3.3 below).

(2) *Composite quotations cited by independent authors*: Hatch devoted particular attention to the phenomenon of quotations which combine two or more OT passages. If these same composite quotations are found in authors literarily independent of one another, then dependence on a third source is indicated.[16] Hatch appears to have envisioned this source as a collection of scriptural *excerpta* whose sequence of texts could be traced in later documents which used this source.

(3) *Argument from analogy*: Hatch admitted that he had no direct evidence for his thesis, yet he maintained that it "is not contrary to analogy."[17] Hatch's reference to the "contemporary habit of making *excerpta*" apparently alludes to contemporary Greco-Roman techniques of making ECs or anthologies.[18] Here Hatch drew on his extensive knowledge of hellenistic culture in the early Christian centuries, placing Christian and contemporary Jewish practices into their wider cultural environment.[19] Hatch was a pioneer in his insistence that the NT is not be studied in isolation, but rather is to be understood in

---

[14] Hatch also suggested a form related to ECs: adapted versions of psalms analogous to modern hymn books ("Early Quotations," 180).

[15] Ibid., 163.

[16] Hatch, "Composite Quotations," 203–4. Hatch offered two major examples of this phenomenon: (1) the composite quotation Jer 2:12–13/Isa 16:1–2 found in *Barn.* 11.3 and Justin *Dial.* 114.5; and (2) a composite quotation from several Psalms and an Isaiah passage found in Rom 3:10–18 and *Dial.* 27.3.

[17] Hatch, "Early Quotations," 186.

[18] Hatch, "Composite Quotations," 203.

[19] See esp. his Hibbert Lectures (1888), published as *The Influence of Greek Ideas*

its Greco-Roman context: his criterion of analogy is simply one aspect of this larger program.[20] In chapter two below, I present examples of Greco-Roman ECs that fill out Hatch's programmatic suggestion.

Hatch pointed out that these collections functioned with the same religious *authority* as the scriptures from which they were adapted. *Barnabas*'s adapted psalms, for example, are introduced with the same quotation formulas (e.g., Δαυὶδ λέγει or λέγει κύριος ἐν τῷ προφήτῃ) as quotations taken directly from scripture.[21] Hatch's observation would again be a starting point for future discussion on the authority of scriptural ECs in early Christianity and contemporary Judaism.

Reaction to Hatch's thesis was immediate.[22] In a glowing review of his friend's *Essays*, Adolf von Harnack agreed that in all probability written OT ECs existed in the first and second centuries.[23] Later, in his monumental *History of Dogma*, Harnack judged that "the hypothesis is not yet quite established, but yet it is hardly to be rejected." He proposed "Jewish catechetical and missionary instruction in the Diaspora" as a likely life-setting for such OT *excerpta*, and adduced Christian apologies and the Sybilline books as evidence for their existence in a Christian milieu.[24] The weighty support of Hatch and Harnack helped ensure that the hypothesis of scriptural ECs would receive continued attention.

Hans Arthur Vollmer took up Hatch's thesis in his important study of Paul's scriptural quotations.[25] Vollmer used the hypothesis of scriptural ECs to account for two phenomena noted by Hatch: LXX-

---

and Usages upon the Christian Church (London: Williams and Norgate, 1890; repr. as The Influence of Greek Ideas on Christianity [New York: Harper, 1957]).

[20] For a review of Hatch's contribution, see Stephen Neill and Tom Wright, *The Interpretation of the New Testament: 1861–1986* (2d ed.; Oxford/New York: Oxford University Press, 1988) 147–50.

[21] Hatch, "Early Quotations," 181, 186.

[22] Neill and Wright note that Hatch's 1880 Bampton Lectures, *The Organization of the Early Christian Churches: Eight Lectures Delivered before the University of Oxford in the year 1880* (London: Rivington, 1881; repr. New York: Burt Franklin, 1972), and *The Influence of Greek Ideas* were quickly translated into German by Harnack and Erwin Preuschen respectively; Hatch is a rare example of an English author who received almost immediate recognition in Germany (*Interpretation*, 147–48).

[23] Harnack, Review of Hatch, *Essays in Biblical Greek*, *TLZ* 15 (1890) 300.

[24] Harnack, *History of Dogma* (New York: Russell & Russell, 1958) 175. Trans. of 3d German ed. (1894).

[25] Vollmer, *Die alttestamentlichen Citate bei Paulus: Textkritisch und biblisch-theologisch gewürdigt nebst einem Anhang ueber das Verhältnis des Apostels zu Philo* (Freiburg/Leipzig: Mohr-Siebeck, 1895).

deviant and composite quotations,[26] and agreed with Hatch that these collections had Jewish roots. Vollmer held that some of Paul's quotations show a knowledge of the original Hebrew, and his composite quotations reflect a "rabbinic custom" of combining texts from the Law, the Prophets, and the Writings on the basis of vocabulary or thematic similarity.[27] Jews combined these texts for "dogmatic" purposes: Hab 2:4 and Gen 15:6, for example, had already been combined under the common theme of "faith" before the time of Paul.[28] Vollmer raised important issues which subsequent *testimonia* studies would address: the relationship of *testimonia* to Jewish exegetical techniques and the role of pre-Christian Jewish collections in developing Christian doctrine.[29]

1.5   *An Alternative to Written Collections:* *"Traditional" Scriptural Proof-Texts*

Not all German scholars accepted Hatch's ideas so readily. William Wrede strongly criticized Hatch in his study of the use of the OT in *1 Clement*.[30] Wrede maintained that *Clement*'s composite quotations do not point to use of *testimonia* collections; rather, they are more likely due to other factors: the author's imprecise memory (which inadvertently combined texts), his loose style of quotation (sometimes introducing quotations with λέγει γάρ που), and his occasional decision to combine texts for his own purposes. Finally, Wrede showed that the criterion of "composite quotations used by independent authors" did not apply in individual cases: the agreement between

---

[26] Ibid., 43.

[27] Ibid., 37–38. Vollmer refers to 2 Cor 9:10, in which texts from Hosea, Isaiah, and Deuteronomy are combined. In Greek there is no obvious connection between the texts; it is only in the Hebrew that the common concept of "rain" would have served to bring these texts together (pp. 41–42).

[28] Ibid., 38. Here Vollmer refers to *Exodus Rabba* (see 23.5) as evidence. The use of later rabbinic texts as evidence of first century (or earlier) Jewish or Christian practices is of course problematic.

[29] Vollmer received qualified support from his contemporary Hans Lietzmann. Lietzmann maintained that the composite quotations cited by Hatch and Vollmer were not completely convincing evidence; the strongest argument for the probability of *testimonia* collections is simply the tendency of the times to make anthologies (*An die Galater* [HNT 10; 2d ed.; Tübingen: Mohr-Siebeck, 1923] 34).

[30] Wrede, *Untersuchungen zum ersten Klemensbriefe* (Göttingen: Vandenhoeck & Ruprecht, 1891) 65–67. Hatch had cited five composite texts from *1 Clement* among his examples.

Rom 3:10–18 and *Dial.* 27:3, for example, is to be explained by Justin's use of an LXX version influenced by Paul, not by a third source used by both.[31] Wrede admitted, however, that *Clement's choice* of OT passages was influenced by a "tradition": he referred to the parallel between *Barn.* 11.3 and *Dial.* 114.5 as traditional anti-Jewish polemic.[32]

Wrede's concession that a "tradition" governed the selection of certain OT passages was echoed and developed by Arthur Freiherr von Ungern-Sternberg.[33] Ungern-Sternberg argued that the early Christians had developed a shared pool of OT texts which they used to "prove" basic Christian beliefs.[34] These beliefs, supported by scriptural quotations, fall into the two major categories of *de Evangelio* and *de Christo*. The *de Christo* passages focused on basic christological beliefs,[35] while the *de Evangelio* texts centered on Christian claims against the Jews: criticism of Jewish ceremonial law, and the contention that Christians had replaced the Jews as God's chosen people.[36] This tradition, however, did not function in a monolithic or mechanical manner. It remained fluid, as texts were added or dropped and themes were developed depending on local circumstances.[37]

The heart of Ungern-Sternberg's argument is a common body of OT proof-texts for each of his *de Christo* and *de Evangelio* categories which he found in the writings of Justin, Irenaeus (especially his *Proof of the Apostolic Preaching*), and Tertullian (in particular his *Against Marcion* and *Against the Jews*).[38] He sought to establish not only that

---

[31] Ibid., 65–67.

[32] Ibid., 66 n. 2.

[33] Ungern-Sternberg, *Der traditionelle alttestamentliche Schriftbeweis "de Christo" und "de Evangelio" in der alten Kirche bis zur Zeit Eusebs von Caesarea* (Halle a. S.: Niemeyer, 1913).

[34] Ungern-Sternberg referred to this process as *traditionelle Schriftbeweis* (SB). The influence of this traditional SB spread over a broad temporal and spatial spectrum: from the time of Paul at least until Eusebius (pp. 191; 295), and over the entire eastern and central Mediterranean coastal lands (p. 230).

[35] Ungern-Sternberg included (1) Christ's pre-existence and divinity; (2) his incarnation (especially the virgin birth); (3) his work as savior and preacher; (4) his humiliation, suffering, and crucifixion; and (5) his resurrection, ascension, and rule at the right hand of the father (p. 47).

[36] Ibid.

[37] Ibid., 141. He rejected the possibility of a written collection of these proof-texts by the second century, as no clear reference to it is made in subsequent literature (p. 140 n. 2).

[38] This is presented in the first part with a wealth of synoptic tables and statis-

the three authors used a common set of OT quotations (*Zitaten-schatz*) which they employed to substantiate the *de Christo* and *de Evangelio* claims, but also that they were independent of one another, and thus dependent on a common tradition.[39] To demonstrate the literary independence of the authors, Ungern-Sternberg noted that: (1) exact agreement in the wording of the quotations and accompanying exegesis is rare; (2) a common order in the presentation of the SB quotations is lacking; (3) the earliest writer, Justin, at times makes a "secondary" use of these texts in comparison with the two later writers.[40]

Ungern-Sternberg's lasting contribution is his detailed collection of OT quotations, showing plainly the existence of a common scriptural tradition in the early church, and his observations on the variety of genres through which this tradition was transmitted: apologies; catechetical material; polemical literature against "pagans," Jews, Marcionites, and gnostic Christians; exegetical and homiletical works; and scriptural ECs and TCs.[41] Christian διδάσκαλοι (see *Barn.* 1.8) and, at a later date, bishops, were the bearers of this tradition. The SB formed an essential part of early Christian instruction (see Origen *Against Celsus* 3.15; Irenaeus *Proof of the Apostolic Preaching*). The major functions of the SB were polemical, apologetical, and didactic.[42] Ungern-Sternberg's conclusions remain valid, although they must be qualified somewhat in the light of recent studies which establish that some kind of literary relationship does in fact obtain between Justin, Irenaeus, and Tertullian.[43]

Concurring with Ungern-Sternberg's model of a common "traditional" use of the OT to witness to major Christian beliefs, Wilhelm Bousset stressed the "school" setting of this activity.[44] Bousset's suggestions were made within the context of his book on Jewish and

---

tics (pp. 4–144). The second part presents further patristic evidence; part three contains evidence for the SB tradition before Justin and concluding observations.

[39] Ibid., 48–49.

[40] Ibid., 49–51.

[41] Ibid., 139–40, 231–33.

[42] Ibid., 233–38.

[43] Oskar Skarsaune argues that Tertullian and Irenaeus show a complex dependence both on Justin directly and on Justin's sources (*Prophecy*, 435–53).

[44] Bousset, *Jüdisch-christlicher Schulbetrieb in Alexandria und Rom: Literarische Untersuchungen zu Philo und Clemens von Alexandria, Justin und Irenäus* (FRLANT n.F. 6/23; Göttingen: Vandenhoeck & Ruprecht, 1915).

early Christian "schools," especially those of Alexandria, which he
argued are the life-setting for many of the exegetical traditions found
in Philo and Clement of Alexandria. Bousset held that the Christian
proof-text collections were *Schulgut* passed down in the form of tractates,[45] developed during the early Christian struggle with the Jews
over the proper interpretation of scripture.[46] For all his emphasis on
the "school," however, Bousset did not discuss the precise structure
or social location of these school activities.[47]

In reaching these conclusions, Bousset argued from essentially the
same core of common texts as had Ungern-Sternberg, drawing his
evidence especially from material common to Justin and Irenaeus's
Demonstration.[48] We see here the importance of the recent publication
of Irenaeus's catechetical work as a catalyst for proposals regarding
early common scriptural traditions.[49] Bousset added a further criterion for detecting the use of a traditional sequence in an author:
when a writer uses a series of quotations without understanding its
original function, he is likely drawing on a previous source.[50]

1.6   *British Support for Hatch's Proposal*

In late nineteenth- and early twentieth-century British scholarship
the proposal that NT writers used authoritative, *written* scriptural
ECs was widely held. Brooke Foss Westcott,[51] William Sanday and

---

[45] For example, in *1 Apology* 31–35; 48–53 Justin follows a tractate featuring scriptural proofs corresponding to events in the life of Jesus.

[46] Ibid., 318.

[47] For a brief critique of Bousset's Alexandrian school thesis as it relates to Philo,
see R. Alan Culpepper, *The Johannine School* (SBLDS 26; Missoula, MT: Scholars
Press, 1975) 204–6.

[48] Ibid., 302–5.

[49] Discovered in 1904, the Armenian text with a German translation was published in 1907 (*Des heiligen Irenäus Schrift zum Erweise der apostolischen Verkündigung: Eis
epideixin tou apostolou kerygmatou, in armenischer Version entdeckt, herausgegeben und in Deutsche
übersetzt von Karapet Ter-Mekerttschian und Erwand Ter-Minassiantz, mit einem Nachwort und
Anmerkungen von A. Harnack* (TU 31, 1; Leipzig, 1906). See below, section 3.4.6, for
discussion of this text.

[50] Ibid., 304 n. 1. For example, Justin uses a sequence of texts to witness to the
divinity of Christ which, Bousset argued (from evidence in Irenaeus), was originally
collected to witness to Christ's ascension (p. 307).

[51] Westcott, *The Epistle to the Hebrews: The Greek Text with Notes and Essays* (2d ed.;
London/New York: Macmillan, 1892; repr. Grand Rapids: Eerdmans, 1955) 476–77,
480. He proposed that Heb 10:30 and 13:5 may derive from a "popular manual"
as envisioned by Hatch.

Arthur C. Headlam,[52] Henry St. John Thackeray,[53] James Drummond,[54] James Moffatt,[55] George Milligan,[56] and Henry Barclay Swete[57] all lent their considerable authority to the thesis. Vincent Henry Stanton offered an important variation to the hypothetical form of TCs in his claim that Matthew's fulfillment citations derive from a "catena of fulfillments of prophecy." This document was written originally in Aramaic; Matthew read it in a Greek translation. This source, Stanton concluded, would not have been a list of quotations alone; rather the scriptural passages must have been accompanied by references to events in the time of Jesus which were understood as the fulfillment of these prophecies.[58]

---

[52] Sanday and Headlam, *A Critical and Exegetical Commentary on the Epistle to the Romans* (ICC; Edinburgh: T. & T. Clark, 1895) 264, 282. In discussing Rom 9:33, they suggest Paul's possible use of a Christian stone collection analogous to Cyprian *Quir.* 2.16 (p. 282; cf. p. 264 on Rom 9:25–26). Nearly twenty years earlier, Sanday had remarked, "We know that types and prophecies were eagerly sought out by the early Christians and were soon collected in a kind of common stock from which every one drew at his pleasure" (*The Gospels in the Second Century* [London: Macmillan, 1876] 272).

[53] Thackeray, *The Relation of St. Paul to Contemporary Jewish Thought: An Essay to which was awarded the Kaye Prize for 1899* (London: Macmillan, 1900) 184–86, 242–45. Thackeray followed Hatch and Vollmer in positing the existence of Jewish anthologies in Paul's time; he found it probable that 1 Cor 2:9 derived from such a collection, though perhaps as an oral tradition. Thackeray, however, did express himself with caution: "The existence of such an anthology [i.e., a Jewish anthology used by Paul] is by no means improbable, but it must be said that no very convincing proofs have yet been brought forward" (p. 184).

[54] Drummond, *An Inquiry into the Character and Authorship of the Fourth Gospel* (London: Williams & Norgate, 1903) 365. Drummond explained some of the LXX-deviant Johannine quotations by postulating the existence of "an anthology of passages useful in controversy."

[55] Moffatt, Introduction, 23–25. Moffatt cited both "internal" (composite quotations; LXX-deviant readings; false attributions) and "external" (i.e., analogous patristic *testimonia* collections) criteria as evidence for *testimonia* collections used in the NT.

[56] Milligan, *The New Testament Documents: Their Origin and Early History* (London: Macmillan, 1913) 207–8. Milligan saw authoritative OT *testimonia* collections, used in "Christian teaching and propaganda," as an important step in the process of developing an "authoritative Christian tradition" which would eventually lead to the canonization of the NT writings.

[57] Swete, *An Introduction to the Old Testament in Greek* (2d ed., rev. R.R. Ottley; Cambridge: Cambridge University Press, 1914; repr. New York: KTAV, 1968) 251–52. Swete, citing Hatch and Westcott approvingly, speculated that Paul may have found the composite quotation he used in Rom 3:10–18 in a *testimonia* collection. Swete also attributed the conflation of Zech 12:10 and Dan 7:13 found in Rev 1:7 (cf. Matt 24:30; John 19:37) to "some collection of prophetic testimonies" or a "book of excerpts" (*The Apocalypse of St. John: The Greek Text with Introduction, Notes, and Indices* [3d ed., London: Macmillan, 1911; repr. Grand Rapids: Eerdmans, 1951] 9–10).

[58] Stanton, *The Gospels as Historical Documents* (3 vols.; Cambridge: Cambridge University Press, 1906–20) 2. 344–45.

1.7   *Papias's* λόγια *and the* Testimonia *Hypothesis*

The weak point of the argument for the existence of scriptural ECs
and TCs in NT times has always been the lack of concrete first-
century evidence. Several scholars around the turn of the century
sought to make up for this lack by appealing to Papias's enigmatic
statement (recorded in Eusebius) concerning the apostle Matthew's
writings: Ματθαῖος μὲν οὖν Ἑβραΐδι διαλέκτῳ τὰ λόγια συνετάξατο
("Matthew put together the oracles in the Hebrew language") (*H.E.*
3.39.16). This collection of τὰ λόγια was taken to be an authoritative
TC, which became the basis for a commentary by Papias himself:
Τοῦ δὲ Παπία συγγράμματα πέντε τὸν ἀριθμὸν φέρεται, ἅ καὶ ἐπιγέγραπται
Λογίων κυριακῶν ἐξηγήσεως ("The writings of Papias in common cir-
culation are five in number, and these are called an Exposition of
Oracles of the Lord") (*H.E.* 3.39.1).[59]

Scholars who held this position included John Burslem Gregory,[60]
Edward Carus Selwyn,[61] F. Crawford Burkitt,[62] and T. Herbert Bindley.[63] A key issue in the scholarly debate was the meaning of the
word λόγια: while J.B. Lightfoot and others held that Papias referred
to a collection of sayings of Jesus, supporters of *testimonia* hypotheses countered that Papias referred to a collection of scriptural "oracles" *about* Jesus. The attractiveness of this hypothesis seems to have
been (1) that it explained phenomena such as LXX-deviant quotations (especially in Matthew) and the common textual core of early

---

[59] Greek text in Gustave Bardy, ed., *Eusèbe de Césarée: Histoire Ecclésiastique*, vol. 1
(SC 31; Paris: Cerf, 1952); ET of frags. in ANF 1. 153–55.

[60] Gregory, *The Oracles Ascribed to Matthew by Papias of Hierapolis: A Contribution to
the Criticism of the New Testament* (London/New York: Longmans, Green, 1894). This
work was originally published anonymously. Gregory was led to the thesis by a
study of Justin's LXX-deviant quotations which converge with quotations in Matthew.

[61] Selwyn, *The Oracles in the New Testament* (London/New York/Toronto: Hodder
& Stoughton, 1912) 396–427. Selwyn argued that Papias referred to a collection
designed to prove that Jesus was the messiah: "a *vade mecum* for devotional, medi-
tative, or controversial purposes" (p. 408).

[62] Burkitt, *The Gospel History and its Transmission* (2d ed.; Edinburgh: T. & T. Clark,
1907) 124–28. Burkitt held that the λόγια were a possible source for the Gospel
of Matthew's quotations. He envisioned the *testimonia* as an originally Hebrew collection in Palestine. Quotations were made "without scrupulous accuracy" and without reference to their source.

[63] Bindley, "Papias and the Matthean Oracles," *CQR* 84 (1917) 31–43. Bindley
argued that the term λόγια at the time of Papias would have been understood as
referring to the OT. The author of this collection was the apostle Matthew, and
his name later became attached to the first Gospel because the evangelist had used
the apostle's collection as a source.

Christian scriptural quotations; (2) that it provided an actual reference for what hitherto had been only hypothetical scriptural ECs; and (3) that it lent the authority of the apostle Matthew to these putative collections. Though based on slim evidence, this interpretation of Papias's statements was accepted widely in England in the early part of this century.

Burkitt (1907) seems to have been the first to use *testimonia* as a technical term in connection with scriptural EC hypotheses.[64] From this time, "*testimonia* hypothesis" became the standard description for scholarly investigations into this area; though, as noted above, general use of the term has at times glossed over important differences in function between ECs and TCs.

1.8   *J. Rendel Harris and* Testimonies

Harris's work presents the classic formulation of the written *testimonia* hypothesis. Harris produced a series of articles on *testimonia* topics, many of which were incorporated into his definitive presentation, the two-volume *Testimonies*.[65]

Harris posited the existence of a written *Testimony Book*, which consisted of select OT passages arranged under different headings. In positing this form, Harris used the models of the extant *testimonia* literature of the patristic period, especially the topically arranged first two books of Cyprian's *To Quirinus* (248 CE) and Ps.-Gregory of Nyssa's *Against the Jews* (ca. 400 CE). Echoing the *de Christo* and *de Evangelio* categories of Ungern-Sternberg, he held that the *Testimony Book* was divided into "Testimonies against the Jews" and "Testimonies concerning the Christ."

For Harris, the *testimonia* genre was closely related to that of the dialogue, specifically the early Jewish-Christian dialogues.[66] These dialogues contain much ancient *testimonia* material, and Harris speculated that the *Testimony Book* employed some of the techniques used

---

[64] So Robert A. Kraft, "Barnabas' Isaiah Text and the 'Testimony Book' Hypothesis," *JBL* 79 (1960) 338 n. 14.

[65] Two of the fifteen chapters in volume one, and three of the thirteen chapters in volume two, were written by Harris's associate Vacher Burch.

[66] In addition to Justin's *Dialogue with Trypho*, Harris also discusses the *Dialogue between Simon the Jew and Theophilus the Christian*, a 5th-century work which, according to Harris, contains ancient material (pp. 1. 94–96).

in the later dialogues. He understood the *Testimony Book*, then, as a collection of OT passages "classified into sections with titles, brief explanations, and frequent insertions of questions and comments by the controversialist editor."[67]

Harris is often criticized for presenting an overly simplistic model of a single *Testimony Book*, but his actual view was more nuanced. He could speak of "phases of evolution" and "editions of the book with expansions and changes,"[68] as well as a "fluid element in the tradition."[69] But at the same time, Harris insisted that the various lines of later *testimonia* tradition could be traced back to the original *Testimony Book*: it was possible to recover "the very headings of the sections under which they were arranged."[70] A large part of Harris's work involves just this tracing of the use of the *Testimony Book* by Greek (Justin, Irenaeus, *Barnabas*), Latin (Tertullian, Lactantius, Novatian and as far as Isidore of Seville [d. 636]), and Syriac authors (Aphrahat and as far as Bar Salibi [d. 1171]).

For Harris, the influence of this original document on developing Christian theology was critical. From its early anti-Jewish function,[71] it developed into a handbook of doctrine.[72] Accepting the "Papias connection" proposed by Bindley and others, he held that the *Testimony Book* was put together by the apostle Matthew and circulated under his name.[73] It is one of the earliest Christian documents, and the earliest writings of the NT must be interpreted in its light.[74] Ultimately, its authority may be traced back to Jesus himself.[75]

In his zeal to find hard evidence for this *Testimony Book*, Harris linked it not only with Papias's λόγοι κυριακοί, but also claimed to have found a direct descendant of the original *Testimony Book* in a sixteenth-century manuscript found on Mount Athos, consisting of five books and attributed to "Matthew the Monk."[76] It is leaps of

---

[67] Ibid. 1. 55.

[68] Ibid. 1. 2

[69] Ibid. 1. 25.

[70] Ibid. 2. 1.

[71] Ibid. 1. 1: *testimonia* collections "arose out of the exigency of controversy," and were employed "for use against the Jews."

[72] "The first handbook of Palestinian Theology" (2. 52); it contained a "developed Christology" (2. 33, 43).

[73] Ibid. 1. 124.

[74] Ibid. 1. 25.

[75] Ibid. 2. 95–100.

[76] Ibid. 1. 100–117, esp. 117. Harris spent an unfortunate amount of time arguing for the Papias and Mt. Athos connections: see 1. 100–132 and an appendix to volume 2 (pp. 109–36).

imagination of this sort that provoked C.H. Dodd's comment, "This final stage of the argument, I fancy, no one, not even Harris himself, took very seriously."[77]

Harris explicitly listed five principles for detecting use of the *Testimony Book* in later literature.[78] The first two, LXX-deviant readings and composite quotations in independent authors,[79] have already been discussed. The other criteria are:

(1) *False attribution*: An author's mistaken attribution of a scripture passage to a given source might be due to misreading the *Testimony Book*. Thus when Mark 1:3 attributes an Isaiah/Malachi conflation to Isaiah alone, this suggests that the evangelist used a collection in which the texts appeared together. It would be easy for a reference to an author to drop out in transmission, or for the evangelist's eye to skip over an ascription in copying his source.[80]

This argument retains some merit, though not in the form that Harris presented it. Study of early Christian quotations has shown that conflation of texts was a common technique in a variety of genres, and thus there is no need to posit that *testimonia* were originally presented in list form. Indeed, Harris himself envisioned the *Testimony Book* not as a bare list, but as a EC with editorial comments. False attribution, however, would still be possible in the transmission of a collection with commentary.

(2) *Editorial (exegetical) remarks*: Here Harris argued that comments and introductions of the Testimony Book editor could be isolated in later authors. An example: the phrase "at his coming," used by both Justin and Irenaeus to introduce a quotation of Isa 35:5, may be attributed to the *Testimony Book* editor.[81] This criterion is closely related to observations of recent critics who study common exegetical traditions.

(3) *Anti-Jewish Polemic*: This criterion reflects Harris's conviction that the *Testimony Book* arose out of the exigencies of polemic against

---

[77] Dodd, *Scriptures*, 25.

[78] Harris, *Testimonies* 1. 8. For ease of comparison with other scholars, I use my own labels for Harris's categories (e.g., my "false attribution" for his "erroneous authorship").

[79] Ibid., 1. 18–19. Two examples offered by Harris are the combination of Psalms 110 and 71 in Bar Salibi, Justin *Dialogue* 45 and 76, and Ps.-Gregory of Nyssa, and the combination of "stone" passages found in 1 Pet 2:6–8 and later in Cyprian and Ps.-Gregory.

[80] Ibid. 1. 21–22.

[81] Ibid. 1. 9; see Justin *1 Apology* 48 (Τῇ παρουσίᾳ αὐτοῦ) and Irenaeus *A.H.* 4.55.2 (*adventu eius*).

the Jews, and led him to suspect that almost any "anti-Jewish" state-
ment was an original part of the *Testimony Book*. The argument is
circular: the *Testimony Book* was anti-Jewish, thus anti-Jewish polemic
is an indication of the *Testimony Book*. This overemphasis on the anti-
Jewish function sometimes led to fundamental misunderstandings.
Harris read Romans, for example, as a dialogue between the "pro-
Gentile" Paul and a Jewish objector.[82] His insistence on the "anti-
Judaic" character of the *testimonia* led him to attribute to a colorless
Jewish interlocutor what is actually Paul's own poignant struggle to
understand God's plan for his people Israel.

A reference in Harris's book to a contemporary controversy sheds
some light on one of the theological implications of the *testimonia* thesis. In an effort to delineate a theory of inspiration without inerrancy,
J. Armitage Robinson had offered Matt 27:9 (which ascribes an
adapted quotation from Zechariah to Jeremiah) as an example of
an error in an inspired work. Harris noted that his thesis provided
an alternative: if Matthew had drawn his quotation from the *Testimony
Book*, then the error of ascription might be due either to the *Book*
itself or to Matthew's use of the *Book*.[83] In positing this intermediary
stage, the evangelist is insulated from any direct misuse of scripture.

While Harris's thesis of a single *Testimony Book* is rightly to be rejected, his contribution in presenting clear *testimonia* criteria, his insights
into the commentary form of these early collections, his speculation
on the influence of scripture collections on developing theology, his
location of this material in a polemical context, and the evidence he
gathered from a wide variety of sources (his special contribution
being the Syriac material) retain their value. Even his rather idiosyncratic thesis of a single *Testimony Book* has a symbolic value: for
Harris, the *Book* represented the original unity of the Christian faith
and was a guarantor of its accurate transmission. It was a powerful symbol of the continuity of Christian beliefs worked out through
scriptural witness and transmitted through the ages.[84]

---

[82] Harris, *Testimonies* 2. 30; Harris refers to such passages as Rom 10:18–19;
11:1, 11.

[83] Ibid. 1. 52–60.

[84] Harris's enthusiasm for the *testimonia* hypothesis continued unabated after the
publication of *Testimonies*; in 1932 (at age eighty!), for example, he argued that
Josephus's *Testimonium Flavianum* shows extensive contact with the *Testimony Book*
(*Nicodemus* [Evergreen Essays 4; Cambridge: Heffer, 1932]). Harris here argued for
a pre-Christian Jewish *Testimony Book* (with messianic proof-texts) and the influence
of this *Book* on Christians.

1.9 *Reactions to Harris*

Reaction to Harris's contentions tended towards either enthusiastic support or strong rejection. Supporters of the single *Testimony Book* thesis included the British scholar J.A. Findlay[85] and the Dutch scholars Daniel Plooij[86] and Adolphine Bakker.[87] G.H. Box cited Harris with approval, but modified his model to include smaller-scale TCs.[88] The extensive influence of Harris's ideas is witnessed by C.H. Dodd, who could write in 1952:

> In fact it may be said that in Great Britain at least Rendel Harris's book was the starting point of modern study of the use of the Old Testament in the New. It has, I believe, been assumed by most recent British writers that some such anthology of quotations was actually in existence at an early period, and that its use by NT writers is the best explanation of the phenomena before us.[89]

---

[85] Findlay, "The First Gospel and the Book of Testimonies," in H.G. Wood, ed., *Amicitiae Corolla: A Volume of Essays Presented to James Rendel Harris, D. Litt., on the Occasion of his Eightieth Birthday* (London: University of London Press, 1933) 57–71. Findlay compared Matthew's quotations to later *testimonia* literature (Justin, Cyprian) and found little correlation in text selection or textual form. Rather than questioning the *testimonia* thesis, however, Findlay concluded that Matthew is "not in the main Testimony-stream" (p. 69).

[86] Plooij (one also sees the variant spelling "Plooy"), *Studies in the Testimony Book* (Verhandelingen der Koninklijke Akadamie van Wetenschappen te Amsterdam, Literature Sect. 32/2; Amsterdam: Noord-Hollandsche Uitgevers-Maatschappij, 1932). Plooij allowed that the *Book* may have begun in oral form (pp. 9, 11). His studies focus on temple traditions found in Paul's Corinthian correspondence and in Hebrews. Drawing on parallel text sequences in Paul and Aphrahat, Plooij suggested that the earliest written form of the *Book* was a Palestinian Aramaic composition. Again we see hints of the theological importance of the thesis: the authority of Jesus himself is behind the OT collections (pp. 11, 26, 34); they shaped the earliest Christian theology; the Aramaic original of the *Book* shows that this earliest theology is grounded in the primitive Palestinian church, not "Hellenistic speculations" (p. 26).

[87] Bakker, "Testimony-Influence in the Old-Latin Gospels," in Wood, ed., *Amicitiae Corolla*, 1–14. Bakker, a student of Plooij, argued that additions to the Old Latin versions of Mark 12:2 (e.g., *et post tridum aliumut excitabitur sine manibus*) derive from a "stone" *testimonia* collection. Bakker also proposed that Hebrews 1–2 is directed against an early Jewish Christian christology (originally in the *Testimony Book*) that proclaimed Christ as the angel of God ("Christ an Angel? A Study of Early Christian Docetism," *ZNW* 32 [1933] 255–65).

[88] Box, "The Value and Significance of the Old Testament in Relation to the New," in Arthur S. Peake, ed., *The People and the Book: Essays on the Old Testament* (Oxford: Clarendon, 1925) 433–67. Box conjectured originally Aramaic TCs before Paul, and drew the conclusion that the method and content of the gospel message were thus pre-Pauline (p. 445).

[89] Dodd, *Scriptures*, 25–26.

The Dutch scholar N.J. Hommes responded to the theories of Harris and Plooij with a book-length critique.[90] Hommes charged Harris with circular reasoning: he constantly returns to the unproven starting point of a single *Testimony Book*.[91] Hommes admitted that the early Christian anti-Jewish literature indeed knew groupings of OT texts combined by catch-words, but these are better understood as the products of a Christian school tradition (Hommes refers to the work of Bousset).[92] These collections were based on the LXX, with certain intentional alterations. This literature developed slowly over many years as authors copied one another and made their own changes in the material.[93]

The German scholar Otto Michel rejected the *testimonia* claims of Hatch, Vollmer, and Harris in his study of Paul's use of scripture.[94] Composite quotations parallel to Paul in 1 Peter and Justin are simply examples of later Pauline influence. Paul himself must have put together most of the composite quotations, as these compositions betray Paul's own theological emphases. Michel saw two dangers in Harris's theory: it devalues the originality of Paul and it denies the influence of Paul on later writers.[95] While Michel's latter point is valid, the former seems part of an unjustifiable tendency among some scholars to find any dependence of Paul upon other sources to be an insult to the apostle's creativity.[96] In a further argument—one that would be made obsolete by the Qumran discoveries—Michel maintained that there is simply no evidence for pre-Christian scriptural *florilegia*, nor evidence for Christian *florilegia* before the apostolic fathers.[97]

---

[90] Hommes, *Het Testimoniaboek: Studien over O.T. Citaten in het N.T. en bij de Patres. Met Critische Beschouwingen over de Theorieen van J. Rendel Harris en D. Plooy* (Amsterdam: Noord-Hollandsche Uitgevers-Maatschappij, 1935). See the summary and review of the book in August Kraemer, *Philologische Wochenschrift* 58 (1938) cols. 73–84.

[91] Hommes, *Testimoniaboek*, 356.

[92] Hommes emphasizes the similarity of this technique and later rabbinic practice (ibid., 304–54).

[93] Ibid., 357.

[94] Michel, *Paulus und seine Bibel* (BFCT 2/18; Gütersloh: Bertelsman, 1929; repr. Darmstadt: Wissenschaftliche Buchgesellschaft, 1972) 37–54.

[95] Ibid., 52–53.

[96] This tendency is noticeable even in G.H. Box, who, though broadly sympathetic to Harris's claim that Paul used the *Testimony Book*, nevertheless cautioned that "one should not disparage Paul's originality" in using scripture, and noted the difficulty of distinguishing between citations dependent on *testimonia* and those selected independently by Paul ("Value and Significance," 463).

[97] Michel, *Paulus*, 43, 52. In his review of Michel's book, Rudolf Bultmann expressly agreed with Michel's observation (*TLZ* 58 [1933] col. 157).

Michel did concede that Paul had taken over previously established interpretive traditions (both Jewish and early Christian) of select passages. Paul understands certain psalms messianically (e.g., Psalms 8 and 110 in 1 Corinthians 15); his interpretation of the faith of Abraham has been anticipated by the use of Gen 15:6 in 1 Macc 2:52 and Philo *De Abrahamo* 262; and he uses a traditional understanding of Isaiah 53 to interpret the death of Jesus (e.g., in Rom 4:25). Such traditions would have their life-setting in missionary preaching in which scriptures were gathered around certain themes (e.g., Hab 2:4 and Gen 15:6 on "faith").[98] Michel thus continued the general German tendency to speak of a broad scriptural tradition and hence avoid the hypothesis of written ECs.

1.10   Testimonia *and Early Anti-Jewish Literature*

Further studies focused on the anti-Jewish nature of early Christian TCs, placing them within the context of Christian anti-Jewish literature as a whole. In 1935, A. Lukyn Williams used the *testimonia* thesis as the starting point of his valuable survey of Christian *apologiae* against Jewish opponents.[99] Williams provided brief summaries of the literature in which these common proof-texts are recorded: ante-Nicene Greek and Latin works (e.g., *Barnabas*, Justin, Tertullian), Syriac writers (e.g., Aphrahat, Bar Salibi), and later Greek, Latin, and Spanish writers (e.g., Chrysostom, Augustine, Isidore of Seville) down to the Renaissance. Williams demonstrated the remarkable durability of these scriptural proof-text traditions. To give only one example: Isidore of Seville's *Against the Jews* (ca. 620) is a large-scale TC (eighty-eight thematic groupings) composed of traditional proof-texts; this work in turn became "a storehouse from which, in all probability, many later tracts, perhaps even down to the nineteenth century, were ultimately drawn."[100] Fifth- and sixth-century Latin dialogues and treatises based on traditional TCs became the script for Christian dramas of the Middle Ages, with actors taking on the roles of prophets like Jeremiah and Isaiah.[101]

---

[98] Ibid., 87–90.

[99] Williams, *Adversus Judaeos: A Bird's Eye View of Christian Apologiae until the Renaissance* (London: Cambridge University Press, 1935).

[100] Ibid., 217. See pp. 282–92 for a summary of Isidore's TC.

[101] Ibid., 321–38. Perhaps the most influential was Ps. Augustine's sermon, "Against

In his study of early Jewish-Christians relations, Marcel Simon showed that the biblical TC was one of the many genres in which Christian anti-Jewish literature expressed itself.[102] Early TCs served as sources for later literature: epistles (*Barnabas*), expositions of doctrine (Tertullian), homilies (Aphrahat), poems (Ephrem), sermons (Chrysostom), and dialogues (Justin).[103] Contrary to the views of scholars such as Harnack, he argued, the great majority of this anti-Jewish literature reflects actual controversies; the polemic should not be understood simply as a literary device.[104]

1.11   Testimonia *and Messianic Debates*

Accepting the main outlines of Harris's theory, B.P.W. Stather Hunt applied the *testimonia* thesis systematically to the composition of the canonical gospels.[105] He maintained that the earliest apostolic preaching (as witnessed in Acts) was "chiefly concerned with proving that Jesus of Nazareth was the long awaited Messiah." This "proof" consisted of matching events in the life of Jesus to messianic prophecies. For example, stories of Jesus healing the blind were collected not so much for their own sake, but because they matched the prophecy in Isa 35:5–6. Occasionally details of an event in the life of Jesus might be altered to fit more closely the scriptural witness.[106] Stather Hunt envisioned a complex development: certain texts

---

the Jews, the Heathen, and the Arians: A Discourse on the Creed" (P.L. 42. 1115–30). Scholars of medieval drama have shown that this sermon served as the basis for various French, German, and English "prophet plays." The Ps. Augustinian sermon had already been included in Christian liturgy (Sarum Breviary: Lectio III Adventus) and thus it was probably this liturgical source from which the plays drew. See Paul Edward Kretzmann, *The Liturgical Element in the Earliest Forms of the Medieval Drama, with Special Reference to the English and German Plays* (Studies in Language and Literature, University of Minnesota 4; Minneapolis: Bulletin of the University of Minnesota, 1916) 23–34.

[102] Simon, *Verus Israel: A Study of the Relations between Christians and Jews in the Roman Empire (135–425)* (Littman Library of Jewish Civilization; Oxford: Oxford University Press, 1986) 140; orig. pub. Bibliotheque des Ecoles françaises d'Athenes et de Rome; Paris: Boccard, 1948).

[103] Ibid., 141–55; esp. 154–55 on *testimonia*.

[104] Ibid., 137–46.

[105] Stather Hunt, *Primitive Gospel Sources* (New York: Philosophical Library, 1951) viii.

[106] See esp. ibid., 74–84. Cf. Jan Willem Doeve's view that Jesus traditions were transmitted along with scriptures of which they were considered the fulfillment. Doeve proposed that these accompanying texts in fact governed the sequence of presentation: e.g., the five controversy stories in Mark 2:1–3:6 are ordered accord-

were emphasized by Jesus (see Luke 24:25–27, 44–48), others were texts both Jews and Christians agreed were messianic,[107] and still others were texts in which Christians found a messianic meaning "in passages that did not really contain one."[108] After presenting his case that the Gospel writers used *testimonia* sources as the framework for their compositions, Stather Hunt offered evidence from patristic sources for use of TCs. A major section is devoted to the dialogues, which Stather Hunt argued preserve *testimonia* traditions that predate the NT.[109]

1.12   C.H. Dodd: Recovering the "Sub-structure" of the Kerygma

C.H. Dodd's classic work, *According to the Scriptures: The Sub-structure of New Testament Theology*, originally delivered as the Stone Lectures at Princeton Theological Seminary in 1950, marked a decisive shift in the understanding of the form and function of OT *testimonia*.[110] Admitting that he had "worked with Harris's hypothesis for many years," Dodd finally rejected the "Testimony Book" thesis as untenable.[111] Dodd's own starting point is his understanding of the "kerygma" as the "common and central tradition of the NT."[112] The kerygma is the proclamation of certain historical events—the ministry, suffering, death, resurrection and ascension of Jesus, as well as the rise of the

---

ing to the sequence of themes in their accompanying text (Isaiah 57–59) (*Jewish Hermeneutics in the Synoptic Gospels and Acts* [Assen: Van Gorcum, 1953] 202–4). Though his overall thesis is viable, the detailed application (as seen in the above example) often strains credibility.

[107] Stather Hunt, *Gospel Sources*, ix.

[108] Ibid., 7.

[109] Ibid., 239–303. Stather Hunt discusses Jason and Papiscus, Simon and Theophilus, Zacchaeus and Apollonius, Athanasius and Zacchaeus, and Timothy and Aquila.

[110] Dodd also presented a more popular version of his conclusions in *The Old Testament in the New* (London: Athlone, 1952).

[111] Dodd, *Scriptures*, 26. Dodd argued that if the "Testimony Book" was really as influential as Harris imagined, it is inexplicable that there are no unambiguous references to it or that it was not included in the canon. Dodd further judged that the evidence adduced by Harris (deviation from the LXX; conflated readings; thematically-grouped passages) was indeed intriguing, but did not constitute a large enough body of evidence to prove a general theory.

[112] In *Scriptures*, Dodd presupposed the basic kerygmatic tradition which he had outlined in *The Apostolic Preaching and Its Developments* (London: Hodder & Stoughton, 1936). Dodd drew on the evidence in the speeches in Acts along with Paul's letters to isolate the common NT kerygma.

church—along with the significance of those events. Early Christians turned to scriptures as a means of expressing this significance: their biblical research clarified meanings for themselves and articulated the message to outsiders.[113] Dodd's project was to determine as precisely as possible which scriptures were used to witness to the kerygmatic events.[114]

Dodd's efforts must be seen within the larger context of contemporary NT scholarship: it paralleled form-critical efforts to recover the oral stages behind the NT writings,[115] and also shared a methodological and theological interest in emphasizing the centrality of the "kerygma" in early Christianity.[116] Dodd's biographer, F.W. Dillistone, offers some further insights into the motivation behind Dodd's efforts to delineate the earliest kerygma.[117] He suggests that it was both a reaction to the emphasis of contemporary NT scholarship on the *diversity* of the early Christian writings, and an attempt to find an objective expression of Christian truth as a standard to protect against subjective claims that emphasized the truth of individual experience.[118] Moreover, the recovery of the original form of the apos-

---

[113] Dodd, *Scriptures*, 14.

[114] Dodd's friend and successor in the Rylands Chair at Manchester, T.W. Manson, had laid out a similar thesis: oral *testimonia* were grouped around items in the kerygma before being written down ("The Argument from Prophecy," *JTS* 46 [1945] 132).

[115] One thinks especially of Martin Dibelius, with his emphasis on Christian preaching as the original *Sitz im Leben* of the Gospel accounts. In fact, Dibelius accepted the likelihood of early collections of scriptural proof-texts: such collections may be reflected in individual or group NT scriptural quotations that stand out from their contexts as independent forms. As examples, he proposed the catena in Rom 3:10–18, the use of Psalm 16 in the Acts speeches, and the use of Isaiah 53 and various psalms in the passion narrative. To recover the early stages of this "halbliterarische" ("semi-literary") effort, Dibelius looked to the apostolic period, where works such as *Barnabas* (he cited Windisch's theory of TCs in *Barnabas*) and *1 Clement* (with its lists of OT *exempla*) demonstrate use of collection techniques taken over from hellenistic Judaism. Early Christians and contemporary Jews also made scriptural ECs for parenetic and homiletical (e.g., Hebrews 11) purposes ("Zur Formgeschichte des Neuen Testaments [auserhalb der Evangelien]," *TR* 3 [1931] 227–29).

[116] Bultmann's program is the most obvious example.

[117] Dillistone, *C.H. Dodd: Interpreter of the New Testament* (Grand Rapids: Eerdmans, 1977) 136–37.

[118] On the latter point, Dillistone quotes from Dodd's commentary on 1 John: "If such experience [i.e., the appeal to the individual inspiration] is made the criterion, persons with little grasp of the central truths of the Gospel may mistake their own 'inspirations' (or bright ideas) for the truth of God, and so the corporate, historical tradition of Christianity is imperiled" (*The Johannine Epistles* [MNTC; London: Hodder & Stoughton, 1946] 63).

tolic preaching satisfied Dodd's dual roles as biblical scholar and preacher: the emphasis on the original unity of the Christian message mirrored Dodd's own ecumenical concerns as a Congregationalist working in the largely Anglican atmosphere of English scholarship.[119] Though rejecting Harris's methods, Dodd completely supported the older scholar's theological vision of an early church unified in its appeal to certain core scriptures.

Dodd's method in isolating the common passages that witnessed to the kerygma (he retained the label "testimonies") involved two steps. First, he collected all OT passages cited by two or more independent NT authors, as these were likely to represent a common early tradition.[120] Dodd pointed out, however, that often NT writers do not cite precisely the same passage, but rather adjacent passages.[121] This observation led to step two: an examination of the wider context of the common passages cited. The claim that in most cases the wider *contexts* of cited passages were also understood as *testimonia* by the NT writers is Dodd's well-known contribution to the *testimonia* discussion.

Dodd set out his results under the rubric, "The Bible of the early church." He grouped the *testimonia* sections under four headings:

(1) *Apocalyptic-eschatological scriptures*: The scriptures informed early Christian expectations of the end times, including the coming of Christ as judge and savior. These texts "moulded the language" of Christian expectations of Christ's past and future work.[122]

(2) *Scriptures of the New Israel*: These scriptures (e.g., Hosea, Isaiah 6–9, and Jeremiah 31) witness to belief in the judgment of Israel, and the understanding of Christians as the "new Israel," i.e., the new covenant people.[123]

(3) *Scriptures of the Servant of the Lord and the Righteous Sufferer*: The pattern of the righteous sufferer who is ultimately glorified by God is seen in these texts (e.g., the Isaian Servant texts and Psalms 22

---

[119] Dodd was the first non-Anglican to hold a divinity professorship at Oxford or Cambridge (the Cambridge Norris-Hulse Chair in 1935) since the Restoration (Dillistone, *C.H. Dodd*, 145).

[120] Dodd, *Scripture*, 28–60. Dodd presented fifteen passages: four from Psalms, five from Isaiah, and one each from Genesis, Deuteronomy, Jeremiah, Joel, Zechariah, and Habakkuk.

[121] Ibid., 57–60. He used the widespread quotations from various parts of Psalm 68 as an example.

[122] Ibid., 62–74, esp. 62–3, 67.

[123] Ibid., 74–88.

and 69). The texts are applied to the life of Jesus, but also to that of every Christian.[124]

(4) *Unclassified Scriptures*: Here Dodd refers to the "messianic" texts of Psalms 8, 110, and 2 and their christological use.[125]

Filled out with their OT references, Dodd's categories appear as follows:[126]

Primary Sources of Testimonies	Subordinate and Supplementary Sources

(1) Joel 2–3;
    Zechariah 9–14;
    Daniel 7
	Mal 3:1–6;
	Daniel 12

(2) Hosea;
    Isa 6:1–9:7; 11:1–10;
    28:16; 40:1–11;
    Jer 31:10–34
	Isa 29:9–14;
	Jer 7:1–15;
	Habakkuk 1–2

(3) Isa 42:1–44:5; 49:1–13;
    50:4–11; 52:13–53:12; 61;
    Psalms 22; 31; 34; 38; 41;
    42–43; 69; 80; 88; 118
	Isa 58:6–10

(4) Psalms 2; 8; 110
    Gen 12:3; 22:18;
    Deut 18:15, 19
	Psalms 32; 132; 2 Sam 7:13–14;
	Isa 55:3; Amos 9:11–12

Dodd then drew together the threads of his study in a presentation of "the fundamentals of Christian theology." The *testimonia* passages and their application to the kerygma provided the starting point for Paul, John, and the author of Hebrews; this common body of material is in fact the "substructure of all Christian theology and contains already its chief regulative ideas."[127] The *testimonia* provide the foundation for christological (Jesus understood as the Son of Man and Servant, as both the representative human and as Lord, and Jesus' death interpreted as expiatory sacrifice) and ecclesiastical (the church understood as the body of Christ and as the new Israel) re-

---

[124] Ibid., 88–103.
[125] Ibid., 104–7.
[126] Ibid., 107–8.
[127] Ibid., 127.

flection.[128] Though he rejected Harris's *testimonia* thesis, Dodd's own model is actually quite similar in proposing a common pre-NT scriptural tradition from which the major categories of Christian theology developed.[129] The key difference is of course Harris's insistence on a written source and Dodd's emphasis on oral tradition in line with such scholars as Ungern-Sternberg.

Dodd's study is open to criticism on many levels. His isolation of the "Bible of the early church" simply does not hold up to statistical analysis,[130] and his insistence on the importance of context is overdrawn.[131] Dodd presented an overly homogenous picture of NT Christianity: his study fails to make clear distinctions between early and late traditions, and he did not account for the fact that the same passage was interpreted in different ways. Finally, Dodd gave no concrete indication of how such scriptural traditions were transmitted, relying overly on the later model of rabbinic oral transmission.[132]

Dodd's lasting achievements, however, should not be overlooked. He was influential, particularly in Britain, in moving the *testimonia* discussion away from a preoccupation with a single "Testimony Book"

---

[128] Ibid., 111–25.

[129] So Albert C. Sundberg, "On Testimonies," *NovT* 3 (1959) 280.

[130] Sundberg showed that actual use of OT passages is more diverse than Dodd had suggested, and demonstrated that different NT authors favored different scriptural books. However, Sundberg's own study is flawed by a failure to reckon with *independent* NT citations. Furthermore, Sundberg's statistics showing the variation of the relative importance of OT books among the different NT works is not strictly relevant to Dodd's thesis: the authors may simply show individual interests within a larger common tradition. More tellingly, Dietrich-Alex Koch points out that only 15 of Paul's 93 scripture quotations fall within Dodd's "Bible of the early church" (*Die Schrift als Zeuge des Evangeliums: Untersuchungen zur Verwendung und zum Verständnis der Schrift bei Paulus*) (BHT 69; Tübingen: Mohr-Siebeck, 1986) 254.

[131] Dodd himself admitted that some citations are interpreted out of context (p. 107 on Gen 12:3; 22:18; Deut 18:15, 19). For further examples, see Sundberg, "Testimonies," 275–78; Koch, *Schrift als Zeuge*, 255.

[132] Dodd provided further explication of his thought in a letter to T.F. Glasson published by the latter ("Old Testament Testimonies and their Transmission," *ExpTim* 87 [1975] 21–22]. In response to Glasson's queries about his thesis, Dodd reiterated his belief that the *testimonia* process "took place mainly in a context of oral tradition" and that testimony books "represent the end-product and not the basis of the biblical research in which early Christian teachers were involved." Dodd does allow that "written memoranda" or "written aides-memoire" were likely used at this early stage, but only as a practical convenience to the largely oral work. This research took place in a setting "something indeed rather like Krister Stendahl's 'School of St. Matthew.'" Dodd's analogy for this oral research, and indeed for his theory of a single passage evoking a whole context, was the work done in "Jewish rabbinic schools" (p. 22).

and into the wider (if more vague) field of oral tradition.[133] His emphasis on considering the wider context of cited passages pointed out a real, if not universal, technique employed by NT writers. Especially valuable is his suggestion that NT writers often have an entire "plot" in mind (e.g., a suffering righteous person will be vindicated) when they refer to specific passages. This move in some ways anticipated modern narrative and intertextual approaches to the use of scripture in the NT. Finally, Dodd's image of a body of scriptural passages and their interpretation as a precondition or "substructure" of subsequent NT theology remains an important model for interpreting the influence of scriptural interpretation on early Christian theological concepts.

1.13   *Barnabas Lindars: The Apologetic Life-Setting of the* Testimonia

In his *New Testament Apologetic*, Barnabas Lindars accepted the main lines of Dodd's *testimonia* argument, but developed it into a more sophisticated model for uncovering the scriptural roots of NT theology. For Lindars, the use of *testimonia* developed as an essential part of the apologetic activity of the early church, an activity functioning primarily to answer Jewish objections to Christian claims.[134] With Dodd, Lindars posited a close relationship between OT passages and the early Christian kerygma; presumably the original scriptural apologetic "answers some objection to the primitive kerygma."[135]

The starting point for Lindars is the resurrection of Jesus. The fact that God had raised Jesus from the dead indicated to his followers that he was the messiah, and the earliest use of OT passages was to confirm that Jesus fulfilled messianic prophecies in his resurrection.[136]

---

[133] A good example of Dodd's influence may be found in the work of Archibald Hunter. In his study of pre-Pauline tradition, originally published in 1940, Hunter accepted the main lines of Rendel Harris's sketch in *Testimonies* (*Paul and his Predecessors* [rev. ed.; Philadelphia: Westminster, 1961], esp. 58–64). In his 1961 appendix, however, Hunter enthusiastically accepted Dodd's model in *According to the Scriptures* as the preferable explanation (pp. 131–34). Other scholars accepted Dodd's proposals more cautiously, C.F.D. Moule, for example, holds that Dodd's theory does not rule out the use of written collections in NT times (*The Birth of the New Testament* [3d ed.; San Francisco: Harper & Row, 1982] 104–5).

[134] Lindars, *Apologetic*, 13.

[135] Ibid., 9, 23–24. Here Lindars explicitly agreed with Harris in emphasizing the anti-Judaic character of much of the primitive *testimonia*.

[136] Ibid., 32–33. Lindars held that this use of scripture "is only possible when the messianic interpretation is common ground between Christians and Jews" (ibid.,

Testimonia were further used in describing Jesus' role as messiah: Ps 110:1 was the basis for the theologoumenon that the messiah sits at the right hand of the Father; Ps 68:19 lies at the basis of the conception that the messiah will give the gifts of the Spirit from this exalted position.[137] Understanding of Jesus was shaped by both previously established messianic interpretations and the modification of those interpretations caused by the life of Jesus.[138]

The next stage of *testimonia* use occurred in the "passion apologetic": Christians defended the claim that Jesus was the messiah against the objection that God would not allow his messiah to suffer and die.[139] A central answer to this objection was the claim that Jesus fulfilled the mission of the Servant, especially as described in Isa 52:13–53:12.[140] Concurrently with its use as an apologetic text, this Isaian passage helped develop the positive doctrine of Christ's death as atonement for sin.[141] In Rom 4:25, for example, Paul can allude to this section with παρεδόθη διὰ τὰ παραπτώματα ἡμῶν; this conception of Christ's atonement underlies all of Romans 5.[142] Echoing Dodd, Lindars stressed the importance of the *pattern* of Psalm 22: it tells the story of God's righteous one who suffers but is vindicated in the end.[143] While Lindars's emphasis on the centrality of Isaiah 53 is open to question,[144] his sketch of a Christian "passion apologetic"

---

84 n. 2). He offered Peter's use of Psalms 16 and 110 in Acts 2:22–36 as an example of this type of argument (pp. 40–45). Lindars is correct that a common interpretive ground is assumed, but to call it "messianic" begs the question. The common ground need only be an agreement that the texts represent God's vindication of an individual.

[137] Ibid., 45–59.

[138] Ibid., 186–87. For example, Psalm 22 first attracted Christian attention not because it was messianic but because it corresponded to the details of Jesus' suffering: "it was these astonishingly accurate details which first drew attention to the psalm, which was then declared to be messianic because it is fulfilled in Jesus, who is acclaimed as the Messiah *on other grounds*" (ibid., 34, emphasis original). Lindars further argued that once the messianic designation is made, the psalm can be used to fill out some details of Jesus' passion (ibid., 91).

[139] Lindars, *Apologetic*, 75–137.

[140] Ibid., 79. Lindars admitted that there were few explicit quotations of this passage in the NT, but nevertheless found it "deeply embedded in the earliest thought of the church."

[141] See ibid., 134–37, for a summary of this position.

[142] Ibid., 82.

[143] Ibid., 90. Lindars also discusses Psalms 31, 34, 41, 69, and 109 as *testimonia* employed in the passion apologetic.

[144] For an argument against the broad influence of Isaiah 53, see Morna Dorothy Hooker, *Jesus and the Servant: The Influence of the Servant Concept of Deutero-Isaiah in the New Testament* (London: SPCK, 1959).

backed by references to scriptural patterns of suffering and vindication remains convincing.

Lindars held that Christians first recognized Jesus as the messiah at his resurrection; only at a later stage were messianic themes "read back" into Jesus' life. Jesus' baptism (interpreted through Ps 2:7 and Isa 42:1), for example, is understood as a messianic designation.[145] Once Christians admitted that Jesus was recognizable as the messiah during his lifetime, however, they would have to explain why so many did not in fact recognize him as such. Lindars argued that the explanation was found in the classic "hardening" text, Isa 6:9–13. This passage was applied to those who could not understand Jesus' parables (Mark 4:12 par.) and to unbelieving Jews as a justification for preaching to the gentiles (e.g., Rom 11:7, 25; 2 Cor 3:14).[146]

Lindars claimed that apologetical stages could be found even within a single quotation. His analysis of the adaptation of Isa 42:1–4 (quoted in Matt 12:18–21) uncovered four "stages" in the application of this passage: (1) The passage was originally applied to the resurrection of Jesus: the opening words, "Behold my servant," were understood as the revelation of Jesus as messiah at this event. (2) The conflation of Isa 42:1 with Ps 2:7 in Matt 12:18 shows that the moment of messianic revelation had now been connected with Jesus' baptism (cf. Matt 3:17 with its use of Ps 2:7). (3) As an explanation for the failure to recognize Jesus as messiah during his public teaching, the quotation of Isa 42:2 in Matt 12:19 emphasizes (through vocabulary changes) the quietness of Jesus' ministry and de-emphasizes (through omissions and vocabulary substitutions) his role as bringer of judgment. (4) An exact LXX quotation of Isa 42:4b in Matt 12:21 shows a concern to defend the mission to the gentiles.[147] This analysis exemplifies key principles of Lindars's approach: he spoke not only of different applications of this text, but of "traces of four successive phases of application."[148] These stages of exegetical shaping all took place *before* Matthew took over this Isaiah passage.[149] Lindars, obvi-

---

[145] Ibid., 139–52.

[146] Ibid., 159–67.

[147] Ibid., 144–51.

[148] Ibid., 151.

[149] This is in contrast to Krister Stendahl's conclusion (in his *School of Saint Matthew*) that the Gospel's reworked quotations reflect the activity of the Matthean school. Though he reaches opposite conclusions regarding the provenance of the quotations, Lindars frequently refers to Stendahl in his book.

ously influenced by the recent publication of the Dead Sea Scrolls (especially the Habakkuk commentary), referred to this shaping as "*pesher*" quotations.

Lindars was also confident of recovering the original form of these apologetical quotations. In discussing the use of Zech 12:10 and Dan 7:13 in Matt 24:30, Rev 1:7, and John 19:37, he offered a reconstruction of the original, non-LXX form from which all were drawn:

> καὶ ὄψονται εἰς ὃν ἐξεκέντησαν
> καὶ κόψονται ἐπ᾽ αὐτὸν πῶσαι αἱ φυλαὶ τῆς γῆς.[150]

Lindars ascribed the close agreements between the three citations (which all deviate from the LXX) to a "living apologetic tradition, oral rather than written," in which the regular use of the text helped to preserve its identity.[151]

Lindars's fluid model of "stages" is both the strength and the weakness of his approach. It offers the important insight that the use of scriptural *testimonia* was not fixed to a certain purpose: texts regularly underwent a "shift in application." At the same time, Lindars's model is often highly speculative, bordering on the arbitrary. His thesis, for example, that texts applied to Jesus' resurrection are the most primitive is put forth with little supporting evidence. Further, while Lindars cautioned that his developmental model should be taken not as a strictly chronological but rather as a "logical" sequence,[152] it is unclear how he distinguishes between the two. His model of linear development is attractive, but in the end is too simple to account for the complexities of early Christian exegetical practices.

There is a tension in Lindars between his reliance on Dodd's model of an oral *testimonia* tradition and his own detailed analysis of what he calls the "*pesher* quotations." The examples cited above are best explained as the result of extensive written exegetical activity and written transmission of exegetical traditions.[153] While some scriptural traditions were probably oral (e.g., the narrative model of the righteous one who is vindicated), Lindars must strain to fit more

---

[150] Lindars, *Apologetic*, 124.

[151] Ibid., 127. In only one case did Lindars accept the necessity of a written *testimonium*: a tradition used by both Rom 9:33 and 1 Pet 2:6 (pp. 179–80 n. 3).

[152] Ibid., 29, 116.

[153] For detailed arguments on these points, see sect. 4.3.2c on Matt 12:18–21 and sect. 5.5 on Zech 12:10.

detailed exegetical traditions into Dodd's model of Christian use of larger scriptural blocks.[154]

Finally, the specific focus of Lindars's book on apologetic efforts can leave the impression that all early Christian doctrine arose from these apologetical concerns. For example, while he is surely correct to emphasize the constructive role of the passion apologetic in shaping early christology, his suggestion that the doctrine of the atonement arose as its positive counterpart undervalues other possible explanations (e.g., the implications of Jesus' own teaching and healings) for the development of this doctrine. Lindars's apologetic is better seen as one part of an extensive Christian exegetical activity which also served liturgical, catechetical, and more broadly didactic purposes.[155]

Lindars's insistence on the variety of interpretations of a single *testimonium* was supported by David M. Hay's work on Psalm 110, *Glory at the Right Hand: Psalm 110 in Early Christianity*.[156] Hay neatly summarized the major uses to which Christians put Ps 110:1:

(1) vindication or glorification of Jesus

(1a) glorification or empowerment of Christians

(2) support for christological titles

(3) subjection of powers to Jesus

(4) intercession or priesthood of Jesus[157]

Unlike Lindars, however, Hay concluded that no simple line of development can be traced in the psalm's interpretation,[158] and he occasionally argued for the use of written TCs in early Christianity (e.g., in *Barn.* 12:10–11 and Heb 1:13/*1 Clement* 36).[159]

---

[154] See the comments of H.F.D. Sparks, Review of Lindars, *New Testament Apologetic*, *JTS* 13 n.s. (1962) 400–401. Sparks concluded his review with a genuine, if backhanded, compliment to Lindars: "All of it is interesting. Much of it is really exciting—not to say fascinating in its ingenuity. And some of it may well be true" (p. 401).

[155] Ibid., 134–37. A few years after the publication of *New Testament Apologetic*, Lindars revised his view in "Second Thoughts IV. Books of Testimonies," *ExpTim* 75 (1964) 173–75. Influenced by Pierre Prigent's work on *Barnabas*, Lindars allowed for a more complex range of pre-NT *testimonia*: not only oral traditions, but also thematic TCs, text-and-commentary collections, and "little gospels" with texts correlated to kerygmatic statements. Some of these documents may have had a fairly wide circulation; others may have been purely local. Lindars concludes, "The question of testimony books is by no means closed" (p. 175).

[156] SBLMS 18; Nashville/New York: Abingdon, 1973.

[157] Hay, *Right Hand*, 45. Hay included a wealth of NT and early Christian references for these positions.

[158] Ibid., 156.

[159] Ibid., 38–39.

1.14 Testimonia *Collections and Other Intermediate Sources of Quotations*

An important aspect of Hay's study on Psalm 110 is his discussion of "intermediary" scriptural sources. He argued that Christian references to Jesus' sitting at God's right hand may not indicate *direct* use of Ps 110:1, but simply use of a hymn or confession which incorporated the verse. While Hay offered such considerations as "rhythmic" prose and "settings indicative of creed-like origin" to distinguish creeds or hymns from TCs,[160] these criteria cannot be used to make absolute distinctions between the genres. A catena of texts may well have been arranged into a hymnic composition and at the same time functioned as a TC.[161]

Similarly, Edward Gordon Selwyn's classic commentary on 1 Peter argued that a hymn rather than a *testimonia* collection is the source for the "stone" citations found in Rom 9:33 and 1 Pet 2:6–8. Selwyn noted that (1) hymns were used as a medium of teaching/catechesis (cf. Col 3:16) and (2) some deviations from the LXX may simply be due to the exigencies of placing citations in a rhythmical structure.[162] In individual cases, then, the distinction between a hymn and a TC may be impossible to draw.

1.15 *Philip Carrington and E.G. Selwyn: Catechetical Patterns in the New Testament*

Philip Carrington sketched out a catechetical pattern which he claimed to find in sections of 1 Thessalonians; Romans; Galatians; 1 Peter; James; Ephesians; and Colossians.[163] For Carrington, this pattern reflected catechesis given in a baptismal life-setting. Using rabbinic models, he argued that these Christian traditions were passed down orally.[164] The common catechesis was based on the image of the new Christian church as community of holiness (derived from Leviticus

---

[160] Ibid., 39–43; tabular summary on p. 42.

[161] See ibid., 39 for the argument that the *testimonia* in Heb 1:5–14 and *1 Clement* 36 were used in early church worship.

[162] Selwyn, *The First Epistle of St. Peter: The Greek Text with Introduction, Notes and Essays* (2d ed.; London: Macmillan, 1947) 273–77.

[163] Carrington, *The Primitive Christian Catechism: A Study in the Epistles* (Cambridge: Cambridge University Press, 1940).

[164] See esp. 67–73.

17–20), and included a parenetic section which contained the following exhortations: (1) Put off (ἀποτίθημι) all evil; (2) submit yourselves (ὑποτάσσω) to the elders (or to God); (3) watch (γρηγορέω) and pray; (4) resist the devil (ἀνθίστημι).

E.G. Selwyn followed a similar procedure in arguing for common catechetical and parenetic patterns underlying the epistles and other NT passages.[165] Selwyn preferred an expanded classification system (referred to by Carrington) which included (1) New Creation/New Birth, and (2) the Worship of God in addition to the four categories noted above.

Although neither work treats the subject of *testimonia* as such, the studies of Carrington and Selwyn have implications for any *testimonia* hypothesis. If the common catechesis is based on certain OT passages such as Leviticus 17–20; this necessarily implies a prior stage in which these passages were selected and adapted to the catechetical context.[166] While the attempt to uncover a specifically baptismal catechesis has been judged unsuccessful,[167] the solid conclusion that independent NT writers shared a parenetic tradition ultimately based on selected scriptures is clearly relevant in assessing the case for early TCs.

1.16   Testimonia *and Jewish Exegetical Techniques*

1.16.1   Testimonia *and Midrash*

N.J. Hommes had argued (against Harris) that Christian collections of scripture were not reflections of a single book, but rather represented individual Christian writers' use of Jewish exegetical techniques in which texts were collected to interpret one another. Subsequent scholars agree that Christians used these "midrashic" techniques, but they are divided as to the implications of this fact for *testimonia* hypotheses.[168]

---

[165] Selwyn, *Peter*, 365–466.

[166] Robert Hodgson discusses NT patterns of parenesis which are based on scriptural collections; see sect. 1.18 below.

[167] See Paul J. Achtemeier, *A Commentary on First Peter* (Hermeneia; Minneapolis: Fortress, 1996) 60–61.

[168] Two major survey articles from the early 1970s discuss the *testimonia* thesis within the larger framework of Jewish exegetical practices: Merrill P. Miller, "Targum, Midrash and the Use of the Old Testament in the New Testament," *JSJ* 2 (1971)

Joseph Bonsirven held that Paul's use of "rabbinic" techniques ruled out his use of TCs. He argued that Paul, trained in memorizing, meditating upon, and repeating scripture, would simply have no need of a written collection of texts.[169] Although Bonsirven's study was pioneering in its systematic effort to understand Paul's scriptural interpretation within a Jewish framework, his pre-Dead Sea Scrolls understanding of first-century Jewish exegesis seriously undervalues the role of written traditions.

C.F. Burney, in contrast, combined an emphasis on Jewish exegesis with a *testimonia* thesis. Referring to Acts 6:7, Burney argued that recently converted Jewish priests may have used their training to compose collections of OT *testimonia* "with the object of meeting Rabbinic Judaism on its own ground."[170] Paul, Burney contends, drew from such a collection at 1 Cor 15:45. His introduction, οὕτως καὶ γέγραπται, is meant to refer both to the quoted scripture Ἐγένετο ὁ πρῶτος ἄνθρωπος Ἀδὰμ εἰς ψυχὴν ζῶσαν (Gen 2:4), and the authoritative deduction that accompanied it in the *testimonia* source: ὁ ἔσχατος Ἀδὰμ εἰς πνεῦμα ζῳοποιοῦν.[171]

The attempt to define the term "midrash" itself has resulted in a fruitful scholarly debate. Renée Bloch's well-known definition proposed that midrash is characterized by (1) scripture as its point of departure; (2) a homiletical style; (3) attention to the details of text; (4) an adaptation of scripture to present concerns; and (5) both haggadic and halakhic purposes.[172] Addison G. Wright's definition also emphasized the scriptural text as starting point: a text is midrashic if it focuses on understanding a biblical passage (cited explicitly or

---

29–82, and D. Moody Smith, "The Use of the Old Testament in the New," in James M. Efird, ed., *The Use of the Old Testament in the New and Other Essays: Studies in Honor of William Franklin Stinespring* (Durham, NC: Duke University Press, 1972) 3–65, esp. 25–35 on *testimonia*.

[169] Bonsirven, *Exégèse Rabbinique et Exégèse Paulinienne* (Bibliothèque de la Théologie Historique; Paris: Beauchesne, 1939) 292, 337. Bonsirven also noted that LXX-deviant citations in Paul were possibly due to different LXX recensions or imprecise citations.

[170] Burney, *The Aramaic Origin of the Fourth Gospel* (Oxford: Clarendon, 1922) 46.

[171] Ibid., 45–46. W.D. Davies, while accepting the probable existence of TCs in Paul's time, argued that Genesis 1–2 is not part of the "well-defined blocks of Scripture" from which *testimonia* were drawn (*Paul and Rabbinic Judaism: Some Rabbinic Aspects in Pauline Theology* [2d ed.; London: SPCK, 1955] 44).

[172] Bloch, "Midrash," *DBSup* 5/29: 1263–80; repr. in William Scott Green, ed., *Approaches to Early Judaism: Theory and Practice* (BJS 1; Missoula, MT: Scholars Press, 1978) 29–50, esp. 31–34.

implicitly); it is not midrashic if it merely cites a scriptural passage in support of another purpose.[173] While Wright's definition is probably too strict,[174] it implies a working distinction between midrash and *testimonia* which I will employ: midrash takes scripture as its starting point and seeks to draw out further meaning; a *testimonium* takes an extra-biblical subject as its starting point and refers to scripture as a witness to this subject, by this process also drawing out further meaning from the scripture.[175]

E. Earle Ellis worked from a similar distinction between midrash and *testimonium*. A midrash begins from scripture and argues exegetically to a certain conclusion (Ellis uses the schematic Scripture > Current Event). The direct application of a scripture to a certain conclusion, without exegetical argument, is a *testimonium* (the schematic is Current Event > Scripture). Ellis argues that the use of a *testimonium* often points to prior midrashic activity which established a cer-

---

[173] Wright, *The Literary Genre Midrash* (Staten Island, NY: Alba, 1967) 144. Wright contends that John 6 is midrashic, while Chronicles and Josephus's *Jewish Antiquities*, though they re-work biblical material, are not midrashic since they are not meant to be read in the context of the cited scripture. Cf. Gary G. Porton's proposal: "Midrash is a type of literature, oral or written, which has its starting point in a fixed canonical text, considered the revealed word of God by the midrashist and his audience, and in which this original verse is explicitly cited or clearly alluded to" ("Midrash: Palestinian Jews and the Hebrew Bible in the Greco-Roman Period," *ANRW* 2.19.2. 112).

[174] See Miller, "Targum," 44. Miller argues that a focus on understanding scripture cannot be neatly separated from the concern to interpret present events. In a Christian context, for example, scripture witnesses to and interprets Christ, even as Christ and the events of his life unveil the deeper meaning of scripture. Cf. also Jacob Neusner (*Midrash in Context: Exegesis in Formative Judaism* [The Foundations of Judaism: Method, Teleology, Doctrine, Part One: Method; Philadelphia: Fortress, 1983] 82–83) who offers a taxonomy of four categories in rabbinic midrashic collections: (1) close exegesis of the words or phrases of a passage; (2) amplification of a larger scriptural unit; (3) focus on a theme, for reflection on which the cited scriptural passage is but a pretext; (4) collection of passages around a given theme ("topical anthologies"). The rabbis, then, employed both midrashic and *testimonia* techniques (as I define them in this section) in their midrash collections.

[175] "Midrashic" literature is related to the targums; there is no hard and fast distinction between a midrashic interpretation and a freer or more periphrastic targum (see E. Earle Ellis, "Midrash, Targum and New Testament Quotations" in E. Earle Ellis and Max Wilcox, eds., *Neotestamentica et Semitica: Studies in Honour of Matthew Black* [Edinburgh: T. & T. Clark, 1969] 63–65; repr. in Ellis, *Prophecy and Hermeneutic in Early Christianity* [Grand Rapids: Baker, 1993] 188–97; orig. pub., WUNT 18; Tübingen: Mohr-Siebeck, 1978]). I understand the *pesher* interpretation of Qumran, with its explicit starting point in the biblical text, as a type of midrash. On this latter point, see Ellis, "Midrash," 62–63. Here Ellis suggests that *pesher* be understood as "haggadic, i.e., non-legal midrash," and points out that the terms "midrash" and *pesher* are identified in 4QFlor 1.14 [4QEschatological Midrash].

tain interpretation of that passage.[176] Ellis here raised the "chicken and the egg" dilemma of *testimonia* study: are TCs prior to or the result of midrashic compilations?[177]

In another study, Ellis compared Paul's use of Hab 2:4 in Gal 3:11 and in Rom 1:17 to illustrate the two uses of scripture. In Galatians, Paul's focus is on interpreting the Habakkuk passage in the wider context of his midrash on Gen 15:6 (Gal 3:6–9): the story of the faith of Abraham illuminates the meaning of the prophet. In Rom 1:17, however, Hab 2:4 is used as a *testimonium*, i.e., its relevance to the current topic is simply asserted, not exegetically established. This shows that Rom 1:17 "presupposes the midrash of Galatians 3 or something like it."[178] Ellis's point is important: a *testimonium*, in order to function as a forensic proof-text, cannot itself stand in need of proof.[179]

Jan Willem Doeve also argues for the priority of midrashic compilations over *testimonia* collections in Christian literature.[180] Doeve emphasized Christian use of the Jewish technique *gezerah shevah*—the practice of bringing scriptural texts together through links of vocabulary or theme for the purpose of mutual interpretation. Since this practice presupposes an understanding of scripture as an organic whole, Doeve rejected the possibility of early Christian or Jewish TCs of diverse passages: "Words lifted from their Scriptural context can never be a *testimonium* to the Jewish mind." Extant *testimonia* collections from the patristic era presuppose a non-Jewish audience unfamiliar with midrashic techniques.[181] Doeve's argument is not cogent,

---

[176] Ellis, "Midrashic Features in the Speeches of Acts," in Albert Descamps and André de Halleux, eds., *Mélanges Bibliques en hommage au R.P. Béda Rigaux* (Gembloux: Duculot, 1970) 308–309; repr. in Ellis, *Prophecy*, 198–208.

[177] Dodd's conclusion was of course unambiguous: "The composition of 'testimony-books' was the result, not the presupposition, of the work of early Christian biblical scholars" (*Scriptures*, 126).

[178] Ellis, "Midrash," 65–66. Ellis gives as a further example 2 Samuel 7, read midrashically in Acts 13:16–41 and used as a *testimonium* in 2 Cor 6:18 and Heb 1:5 (pp. 66–68). See also Ellis, "Speeches," 310–12.

[179] Cf. Dodd's observations on this distinctions: in Hebrews 3–4, the author must argue for the applicability of Ps 95:11 to contemporary concerns, while Heb 2:12 simply assumes the applicability of Ps 21:23 to the point that Jesus is not ashamed to call believers brothers and sisters. Similarly, Paul *argues* that Deut 30:12–13 is applicable to his gospel message (Rom 10:6–10); he *assumes* that passages from Isaiah 8 and 27 (Rom 9:33) can be applied to the Christ events (*Scriptures*, 22–23).

[180] Doeve, *Jewish Hermeneutics*.

[181] Ibid., 115–16. Cf. Miller ("Targum," 55), who likewise considers midrash collections to be earlier than Christian TCs.

however, for the same process involved in the "midrashic" *gezerah shevah* is evident in TCs: lifting a passage out of its scriptural context and creating a new context of combined scriptures, whether in a *testimonia* list or a midrashic composition.

Use of a scripture as a forensic *testimonium*—without exegetical argument—presupposes that an intended audience will accept the cited passage as *authoritative*. The author assumes *either* that the cited passage self-evidently is relevant to the point to be proved *or* that the reader knows an authoritative interpretation of it which makes it relevant to the proof at hand.

1.16.2   Testimonia *and Jewish Homiletical Forms*

A variant of the above *testimonia*/midrash discussion centers on the distinction between TCs and midrashic homilies. J.W. Bowker isolated two homiletical forms in the speeches of Acts: the "proem" and the *yelammedenu*.[182] These forms are related to the synagogue lectionary readings: the *seder* (the central reading from the Torah) and the *haftarah* (secondary readings from the Prophets). The "proem" homily form begins with a scriptural text, which is interpreted with a string of texts related to the *haftarah* and leading towards the *seder*. The related *yelammedenu* form begins with a question which is then answered with a string of texts that lead to the *seder* of the day.[183] Bowker concluded that various speeches in Acts have elements of these homily forms. Paul's speech in Acts 13:17–41, for example, was originally a homily in which the *seder* was Deut 4:25–46, a *haftarah* 2 Sam 7:6–16, and a proem text 1 Sam 13:14; the whole composition shows indications of an Aramaic original. The major difficulties with Bowker's study are that our evidence for these rabbinic forms is late,[184]

---

[182] Bowker, "Speeches in Acts: A Study in Proem and Yelammedenu Form," *NTS* 14 (1967–68) 96–111.

[183] Ibid., 99–101. The classic work seeking to relate the Palestinian lectionary cycle to extant homiletic midrashim is Jacob Mann's *The Bible as Read and Preached in the Old Synagogue: A Study in the Cycles of the Readings from the Torah and Prophets, and in the Structure of the Midrashic Homilies* (2 vols.; Cincinnati, 1940; New York, 1966; repr. Library of Biblical Studies; New York: KTAV, 1971).

[184] See Charles Perrot, "The Reading of the Bible in the Ancient Synagogue," in Martin Jan Mulder, ed., *Mikra: Text, Translation, Reading and Interpretation of the Hebrew Bible in Ancient Judaism and Early Christianity* (CRINT 2/1; Assen/Maastricht: Van Gorcum; Philadelphia: Fortress, 1988) 158. Perrot notes that the extant *yelammedenu* sermons are "hardly earlier than the fifth century CE" Yet if the fixed liturgical reading patterns of the Talmudic period cannot be read back into the pre-70 CE period, nevertheless "beyond the gaps in history, there are continuities to be found (p. 157)."

that lectionary readings differed from region to region,[185] and that as the sermons made only indirect allusions to the *seder* and *haftarah* readings, isolating the exact references is difficult.

If the above difficulties make a precise fixing of lectionary readings with extant texts a dubious task, nevertheless certain fixed commentary patterns in the literature may suggest an original life-setting of liturgical readings and explication. Peder Borgen's study of a homiletical form in John 6 is especially valuable since he does not rely on rabbinic evidence but is able to show parallel structures in the contemporary Philo.[186] Recently, a Lawrence Wills's study isolated a "word of exhortation" sermon form in the NT and other early Christian and contemporary Jewish literature.[187] Yet even granted that a homiletical form is present already in the NT, this does not solve the *testimonia* issue: were texts (e.g. in Acts 13) brought together because of a fixed lectionary schedule, the homilist's (or a later editor's) own interest, or did a previous scriptural tradition (oral or written) dictate the selection? Does a homilist establish the significance of a base text by exegetical argument or does he take over an already established *testimonium*?

1.16.3   Testimonia *and the Dead Sea Scrolls*

In my discussion of Barnabas Lindars above, I noted the influence of the *pesher* commentary on Habakkuk as a model for his understanding of early Christian exegesis. Krister Stendahl, in his classic study *The School of Saint Matthew and its Use of the Old Testament* (1954), also used the Habakkuk commentary as a model for his analysis of Matthew's "fulfillment" quotations. Rejecting the claims of a long line of scholars who argued that these quotations represent a TC taken over by the evangelist,[188] Stendahl understood them as an integral part of the Gospel, produced by the Matthean "school."[189]

The school used the exegetical techniques evident at Qumran:

---

[185] See Ellis, "Speeches," 305 n. 3.

[186] Borgen, *Bread from Heaven: An Exegetical Study of the Concept of Manna in the Gospel of John and the Writings of Philo* (NovTSup 10; Leiden: Brill, 1965).

[187] Wills, "The Form of the Sermon in Hellenistic Judaism and Early Christianity," *HTR* 77 (1984) 277–99. Wills also uses Paul's speech in Acts 13 as an example of this form.

[188] The LXX-deviant character and striking introduction formulas in these Matthean quotations had already attracted the attention of Credner, Gregory, Burkitt and Harris.

[189] Stendahl, *School*, 31.

deliberate alteration of the scriptural text and the selection of variant readings congenial to their own interpretations.[190] For example,
Stendahl maintained that the quotation of Isa 42:1–4 (Matt 12:18–21)
shows knowledge of traditions reflected in the MT, LXX, Theodotion,
targums, and the OT Peshitta. The school carefully chose these variants and blended them into a theological whole.[191] This sort of detailed analysis of the quotations and the comparison of them with
various scriptural traditions is the strength and lasting value of Stendahl's work. His attempts to show that the quotations are products
of the Matthean school and thus fit smoothly into their current context in the Gospel are less convincing.

Stendahl portrays the "school" as an alternative to *testimonia* hypotheses.[192] Again, however, the two options are not mutually exclusive.
The real question is why certain texts were chosen by a "school"
or by any other early Christian—has a tradition already privileged
certain texts or established a Christian interpretation for these texts?
Stendahl in fact admits that this is the case: OT citations in Matt
3:3 and 11:10 (linked with John the Baptist), 24:30, and 26:31 probably had an independent existence as Christian *testimonia* before their
incorporation into Matthew.[193]

Norman Perrin, adopting the "stage" development model of Lindars,
also focused on the development of Christian *pesher* traditions.[194] He
argues that the conflation of Ps 110:1 and Dan 7:13 (read with Zech
12:10) in Mark 14:62 is the result of the merging of two Christian
pesher traditions which utilized Jewish "messianic" interpretations of
Dan 7:13. Mark 14:62 is a result of the "historicization" of these
traditions, i.e., placing later formulations on the lips of the Jesus.

---

[190] See ibid., 183–202.

[191] Ibid., 107–15, 127. Robert Horton Gundry, in his own detailed study, also
concludes that the quotations in Matthew (both "fulfillment" and other non-Markan
quotations) show a knowledge of a variety of scriptural traditions, but held that this
knowledge goes back not to a Matthean school but to the apostle Matthew himself (*The Use of the Old Testament in St. Matthew's Gospel with Special Reference to the
Messianic Hope* [NovTSup 18; Leiden: Brill, 1967]).

[192] See Stendahl, *School*, 216–17, for the argument that use of midrashic and
homiletical techniques are a better explanation for composite quotations than a *testimonia* hypothesis.

[193] Ibid., 47–51, 83, 212–14.

[194] Perrin, "Mark XIV. 62: The End Product of a Christian Pesher Tradition?"
NTS (1965–66) 150–55. See also his *Rediscovering the Teachings of Jesus* (New York/
Evanston: Harper & Row; London: SCM, 1967) 172–85, which presupposes the exe-
getical results of the earlier article.

As was the case with Lindars, Perrin's recovery of the stages of the *pesher* remain speculative. His use of late midrashic collections as evidence for pre-Christian Jewish messianic readings is unacceptable (though his use of Enoch traditions is on firmer ground). His position on the "historicization" of the *pesher* rules out the possibility that these traditions began in the teachings of Jesus—an unnecessarily skeptical exclusion. At the same time, Perrin is right to bring out the close connections between established Jewish traditions, Christian exegetical activity in combining *testimonia*, and the influence of this activity on christology.

Similarly, Matthew Black sees a midrashic tradition of combining texts as the background to various christological titles.[195] The Χριστός title is based on "messianic" texts: Amos 9:11, 2 Sam 7:11–14, and Ps 2:7;[196] the Son of Man christology (both Synoptic and Johannine) results from traditions combining Dan 7:13, Isa 52:13, Ps 118:22, and Hos 6:2; the κύριος christology has an important source in a midrash on *1 Enoch* 1:9 (cf. Jude 14). Black is keen to show that many of these exegetical traditions go back to pre-Christian times (he often proposes an Aramaic background to the texts).[197] While Black used the term *testimonia* in his studies, it is unclear whether he refers to written collections or oral traditions.

The 1956 publication of 4QTestimonia renewed interest in written *testimonia* hypotheses.[198] In its initial publication, John M. Allegro explicitly invoked the classic thesis: "There can be little doubt that we have in this document a group of *testimonia* of the type long ago proposed by Burkitt, Rendel Harris, and others to have existed in the early Church."[199] Joseph A. Fitzmyer's influential 1957 article, "'4QTestimonia' and the New Testament," provided additional impetus for reconsideration of use of TCs in the NT in the light of 4QTestimonia, 4QFlorilegium, and *Papyrus Rylands Greek 460*.[200]

---

[195] Black, "The Christological Use of the Old Testament in the New Testament," *NTS* 18 (1971–72) 1–14.

[196] Ibid., 1–4.

[197] See also Black's study of the Semitic background to the Psalm 110 and Daniel 7 *testimonia*, "Πᾶσαι ἐξουσία αὐτῷ ὑποταγήσονται (Ps 110:1; Dan 7:13; 1 Cor 15:24–27; Eph 1:20–21; 1 Pet 3:22)," in M.D. Hooker and S.G. Wilson, eds., *Paul and Paulinism: Essays in Honour of C.K. Barrett* (London: SPCK, 1982) 74–82.

[198] The document cites a string of scriptural texts without intervening comment. For details, see below, sect. 2.7.5.

[199] Allegro, "Further Messianic References in Qumran Literature," *JBL* 75 (1956) 186.

[200] Fitzmyer, "4QTestimonia." Fitzmyer stressed the similarity of the NT composite

1.17   *Patristic Studies*: Barnabas, *Justin, and* Testimonia *Collections*

1.17.1   *Pierre Prigent and* Barnabas

Pierre Prigent's 1961 work on *Barnabas, Les Testimonia dans le christianisme primitif: L'épître de Barnabé I–XVI et ses sources*, sparked a renewed
discussion of patristic TCs that has continued until the present day.
Prigent's central goal was to define more closely the phenomenon
of *testimonia*; he chose *Barnabas*, with its numerous scriptural quotations,
as a test case.[201] Prigent rightly began by addressing the lack of scholarly agreement on the precise form of the *testimonia*: Hatch referred
to manuals, Vollmer to small collections; others to exegetical traditions
linked to certain texts.[202] Though nowhere offering his own formal
definition, Prigent works with the model represented by Cyprian's
To Quirinus: proof-texts grouped around a word or theme, unac-
companied by exegetical remarks. He recognizes that the quotations
often deviate from texts represented by the MT or LXX.[203] He uses
standard scholarly criteria for detecting *testimonia*: composite quotations, false attributions, LXX-deviant readings, same series of quotations in independent authors, and a series of quotations used by
an author for a purpose clearly different from the original purpose
of that series.[204]

Prigent differentiated between *Barnabas*'s use of *testimonia* sources
(which he divided into "messianic" and "anti-cultic") and its use of
"midrashic" sources.[205] The "anti-cultic" source (found, e.g., in *Barn.*
3:1–5) is a single document, whose chapters systematically treat such
Jewish rituals as fasting and sabbath observance. Prigent argued that
this *testimonia* source had a particular theology: a spiritualizing interpretation of the OT which denied that the Jewish cult ever had
legitimacy. The "messianic" *testimonia* are divided into "christological"
(e.g., *Barn.* 6:1, 2–4) and "universal" (e.g., *Barn.* 12:10–11) categories;

---

quotations and these three documents. On 4QFlorilegium, see sect. 2.7.7a below;
on *P. Ryl. Gk. 460*, see sect. 3.6.1 below.

[201] Prigent, *Testimonia*, 28.

[202] Ibid., 16–28.

[203] Ibid., 82, 204 n. 4.

[204] Ibid., 28. Prigent refers to this last criterion as his own contribution, yet
Bousset and Ungern-Sternberg had already used it in their own studies of Justin.

[205] While these are Prigent's main categories, he also attributes some quotations
to other sources: "Jewish apocalyptic" traditions (pp. 70, 219); a Syrian Christian
tradition (p. 70); a source influenced by the "two-ways" tradition (p. 157); a Christian
apocalypse (p. 158); and "targumic paraphrases" (p. 66).

Prigent is less clear on the exact form of these *testimonia*. The midrashic source (e.g., in *Barnabas* 7–8) is typological, less anti-Jewish, shows an interest in the Christian sacraments, and was apparently developed for internal Christian use in a catechetical or liturgical setting.[206]

In a lengthy excursus, Prigent attempted to show that the messianic *testimonia* are part of the wider Christian use of *testimonia* in the first two centuries.[207] These texts were originally collected to recount the passion through prophecy and to present summaries of the Christian faith. Prigent follows earlier *testimonia* scholars in proposing that these putative collections were considered authoritative: they were derived from the apostles and formed the basis for later confessions of faith.[208] Similar uses of "messianic" *testimonia* are found in Irenaeus (ancient formulas of faith and lists of OT prophecies applied to the life of Jesus)[209] and indeed already in the NT.[210]

Prigent's work has been rightly criticized for lack of clarity in his definition of *testimonia*.[211] The form of his putative messianic *testimonia* is especially vague. More importantly, Prigent does not explicitly include the *function* of the *testimonia* in his definition, a distinction which would help to distinguish it more clearly from "midrash."

Prigent's definition mixes formal and content categories. While the terms *testimonia* and midrash involve formal distinctions, "anti-cultic" and "messianic" refer only to content.[212] This confusion is apparent in Prigent's attribution of an anti-Jewish theology to his proposed *testimonia* source. This attribution led Prigent to classify the strongly anti-Jewish retelling of Moses breaking the tablets (*Barn.* 4:7–8; 14:1–3) as part of his *testimonia* source, notwithstanding its clearly midrashic character.[213]

---

[206] Ibid., 218.

[207] Ibid., 183–216.

[208] Ibid., 218.

[209] Ibid., 183–90. Here Prigent employs the criterion of common texts in a sequence.

[210] Ibid., 204–7. Prigent refers to the passion predictions in Mark 9:31, 10:33 par., which he argues are based on small literary units announcing the passion, death, and resurrection of Christ through prophecy.

[211] See H. Stegemann, Review of Prigent, *Testimonia*, *ZKG* 73 (1962) 144; Jean-Paul Audet, "L'hypothèse des Testimonia: Remarques autour d'un livre récent," *RB* 70 (1963) 400.

[212] See Stegemann, Review, 144, 147. Stegemann rightly holds that one cannot establish a source simply on grounds of content.

[213] See also the critique in James Carleton Paget, *The Epistle of Barnabas: Outlook and Background* (WUNT 2/64; Tübingen: Mohr-Siebeck, 1994) 175.

Jean-Paul Audet and H. Stegemann offer important challenges to
the criteria used to establish use of written TCs. Stegemann attacked the
criteria on two fronts: (1) with many other scholars, he held that the
phenomena of composite texts and common sequences may simply
point to use of common scriptural tradition, and (2) if the criteria
do indeed indicate a written or oral collection, this does not necessarily imply that the collection functioned as *testimonia*. These collections may have been used in biblical commentaries, targumic or
midrashic rewritings of scripture, or in liturgical or catechetical settings.[214] The key distinction is an informed judgment on the *function*
of a scriptural collection.

Audet notes that the literary independence of common witnesses—
a key to most of the criteria for use of TCs—is difficult to establish. Audet argued that the ancient world in general, and Christians
in particular, placed little value on the careful citation of sources.[215]
Audet's warning is important, but it cuts both ways: if an author
does not bother to acknowledge that her scriptural quotations are
taken from *1 Clement*, for example, neither would that same author
bother to acknowledge her use of a TC.

Audet also offers an alternative explanation for the phenomenon
of common LXX-deviant quotations in independent authors: these
writers used a "popular transmission of the Greek OT."[216] Skarsaune
correctly points out, however, that the hypothesis of popular versions of scripture that deviate strongly from the LXX and the MT
(as *Barnabas*'s quotations so often do) is more speculative than the
hypothesis of smaller scale TCs.[217]

Audet makes a further important distinction between the use of
private and public scriptural ECs. The practice of making personal
notes or memory aids in the ancient world must be distinguished
from that of creating ECs designed for wider publication. Audet
maintains that there is no evidence for Christian ECs of this latter

---

[214] Stegemann, Review, 152; Audet, "L'hypothèse," 394; see also Robert A. Kraft,
Review of Prigent, *Testimonia*, *JTS* n.s. 13 (1962) 405.
[215] Ibid., 393–94. He notes that *Barnabas* itself was probably originally anonymous. Audet (p. 393 n. 13) refers to Pliny the Elder, who prided himself on an
honest acknowledgment of his sources, in contrast to most of his contemporaries
(see Pliny, *Natural History*, preface, 21–22).
[216] Audet, "L'hypothèse," 395.
[217] Skarsaune, *Prophecy*, 22 n. 29.

type before Melito (ca. 170) and Cyprian (ca. 250).[218] It is anachronistic to use Cyprian's extensive, written collection in *To Quirinus* as a model for the first Christian centuries.[219] Audet's point has implications for the issue of authority: even if use of a scriptural EC or TC is detected in a work, we cannot jump on this basis alone to conclusions concerning its authority for a wider community.

Finally, Prigent's work has been faulted for taking the problem of *testimonia* as its starting point. Audet suggests that this singular focus on the *testimonia* question excluded Prigent from seriously considering other possibilities.[220]

L.W. Barnard is another scholar who studied *Barnabas* with an eye towards the *testimonia* question, using Dodd's model of the common use of wider scriptural contexts.[221] Barnard employed an evolutionary schema in which oral traditions were built up gradually into more complex written collections. For example, his analysis of the "stone" *testimonia* posits that Jesus first applied Ps 118:22–23 to himself (Mark 12:10–11); additional texts from Isaiah were then added (witnessed in Romans 9 and 1 Peter 2); Luke may have added Dan 2:34, 44–45; and finally the author of *Barnabas* added three new texts when he quotes the *testimonium* in *Barn.* 6:2–4.[222] After reviewing several other *testimonia* complexes in *Barnabas*, Barnard concluded that *Barnabas*'s *testimonia* are based on "a strong oral tradition and a variety of partial transcripts."[223] Barnard's fluid model of gradually evolving collections is important, although again his principle that the earliest collections were oral is not necessarily correct.

---

[218] Audet, "L'hypothèse," 403–5.

[219] Ibid., 401.

[220] Ibid., 386. Prigent went on to study the use of OT quotations in Justin: *Justin et l'Ancien Testament: L'Argumentation scripturaire du traité de Justin contre toutes les hérésies comme source principale du dialogue avec Tryphon et de la première apologie* (Paris: Gabalda, 1964). Against his own initial expectations, Prigent concluded that Justin did not depend directly on TCs in *1 Apology* and *Dialogue*, but rather used his own earlier (no longer extant) work, the *Syntagma Against all Heresies*. Prigent declined to speculate on whether this earlier work was itself based on TCs.

[221] Barnard, "The Use of Testimonies in the Early Church and in the Epistle of Barnabas," in idem, *Studies in the Apostolic Fathers and Their Background* (New York: Schocken, 1966) 109–35.

[222] Ibid., 115–22.

[223] Ibid., 133. Barnard argues that the quotation of Ps 51 (50):19 in *Barn.* 2:10, with its parallels in Irenaeus and others, derives from a written source (p. 128); in *Barnabas* 9 the epistle's "more discursive" style indicates that its author is working with "traditional material" (p. 130).

Robert A. Kraft's studies also support the conclusion that *Barnabas* makes use of small scale TCs.[224] His analysis of six quotations in *Barnabas* with major deviations from the LXX reveals a highly complex relationship between these quotations and their parallels in other Christian authors (esp. Justin, Irenaeus, Cyprian, Tertullian, and Ps.-Gregory). While one author will agree with *Barnabas* in quoting a particular non-LXX form, that same author will agree with the LXX over against *Barnabas* in other quotations.[225] Kraft envisioned "testimony note sheets"[226] which were later gathered together and revised into larger collections. The mixed record of agreement and variation in the extant witness of the *testimonia* literature would be due to the chance preservation or loss of these note sheets.[227]

1.17.2 *Jean Daniélou's* Testimonia *Studies*

A good part of the work of the prolific French scholar and cardinal, Jean Daniélou, specifically addresses the patristic use of scriptural *testimonia*.[228] Daniélou saw himself continuing the tradition of previous *testimonia* scholars such as Harris, Dodd, Lindars, and the contemporary studies of Prigent. He accepted the criteria for detection of written TCs articulated by earlier scholars, emphasizing especially LXX-deviant readings (interpreted as deliberate, "Christianizing" alterations) and conflated citations.[229] His own approach involved the study of the history of interpretation of a particular OT text, fol-

---

[224] See esp. Kraft, "Isaiah," 350.

[225] Ibid., 348. Thus Irenaeus is the only other ante-Nicene witness to *Barnabas*'s peculiar reading of Isa 50:8–9 (p. 348), but he lacks a variation (ἱμάτια [garments] read for ἰάματα [healings]) in quoting Isa 58:8 which *Barnabas* and several other early authors read and interpreted in a Christian sense (pp. 342–43).

[226] He suggests 4QTestimonia as a possible example of a "note sheet" (ibid., 350).

[227] Ibid., 349–50. See also Kraft's critical notes, "Barnabas' Isaiah Text and Melito's *Paschal Homily*," *JBL* 80 (1961) 371–73 and "A Note on the Oracle of Rebecca (Gen xxv.23)," *JTS* n.s. 13 (1962) 318–20, where he provides additional evidence (drawn from peculiar readings in Melito and Irenaeus paralleled in *Barnabas*) for *testimonia* circulating in various textual forms.

[228] Some of his most important essays on this topic are collected in *Études d'exégèse judéo-chrétienne (Les Testimonia)* (Théologie Historique 5; Paris: Beauchesne, 1966).

[229] Daniélou refined the LXX-deviant criterion: sometimes we have proof that an author knows the LXX but chooses to cite another version. *Barnabas*, for example, reads the LXX of Isa 50:7 in 5:14, but later cites an LXX-deviant text of the same passage as scripture (6:3). This variant reading is paralleled in *Odes Sol.* 31:11 (*The Theology of Jewish Christianity* [The Development of Christian Doctrine before the Council of Nicaea 1; London: Darton, Longman & Todd, 1964] 92).

lowing its development from the NT well into the patristic era.[230]

Daniélou placed the *testimonia* within the framework of his understanding of "Jewish Christianity." Jewish-Christian quotations are characterized by intentional, interpretive alterations from an LXX *Vorlage*; this freedom with the text reflects contemporary Jewish exegetical practices. These altered texts were considered to have the same authority as scripture—showing a typically Jewish-Christian understanding of scripture as both the sacred text and its authoritative interpretation.

Daniélou argued that often these Jewish-Christian collections were derived from previous Jewish sources. The Christian use of Lam 4:20 in combination with Deut 30:15 (by Justin, Tertullian, Origen), for example, derives from a Jewish collection on the "two ways."[231] The anti-cultic collection (witnessed in *Barn.* 2:4–10), drawn together by the thesis that almighty God has no need of sacrifices, was originally put together in the Qumran community.[232]

Daniélou spoke of a wide variety of life-settings in which the *testimonia* were employed: teaching, catechesis, apology, liturgy.[233] In the manner of Lindars, Daniélou showed that a single *testimonium* text could serve a variety of functions in different contexts. Psalm 22 (21), for example, was first understood messianically, then employed in a liturgical (particularly baptismal) setting, and finally interpreted mystically as presenting stages of spiritual progress.[234]

Daniélou envisioned the original form of TCs as groupings based on common themes (e.g., on the unbelief of the Jews; on Christ's Passion) and catch-words (e.g., λίθος, ῥάβδος, ξύλον) collections. Arguing that traces of such TCs are to be found in the NT,[235] Daniélou, with Barnard and Kraft, posited a development in which these smaller collections were gathered up into the more global works of Cyprian and Ps.-Gregory. At a still later stage, OT *testimonia* were arranged by scriptural books, rather than thematically.[236] In addition to his

---

[230] Daniélou, *Testimonia*, 5–6.

[231] Ibid., 88–89.

[232] Ibid., 167.

[233] Ibid., 6.

[234] "Le Psaume 22 et les étapes de l'initiation," in *Etudes*, 141–62.

[235] E.g., "Χριστὸς Κύριος" (Luke 2:11) depends on a *testimonium* reading of Isa 45:1 (*Testimonia*, 90–93).

[236] Daniélou cites the *Prophetic Extracts* of Clement of Alexandria and Eusebius of Caesaria as examples (*Testimonia*, 9–10). For Clement, see sect. 3.4.7 below; for Eusebius, sect. 3.6.3.

main focus on the Jewish Christian milieu, Daniélou also discussed a Latin tradition of *testimonia*.[237]

With Prigent, he recognized Christian midrash as distinct from *testimonia* sources, without clearly distinguishing between the two.[238] For example, he held that Ezek 37:1–14 was "a part of the most ancient collections of *Testimonia* on the resurrection," at the same time showing that Ezekiel 37 quotations in Justin and Tertullian may well have derived from the midrashic *Apocryphon of Ezekiel*.[239] This last example reflects Daniélou's wide understanding of *testimonia*, as witnessed by his definition of a *testimonium* as "a verse found in circulation in the milieus of the ancient Church," not necessarily dependent on previous collections of verses.[240]

With Dodd and Lindars, Daniélou was convinced of the importance of the *testimonia* for the development of Christian theology. His study of Ps 110:1, for example, concludes that the text was used to develop concepts regarding Christ's divinity and his ascension and enthronement at God's right hand: "indeed the *testimonia* furnished to a very large extent the categories through which the first Christians expressed the significance of the events of the life of Jesus."[241] Yet this judgment needs further scrutiny: did the texts help to form the theological beliefs, or were they simply witnesses to, or proofs of, already established beliefs? This issue is a variant of the above discussion regarding the distinction between quotations used as *testimonia* and quotations used constructively (midrashically) to establish a certain point of interpretation.

1.17.3   *Oskar Skarsaune: Justin's Use of* Testimonia *Collections*

Oskar Skarsaune's recent massively detailed study of Justin's quotations concludes that the apologist's short non-LXX quotations are

---

[237] Daniélou, "Les 'Testimonia' de Commodien," in Antonio Maddalena, et al., eds., *Forma Futuri: Studi in Onore de Cardinale Michele Pelligrino* (Turin: Bottega de Erasmo, 1975) 59. He posits that Commodian is not dependent on Cyprian for his *testimonia*; rather both depend on an earlier Latin collection of *testimonia*. See also his *The Origins of Latin Christianity* (A History of Early Christian Doctrine before the Council of Nicaea 3; London: Darton, Longman & Todd; Philadelphia: Westminster, 1977), esp. pp. 261–95 on Latin *testimonia* traditions.

[238] Daniélou, *Theology*, 97–107.

[239] "La vision des ossements desséchés," in *Testimonia*, 111–21, esp. 111, 118–21.

[240] Daniélou, *Testimonia*, 165.

[241] "La session à la droite du Père (Psaume 109, 1–2)," in *Testimonia*, 42–49; see esp. p. 42.

taken from written Christian *testimonia* sources, while his long LXX quotations are taken from biblical manuscripts.[242] Skarsaune operates with a deliberately broad definition: "I use the term 'testimony source' in a very wide meaning: *source of OT quotations other than a Biblical MS*, implying no prejudice deriving from the traditional account of 'testimony collections.'"[243] Skarsaune, then, can refer to Romans, Galatians, *1 Clement*, and Matthew as some of Justin's *testimonia* sources.[244] At the same time, however, Skarsaune clearly argues that Justin used written collections of OT texts based on themes or catch-word, though he judges that these collections were accompanied by exegetical comments.[245] He cautiously accepts *testimonia* criteria worked out by earlier scholars.[246] Skarsaune's achievement here is to move the discussion beyond the sterile either-or dichotomy of previous positions: the certainty that an author depends literarily on known NT and patristic sources does not rule out the possibility that that author *also* uses non-extant written TCs.[247]

I will reserve a more detailed examination of Skarsaune's analysis of Justin's *testimonia* sources for chapter three (sect. 3.4.1 below). For the present, I simply note two of Skarsaune's most important conclusions: Justin uses a "kerygmatic source" in which *testimonia* were arranged into a creedal pattern to correspond to the life and work of Jesus Christ and a "recapitulation source" in which *testimonia* were arranged in dialogue form (cf. Harris's conclusions concerning the connection between *testimonia* and the dialogue form). While Skarsaune's work is not directly relevant to the issue of the use of TCs in the NT, his evidence for Justin's use of *authoritative* TCs in the middle of the second century indicates that these collections attained this authority at a very early date.

---

[242] Skarsaune, *Prophecy*, 8. See ibid., 21–22, for a general discussion of the *testimonia* hypothesis.

[243] Ibid., 22 n. 29. Emphasis original.

[244] See ibid., 30, 57, 100.

[245] Ibid., 91.

[246] Ibid., 22 n. 29. Skarsaune also offers a further, more general, criterion: evident lack of awareness of the original scriptural context in a quotation. While admitting that this criterion is unsafe in the case of ancient authors with "atomistic" approaches to scripture, he maintains that in Justin at least "there is a conscious effort to place Biblical texts in their proper contexts," and thus the criterion is relevant for detecting Justin's use of *testimonia* sources.

[247] Skarsaune's broad definition of *testimonia* model is adopted explicitly in Carleton Paget, *Barnabas*, 94.

1.18   *Robert Hodgson and the* Testimonia *Hypothesis*

Robert Hodgson's 1979 *JBL* article, "The Testimony Hypothesis," is an explicit attempt to renew the debate on the use of written TCs in the NT.[248] Hodgson presents two bodies of evidence for *testimonia*: (1) extra-biblical anthologies (especially Qumran documents) and (2) scholarly studies of possible *testimonia* use in the NT, categorized under the criteria used by Harris to detect the use of written TCs (non-standard scriptural readings; common sequences;[249] false ascriptions; anti-Jewish material; and editorial comments reflective of a TC). Hodgson then presents his own constructive argument for TCs as a source for the parenetic sequences in 1 Thess 4:1–12 and 1 Pet 1:13–2:3, 11–12.[250]

The latter argument rests on three considerations: (1) the analogy of *Ps.-Phocylides* and 4QOrdinances as parenetic scriptural ECs;[251] (2) content parallels with scriptural passages (especially Leviticus 18–19); and (3) formal parallels (use of imperatival infinitives and participles) with the Decalogue and rabbinic law codes.[252]

---

[248] The article is a revision of a section of Hodgson's dissertation, "Die Quellen der paulinischen Ethik" (Th.D. diss., Heidelberg University, 1976) 1–35. I gratefully acknowledge Hodgson's article for providing many fruitful starting points for my own investigations.

[249] Ibid., 370–71. Hodgson extends this criterion to include common sequences of *allusions* to scripture. One example: Ps 77:2 is combined with an allusion to Isa 6:9–10 in 1 Cor 2:7–9 and Matt 13:14–15. Hodgson is not the first to argue in this manner: Lucien Cerfaux had speculated on a TC underlying 1 Cor 1:18–31, produced in a hellenistic Jewish milieu with the aim of rejecting the "wisdom" of Greek philosophy. Cerfaux had argued from non-LXX citations and allusions which are witnessed in Justin and esp. Clement of Alexandria ("Vestiges d'un florilège dans I Cor., I, 18–III, 23," *RHR* 27 [1931] 521–34; repr. in idem, *Recueil Lucien Cerfaux: Etudes d'Exégèse et d'Histoire Religieuse de Monseigneur Cerfaux* [2 vols.; BETL 6–7; Gembloux: Duculot, 1954] 319–32). The study of allusions in *testimonia* research, while a valid activity in itself, necessarily makes any conclusions more uncertain.

[250] Hodgson ("1 Thessalonians 4:1–12 and the Holiness Tradition [HT]," in Kent H. Richards, ed., *SBL 1982 Seminar Papers* [SBLSP 21; Chico, CA: Scholars Press, 1982] 199–215) gives a fuller argument that 1 Thess 4:1–12 is part of a "tradition of ethical exposition of the Holiness Code in Leviticus 17–26" (p. 199). Hodgson traces this tradition (including similar foundational statements, concrete demands, and motivations) through the LXX of Leviticus, Ps.-Phocylides, and the Damascus Document. Hodgson argues that Paul may have known this tradition in the form of an EC drawn from the Holiness Code (p. 214). Although he demonstrates significant connections (e.g., common use of an imperatival infinitive) between the documents, Hodgson does not offer adequate criteria to distinguish between use of this tradition and the direct use of Leviticus itself.

[251] See sects. 2.6.2 and 2.7.4 below for discussion of these texts.

[252] Hodgson, "Testimony," 376–78.

Hodgson's review of the literature is valuable, surveying both the older *testimonia* literature and more recent applications of the hypothesis in studies such as those of Traugott Holtz[253] on Luke-Acts and Georg Strecker[254] on Matthew's fulfillment quotations. Nevertheless, Hodgson's summary statements and his own constructive example lack precise terminology. He uses the term "testimony" not only of forensic proof-texts, but also of texts which function "in the most diverse spheres of church life: worship, evangelization, catechetics, parenesis, and apologetics."[255] Hodgson also blurs the distinction between written and oral *testimonia*: while his article is structured around the classic criteria to establish use of written collections, his summary statements speak more vaguely of "a primitive Christian testimony cycle."

Hodgson pursued his interest in the *testimonia* hypotheses and a more general interest in ECs in later articles. Isolating twenty-two scriptural quotations and allusions in the sayings collection Q, Hodgson argued that Q has taken over a *testimonia* tradition that included thematic collections on tithing and table fellowship (reflecting contact with Pharisees), judgment, and preaching the good news.[256] His study of Paul's lists of tribulations sketches a history of religions background (in Josephus, Nag Hammadi documents, the Mishnah, and Plutarch) to this genre.[257] Hodgson also devoted two articles to Valerius Maximus, a first century CE Roman anthologist who collected literary extracts into nine books of *exempla*. Hodgson then draws implications of Valerius's collection for study of the NT.[258] These later articles

---

[253] Holtz, *Untersuchungen über die alttestamentlichen Zitate bei Lukas* (TU 104; Berlin: Akademie, 1968).

[254] Strecker, *Der Weg der Gerechtigkeit: Untersuchung zur Theologie des Matthäus* (FRLANT 82; 3d ed.; Göttingen: Vandenhoeck & Ruprecht, 1971).

[255] Hodgson, "Testimony," 375.

[256] Hodgson, "On the Gattung of Q: A Dialogue with James M. Robinson," *Bib* 66 (1985) 73–95. Given that the existence of Q itself is a hypothesis, Hodgson's reconstruction is on quite shaky ground.

[257] "Paul the Apostle and First Century Tribulation Lists," *ZNW* 74 (1983) 59–80.

[258] The anthology is *Factorum et Dictorum Memorabilium Libri Neuem* (Of Noteworthy Deeds and Sayings: Nine Books); see Hodgson, Valerius Maximus and Gospel Criticism," *CBQ* 51 (1988) 502–10; idem, "Valerius Maximus and the Social World of the New Testament," *CBQ* 51 (1989) 683–93. The former article offers useful correctives to contemporary scholarship on pronouncement stories (Valerius has many more action *exempla* than might be expected); the latter shows how Valerius's work sheds light on emperor worship and other aspects of first-century Roman religion.

provide insight into literary genres relevant for the study of early
Christianity, although they do not reflect on *testimonia* hypotheses in
any sustained manner.

1.19   Testimonia *and Recent Discussion on the Nature of*
Christian-Jewish Relations and Messianic Debates

1.19.1   *Jewish-Christian Conflict: Reality or Literary Fiction?*

Recent scholars have continued the Harnack-Simon debate as to
whether anti-Jewish literature, especially in the patristic era, represents actual Jewish-Christian conflict or is merely a literary device.
The recent detailed investigation of *Barnabas* by Reidar Hvalvik concludes that the author (he dates *Barnabas* to ca. 130 CE) wrote in a
setting of actual Jewish-Christian competition.[259] Rosemary Radford
Ruether, on the other hand, argues that the anti-Jewish TCs are to
be seen as an essential part of early Christian anti-Jewish, and eventually anti-Semitic, tradition in which the "Jewish protagonist is a
straw figure for the Christian apology."[260] She argues that this anti-
Jewish polemic is the dark side of what Ungern-Sternberg called the
de Evangelio tradition: God has chosen the Christians as the new
Israel, but has rejected the Jews. The Jew becomes the archetype of
materialistic, narrowly parochial, and unredeemed humanity, acting
as a foil to the spiritual, universal, and redeemed Christian.

Hvalvik's and Ruether's studies need not be seen as mutually exclusive. If Hvalvik shows that the *adversus Judaeos* literature reflects a situation of actual conflict with Jewish opponents, Ruether shows how
this polemic often developed into a caricature of the Jew as the

---

[259] Hvalvik, *The Struggle for Scripture and Covenant: The Purpose of the Epistle of Barnabas
and Jewish-Christian Competition in the Second Century* (WUNT 2/82; Tübingen: Mohr-
Siebeck, 1996). Hvalvik concludes that *Barnabas* is a λόγος προτρεπτικός, written to
exhort members of *Barnabas*'s community to have nothing to do with the Jewish
law or its adherents (see esp. pp. 158–65). Part three of Hvalvik's work (pp. 213–321)
lays out evidence that various forms of Judaism were in direct competition with
early Christian churches.

[260] Ruether, "The *Adversus Judaeos* Tradition in the Church Fathers: The Exegesis
of Christian Anti-Judaism," in Paul E. Szarmach, ed., *Aspects of Jewish Culture in
the Middle Ages* (Albany: State University of New York Press, 1979) 27–50; repr. in
Jeremy Cohen, ed., *Essential Papers on Judaism and Christianity in Conflict: From Late
Antiquity to the Reformation* (New York/London: New York University Press, 1990)
174–89.

embodiment of all anti-Christian values. Both works are important contributions to Christian reflection on the extent to which early Christian self-identity as the new people of God necessarily involved the complementary conclusion that God had rejected the Jews.

1.19.2 Testimonia *and Messianic Debates Revisited*

A more specific question in this larger debate is the extent to which early Jews and Christians actually engaged in debate on the application of "messianic" scriptures to Jesus. The first point to clarify in this issue is the precise meaning of "messianic." Since Stather Hunt wrote, scholars have become increasingly aware of the variety of "messianic" concepts in the early church and contemporary Judaism.[261] At a minimum we must speak with John J. Collins of "four basic messianic paradigms" of an eschatological figure (i.e., king, priest, prophet, and heavenly messiah), and realize that the specific title "anointed one" (משיח, χριστός) was not always applied to these figures.[262] Scholars such as Richard A. Horsley, emphasizing that variety of popular prophetic and "messianic" movements in late Second Temple Judaism, conclude that there was no standard messianic expectation; Horsley goes so far as to say that "there was little interest in a Messiah, Davidic or otherwise."[263]

Although David T.M. Frankfurter does not speak of "messianic" expectations, his argument that miracle-lists, describing characteristics of the eschatological "prophet-like-Moses," circulated orally and in written form in the first and second centuries is a recent example of a scholarly tendency to reconstruct an oversimplified, generic Jewish expectation. Frankfurter maintains that it was to fulfill such a fixed expectation that early summaries of Jesus' miracles arose (e.g., Luke 7:22 = Q); these summaries in turn influenced the selection and arrangement of the miracle catenae underlying Mark 6–8 and

---

[261] On this general topic, see Jacob Neusner, William Scott Green, and Ernest S. Frerichs, eds., *Judaisms and Their Messiahs* (Cambridge: Cambridge University Press, 1987); James H. Charlesworth, ed., *The Messiah: Developments in Earliest Judaism and Christianity: The First Princeton Symposium on Judaism and Christian Origins* (Minneapolis: Fortress, 1992); John J. Collins, *The Scepter and the Star: The Messiahs of the Dead Sea Scrolls and Other Ancient Literature* (AB Reference Library; New York/London: Doubleday, 1995).

[262] Collins, *Scepter*, 12.

[263] Horsley, "'Messianic' Figures and Movements in First-Century Palestine," in Charlesworth, ed., *Messiah*, 295, see also 278–80.

John's *semeia* source.[264] Frankfurter's model, however, is a conflation of distinct first-century eschatological traditions: speculations on Elijah, traditions evident in popular oracular and "signs" prophets, and Samaritan interpretations of Deut 18:15–19. Horsley, in fact, can conclude that "expectations of an eschatological prophet or of the coming of a prophet like Moses, if present in the minds of some, were not important factors in Jewish literature at the time of Jesus."[265]

While Collins, Horsley, and others are correct to underline the variety of late Second Temple conceptions that have previously been homogenized under the untenably general rubric "first-century Jewish expectations," I shall argue (with such scholars as Donald Juel and Pierre Prigent) that alongside the plethora of these "messianic" or eschatological figures, there was still a relatively stable expectation of a royal messiah of the line of David. This tradition of a messianic king was supported by a core group of *testimonia* which included Gen 49:9–12, Num 24:17, Isaiah 11:1, 10 and 2 Sam 7:10–14; these royal messianic texts were applied to Jesus by his earliest followers and were key in the earliest christological beliefs.[266] I shall argue these points in some detail in sect. 5.2 below; Juel's arguments for the centrality of early Christian understanding of Jesus as the Davidic messiah are discussed in sect. 1.19.3 below.

It is a separate question, however, to ask to what extent messianic and other scriptural passages actually served as a basis for debate between Jews and Christians. As will become clear, this study finds no unambiguous evidence suggesting that such debates actually occurred. On the contrary, the *testimonia* seem to have played an internal role, helping Christians to develop and clarify their particular

---

[264] Frankfurter, "The Origin of the Miracle-List Tradition and Its Medium of Circulation," in David J. Lull, ed., *SBL 1990 Seminar Papers* (SBLSP 29; Atlanta: Scholars Press, 1990) 344–74.

[265] Horsley, "'Like One of the Prophets of Old': Two Types of Popular Prophets at the Time of Jesus," *CBQ* 47 (1985) 443.

[266] See Juel, *Messianic Exegesis: Christological Interpretation of the Old Testament in Early Christianity* (Philadelphia: Fortress, 1988) 11. Prigent's study ("Quelques testimonia messianiques: Leur histoire littéraire de Qoumrân aux Pères de l'église," *TZ* 15 [1959] 419–30) traces the use of combinations of Gen 49:9–10 (the scepter and lion of Judah); Num 24:17 (the star of Jacob), and Isaiah 11:1, 10 (the root of Jesse) from Qumran, through passages such as *Testament of Levi* 18 and *Testament of Judah* 24, to Justin (*1 Apology* 32; *Dialogue* 52), Irenaeus, and on to Cyprian and Eusebius. See further evidence and references regarding Jewish and Christian use of these texts in sect. 5.2 below.

beliefs (Dodd's "sub-structure" of Christian theology) rather than being applied for apologetic or polemic purposes.

1.19.3 *Donald Juel and Messianic Exegesis*

Juel, with many recent scholars, recognizes the central role that scriptural reflection played in the developing Christian understanding of Jesus. His specific contribution, however, is to argue that the understanding of Jesus as the royal Davidic messiah who was crucified and rose again was the central paradigm that guided the earliest followers of Jesus in their "search of the scriptures."[267] Juel builds here on the argument of his teacher Nils Dahl, who held that the crucifixion of Jesus as a messianic pretender is the firm fixed point from which any reconstruction of the life of Jesus and earliest Christian thought must begin.[268] Juel contends that followers of Jesus would have first used royal messianic *testimonia* (e.g., 2 Sam 7:10–14, Gen 49:10–12, Num 24:17, Psalm 2, Isaiah 11, Zech 6:12, Jeremiah 33) in developing their christology.[269] Against Lindars, Juel sees this process not as an apologetic to persuade non-Christian Jews, but rather as a natural internal development in which the followers of Jesus tried to make sense of events through their scriptures.[270]

Juel's first step is to show that the above texts were in fact interpreted messianically in late Second Temple Judaism. He accomplishes this by presenting evidence from Qumran and (more questionably) from later rabbinic interpretations.[271] In the few cases where Christians simply apply such interpretations to Jesus, Juel's argument is straightforward (e.g., the quotation of Ps 2:7 and 2 Sam 7:14 in a TC showing that Jesus is God's son [Heb 1:5]). Admitting that such direct messianic quotations are rare, Juel outlines a more subtle process in which early followers of Jesus used Jewish midrashic techniques to combine messianic texts with other related scriptural

---

[267] See Juel's thesis statement, "The beginnings of Christian reflection can be traced to interpretations of Israel's scriptures, and the major focus of that scriptural interpretation was Jesus, the crucified and risen Messiah" (*Exegesis*, 1).

[268] See Dahl, "The Crucified Messiah," in idem, *The Crucified Messiah and other Essays* (Minneapolis: Augsburg, 1974) 10–36; repr. in Donald H. Juel, ed., *Jesus the Christ: Historical Origins of Christological Doctrine* (Minneapolis: Fortress, 1991) 27–47.

[269] See Juel, *Exegesis*, 11 n. 15, for his list of messianic passages.

[270] Ibid., 140.

[271] See ibid., 61–75 on interpretation of 2 Sam 7:10–14 at Qumran; pp. 105–7 on rabbinic interpretation of Psalm 89.

texts to expand their vision of Jesus and his significance.[272]

In Mark's account of the Jesus' baptism (1:9–11), for example, Juel concurs with many other scholars in seeing the influence of Ps 2:7, Isa 42:1, and perhaps of the account of the near sacrifice of Isaac in Genesis 22.[273] Yet he argues that the royal messianic image from Ps 2 is primary: one can see how the royal messianic imagery would have been filled out with references to Jesus as servant (Isaiah) or to the sacrifice of Isaac, but the opposite process of understanding Jesus first as a servant and then adding on royal imagery is harder to credit. Juel thus sees the influence of messianic texts as the primary factor in the development of the title "Son of God" as reflected in the Markan passage and in Rom 1:3.[274]

A key test case for Juel's theory is the use of non-messianic psalms in the passion narratives. Rightly pointing out that the overall imagery in the passion narratives is royal, Juel argues that allusions to Psalms 22, 31, and 69 do not depend on an image of Jesus as the paradigmatic righteous sufferer, but are used because they were understood as messianic.[275] Attempting to trace the process by which these non-messianic texts came to be understood messianically, Juel offers Psalm 89 as a key.[276] The speaker identifies himself as the Lord's "anointed" (Ps 89:38), yet he is depicted as undergoing suffering and humiliation. This fact, together with vocabulary links between Psalm 89 and the passion psalms, would have supplied exegetical warrant for applying these latter psalms to the Lord's messiah Jesus. Admitting that there is no extant evidence for a messianic interpretation of

---

[272] See ibid., 31–56 on the "rules of the game" for scriptural interpretation in the first century.

[273] Ibid., 79–80.

[274] Juel's point receives support from Joel Marcus's analysis of the baptism story (*The Way of the Lord: Christological Exegesis of the Old Testament in the Gospel of Mark* [Louisville, KY: Westminster/John Knox, 1992] 56–72). Marcus shows that the title "Son" given at Jesus' baptism would be seen by Mark's audience primarily as a reference to Ps 2:7, thus alluding to Jesus as the royal messiah in the eschatological age. Marcus does, however, later distance himself from Juel's suggestion that "Son of God" is primarily a messianic title in his exegesis of Mark 12:35–37 (ibid., 142).

[275] Juel, *Exegesis*, 102. Juel here disputes the views of Hartmut Gese, A.H. Harvey, Klaus Berger and others (references in ibid.).

[276] Ibid., 104–111. See also Juel's article, "The Social Dimensions of Exegesis: The Use of Psalm 16 in Acts 2," *CBQ* 43 (1981) 543–56, esp. 547–50, for a similar argument that interpretation of Psalm 89 paved the way for the use of Psalm 16 in Peter's messianic argument in Acts 2.

Psalm 89 in Second Temple Judaism, Juel cites later rabbinic messianic interpretations to demonstrate that the Psalm had at least the potential for this messianic exegesis.

Juel's argument is ingenious, but perhaps overly so. While Juel is surely correct to criticize the "paradigmatic righteous sufferer model" as too general,[277] there is little need to resort to highly imaginative reconstructions. One may simply posit that the (admittedly ironic) image of Jesus as royal messiah in the passion narrative has been supplemented by reflection on psalms that highlight suffering. Even granted that the messianic image is primary, it does not follow that the psalms themselves were understood as messianic. The key is the effect of combining the messianic image with psalms of suffering: both messianic and "righteous sufferer" paradigms are modified.

Juel's strongest arguments for the centrality of the messianic understanding of Jesus in earliest Christianity are those he takes over from Dahl: (1) the massive fact that "Christ" is simply assumed as the fundamental title of Jesus, becoming virtually a part of his name in most of the New Testament, and (2) the guiding imagery of the passion narratives (both Synoptic and Johannine) is a royal one: Jesus is condemned and executed as King of the Jews. Since the "messiahship" of Jesus is simply assumed, however, the use of messianic scriptures is often at a more subtle level of allusion, as shown by Juel.[278] Discussions of early Christian use of scripture, then, should be more aware of the messianic background.

At the same time, however, Juel places perhaps too much emphasis on a chronological logic: *first* messianic scriptures were applied to Jesus, and then other scriptural passages were attracted to this core. The process was likely a more simultaneous one: Jesus was recognized as the royal messiah, but this would not have precluded

---

[277] Juel cites an observation by Martin Hengel that is well worth reproducing here: "The pattern of humiliation and exaltation of the righteous is far too general and imprecise to interpret the event which Mark narrates so skillfully and with such deep theological conviction. He is concerned with the utterly unique event of the passion and crucifixion of the Messiah of Israel which is without any parallel in the history of religion. For Mark, the few psalms of suffering which illuminate individual features of the suffering and death of Jesus, like Psalms 22 and 69, are exclusively *messianic* Psalms, such as Ps 110 and 118. . . . The suffering "of the righteous" is to be integrated completely into the sufferings of the Messiah (Hengel, *The Atonement: The Origin of the Doctrine in the New Testament* [Philadelphia: Fortress; London: SCM, 1981] 41); see Juel, *Exegesis*, 103.

[278] See also my discussion below (sect. 5.2.2) on the allusive use of messianic *testimonia* in the NT.

understanding him through the use of other scriptural passages (e.g., psalm passages of the righteous sufferer). Juel is correct to insist, however, that these other conceptions often (always?) presuppose, or are combined with, royal messianic conceptions.

1.20   Transmission of Tradition in Early Christianity

The proposed model of small-scale scriptural TCs transmitted in early Christianity (Kraft, Barnard) fits in well with recent studies demonstrating that the major aspects of the Jesus tradition—sayings, miracle, and passion traditions—were transmitted both orally and in smaller scale written collections. I shall refer briefly to key studies in these three categories.[279]

1.20.1   Sayings Traditions

John Kloppenborg's work has placed the sayings source Q firmly within the genre of Greco-Roman and Near Eastern sayings collections.[280] Helmut Köster has shown that synoptic traditions were often transmitted independently of what would become canonical literature.[281] In addition to the larger collections of Q and the *Gospel of Thomas*, scholars have argued convincingly that the aphorisms of Jesus were transmitted in smaller thematic clusters.[282] Moreover, there is

---

[279] On the general argument for small-scale written transmission of early Christian tradition see J.C. O'Neill's provocative article, "The Lost Written Records of Jesus' Words and Deeds Behind Our Records," *JTS* 42 n.s. (1991) 483–504, esp. 496–8 where he argues for a variety of small narrative and sayings collections used by Matthew, Justin, Luke, and Thomas.

[280] Kloppenborg, *The Formation of Q: Trajectories in Ancient Wisdom Collections* (Studies in Antiquity and Christianity; Philadelphia: Fortress, 1987), esp. 263–316.

[281] Köster, *Synoptische Überlieferung bei den Apostolischen Vätern* (TU 65; Berlin: Akademie, 1957). *Barnabas* 7:3–9, for example, draws on "school" TCs for its scriptural references (pp. 149–55). Köster's conclusions have of course been challenged: a classic study arguing for widespread *dependence* of early Christian writers on the Gospel of Matthew is Edouard Massaux, *The Influence of the Gospel of Matthew on Christian Literature before St. Irenaeus* (ed. Arthur J. Bellenzoni; 3 vols.; Macon, GA: Mercer University Press, 1990; orig. pub., Universitas Catholica Lovaniensis Dissertationes; Louvain: Universitaires de Louvain, 1950). Massaux's study, however, tends towards an uncritical acceptance of Matthean influence. See now the work of Wolf-Dietrich Köhler, *Die Rezeption des Matthäusevangeliums in der Zeit vor Irenäus* (WUNT 2/24; Tübingen: Mohr-Siebeck, 1987), which takes an intermediate position between Köster and Massaux.

[282] See Julian V. Hills, "The Three 'Matthean' Aphorisms in the *Dialogue of the Savior* 53," *HTR* 84 (1991) 43–58; David E. Aune, "Oral Tradition and the Aphorisms

evidence that Jesus's parables were transmitted in thematic clusters,[283] that Matthew knew the Sermon on the Mount as a written source,[284] and that the eschatological discourse (Mark 13 par.) existed as an independent document.[285] Birger Gerhardsson has argued for an early written transmission of the teachings of Jesus, though his thesis has not gained wide acceptance.[286]

1.20.2 *Miracle Traditions*

Scholars have argued for narrative collections of Jesus' miracles underlying the Gospel of Mark[287] and a "semeia" source underlying John.[288] Recently, Julian V. Hills has argued that miracle lists were also transmitted independently of the NT Gospels.[289] Hills show that the miracle lists often function in ways strikingly similar to scriptural TCs: they are used as prophecies (Sibylline Oracles), as anti-Jewish polemic (Acts of Andrew 10), as proofs of the divinity of Jesus (Tertullian *Apology* 21), and as part of a review of the life of Christ (Hippolytus *C. Noet.* 18.6–7).[290] Perhaps most significantly, Hills has shown that the miracle lists often seem to be part of a catechetical structure which reflects a community's rule of faith.[291] I shall discuss

---

of Jesus," in Henry Wansbrough, ed., *Jesus and the Oral Gospel Tradition* (JSNTSup 64; Sheffield: JSOT, 1991) 239–40.

[283] See Philip Sellew, "Oral and Written Sources in Mark 4.1–34," *NTS* 36 (1990) 234–67, esp. pp. 237–39 for older proposals of parable collections and pp. 260–61 on Sellew's own conclusions that Mark used an oral collection of seed similitudes that may have been written down before its incorporation into the Gospel.

[284] See Hans Dieter Betz, *Essays on the Sermon on the Mount* (Philadelphia: Fortress, 1985).

[285] David Wenham, *The Rediscovery of Jesus' Eschatological Discourse* (Gospel Perspectives 4; Sheffield: JSOT, 1984).

[286] Gerhardsson's original argument was set forth in *Memory and Manuscript: Oral Tradition and Written Transmission in Rabbinic Judaism and Early Christianity* (Lund: Gleerup, 1961) and updated in *The Origins of the Gospel Traditions* (Philadelphia: Fortress, 1979) and *The Gospel Tradition* (Mälmo: Gleerup, 1986).

[287] Paul J. Achtemeier, "Towards the Isolation of Pre-Markan Miracle Catenae," *JBL* 89 (1970) 265–91; idem, "The Origin and Function of the Pre-Marcan Miracle Catenae," *JBL* 91 (1972) 198–221.

[288] See Robert T. Fortna, *The Fourth Gospel and its Predecessor* (Philadelphia: Fortress, 1988).

[289] Hills, *Tradition and Composition in the Epistula Apostolorum* (HDR 24; Minneapolis: Fortress, 1990) 38–44 (pp. 40–44 presents a selection of early Christian miracle lists); see also idem, "Tradition, Redaction, and Intertextuality: Miracle Lists in Apocryphal Acts as a Test Case," in Lull, ed., *SBLSP 1990*, 375–90 (pp. 377–87 presents a selection of miracle lists in the OT, NT, and apocryphal Acts).

[290] Hills, *Tradition*, 38–39.

[291] See Hills, "Miracle Lists," 388.

in chapter three how many early Christian TCs follow a "creedal" outline which was likely developed in a catechetical life-setting.

1.20.3   *Passion Traditions*

John Dominic Crossan has proposed a bold vision of the development of the original narrative of Jesus' passion. The tradition began with lists of prophetic texts (Crossan refers to them as *testimonia*), developed into "exegetical discourses" (e.g., the midrash on the scapegoat ritual in *Barnabas* 7), and was finally written up into a coherent passion narrative.[292] Proposed early collections of prophetic texts applied to Jesus' passion have of course been a staple of various *testimonia* theories.[293]

An important achievement of Crossan's 1988 work *The Cross That Spoke: The Origins of the Passion Narrative*, is to show the continuity between NT passion *testimonia* and patristic *testimonia* collections.[294] He argues plausibly that these scriptural proof-texts collections were transmitted independently of a narrative passion framework up until the third century.[295] Crossan's method of using patristic evidence to illustrate a pattern of *testimonia* use in the NT is of course risky, but his detailed investigations bear out the value of his approach. I will discuss in detail Crossan's interpretation of *Barnabas* 7 below (sect. 5.5.7).

Crossan's work is a strong challenge to the historicity of any part of the passion narrative. His position is a radicalization of positions of previous *testimonia* scholars, who had long recognized that in some cases *testimonia* not only shaped the selection and presentation of Jesus traditions (Stather Hunt, Doeve) but at times provided details that

---

[292] See Crossan's sketch of this development in "Lists in Early Christianity: A Response to *Early Christianity, Q and Jesus*," *Semeia* 55 (1991) 241–43. Crossan's more detailed argument is presented in *The Cross That Spoke: The Origins of the Passion Narrative* (San Francisco: Harper & Row, 1988); a more popular version of the same argument is Crossan's *Who Killed Jesus? Exposing the Roots of Anti-Semitism in the Gospel Story of the Death of Jesus* (San Francisco: HarperSanFrancisco, 1995). The *Semeia* article is a richly suggestive proposal that Christian literature developed out of an original triad of sayings, miracle, and prophetic lists.

[293] See for example Prigent, *Testimonia*, 204–7, on small literary units announcing the passion, death, and resurrection of Christ which form the basis for the passion predictions in Mark.

[294] I leave aside as irrelevant for present purposes Crossan's proposal that an original "Cross Gospel" (now embedded in the Gospel of Peter) was used by NT gospel writers; suffice it to say that his theory has not found widespread support.

[295] Crossan, "Lists," 241.

were incorporated into the gospel accounts (Lindars). While Crossan's complete historical skepticism is unwarranted, his work represents additional support for the insight of many *testimonia* scholars that both individual quotations and larger scriptural patterns (e.g., the suffering and vindicated righteous one) are central to the NT portrayals of Jesus.[296]

In sum, if early Christians indeed passed down collections of selected scriptures, this practice fits well into the larger pattern of oral and literary activity being sketched by this wide range of current scholarship.

1.21 *Conclusions: Central Issues Raised by the* Testimonia *Hypothesis*

(1) *Basic Argument*: The core of all *testimonia* hypotheses is the claim that early Christians did not use the Jewish scriptures as an undifferentiated whole, but rather selected, shaped, and interpreted certain passages in support of emerging Christian beliefs.

(2) *Influential Passages*: The fact that certain passages (e.g., Psalms 22 and 110) were quoted more often and were more influential on early Christian thought than others is incontestable. The debate involves the precise nature of these "selected passages" (form; function; life-setting; authority).

(3) *Extract Collections and Testimonia Collections*: The *testimonia* debate has often been hindered by a lack of precise terminology. I have proposed an initial distinction between general scriptural extract collections (ECs), which may have functioned in liturgical, catechetical, or homiletical life-settings, and *testimonia* collections (TCs), in which the texts function forensically to "prove" certain claims. ECs and TCs may share the same form, but distinctions must be made in function.

(4) *Testimonia Collection as a Distinct Genre*: Further distinctions must be made between *testimonia* collections and related genres (e.g., midrash,

---

[296] A recent study by Reinhold Liebers, *Wie Geschrieben Steht: Studien zu einer besonderen Art frühchristlichen Schriftbezuges* (Berlin/New York: de Gruyter, 1993) again corroborates these insights. In a detailed investigation of NT quotations that reference no specific text (e.g., "as it is written", Mark 14:21), Liebers isolates four passages (1 Cor 15:3b–5; Mark 9:11–13; 14:21; 14:48–49) which he argues refer not to specific passages, but to the general scriptural *pattern* of the suffering, death, and eventual glorification (by resurrection) of the righteous. See below, sect. 4.2.1b for further discussion of Liebers's proposal.

homilies) that quote scripture. Although no absolute distinctions can be made, midrash may be defined as an approach that begins with the scriptural text and applies it to extra-scriptural events, while a *testimonium* begins with an extra-scriptural event and appeals to scripture for "proof" of this event. Use of scripture as a *testimonium* should also be distinguished from a compositional use of scripture, i.e., use of scriptural patterns or "plots" in order to portray or interpret non-scriptural figures or events. In the NT, the pattern of the righteous suffering one (Psalms, Isaiah), for example, has been applied to Jesus.

(5) *Self-Evident or Previously Established Significance*: An essential characteristic of a *testimonium* is that its significance must be self-evident. In the NT, we can distinguish between quotations whose meanings must be established by exegetical argument (e.g., Ps 95:7–11 in Hebrews 3–4) and *testimonia* whose significance is either obvious or has been previously established. An important subset of this category is the discussion on the existence of generally accepted messianic *testimonia* in NT times.

(6) *Oral v. Written Testimonia*: Much of the *testimonia* discussion has centered on the distinction between written and oral traditions. Beginning with Hatch, a long line of scholars has proposed and refined criteria to detect the use of written ECs and TCs in early Christian and contemporary Jewish authors. An equally long line of scholars (Ungern-Sternberg, Dodd, Lindars) have advanced an alternative model of a more general oral tradition in which certain scriptures and their interpretations attained authoritative status.

(7) *Criteria to Detect Written Collections*: The basic argument for written TCs is that a given quotation is not drawn from a scriptural manuscript, but from an EC. The major criteria are (1) quotations that deviate considerably from known scriptural texts (LXX or LXX recensions, MT), especially in a Christianizing direction; (2) composite quotations; (3) false attributions; (4) use of the same series of texts in independent authors; (5) editorial or interpretive comments indicative of a collection; (6) evident lack of awareness of the biblical context of a quotation; (7) use of the same exegetical comments in independent authors. Though not strictly criteria, two further considerations are relevant: (1) the existence of numerous ECs and TCs in Second Temple Jewish, ancient Greco-Roman, and patristic literature furnishes analogous or indirect evidence for the likely existence of early Christian scriptural ECs and TCs, and (2) practical

considerations; e.g., for a Christian missionary, a written TC would be easier to transport and reference than bulky, expensive scrolls.

It should be noted that most of these criteria focus specifically on the form of a *collection*; possible use of individual *testimonia* is not in view. The probative force of all (except the last two) these indicators is greatly strengthened if the same phenomenon is found in literarily independent texts. Yet even if a non-scriptural source is indicated one cannot simply assume a TC; the function of the particular collection must first be determined.

(8) *Objections to Written Collection Criteria*: The major objections and alternative models to putative written TCs are (1) the influence of a more general oral tradition; (2) the lack of direct evidence of Christian TCs before the third century (extant texts or unambiguous references); (3) the intentional alteration or conflation of quotations by a given author; (4) faulty memory or "loose" quotations; (5) use of a non-standard textual tradition (on analogy with the targums); (6) the dependence on a non-scriptural source other than a TC (quotations by other authors, scriptural commentaries, liturgical collections). This last objection should not be understood as presenting mutually exclusive options: a TC could easily take the form of a hymn, for example.

(9) *Christological and Anti-Jewish TCs in the Patristic Era*: The existence of widespread Christian oral and written *testimonia* traditions by the second and third centuries is established. These traditions supported and illustrated two major categories of beliefs: (1) christological doctrines (e.g., Jesus' divine status; the scriptural necessity of his suffering) and (2) anti-Jewish positions, with the concomitant belief that Christians had replaced Jews as God's chosen people. A scholarly consensus recognizes that in the second century *Barnabas* and Justin were using written TCs. Irenaeus's *Proof*, Tertullian's *Against Marcion* and *Against the Jews*, and Cyprian's *To Quirinus* are witnesses for the continuity of the *testimonia* tradition into the third century. The unresolved question is the extent to which these *testimonia* traditions, especially written collections, have their beginnings in the first century.

(10) *Creedal Form of Testimonia Collections*: In most of these patristic TCs, a creedal form can be identified, i.e., *testimonia* are arranged around creedal beliefs concerning the life and work of Christ and the Christian church.

(11) *Flexible Applications of Testimonia*: The *testimonia* did not function statically, but could be applied to different situations. This shift in application is evident already in the NT (Lindars, Hay).

(12) *Relationship of Testimonia and Early Christian Narrative and Theology*: The influence of certain scriptural passages on emerging Christian narratives and theological concepts is recognized as central. The scriptural pattern of the suffering righteous one who is vindicated (Psalms, Isaiah, Wisdom), the role of Ps 110:1 in understanding Jesus' exaltation, and the scriptural background to the various christological titles are clear examples. Given this, however, open questions abound. Which is earlier in Christian narratives: the explicit quotation (e.g., Matthew's fulfillment quotations) or the implicit scriptural pattern? Were scriptural patterns primary, and narratives about Jesus conformed to or even created to match these patterns (Crossan)? Or did events in the life of Jesus and the early church govern the selection of scriptural *testimonia*? Did Christians take over previous Jewish *testimonia* collections? Can *testimonia* be traced to Jesus' own self-understanding and teaching? To what extent did *testimonia* like Ps 110:1 simply *witness* to Christian beliefs, and to what extent did they *shape* those beliefs?

(13) *Authority of the Testimonia Collections*: Closely related to the question of influence is that of authority. Many scholars have traced the ultimate authority for *testimonia* back to Jesus' and the apostles' own use of scripture. *Barnabas* and Justin quote TCs with the full authority of scripture. The *testimonia* may have derived their authority from their presence in catechetical or even creedal sequences. Distinctions must be drawn between local or private TCs and those collections which were intended for wider circulation and carried greater authority.

(14) *Limitations of the Apologetic Model*: Proposals for the life-setting of early Christian TCs have long been dominated by the model of Christian apologetic or polemic aimed at the Jews (Harris; Lindars). This proposal requires significant modification: clarification of first-century messianic or more broadly eschatological expectations based on scripture; a distinction between actual Jewish-Christian conflict and literary fictions; and a realization that anti-Jewish debate is only one factor in the early Christian use of scripture. Broader teaching/catechesis and worship settings must also be considered even for TCs.

(15) *The School Life-Setting*: The most unsuccessful aspect of *testimonia* research was the early attempt to trace *testimonia* to a single

"Testimony Book." Much more plausible are models of small-scale written TCs developed in a "school" life-setting (Bousset, Kraft, Skarsaune). The scribal activity of Qumran provides one "school" model, but further investigation is necessary. This scribal activity is not necessarily an alternative to *testimonia* theses (*pace* Stendahl): the issue is why certain texts first became the object of scribal scrutiny.

(16) *TCs within Transmission of Tradition*: The model of small-scale written TCs fits well with recent studies that have identified smaller groupings of traditional material transmitted independently of the NT Gospels: collections of Jesus' sayings, Jesus' parables, miracle stories and lists, and passion traditions (Kloppenborg, Achtemeier, Hills, Crossan).

(17) *Form of the Testimonia Sources*: The form of these small-scale TCs need not be limited to a bare collection of passages arranged by theme or catch-word. *Testimonia* were likely transmitted with comments or in a variety of forms: as dialogues, homilies, or hymns.

CHAPTER TWO

THE LITERARY BACKGROUND TO CHRISTIAN *TESTIMONIA* COLLECTIONS: ANCIENT GRECO-ROMAN AND JEWISH EXTRACT COLLECTIONS AND THEIR FUNCTIONS

2.1 *Overview of the Chapter*

I begin this chapter by considering the function of *testimonia* collections within the context of ancient Greco-Roman rhetoric and literary genres. This background is particularly important in answering questions about how the first Christians understood the force of their *testimonia*: were they considered to be prophecies that "proved" that the Christ events were ordained by God, or were they thought of as paradigms and examples which shed light on the Christ events but did not "prove" them in a forensic sense?

Beginning with Hatch, supporters of *testimonia* hypotheses have often appealed to Greco-Roman literature for formal analogies. In this chapter, I present a variety of Greco-Roman genres in which excerpt collections are found. As I proceed, I reflect on similarities and parallels between the function, form, and life-setting of these excerpt collections and the corresponding aspects of extant and hypothetical scriptural *testimonia* collections.

I then turn to a consideration of the place of *testimonia* within Second Temple Jewish literature, with particular attention given to the Qumran documents. Here many analogies of form can be found: the Qumran literature is especially rich in a variety of scriptural excerpt collections. Of particular importance is the consideration of the function of these collections, and the location of *testimonia* collections within this variety of function.

2.2 *Functions of Extracts within Classical Rhetorical Categories*

To shed light on the function of TCs as "proofs" of the Christian message, I now consider them from the point of view of Greco-Roman rhetorical categories. Aristotle divides rhetoric into three types:

deliberative (συμβουλευτικόν, persuading or dissuading speech); forensic (δικανικόν, speech attacking or defending someone); and epideictic (ἐπιδεικτικόν, speech blaming or praising someone [*Rhet.* 1.3.3]).[1] I will also use a more general category, the didactic genre (γένος διδακτικόν), for classification purposes.[2] The TCs and related genres which I discuss below fall into all four of these rhetorical categories.

Forensic speech deals with establishing the justice or injustice of some past action (*Rhet.* 1.3.5). The use of proofs is vital to the proper establishment of justice; Aristotle lists laws, witnesses (μάρτυρες), contracts, (confession under) torture, and oaths as examples of proper forensic proofs (πίστεις, *Rhet.* 1.15.3).[3] Witnesses are of two kinds: ancient and recent; ancient witnesses—poets, soothsayers, and proverbs—are the most trustworthy, for they cannot be corrupted. Aristotle further distinguishes between ancient written authorities that may be used to witness to a *past* action, and those one can appeal to as "interpreters of oracles (χρησμολόγοι) for the *future*" (*Rhet.* 1.15.13–17).[4] Similarly, the Roman rhetorician Quintilian (ca. 35–95 CE) refers to "supernatural witness" (*divina testimonia*) given in oracles, prophecies, and omens (5.7.35).[5] It is no surprise, then, that early Christians often understood scripture within this forensic category: Justin calls his biblical quotations μαρτύρια (e.g., *1 Apol.* 53.2); already in the NT, scripture is said to witness (μαρτυρέω) to Jesus (John 5:39) and to the new covenant (Heb 10:15).[6] Christian use refers both to past actions (prophesied events fulfilled in the life of Christ) and future fulfillment of prophecy in the last days (e.g., the coming of Christ as judge).

Aristotle's contention that contracts (συνθῆκαι) are also a type of forensic proof is relevant to a polemical point often made in Christian

---

[1] Greek text and ET in John Henry Freese, ed., *Aristotle: The "Art" of Rhetoric* (LCL; London: Heinemann; New York: Putnam, 1926).

[2] I follow here the literary categories employed in Klaus Berger, "Hellenistische Gattungen im Neuen Testament," *ANRW* 2.25.2. 1031–1432. The didactic form is a more general category, and may in fact subsume examples of the other three types within it.

[3] Aristotle calls these "inartificial" (ἄτεχνοι) proofs.

[4] In reference to a past action, Athenians supported their claim to Salamis by referring to a passage in the *Iliad*; Themistocles supported his argument for a sea battle by referring to the oracle of the wooden wall (*Rhet.* 1.15.13–14).

[5] Latin text and ET in H.E. Butler, ed., *The Institutio Oratoria of Quintilian*, vol. 2 (LCL; Cambridge, MA: Harvard; London: Heinemann, 1939).

[6] Cf. also 1 *Clem.* 23:5, where scripture bears witness (συνεπιμαρτυρέω) to the swift accomplishment of the Lord's will.

TCs: Christians, not Jews, are the true inheritors of the covenant (διαθήκη) and promises of God (e.g., Acts 13:34–39). Scripture passages serve prominently as "witnesses" to this assertion in Luke-Acts and in later Christian works such as *Barnabas*.[7]

It must be admitted, however, that boundaries between categories are not always clear. Collections with a clearly forensic purpose often also serve a didactic function.[8] Another important borderline case is use of examples (παραδείγματα; *exempla*): while generally classed in the deliberative category (e.g., famous examples of morality to exhort the reader to similar behavior), they may also serve as a kind of forensic argument. Aristotle, granting that inductive examples lack the persuasive power of deductive enthymemes, nevertheless allows them as a lesser kind of proof:

> If we have no enthymemes, we must employ examples as demonstrative proofs (ἀποδείξεις), for conviction (πίστις) is produced by these; but if we have them, examples must be used as evidence (μαρτύρια) and as a kind of epilogue to the enthymemes . . . if they stand last they resemble evidence, and a witness (μάρτυς) is in every case likely to induce belief. (*Rhet.* 2.20.9)

Cicero (106–43 BCE) accepts the effectiveness of examples (*exempla*) in legal argument (*Topics* 10.44),[9] while Quintilian follows Aristotle in classing the παραδείγματα as a type of proof, calling them rhetorical induction (ῥητορικὴν ἐπαγωγήν; 5.11.1–2). The author of the *Rhetorica ad Herennium* (ca. 80 BCE) is more cautious; while admitting that in some authors "an example (*exemplum*) is used just like testimony to prove a point" (4.1.1–2.2), he himself holds that "examples are set forth, not to confirm or bear witness (*nec confirmandi neque testificandi causa*) but to clarify (*sed demonstrandi*)" (4.3.5).[10]

I shall present below Jewish and Christian *exempla* collections of

---

[7] On Luke-Acts, see William Stephen Kurz, "The Function of Christological Proof from Prophecy for Luke and Justin" (Ph.D. diss., Yale University, 1976) 107, 113; sees *Barn.* 4:6–8.

[8] The proof-texts in *Barnabas* "prove" that God has rejected the Jews; at the same time, they function as salutary warnings to Christians (see 2:10; 4:1–2).

[9] Latin text and ET in H.M. Hubbell, ed., *Cicero: Topica* (LCL; Cambridge, MA: Harvard University Press, 1949).

[10] Latin text and ET in Harry Caplan, ed., *Rhetorica ad Herennium* (LCL; Cambridge, MA: Harvard University Press, 1954). My examples are a summary of the work presented by Michael R. Cosby, *The Rhetorical Composition and Function of Hebrews 11 in Light of Example Lists in Antiquity* (Macon, GA: Mercer University Press, 1988) 93–105.

scriptural heroes and events (e.g., Sirach 44–50 and Hebrews 11), discussing in each case whether their purpose is forensic or deliberative.

2.3   *Extract Collections in Ancient Greco-Roman Literature*

In the remainder of this chapter, I present collections found in several types of ancient Greco-Roman and Second Temple Jewish literature. These collections provide detailed support to the criterion of analogy: since the technique of gathering written excerpts into collections is widespread in this contemporary literature, it is likely that early Christians also participated in this practice by making scriptural ECs.[11] For the most part, these examples are *formal* analogies: collections of excerpts, often arranged topically. Yet I also present analogies of *content*: Jews made collections of scripture and Greeks and Romans collected oracles and other sacred writings. Finally, analogies of *function* are also evident: while a majority of the collections have a generally didactic function, specific examples of deliberative, epideictic, and, most importantly, of forensic collections will also be presented.

2.3.1   *The Didactic Anthology*

The primary purpose of the ancient Greek anthology was didactic: it was used both for practical instruction and for moral training.[12] The earliest reference is in Plato, where the pedagogical use of collected "selected passages" is discussed as a firmly established practice (*Laws* 811a).[13] Anthologies were used at the primary level to

---

[11] Hodgson comments, "Primitive Christianity must emerge as a foreign body in a world replete with compilations of proverbs and sayings of ancient worthies, should the spirit of the anthologist be found wanting" ("Testimony," 363).

[12] I understand "anthology" as an extensive collection of extracts taken from a work or works of one or more authors. It normally stands independently as a discrete work. (Cf. *Webster's Third New International Dictionary*: "a usually representative collection of literary pieces or passages.")

[13] Greek text and ET in R.G. Bury, *Plato: Laws*, vol. 2 (LCL; Cambridge, MA: Harvard University Press; London: Heinemann, 1926). Plato's discussion concerns the proper education of the young: some assert that the young should learn whole poets by heart; others recommend compiling (ξυναγαγοωντες) select summaries (κεφαωλαια ἐκλεωχαντες) for memorization. See the discussion in Henri I. Marrou, *A History of Education in Antiquity* (Wisconsin Studies in Classics; Madison: University of Wisconsin Press, 1982) 71. Werner Jaeger also refers to this passage in concluding that an anthology of poetic sayings was in use "at latest, towards the end

teach children to read;[14] at higher levels students used philosophical and rhetorical handbooks consisting of extracts.[15] Collections of maxims (dating from the 3d cent. BCE) culled from the poets and playwrights and grouped around various moral themes, were intended for moral instruction.[16] In a classical Greek educational system whose goal was to preserve the glories of its past literature, anthologies were a popular method of selecting certain passages and whole books deemed worthy of inclusion in the educational scheme, thus in effect developing a "canon."[17]

Plutarch's (ca. 46–120) essay "How the Young Man Should Study Poetry," in which he argues that study of the poets is an essential part of a young man's education, is itself largely a series of poetic extracts on which Plutarch comments.[18] To help the young distinguish good from bad poetry, he recommends balancing immoral passages with selected noble ones (*Moralia* 20).

Seneca (ca. 4 BCE–65 CE) also discusses the pedagogical use of excerpt collections in his letters to Lucilius.[19] Stoics, he asserts, are not interested in "choice extracts" (*flosculos*); instead, they concentrate on the strength of the whole work (*Ep.* 33.1). He advises Lucilius not to ask for extracts and quotations (*excerpta et repetita*) nor learn through epitomes (*summatim*); the proverb and the χρεία are properly for children (33.3–7). Here Seneca confirms the use of collected

---

of the fifth century or the beginning of the fourth century" (*Paideia: The Ideals of Greek Culture* [3 vols.; 2d ed.; New York: Oxford University Press, 1945] 1. 189).

[14] See Marrou, *Education*, 153. A well-known example of a primary textbook is a 3d cent. BCE Egyptian papyrus whose text begins with lists of syllables, followed by a word list and finally excerpts from poetical works. See O. Guéraud and P. Jouget, eds., *Un Livre d'écolier du IIIe siècle avant J.-C.* (Publications de la Société royale égyptienne de Papyrologia, textes et documents; 2 vols.; Cairo: Institut française d'archéologie orientale, 1938). This work includes a history of the hellenistic school anthology (xxiv–xxxi).

[15] See below, sect. 2.3.2, for examples.

[16] For examples, see Henry Chadwick, "Florilegium," *RAC* 7 (1969) cols. 1131–33.

[17] Marrou, *Education*, 162. For example, of the large number of plays by Aeschylus and Sophocles, only the seven which were chosen for teaching purposes are still extant.

[18] Greek text and ET in Frank Cole Babbit, ed., *Plutarch's Moralia*, vol. 1 (LCL; London: Heinemann; New York: Putnam, 1927) 72–197. It is virtually certain that Plutarch used thematically grouped poetic anthologies as sources in works such as *Consolation to Apollonius*. See Jean Hani, ed., *Plutarque Consolation à Appollonios* (Etudes et Commentaires 78; Paris: Klincksieck, 1972) 49–50.

[19] *Ep.* 33; Latin and ET in Richard M. Gummere, ed., *Seneca Ad Lucilium Epistulae Morales*, vol. 1 (LCL; Cambridge, MA: Harvard University Press; London: Heinemann, 1917).

extracts at the primary level; yet his sharp criticism implies that many adults also found them convenient.

Alongside their educational function, anthologies were also put together for more purely aesthetic purposes.[20] The first comprehensive example of this type is Melanger's *Garland*, a collection of epigrams compiled around 100 BCE at Cos. The word anthology itself (ἄνθη λέγειν: "to gather flowers"), though not attested before Diogenian in the second century CE, betrays this aesthetic intent.[21] The great anthology of John Stobaeus (5th cent. CE) preserves many of these earlier collections.

2.3.2   *Other Didactic Collections*

If the anthology was associated for the most part with primary education, other types of ECs or condensed versions of originals were used in Greco-Roman higher education, especially in the philosophical and rhetorical schools. The following are examples of these other genres.

(a) The Epitome (ἐπιτομή)
This is simply a condensed version of a larger work or works. A famous example is Epicurus's *Kyriai Doxai* (ca. 300 BCE), a collection of forty select sayings, probably made by Epicurus himself, which serves as a summary of his philosophical works.[22] Hans Dieter Betz makes the bold claim that the Sermon on the Mount is Matthew's epitome of Jesus' teaching.[23]

(b) The Philosophical Handbook (διδασκάλικος)
The best known example of this popular didactic tool is Alcinous's *Handbook of Platonism* (ca. 150 CE), which attempts to summarize and

---

[20] On this distinction, see Alan Cameron, *The Greek Anthology from Meleager to Planudes* (Oxford: Clarendon, 1993) 6–7; John Barns, "A New Gnomologium: With Some Remarks on Gnomic Anthologies," *Classical Quarterly* 44 (1950) 134–35.

[21] Cameron, *Anthology*, 5. Cameron also discusses evidence of anthologies before Melanger (pp. 6–10).

[22] The text is preserved by Diogenes Laertius. Greek text and ET in R.D. Hicks, ed., *Diogenes Laertius: Lives of Eminent Philosophers*, vol. 2 (LCL; London: Heinemann; New York: Putnam, 1925) 10.139–54. Chadwick calls it the earliest dogmatic florilegium ("Florilegium," col. 1138). Epicurus also composed other epitomes; he wrote the *Epistle to Herodotus* as "an epitome of the whole system" for "those who are unable to study carefully all my physical writings, or to go into the longer treatises at all" (*Lives* 10.35).

[23] Betz, "The Sermon on the Mount: Its Literary Genre and Function," *JR* 59 (1979) 285–97; repr. in idem, *Essays on the Sermon on the Mount* (Philadelphia: Fortress, 1985) 11–15.

synthesize Plato's writings under various categories.[24] John Dillon understands this work as part of a long process in which Plato's dialogues were distilled into *dogmata* by editing and splicing together various Platonic passages related to the same subject.[25] Handbooks summarizing the positions of other philosophical schools were also available "at least as early as the first century [BCE]"; Arius Didymus, for example, a teacher of the emperor Augustus, authored a compendium of Stoic and Peripatetic ethics.[26]

(c) The Doxography

The doxography is closely related to the handbook; it presents "lists of the views of philosophers and schools, summarized and arranged under subject-headings."[27] A doxographic edition commonly used in the early centuries CE, first compiled by Aetius, is still extant.[28]

(d) Rhetorical Source Books and Handbooks

The sourcebook is comprised of *exempla* used by students as models for their own compositions and orations. Valerius Maximus's *Facta et Dicta Memorabilia* (published 31 CE) and a non-extant collection in Cornelius Nepos (99–24 BCE) are two anthologies of *exempla*.[29] Rhetorical handbooks often included examples from various authors to illustrate literary techniques. Use of the same examples in both handbooks and sourcebooks led to the development of standard *exempla* which were used to prove or illustrate certain points.[30]

As can be seen from the above discussion, the didactic EC is a

---

[24] See John Dillon, ed., *Alcinous: The Handbook of Platonism* (Clarendon Later Ancient Philosophers; Oxford: Clarendon, 1993).

[25] Ibid., xxix–xxx.

[26] See A.A. Long, *Hellenistic Philosophy: Stoics, Epicureans, Sceptics* (New York: Scribner, 1974) 117. Long allows that Diogenes Laertius "probably" drew on such collections, while Cicero "perhaps" made use of collections in addition to original sources.

[27] Robert M. Grant, "Irenaeus and Hellenistic Culture," *HTR* 42 (1949) 41.

[28] See the edition of Hermann Diels: *Doxographi Graeci* (4th ed.; Berlin: de Gruyter, 1965). The collection was edited in the 2d cent. under the name of Plutarch; John Stobaeus preserves another form of it (Grant, "Irenaeus," 41).

[29] Valerius Maximus collected over one thousand anecdotes and arranged them topically in nine books. For a brief introduction to Valerius Maximus and his relevance to NT studies, see Hodgson, "Valerius Maximus and Gospel Criticism" and "Valerius Maximus and the Social World of the New Testament."

[30] See Cosby (citing the work of Bennett J. Price), *Rhetorical Composition*, 93; Hani, *Consolation*, 30. George A. Kennedy judges that the earliest written rhetorical handbooks were "largely made up of illustrative examples, arranged by the parts of the oration in which they might be used," thus resembling "the collections of commonplaces and other passages for imitation made by Protagoras or Thrasymachus and the *Dissoi Logoi* or the *Tetralogies* attributed to Antiphon [late 5th cent.]" (*A New History of Classical Rhetoric* [Princeton, NJ: Princeton University Press, 1994] 34–35).

standard feature in the classical and hellenistic educational systems. By analogy, we would expect to find a similar method used in early Christian "school" settings; and in fact a consensus of scholars agree that the scriptural collections used by Justin and *Barnabas*, for example, were composed in a didactic setting. The training necessary to isolate, edit, and perhaps comment on scriptural ECs and TCs presupposes a learned scribal environment, and the widespread transmission of these Christian collections presupposes such institutions as Justin's school in Rome.[31]

These didactic collection genres share important similarities with extant Christian ECs and TCs. The formal similarities (collections of extracts, topically arranged) are obvious; even more intriguing are parallels in compositional techniques: both Greco-Roman and Christian writers often felt free to *alter the original* text when they placed it in the collection.[32] A further similarity in *function* can also be noted: just as Alcinous's collection molded scattered passages of Plato into coherent propositions (*dogmata* in Dillon's phrase), so too Christian ECs molded scattered biblical passages into coherent theological (often anti-Jewish), christological, and moral propositions.

2.3.3 *Greek Sayings Collections* (Gnomologia)

The Greek penchant for anthologizing resulted in the preservation of a great amount of sayings (γνῶμαι) material; I list a few representative collections below. A didactic purpose is apparent behind many of the them, sometimes combined with other functions. The broad scope of these collections can be appreciated by reviewing the material presented by Chadwick, Kloppenborg, and Max Küchler; I am indebted to all three in compiling the following list.[33]

---

[31] See sections 3.2 and 3.3 below for detailed arguments on these points.

[32] This is a major conclusion of Christopher D. Stanley's study of 1st cent. Greco-Roman authors (*Paul and the Language of Scripture: Citation Technique in the Pauline Epistles and Contemporary Literature* [SNTSMS 69; Cambridge: Cambridge University Press, 1990] 290–91). Grammatical adaptations, clarifications, elimination of extraneous material, and, occasionally, the combination and conflation of quotations are all standard techniques.

[33] See Chadwick, "Florilegium"; Kloppenborg, *Formation of Q*, 289–316 (see also his Appendix 1); and Küchler, *Frühjüdische Weisheitstraditionen: Zum Fortgang weisheitlichen Denkens im Bereich des frühjüdischen Jahweglaubens* (OBO 26; Freiburg: Universitätsverlag; Göttingen: Vandenhoeck & Ruprecht, 1979) 240–58.

(a) Oracle Collections

The "Delphic Precepts"[34] and the "Sayings of the Seven Sages"[35] are among the earliest extant collections of oracles (4th cent. BCE). This is a close *content* analogy to Jewish or Christian scriptural collections: writings which record divinely inspired speech.

(b) Admonitions on Proper Conduct: Ps.-Isocrates *To Demonicus*

This is the oldest extant Greek prose sayings collection (4th cent. BCE), consisting of admonitions on the proper conduct of life.[36] The deliberative purpose of the collection is clear; it can be compared with the NT *Haustafeln* and Cyprian's thematic scriptural collection on the Christian moral life (*To Quirinus* Book 3).

(c) Multi-author Thematic Collections

These offer close *formal* analogies to Christian collections. From the third century BCE, we have a collection on noble heritage and riches; the sayings are drawn from Euripides, Ps.-Epicharmus, and Menander, and are arranged topically.[37] A second-century BCE collection on "fate" (τύχη) consists of excerpts from Euripides, Demosthenes, Menander, and "Theophrastus or Anaximenes,"[38] while two collections on women and marriage from the same century use sayings from Menander, Epicharmus, Euripides, and Plato Comicus, among others.[39]

2.3.4   Chreiai *Collections*

Closely related to the gnomic saying is the *chreia*. Ancient rhetoricians distinguished between gnomic sayings (γνῶμαι) and *chreiai* (χρεῖαι); *chreiai* are attributed to a named source and show biographical

---

[34] The inscription at Thera is published in *Inscriptiones Graecae* 12/3 (Berlin: Reimer, 1920) no. 188, p. 1020.

[35] Preserved in John Stobaeus (apud Demetrius of Phaleron). See Otto Hense and C. Wachsmuth, eds., *Ioannis Stobaei Anthologium* (5 vols.; Berlin: Weidmann, 1884²–1912; repr. 1968) 3. 111–25.

[36] Greek text and ET in George Norlin, ed., *Isocrates*, vol. 1 (LCL; Cambridge, MA: Harvard University Press, 1928) 4–35.

[37] *P. Hibeh* 1.7, in Bernard P. Grenfell and Arthur S. Hunt, eds., *The Hibeh Papyri* (Egypt Exploration Society, Graeco-Roman Memoirs 7, 32; 2 vols.; London: Egypt Exploration Fund, 1906, 1955); see also Robert Ambrose Pack, ed., *The Greek and Latin Literary Texts from Greco-Roman Egypt* (2d ed.; Ann Arbor: University of Michigan Press, 1965) 2. 1569.

[38] Published in Barns, "Gnomologium," 126–32.

[39] *P. Berol.* 9772 (Pack, *Literary Texts* 2. 1568) and *P. Berol.* 9773 (Pack, *Literary Texts* 2. 1573) in W. Schubart and U. von Wilamowitz-Moellendorff, eds., *Griechische Dichterfragmente* (2 vols.; Berliner Klassikertexte 5; Berlin: Weidmann, 1907) 2. 123–30.

interest.[40] *Chreiai* collections are found in a variety of literary sources: lives (βίοι), "successions" (διαδοχαί), reminiscences (ἀπομνημονεύματα), and in *chreiai* collections proper.[41] The earliest collection was made by Metrocles of the *chreiai* of Diogenes of Sinope (4th cent. BCE).[42] Lucian's *Life of Demonax* (2d cent. CE) consists mainly of a long series of *chreiai*. The analogy between *chreiai* collections and the pronouncement stories in the Gospels has often been noted by NT scholars.

2.3.5   *The Cento: Composition from Extracts*

The cento (κέντρων) is a literary technique which builds a new work by piecing together excerpts from older works. In classical times, the works of Homer and Vergil were the most popular sources for the centoist's art.[43] Again we have an analogy to scriptural collections: the *Iliad* and *Odyssey* as well as the *Aeneid* were considered in some sense as divine or oracular texts, and were thus a mine for extract collections and compositions. At the same time, later Christian authors recognized the dangers of this method of selection and re-arrangement: Irenaeus, Tertullian, Clement of Alexandria, and Jerome all associate scriptural centos with heretical misreading of the true sense of scripture.[44]

2.3.6   *Private Excerpt Collections (Notebooks)*

In addition to the above examples of excerpt collections intended for a wider audience, individuals also wrote down excerpts for later reference in the course of their private reading. The following passages illustrate this practice.[45]

---

[40] In practice, the distinction between the two categories is not always clear; see the discussion in Kloppenborg, *Formation of Q*, 290–92.

[41] See the discussion, with many primary references, in Ronald F. Hock and Edward N. O'Neil, *The Chreia in Ancient Rhetoric. I. The Progymnasmata* (SBLTT 27; Graeco-Roman Religion Series 9; Atlanta: Scholars Press, 1986) 8–9. Plutarch (*Moralia* 78F) refers to the habit of some beginning philosophers who make "collections of apophthegms and anecdotes (χρεῖαι καὶ ἱστορίαι) (Greek text and ET in Babbitt, *Plutarch's Moralia*, vol. 1.

[42] See Diogenes Laertius *Lives* 6.33.

[43] See K.H. Schelke, "Cento," *RAC* 2 (1954) cols. 972–73.

[44] See sect. 3.7 below and the references there.

[45] I am indebted to Christopher D. Stanley, "The Importance of 4QTanḥumim (4Q176)," *RevQ* 15 (1992) 578–79 for all of the following references, except the second quotation from Plutarch and that of Seneca.

(a) Greek Examples

Xenephon (ca. 435–355 BCE) has Socrates say, "And the treasures that the wise men of old have left us in their writings I open and explore with my friends. If we come on any good thing, we extract it (ἐκλεγόμεθα)" (*Memorabilia* 1.6.14).[46] Aristotle encourages his readers "to make extracts also from written works (ἐκλέγειν . . . ἐκ τῶν γεγραμμένων λόγων)" (*Topics* 1.14).[47] In answer to a friend's request to write a treatise, Plutarch relates that "I gathered together from my note-books (ὑπομνήματα) those observations on tranquillity of mind which I happened to have made for my own use" (*Moralia* 464F). Gathering literary extracts was in fact a habit for Plutarch: "For this reason I always strive to collect (συνάγειν) and peruse (ἀναγινώσκειν), not only those sayings and deeds of the philosophers, who are said by fools to have no bile [i.e., "guts"], but even more those of kings and despots (*Moralia* 457D–E).[48]

(b) Latin Examples

Cicero reports that when he decided to write his own textbook of rhetoric, he chose not a single model "but after collecting all the works on the subject I excerpted (*excerpsimus*) what seemed the most suitable precepts from each, and so culled the flower of many minds" (*On Invention* 2.4).[49] Seneca advises that a person should alternate reading and writing, "so that the fruits of one's reading (*quicquid lectione collectum est*) may be reduced to concrete form by the pen" (*Ep.* 84.2).[50] Pliny the Younger describes the custom of his uncle, who made extracts and observations (*adnotabat excerpebatque*) as books were read aloud to him. On his journeys, a shorthand writer (*notarius*) with wax tablets (*pugillares*) accompanied him to take these notes (*Ep.* 3.5).[51] The younger Pliny himself relates making excerpts (*excerpto*) from a volume of Livy (*Ep.* 6.20).

---

[46] Greek text and ET in E.C. Marchant, ed., *Xenephon: Memorabilia and Oeconomicus* (LCL; London: Heinemann; New York: Putnam, 1923).

[47] Greek text and ET in Robin Smith, trans., *Aristotle: Topics: Books I and VIII* (Clarendon Aristotle Series; Oxford: Clarendon, 1996).

[48] Greek text and ET in W.C. Helmbold, ed., *Plutarch's Moralia*, vol. 6 (LCL; London: Heinemann; Cambridge, MA: Harvard University Press, 1939).

[49] Latin text and ET in H.M. Hubbell, ed., *Cicero De Inventione, De Optimo Genere Oratorum, Topica* (LCL; London: Heinemann; Cambridge, MA: Harvard University Press, 1949).

[50] Latin text and ET in Richard M. Gummere, ed., *Seneca Ad Lucilium Epistulae Morales* vol. 2 (LCL; Cambridge, MA: Harvard University Press; London: Heinemann, 1917).

[51] Latin text and ET in W. Melmoth and W.M.L. Hutchinson, eds., *Pliny: Letters*, vol. 1 (LCL; London: Heinemann; New York: Macmillan, 1915).

These examples of private note-taking provide further evidence for the existence of excerpt collections, but at the same time demonstrate that such collections were often made solely by an individual and not intended for wider publication. In evaluating *testimonia* hypotheses, one must take this distinction into account: any single scriptural collection need represent no more than one individual's selection of texts; further evidence is necessary to show that a particular collection was valued in a wider community.[52]

2.4   *Function of Extracts within Jewish Literary Categories*

In chapter one, I drew the working distinction between the midrashic genre (which takes scripture as its starting point and applies it to a contemporary reality) and a *testimonia* genre (which takes an event or proposition outside of scripture as its starting point and refers back to scripture as a witness to the event or proposition).[53] As note above, in concrete cases a clear distinction between these two functions is often difficult to maintain.

A related distinction should be made between *explicit* and *compositional* functions of scripture in Second Temple literature.[54] Explicit citations of scripture may of course function either within a midrashic or in a *testimonia* argument. In compositional use, scripture is woven indirectly into the text through allusions, the use of biblical motifs and models, or the re-writing or expansion of a base biblical text.[55] In the following section, I will provide further discussion and examples. Although *testimonia* hypotheses have usually focused on collections of explicit scripture quotations, we must consider the possibility that particular compositional uses of scripture may be based upon an earlier explicit collection. Conversely, of course, TCs may simply

---

[52] On this point, see Audet, "L'hypothèse," 391–92.

[53] See the related distinction of Geza Vermes between "pure" and "applied" exegesis (*Post-Biblical Jewish Studies* [SJLA 8; Leiden: Brill, 1975] 63–90).

[54] Cf. the terms used by Devorah Dimant, who contrasts the *expositional* and the *compositional* functions of scripture ("Use and Interpretation of Mikra in the Apocrypha and Pseudepigrapha," in Mulder, ed., *Mikra*, 382.

[55] What is called here the compositional use of scripture is also closely related to intertextual reading of scripture; I use the terms interchangeably. For an influential study applying intertextual method to Paul's quotations of scripture see Richard B. Hays, *Echoes of Scripture in the Letters of Paul* (New Haven/London: Yale University Press, 1989), esp. 1–33.

make explicit the implicit texts used compositionally in earlier work.

Finally, the related distinction between *halakhic* and *haggadic* functions of scriptural use should be emphasized. Halakhic functions involve the myriad *legal* questions of scriptural interpretation, including efforts both to systematize laws and to apply general laws to specific cases. In the broadest sense, haggadic use of scripture involves the *non-legal* interpretation of scripture, including moral or homiletical interpretations.[56] Halakhic interpretation usually has to do with explicit, expositional uses of scripture; haggadic readings are often implicit and may involve a compositional re-working of a base scriptural text. Although I have emphasized the forensic function as an essential element of *testimonia*, this does not imply that this genre is relegated to halakhic interpretation; a haggadic interpretation may very well be employed as a kind of proof of a certain argument (e.g., Paul's use of the Abraham narratives to demonstrate his point about faith).

This discussion of *testimonia* in the light of Jewish interpretive categories should not be held separate from the discussion of classical rhetorical categories, since the categories of forensic, epideictic, deliberative, and didactic function are broad enough to be readily applied to both a Jewish and a Greco-Roman milieu. At the same time, the particular emphases of Jewish rhetorical categories and literary techniques must be analyzed in their own right. Given the complex relationships between Greco-Roman and Jewish culture in early Christian history, the student must be aware of the literary categories of both cultures and decide in each case which categories are most appropriate for use in analysis.

2.5   *The Compositional Use of Scripture*

2.5.1   *"Re-written Bible"*

This genre is represented by *Jubilees* (2d cent. BCE), the *Genesis Apocryphon* (ca. turn of the era), and Ps.-Philo's *Biblical Antiquities* (ca. 70 CE).[57] These works generally follow the scriptural sequence, but freely delete,

---

[56] See the discussion in Michael Fishbane, *Biblical Interpretation in Ancient Israel* (Oxford: Clarendon, 1985) 281–83.

[57] For an overview of the genre, see George W.E. Nickelsburg, "The Bible Rewritten and Expanded," in Michael E. Stone, ed., *Jewish Writings of the Second*

expand, paraphrase, and occasionally quote verbatim various biblical sections. Although this genre does not involve the collections of texts, the selection and adaptation of certain passages for a particular rhetorical purpose is analogous to the form and function of extant Christian *testimonia* collections.[58] The authority to re-work scripture is stated most boldly in *Jubilees*: it claims to be a revelation of God to Moses on Mount Sinai.

2.5.2   *Use of Scriptural Allusions, Implicit Quotations, and Models*

The composition of texts in a scriptural style is ubiquitous in Second Temple Jewish literature. Wisdom of Solomon's allusions to Psalm 2 and Proverbs 1–9; the character of Tobit sketched on the model of Job; and the modeling of the Qumran community hymns (*Hodayoth*) on the Psalms are only a few examples.[59] Even in a historical text (1 Macc 5:48), the author models his narration of Judas's rejected request for safe passage through the city of Ephron on the narrative in Numbers 20–21, where the Israelites are refused safe passage. Dimont shows that the very words of Judas's request are in fact an implicit conflated quotation of Deut 2:26–29; Judg 11:19; and Num 21:22—three versions of the Israelites request to King Sihon of the Amorites. With this technique, the author of Maccabees demonstrates implicitly that Judas is taking part in the divinely guided history recorded in scripture.[60] At Qumran, this same technique is applied to a future event: the eschatological battle between the Sons of Light and the Sons of Darkness is modeled on scriptural accounts of battles between Israel and its enemies.[61]

Temple Period: Apocrypha, Pseudepigrapha, Qumran Sectarian Writings, Philo, Josephus (CRINT 2/2; Assen: Van Gorcum; Philadelphia: Fortress, 1984) 89–156.

[58] For example, the re-working of the text in *Jubilees* often functions to support certain halakhic propositions; *Biblical Antiquities* arranges the biblical material around its view of patterns of sin, punishment, repentance, and divinely chosen leaders in history (see ibid., 97–110).

[59] See Dimont, "Mikra in the Apocrypha," 410–19, for the first two examples.

[60] Ibid., 407.

[61] E.g., 1QM 11:6b–7a is based on Num 24:17–19; see Wayne O. McCready, "A Second Torah at Qumran?" *SR* 14 (1985) 10.

2.6   *Scriptural Excerpt Collections in Second Temple Jewish Literature*

2.6.1   *Hebrew and Near Eastern Instruction, Proverb, and Sentence Collections*

These collections are closely related to the Greco-Roman sayings collections presented above. Jewish sayings collections such as Proverbs and Sirach stand within a tradition of Near Eastern sayings collections which date back to the third millennium in Egypt, forming part of the broad category of Near Eastern "wisdom" literature.[62] The organization of the instructions was often based on catch-word or thematic structures.[63] The original purpose of the instruction was probably to train public officials for the royal court. In contrast to a collection of proverbs (whose content could be a subject for deliberation or debate) the admonitions of the instruction are given as authoritative commands requiring obedience.[64] Proverbs 1–9 is an instruction notable for its claim to speak with the divine authority of Wisdom.

The analogies to Christian TCs are clear: the collection of excerpts from other literary works, the catch-word or thematic structure, the pedagogical setting, the authority (even divine authority) of the collection. For the most part, however, these collections served didactic and deliberative rather than forensic functions.

2.6.2   *A Didactic Sayings Collection*: Ps.-Phocylides

Ps.-Phocylides is an arresting example of the combination of Jewish and Greco-Roman sayings traditions.[65] This poetic collection, composed around the turn of the era, is drawn from both the Pentateuch and Greek ethical sayings; half of its verses have parallels in Greek *gnomologia*. The sayings are grouped thematically, treating sexual ethics, modesty, greed, care for the poor and needy, and honesty. Much

---

[62] See, for example, William McKane, *Proverbs: A New Approach* (Philadelphia: Westminster, 1970) 51–182, and Jack T. Sanders, *Ben Sira and Demotic Wisdom* (SBLMS 28; Chico, CA: Scholars Press, 1983).

[63] See Kloppenborg, *Formation of Q*, 264–89. Sirach 38:1–23, for example, is a topical grouping on sickness and death.

[64] Ibid., 263.

[65] Greek text in D. Young, ed., *Theognis, Ps.-Pythagoras, Ps.-Phocylides, Chares, Anonymi Aulodia, Fragmentarum Teleiambicum* (Biblioteca Script. Graec. et Rom. Teubneriania; 2d ed.; Leipzig: BSB Teubner, 1971); ET in P.W. van der Horst, ed., *The Sentences of Pseudo-Phocylides* (SVTP 4; Leiden: Brill, 1978).

of the material is paralleled in the "summaries of the Law" found in Philo and Josephus,[66] leading to speculation that these authors drew on a common catechetical source.[67] Pieter W. van der Horst plausibly identifies the collection's purpose: to demonstrate to a hellenized Jewish audience that Greek ethics and culture are compatible with scriptural ethics.[68] The work is deliberative and was probably composed for use in an educational setting.[69]

2.6.3 *Scriptural* Exempla *Collections*

Like their Greco-Roman counterparts, Second Temple Jewish *exempla* collections served a variety of purposes. Michael R. Cosby identifies six functions, ranging from the didactic genealogy (e.g., Gen 5:1–22) to the epideictic encomium (Sirach 44–50).[70] The deliberative function of providing models for the reader's imitation is widely attested: CD 2:14–3:19 (heroes who walked with God); 1 Macc 2:51–60 (virtues of the ancestors); 3 Macc 6:1–9 (God's punishment of the wicked and support of the righteous); 4 Macc 16:16–23 (examples of courage). Of particular interest is 4 Macc 18:7–19, where the mother of the seven martyrs reminds them of their father's teaching, listing examples of heroes together with direct scriptural quotations. History is understood as the moral drama in which God's purpose is played out (see, e.g., Wisdom 10 on Wisdom's role in historical events). The *exempla* genre passed on into Christian literature: *1 Clem.* 4.7, for example, provides negative and positive examples of jealousy and repentance. The collection in Hebrews 11 is noteworthy for its lack of an explicitly deliberative purpose; its scriptural examples function as forensic proof of the thesis that "faith is the assurance of things hoped for, the conviction of things not seen" (Heb 11:1).

---

[66] Philo *Hypothetica* (apud Eusebius *P.E.* 8.7.1–9) and Josephus *Against Apion* 2.190–219.

[67] See Karl-Wilhelm Niebuhr, *Gesetz und Paränese: Katechismusartige Weisungsreihen in der frühjüdischen Literatur* (WUNT 2/28; Tübingen: Mohr-Siebeck, 1987) 42–43. Niebuhr holds that lack of agreement in precise wording and in the arrangement of the texts makes literary dependence doubtful.

[68] Van der Horst, "Pseudo-Phocylides," *ABD* 5. 348.

[69] Van der Horst, *Pseudo-Phocylides*, 77–80.

[70] Cosby, *Rhetorical Composition*, 14.

2.7   *Scriptural Excerpt Collections at Qumran*

The Qumran discoveries provide an unparalleled opportunity to study scriptural use in a Jewish community that existed at the same time as early Christianity. In the following, then, I present in some detail examples of scriptural collections found in the Dead Sea Scrolls.

2.7.1   *Selection of Passages: 1QIsaiah^a Scroll*

One of the earliest of the Qumran finds, the 1QIsaiah^a scroll, is marked "with some ten or twelve different symbols inserted against passages which the Covenanters must have regarded as important."[71] Several passages, for example, which refer to leaders (kings, the Lord's servant, Cyrus) are marked with an "X." The significance of passages marked with other symbols is unclear, but may have to do with the community's own interpretation of its history. Perhaps marking the passages was the first step in gathering texts into a collection; the technique in any case demonstrates the principle of selecting certain scriptural passages for a special purpose.

2.7.2   *Liturgical Collections: Phylacteries; 4QDeuteronomy^n (4Q41)*

The phylacteries found at Qumran contain various combinations of pentateuchal texts, especially Exod 13:1–16; Deut 5:1–6:3; 6:4–9; and 11:13–21.[72] The thematic link is the reference to the teachings, above all the Decalogue, which should be "as a sign on your hand and as a reminder on your forehead."[73]

4QDeuteronomy^n (the "All Souls Deuteronomy," dated ca. 30 BCE) consists of six columns written on a leather sheet.[74] Column one con-

---

[71] G.R. Driver, *The Judean Scrolls: The Problem and a Solution* (New York: Schocken, 1965) 527–30. Driver cites an analogous example in Epiphanius, who provides a list of signs used by Christians to mark important scripture passages, including a cross to mark those with christological significance (*On Weights and Measures* 1). Hebrew text of the Isaiah^a scroll in Millar Burrows, J.C. Trever and W.H. Brownlee, eds., *The Dead Sea Scrolls of St. Mark's Monastery* (New Haven, CT: The American Schools of Oriental Research, 1950).

[72] The contents of twenty-one phylacteries are published in DJD 6. 47–79. Summary of scriptural contents in Florentino García Martínez, *The Dead Sea Scrolls Translated: The Qumran Texts in English* (2d ed.; Leiden/New York/Cologne: Brill; Grand Rapids: Eerdmans, 1996) 483–84 [hence: *Scrolls*].

[73] See Michael Fishbane, "Use, Authority and Interpretation of Mikra at Qumran," in Mulder, ed., *Mikra*, 351–52.

[74] Hebrew text in DJD 14. 117–28.

tains Deut 8:5–10 and columns 2–6 have Deut 5:1–6:1 (the Decalogue and surrounding material). Recent studies offer strong evidence that this is not a biblical manuscript, but a collection of excerpts, possibly compiled for liturgical use.[75] The following arguments have been presented for understanding the document as an excerpted collection rather than a biblical manuscript: (1) Deuteronomy 8 precedes Deuteronomy 5;[76] (2) Deut 8:5–10 is marked off by spacing; the same text is similarly marked off in 4QDeut[j] and in manuscripts of the Samaritan tradition;[77] (3) 4QDeut[j], 4QDeut[kl], the phylacteries, and *mezuzot* all contain text collections similar to that of the All Souls scroll; all likely had a liturgical setting;[78] (4) the text of the Decalogue harmonizes the versions in Exodus 20 and Deuteronomy 5: this tendency to harmonize Exodus and Deuteronomy is characteristic of excerpted collections;[79] and (5) the size of the manuscript is significantly smaller than typical biblical manuscripts from Qumran, indicating that it was planned to contain select passages of Deuteronomy rather than the whole book.[80] Moshe Weinfeld proposes that Deut 9:5–10 served as a basis for grace after meals at Qumran community;[81] Esther Eshel concludes that 4QDeut[n] may be considered a "Prayer Book."[82]

These Qumran collections may be compared with the Nash papyrus (ca. 100 BCE), a single sheet, found in Egypt, which contains the

---

[75] See Sidnie Ann White, "4QDt[n]: Biblical Manuscript or Excerpted Text?" in Harold W. Attridge, John J. Collins, and Thomas H. Tobin, eds., *Of Scribes and Scrolls: Studies on the Hebrew Bible, Intertestamental Judaism, and Christian Origins Presented to John Strugnell* (College Theology Society Resources in Religion 5; Lanham, MD/New York/London: University Press of America, 1990) 13–20; Moshe Weinfeld, "Grace After Meals in Qumran," *JBL* 111 (1992) 427–29; Esther Eshel, "4QDeut[n]—A Text That Has Undergone Harmonistic Editing," *HUCA* 62 (1991) 148–52; Julie A. Duncan, "Considerations of 4QDt[j] in Light of the 'All Souls Deuteronomy' and Cave 4 Phylactery Texts," in Julio Trebolle Barrera and Luis Vegas Montaner, eds., *The Madrid Qumran Congress: Proceedings of the International Congress on the Dead Sea Scrolls* (STDJ 11; 2 vols.; Leiden/New York/Cologne: Brill; Madrid: Editorial Complutense, 1992) 1. 199–215.

[76] Cf. also 4QExodus[d] (4Q15) where Exod 13:15–17 is followed directly by Exod 15:1.

[77] Duncan, "Considerations," 202–3; White, "Biblical Manuscript," 15.

[78] Eshel, "Harmonistic Editing," 150; Weinfeld, "Grace After Meals," 428; White, "Biblical Manuscript," 15; Duncan, "Considerations," 201–6. Common texts include combinations of Deuteronomy 5–6; 8:5–10; 11; 32; and Exodus 12–13.

[79] White, "Biblical Manuscript," 15; Eshel, "Harmonistic Editing," *passim*.

[80] White, "Biblical Manuscript," 16–17; Eshel, "Harmonistic Editing," 150–51.

[81] Weinfeld ("Grace After Meals," 428) points to a parallel usage in b.Ber. 44a.

[82] Eshel, "4QDt[n]," 151.

Decalogue (Exodus version) together with the Shema.[83] While the liturgy is the most likely life-setting for these collections, they may also have been used for individual study, memorization, or teaching.[84]

2.7.3   *A Harmonizing Collection: 4QReworked Pentateuch^a (4Q158)*

A well-attested technique at Qumran was to gather related excerpts from scripture in an attempt to harmonize/integrate them. In 4Q158, fragments 6–12, for example, the following sequence occurs: Exod 20:19–21; Deut 5:28–29; Deut 18:18–22; Exod 20:12, 16, 17; Deut 5:30–31; Exod 20:20–26; Exod 21:1, 3–6, 8, 10.[85] Michael Fishbane sees this as an attempt to harmonize and integrate various texts concerning the revelation of the law and the role of Moses and his successors. He compares it to the Samaritan text of the Decalogue in Exodus 20, which is combined tendentiously with material from Deuteronomy 5, 18, and 27:4–7 in order to witness to particular Samaritan beliefs regarding the prophet to come and the sanctuary at Shechem.[86]

2.7.4   *Halakhic Collections: 4QOrdinances^a (4Q159) and 11QTemple Scroll (11Q19–20)*

4QOrdinances is a halakhic document, perhaps the legislation followed by a community associated with Qumran.[87] It consists of rephrased biblical precepts (Deut 23:25–26; Exod 30:12; Lev 25:42; Deut 22:5, 13–14) organized under different cultic and ethical categories. For Hodgson, 4QOrdinances is an example of one of the scriptural (as well as popular philosophical) collections which lay behind vice and virtue catalogs, *Haustafeln*, and parenetic texts like 1 Thess 4:1–12 and Rom 13:1–7.[88]

---

[83] See W.F. Albright, "A Biblical Fragment from the Maccabean Age: The Nash Papyrus," *JBL* 56 (1937) 145–76.

[84] See White, "Biblical Manuscript," 17. See also C. Ernest Wright, who comments that the Nash papyrus was used in teaching or in worship (*Biblical Archaeology* [rev. ed.; Philadelphia: Westminster; London: Duckworth, 1962] 216).

[85] Hebrew text in DJD 5. 1–6; ET in *Scrolls*, 219–22.

[86] Fishbane, "Mikra at Qumran," 352–53.

[87] Hebrew text in DJD 5. 6–9; ET in *Scrolls*, 86–87. For a detailed presentation of this position, see Francis D. Weinert, "4Q159: Legislation for an Essene Community outside of Qumran?" *JSJ* 5 (1974) 179–207. Weinert concludes: "Hence the legislation contained in 4Q159 was not intended as a simple repetition of already known biblical law, but as an affirmation of specific biblical laws being interpreted in a new way" (p. 181).

[88] Hodgson, "Testimony," 365.

The Temple Scroll harmonizes and integrates related material from different sections of scripture.[89] In 11QTemple 66:8–9 two rules (Exod 22:15 and Deut 22:28–29) regarding the consequences for rape are harmonized. Prescriptions for the festival of unleavened bread integrate material from Lev 23:6–8; Num 17:10–16; 28:17–25; Deut 16:8; and Ezra 16:8. The sequence in 11QTemple 51–52 is an extended example of this procedure: it presents the laws of Deuteronomy 16–17 together with some exegetical additions and combinations from other pentateuchal laws. A re-interpreted form of Torah is the result.[90]

2.7.5 *Thematic Collection on the Eschatological Struggle: 4QTestimonia (4Q175)*

This document consists of the following sequence of quotations, cited without introduction and without intervening comment: conflation of Deut 5:28–29 and Deut 18:18–19;[91] Num 24:15–17; Deut 33:8–11; conflation of Josh 6:26 and a passage from the sectarian *Psalms of Joshua*.[92] Several catch-word connections link the texts: שמע (Deut 5:28–29; 18:16–19; Num 24:15–17); קום (Deut 18:18–19; Num 24:15–17; Deut 33:8–11), and עם (Deut 5:28–29; Josh 6:26).

As noted above, this document's editor saw this as a confirmation of Burkitt's and Harris's *testimonia* theories.[93] It is often assumed to be a collection of "messianic" texts,[94] but this does not account for the presence of the last quotation. George J. Brooke's interpretation is more convincing: the first three texts refer to the eschatological figures of the prophet, royal messiah, and priest; the whole refers to the fortunes of those who will participate in the eschatological

---

[89] Hebrew text in Yigdal Yadin, *Megillat ham-migdash (The Temple Scroll)* (3 vols. and supp.; Jerusalem: Israel Exploration Society, 1977); ET in *Scrolls*, 154–84.

[90] See Fishbane, "Mikra at Qumran," 353–54. This harmonizing halakhic activity can also be seen in *Jubilees* (see above 2.5.1.a). For a discussion on whether the Temple Scroll is primarily a clarification or harmonization of the "Torah of Moses" or whether it represents a new or second Torah, see McCready, "Second Torah," esp. 12–15.

[91] Patrick W. Skehan shows that this combination reflects the conflated text read in the Samaritan Pentateuch at Exod 20:21 ("The Period of the Biblical Texts from Khirbet Qumran," *CBQ* 19 [1957] 435).

[92] Hebrew text in DJD 5. 57–60; ET in *Scrolls*, 137–38.

[93] Allegro, "Messianic References," 186.

[94] E.g., Geza Vermes labels it "A Messianic Anthology or Testimonia" in *The Dead Sea Scrolls in English* (3d ed.; Sheffield: JSOT, 1987) 295.

struggle.[95] Brooke is correct to see the outlines of an eschatological narrative here, indeed I understand it as the scriptural substructure to an eschatological narrative: perhaps the first stage of collecting texts from which a narrative would be composed. Its physical form (a single unattached sheet) and its epigraphy ("characterized by carelessness and a rather strange orthography")[96] suggest that it was not intended for wider distribution, but was compiled by an individual for his own reference.

2.7.6   Thematic Collection on "Consolation": 4QTanhumim (4Q176)

This fragmentary document consists of a sequence of excerpts taken from the book of Isaiah with no apparent adaptation and no intervening comments.[97] The texts (Isa 40:1–5; 41:8–9; 43:1–6; 49:7; 49:13–17; 51:22–23; 52:1–3; 54:4–10) are all words of comfort (tanhumim) spoken by the Lord in the first person to his people. Stanley is surely correct in understanding this composition as the work of a reader, interested in the Lord's promises of comfort, who excerpted these texts in the course of a sequential reading through the text of Isaiah 40–55.[98] The final purpose of this collection (liturgical reading, notes for future compositional use) remains a matter of speculation.

2.7.7   Prophetic Testimonia on the Future Struggle and the Community's Past History

The following are examples of collections of scripture, together with interpretive comments, which function as proof-texts for particular eschatological or historical views.

(a) Midrash on Eschatological Scriptures: 4QEschatological Midrash (4QEschatMidr^{a,b}) = 4QFlorilegium (4Q174)[99] and 4QCatena^a (4Q177)[100] Annette Steudel's recent study demonstrates that these two fragmentary texts (4QFlorilegium and 4QCatena^a) are in fact parts of the same

---

[95] Brooke, Exegesis at Qumran: 4QFlorilegium in its Jewish Context (JSOTSup 29; Sheffield: JSOT, 1985) 311–19. John Lübbe also argues against a messianic interpretation ("A Reinterpretation of 4Q Testimonia," RevQ [1986] 187–97).

[96] Allegro, "Messianic References," 182.

[97] Hebrew text in DJD 5. 60–67; ET in Scrolls, 208–9.

[98] Stanley, Language of Scripture, 77. See his detailed study in "4QTanhumim," 569–82.

[99] Hebrew text in DJD 5. 53–57; ET in Scrolls, 136–37.

[100] Hebrew text in DJD 5. 67–74; ET in Scrolls, 209–11.

document, which has been labeled the "Eschatological Midrash."[101] The label "Florilegium," assigned by 4Q174's editor, John Allegro, is misleading, since the text has a midrashic structure.[102] The first part (1:1–13) is a midrash on Nathan's oracle (2 Sam 7:10–14): parts of this text are quoted and interpreted with exegetical remarks (without the word *pesher*) and with other scriptural texts (Exod 15:17–18 and Amos 9:11). The second section (1:14–2:6) quotes Ps 1:1, interpreting it with exegetical comments (using the word *pesher*) and other scriptures (Isa 8:11 and Ezek 44:16), and then quotes Ps 2:1, which is applied to "the elect of Israel in the last days."[103] The third section (4QCatena) can be understood as a midrash (it uses the word *pesher*) on Psalms 11–17.[104] The theme of "the last days" links the composition.

The document is a collection of texts and commentary which relates a prophetic narrative of the last days. It doubtless also served a deliberative function, encouraging the members of the community to endure patiently until the end. While the composition is formally midrashic (interpretation of base scriptural texts), it functioned most likely as a prophetic "proof" that the narrated events would take place in the last days.

(b) *Thematic Collection on the Eschatological Jubilee Year and Melchizedek: 11QMelchizedek (11Q13)*

This text combines the following scriptures, together with interpretive remarks (often with the word *pesher*): Lev 25:13; Deut 15:2; Ps 82:1; Ps 7:8–9; Ps 82:2; Isa 52:7; Isa 61:2–3; Isa 52:7; Lev 25:9.[105] Fitzmyer holds that the base text is Leviticus 25,[106] while Merrill P.

---

[101] Steudel, *Der Midrasch zur Eschatologie aus der Qumrangemeinde (4QMidrEschat^{a,b}): Materielle Rekonstruktion, Textbestand, Gattung und traditionsgeschichtliche Einordnung des durch 4Q174 ("Florilegium") und 4Q177 ("Catena A") repräsentierten Werkes aus den Qumranfunden* (STDJ 13; Leiden/New York/Cologne: Brill, 1994) 127–60.

[102] Allegro, "Messianic References," 176.

[103] For analysis of 4QFlorilegium's structure, see William R. Lane, "A New Commentary Structure in 4Q Florilegium," *JBL* 78 (1959) 343–46, and Brooke, *Exegesis at Qumran*, esp. 129–66.

[104] See John J. Collins, Review of A. Steudel, *Midrasch, JBL* 114 (1995) 315.

[105] First published by A.S. van der Woude, "Melchisedek als himmlische Erlösergestalt in den neugefundenen eschatologischen midraschim aus Qumran-Höhle XI.," *OTS* 14 (1965) 354–73. Various reprints with suggested restorations have appeared, e.g., Joseph A. Fitzmyer, "Further Light on Melchizedek from Qumran Cave 11," *JBL* 86 (1967) 26–27; repr. in idem, *Semitic Background*, 247–51; ET in *Scrolls*, 139–40.

[106] Fitzmyer, "Further Light," 251.

Miller argues that the interpretive comments can all be related to Isa 61:1–2.[107] The most important observation, however, is that the anonymous author has collected a series of texts connected with the eschatological jubilee year, associated these texts with the role of God's agent Melchizedek, and created an eschatological narrative.[108]

(c) *Proof-texts on the Community's History: Damascus Document (CD) 6–7*

In contrast to the future prophetic proofs discussed above, this text employs Num 21:18; Isa 54:16; Mal 1:10; Isa 7:17; Amos 5:26–27; 9:11; and Num 24:17 as prophetic proof-texts to the narrative describing the *past* exile of the community.[109] The texts function not so much as proof that these events occurred, but rather to support a certain interpretation of these events: the establishment of the Qumran community and its leaders was foretold in scriptures, and is thus a part of God's plan.

The above selection of documents shows beyond doubt that the gathering of scriptural extracts into written collections was a well-established techniqu at Qumran. In addition, these documents demonstrate the wide range of uses to which these collections were put: prophetic proof-texts or *testimonia* (4QEschatMidr, 11QMelch), liturgical collections (the phylacteries, 4QDeut[n]), harmonizing collections (4QReworked Pentateuch[a]), and halakhic collections (4QOrd[a]; 11QTemple). The markings on the Isaiah scroll, 4QTanḥumim, and perhaps 4QTestimonium afford us precious glimpses into the actual mechanics of how these texts were first collected.

2.8   *Private Collections (Notebooks)*

Birger Gerhardsson offers rabbinic evidence for the use of notebooks or "scrolls of secrets" to facilitate pupils' memorization of their rabbis' teachings.[110] The difficulty with Gerhardsson's references, of course,

---

[107] Miller, "The Function of Isa 61:1–2 in 11Q Melchizedek," *JBL* 88 (1969) 467–69.

[108] Surprisingly, neither of the biblical passages (Gen 14:18–20 and Ps 110:4) in which the name Melchizedek explicitly appears are used in this text.

[109] Damascus Document manuscripts: CD[a.b] = copies of the Damascus Document from the Cairo Genizah; Qumran frags. = 4Q266–4Q273 (4QD[a–h]); 5Q12 (5QD); 6Q15 (6QD); see *Scrolls*, 494–95 for the complex publishing bibliography; ET in *Scrolls*, 33–71.

[110] Gerhardsson, *Memory and Manuscript*, 160–62.

is that all date after the year 200 CE, and he has often been roundly criticized for reading later rabbinical practices back into the first century. The Qumran evidence suggestive of personal scriptural collections (4QTanhumim, perhaps 4QDeut[n] and 4QTest), however, cautions against dismissing Gerhardsson too quickly.

2.9   *Christian Use of Non-biblical Excerpt Collections: Poetic Anthologies and Secondary Philosophical Sources*

To conclude my sketch of the literary environment in which ECs and TCs were standard working tools, I present evidence for early Christian use of non-biblical ECs. I have already referred above (sect. 1.20) to an extensive body of scholarship that demonstrates the extent to which Christian tradition (sayings, parables, miracle stories, eschatological discourses) was passed down in small-scale collections. I now offer further examples of Christian use of non-Christian collections.

It is reasonably certain that the apostle Paul drew his quotation of Menander (1 Cor 15:33) from a poetic anthology.[111] It is also probable that the two classical citations quoted in Acts 17:28 were already found together in an anthology.[112] In the second century, Theophilus of Antioch and Clement of Alexandria made use of poetic anthologies.[113]

Nicole Zeegers-Vander Vorst approaches her study of poetic citations in second-century Christian apologists (Clement of Alexandria, Theophilus, Athenagoras, Tatian, and Ps.-Justin) employing a method similar to that used in *testimonia* research. She isolates (1) common sequences shared by the apologists and non-Christian philosophical works and (2) common exegesis of passages. The common sequences

---

[111] Chadwick, "Florilegium," col. 1143. The quotation is already found in the 3d cent. BCE collection (*P. Hibeh* 1.7) referred to above (sect. 2.3.3c). Hans Conzelmann also cautions that Paul's quotation of Menander does not allow us to assume his first–hand knowledge of the poet (*First Corinthians* [Hermeneia; Philadelphia: Fortress, 1975] 278 n. 139).

[112] Chadwick, "Florilegium," col. 1143.

[113] Ibid., cols. 1143–45. Chadwick notes parallels between quotations in these authors and the collections in John Stobaeus. On Theophilus's use of anthologies, see also Gustave Bardy, "Introduction," to idem, ed., *Théophile d'Antioche: Trois Livres à Autolycus* (SC 20; Paris: Cerf, 1948) 11 (noting several false attributions in quotations), and Robert M. Grant, "Introduction," in idem, ed., *Theophilus of Antioch: Ad Autolycum* (Oxford Early Christian Texts; Oxford: Clarendon, 1970) xi–xii.

are in effect TCs "proving" such propositions as the existence of one
God. Dismissing as too vague previous attributions of this common
material to a "florilegia" source, Zeegers-Vander Vorst instead posits
common use of philosophical tractates (e.g., "On Providence"; "Against
the Impiety of Homer"), and classic collections of texts and commentary (e.g., Plutarch's *Moralia*). These thematic collections, already
well-known due to a long history of use in philosophical circles,
added authority to the claims of the apologists. The apologists also
drew on hellenistic Jewish tractates and the Sibylline Oracles.[114]

Early Christian authors also used intermediary philosophical collections. Three second-century works, Athenagoras's *Supplication*, Theophilus's *To Autolycus* and Irenaeus's *Against Heresies*, all make use of
the doxographical edition first edited by Aetius.[115] The writers cite
the conflicting philosophical opinions in the doxography as evidence
for the limitations of philosophical thought and the consequent need
for reliance on God. Hippolytus's sources for his summary of philosophy (*Refutation of All Heresies*, Book 1, early 3d cent.) span the range
of available intermediary collections: Alcinous's handbook, a doxography, summaries by Sextus Empiricus, various commentaries, and
an anthology which included Heraclitus.[116]

Christian writers themselves made ECs and TCs from non-biblical
materials. To each of his summaries of gnostic heresies, Hippolytus
appends selected representative extracts from their writings, and
finishes his presentation with an epitome of each group's system.[117]
The earliest collection of the writings of a non-biblical Christian
writer is the *Philocalia*, a selection from Origen's works made by Basil
and Gregory Nazianzus (4th cent.).[118]

---

[114] Nicole Zeegers-Vander Vorst, *Les Citations des Poètes grecs chez les apologistes chrétiens du IIe siècle* (Université de Louvain Recueil de Travaux d'Histoire et de Philologie
4/47; Louvain: Universitaires de Louvain, 1972); see esp. 288–92.

[115] Grant, "Irenaeus," 42–44. These Christian authors follow the sequence of the
doxography and use many of its subject headings.

[116] See Miroslav Marcovich, ed., *Hippolytus Refutatio Omnium Haeresium* (Patristische
Texte und Studien 25; Berlin/New York: de Gruyter, 1986) 17–31. That an anthol-
ogy is used in 9.9–10 is shown by Hippolytus's use of the word κεφάλαιον (9.10.8)
to refer to a section or chapter in the anthology; see further Miroslav Marcovich,
"Hippolytus and Heraclitus," in F.L. Cross, ed., *Studia Patristica*, vol. 7 (TU 92;
Berlin: Akademie, 1966) 255. On Hippolytus's use of a doxography, see Diels,
Doxographi, 133–56.

[117] See Marcovich, *Hippolytus*, 33.

[118] Chadwick, "Florilegium," col. 1149.

2.10   *Conclusions*

(1) Early Christian use of scriptural passages as witnesses (μαρτύρια) for their beliefs has an important background in classical rhetorical theory; already in the NT authors present forensic arguments in which the witness of scripture is key.

(2) In order to place early Christian TCs in their literary context, evidence was presented showing the ubiquitous contemporary Greco-Roman technique of gathering written extracts into thematic collections, ranging from the primary anthology to more advanced philosophical and rhetorical handbooks. A didactic or "school" setting is evident for most of these collections.

(3) Analogies between Christian scriptural TCs and Greco-Roman collections can be drawn in several aspects: in content (oracle and moral maxim collections); in form (thematic collections); in compositional technique (conflated and adapted texts), and in function (didactic functions; molding scattered texts into more systematic, even doctrinal, statements). This latter analogy is relevant for claims that TCs influenced developing theological concepts.

(4) The Jewish evidence also presents many points of contact, especially by providing concrete examples of scriptural ECs and TCs. Several examples of collections with no intervening comments are extant. Examples of excerpt collections with comments (e.g., in midrash collections) are even more numerous. The Jewish collections served a variety of functions: we find harmonizing and halakhic, liturgical, didactic, deliberative *exempla*, and prophetic proof-text collections. Halakhic evidence is especially relevant in evaluating claims that early Christian parenesis is based on previous collections of scripture (Hodgson); the use of prophetic proof-texts is an invaluable parallel to similar Christian techniques employed in the NT and in other early literature.

(5) Careful distinctions must be made in discussing genres of midrash, *testimonia* and the compositional use of scripture. While 4QEschatological Midrash, for example, is formally midrashic, its texts function as prophetic proofs of eschatological events, and provide a schematic narrative of those events. I suggest that thematic collections with no commentary (e.g., 4QTestimonia and 4QTanhumim) may have functioned as the substructure from which a subsequent narrative was composed. This evidence is important in

evaluating recent claims that NT narratives are based on previous *testimonia* collections.

(6) Evidence of private excerpt collections in both Greco-Roman and Jewish literature has an important implication for any *testimonia* hypothesis: they remind us that any given collection may reflect only the concerns of an individual or small group, and not necessarily those of a community as a whole.

(7) In contrast to this last point, however, the claim to religious authority implicit in the very process of excerpting and re-arranging scripture must be recognized. This claim is occasionally explicit, as in the case of the halakhic re-writing of scripture in *Jubilees* and in the *Temple Scroll*. Gauging the authority and influence of early collections of scripture is an important aspect of evaluating *testimonia* hypotheses.

(8) We have evidence that Christians of the first and second centuries used poetic and philosophical ECs; by analogy we might expect that they were also employing scriptural ECs and TCs.

CHAPTER THREE

CHRISTIAN *TESTIMONIA* COLLECTIONS IN THE PATRISTIC PERIOD

3.1 *Overview of the Chapter*

I begin this chapter by laying out some of the practical arguments for the probable use of scriptural ECs in early Christianity. I will then proceed to the heart of the chapter: the presentation of concrete examples of a variety of patristic TCs. I begin with a detailed examination of Justin's *1 Apology* and *Dialogue* and of *Barnabas*, since these works offer clear, early evidence for the use of extensive TCs which had the authority of scripture. The chapter then presents examples of *testimonia* collections in various Greek, Latin, Coptic, and Syriac texts. Finally, I present two examples of broader *testimonia* traditions: a case study on an anti-cultic collection used by *Barnabas*, Irenaeus, Clement of Alexandria, and Ps.-Gregory, and a short excursus on collections, relating to Jesus's crucifixion, which evolved around the catch-word "wood."

In presenting these examples, I wish (1) to provide a representative overview of the broad extent of the *testimonia* tradition, a tradition which transcended barriers of time and culture; (2) to present in detail the pattern of precise parallels and individual differences between various TCs (for ease of comparison, I have focused on passion *testimonia*); (3) to establish that, in most cases, a given TC cannot be attributed simply to general oral tradition or to direct borrowing from other Christian authors; rather these TCs presuppose authoritative, written collections of proof-texts which circulated, independently from the NT and other early Christian writings. In the last two chapters of my study, I hope to show that the beginnings of some of these authoritative written traditions are already visible within the NT itself.

For each TC, I will present a brief introduction to the work in which the TC appears; a discussion on the TC's function within the work; concrete evidence that the collection is derived from a written *testimonia* source; and discussion of the original form of that *testimonia* source.

3.2   Early Christian Use of Scriptural Extract Collections:
Practical Considerations

Proponents of *testimonia* hypotheses have long argued that small-scale scriptural ECs would have been practical for early Christian missionaries, who would use them to illustrate or prove particular points.[1] Scrolls of scriptural books were expensive, difficult to transport, and cumbersome to use.[2] ECs would facilitate the apologetic task of the missionaries.

What form would these ECs have taken? The codex (leaf book, the prototype of the modern book) gradually replaced scrolls between the second and fourth centuries.[3] It is a remarkable fact, however, that in a second-century Greco-Roman and Jewish environment still dominated by the book in scroll form, the earliest Christian books were almost without exception made in codex form. Of the Greek books which can be dated before the third century, ninety-eight percent are scrolls, yet virtually all Christian books in this period are codices.[4]

If, as these practical considerations suggest, early Christians used ECs, these collections would have been in codex form. This conclusion is supported by the following considerations: (1) the general Christian predilection for the codex; (2) *excerpta* were commonly copied down in codex notebooks;[5] (3) the compact codex was more convenient for travelers and missionaries;[6] and (4) since its pages could be

---

[1] See Harris, *Testimonies* 1. 1; Stather Hunt, *Sources*, 16–17; more recently, Gamble, *Books and Readers*, 27.

[2] For a brief discussion on the expense of books in the ancient world, see William V. Harris, *Ancient Literacy* (Cambridge, MA; London: Harvard University Press, 1989) 225.

[3] Gamble, *Books and Readers*, 43.

[4] Ibid., 49. See also the discussion, with statistics, in S.R. Llewelyn, ed., *New Documents Illustrating Early Christianity*, vol. 7 (The Ancient History Documentary Research Centre, North Ryde, New South Wales, Australia: Macquarie University, 1994) 251.

[5] As shown by Pliny's comment that his uncle's secretary copied down his excerpts and notes on *pugillares* (wax tablets in codex form) (*Ep.* 3.5); see sect. 2.3.6b. Gamble maintains that the codex was not recognized among the ancients as a proper book: it was considered a mere notebook, with private and practical associations (*Books and Readers*, 49–50).

[6] The Roman poet Martial (ca. 85 CE) recommended parchment (*membranas*) pages in codex form for readers who wished to carry his poems with them on journeys (*Epigr.* 1.2; see Gamble, *Books and Readers*, 52). The use of the codex by missionaries is clear from 2 Tim 4:13: the author asks Timothy "to bring the cloak that I left with Carpus at Troas, also the books, and above all the parchments" (καὶ τὰ

marked, the codex facilitated looking up references: no small advantage for the Christian preacher or apologist.[7]

A wealth of hypotheses have been presented to account for this overwhelming Christian predilection for the codex, none of which is completely satisfactory.[8] I propose that the most likely explanation is that scriptural ECs and TCs in codex form were among the first authoritative Christian documents. Such codex collections, used in worship, polemic, and instruction, might well have influenced the physical form which other Christian writings took.[9]

A scriptural EC would also make practical sense in a worship life-setting. While full scrolls were certainly used for public reading of scripture (see, e.g., Luke 4:17–20), the Qumran evidence presented above suggests that ECs were also produced for liturgical purposes.[10] Although Christians used scripture in their worship services from the earliest times, we possess no LXX manuscript clearly produced by Christians before about the middle of the second century.[11] Only in the later second century do we find evidence of Christian *scriptoria*.[12] A partial explanation for these facts is that many Christian communities had no access to Jewish produced scriptures (because of hostile relations or simple lack of proximity) and would have made do with ECs or TCs of passages considered especially relevant.[13]

βιβλία μάλιστα τὰς μεμβράνας). This last word refers to a parchment codex (Gamble, *Books and Readers*, 64), although there is no compelling reason to suppose that it refers specifically to a TC, *pace* C.H. Roberts, "Books in the Graeco-Roman World and in the Old Testament," in P.R. Ackroyd and C.F. Evans, eds., *The Cambridge History of the Bible*, vol. 1: *From the Beginnings to Jerome* (Cambridge/New York: Cambridge University Press, 1970) 53.

[7] Harris, *Literacy*, 296. Harris cites a late example from Augustine which describes this technique: "I took up the codex (*codicem*) and read out each place" (*Letters* 29.4–10).

[8] See Gamble, *Books and Readers*, 54–66; Llewelyn, *Documents*, 251–56. The explanation favored by Gamble, that a codex collection of Paul's letters influenced other early Christian literature, does not explain why a letter collection would influence the physical form of other Christian writings (including the gospel genre). Practical explanations (e.g., ease of reference and transport) would equally apply to non-Christian groups that continued to use scrolls. The argument that poor Christians could not afford scrolls ignores evidence that early Christianity included a range of social classes.

[9] This conclusion is also reached by Gerhardsson, who argues that the gospel tradition began with records in codex-style notebooks; these documents influenced the choice of the codex for later Christian literature (*Memory and Manuscript*, 201–2).

[10] See sect. 2.7.2 above.

[11] Gamble, *Books and Readers*, 27 n. 89. See also the discussion in Roberts, "Books," 62.

[12] Ibid., 65.

[13] See sect. 3.4.4 below for evidence that Melito's community in Sardis lacked

3.3   *Excursus on the LXX-deviant Criterion*

Before considering the patristic evidence for ECs and TCs, some
remarks on the criterion of LXX-deviant texts for detecting use of
ECs are necessary.[14] The essential logic of this criterion is that quotations that deviate significantly from the LXX are attributable either
to (1) intentional changes by an author or (2) use of a non-scriptural
source. This criterion has been challenged on the grounds that since
we know little about various text traditions available in the first
centuries CE, we cannot attribute a "deviation" to an EC or TC—
it may simply derive from an unknown text tradition.[15] How valid
is this objection?

Two basic models have dominated the discussion of the development of the LXX: Paul de Lagarde's thesis of an original archetype translation for each book from which later revisions were made,
and Paul Kahle's claim that the LXX developed from multiple
early translations (on analogy with Aramaic targums) which were
only gradually shaped into a unified tradition.[16] Recent scholarship
has tended to support Lagarde's position: we can speak of a relatively unified LXX text in the first centuries CE; deviations from it
are to be explained by systematic attempts to revise the translation
towards the Hebrew. The so-called καίγε text tradition (represented
by a first-century scroll of the Twelve Prophets found at Nahal Hever),
for instance, is an example of this revision towards the Hebrew;[17]
second-century translations (e.g., Aquila) were in fact revisions of the
καίγε tradition towards contemporary rabbinic Hebrew.[18] The upshot

---

access to scriptural manuscripts. It is also worth noting that we can date no Christian
commentary on an entire OT book before the beginning of the third century
(Hippolytus and Origen): see Martin Hengel, "The Old Testament in the Fourth
Gospel," *HBT* 8 (1990) 23.

[14] I understand "LXX" in its broadest definition as including the original Greek
("Old Greek") translations of Hebrew scriptures (beginning 3d cent. BCE), some later
revisions (towards the Hebrew) of these translations, and other "apocryphal" books,
whether composed originally in Hebrew (e.g., Sirach) or in Greek (e.g., Wisdom of
Solomon). See Emanuel Tov, *Textual Criticism of the Hebrew Bible* (Minneapolis: Fortress;
Assen/Maastricht: Van Gorcum, 1992) 135.

[15] See Audet, "L'hypothèse," 394–95.

[16] See Ernst Würthwein, *The Text of the Old Testament: An Introduction to the Biblia
Hebraica* (2d ed.; Grand Rapids: Eerdmans, 1995) 61–66.

[17] Published by Dominique Barthélemy, *Les Devanciers d'Aquila: Première publication
intégrale du texte des fragments du Dodécapropheton* (VTSup 10; Leiden: Brill, 1963); see
Würthwein, *Text*, 65.

[18] See Frank Moore Cross, "The History of the Biblical Text in the Light of

is that a reading which deviates significantly from the LXX, and
which cannot be explained as a revision towards the Hebrew, may
legitimately be considered as possible evidence for the use of a non-
biblical collection.[19]

3.4   *Early Greek* Testimonia *Collections (Second Century)*

3.4.1   *Justin* First Apology *and* Dialogue with Trypho

Justin was born in Samaria, lived for a time in Ephesus, conducted
a school for Christians in Rome, and was martyred around 165 CE.
Two major writings are extant: the *First Apology*,[20] written between
150 and 156 and addressed to the Roman emperor Antoninus,
and the *Dialogue with Trypho*, a discussion between Justin and a Jewish opponent concerning the truth of Christianity, written shortly
afterwards.[21]

(a) *Function of* Testimonia
Justin quotes extensively from scripture. He calls his quotations "testimonies" (μαρτύρια) and uses them to "prove" the truth of the
Christian religion to the emperor and to Trypho, respectively. The
following passage is representative:

> For with what reason should we believe of a crucified man that He
> is the first-born of the unbegotten God, and Himself will pass judg-
> ment on the whole human race, unless we had found testimonies

---

Discoveries in the Judean Desert," in idem and Shemaryahu Talmon, eds., *Qumran
and the History of the Biblical Text* (Cambridge, MA/London: Harvard University Press,
1975) 179.

[19] The LXX-deviant criterion by itself is of course not adequate to establish the
use of an EC; it must be used in conjunction with other criteria.

[20] Greek text in Miroslav Marcovich, ed., *Iustini Martyris Apologiae pro Christianis*
(Patristische Texte und Studien 38; Berlin/New York: de Gruyter, 1994); ET in
ANF 1. 163–87. The *Second Apology* is generally considered to be a supplement or
postscript to the first, written a short time after the latter's completion (Marcovich,
Apologiae, 11). Marcovich's edition cites extensive early Christian parallels with Justin's
quotations, together with important secondary discussions (including those of Prigent
and Skarsaune).

[21] Greek text in Miroslav Marcovich, ed., *Iustini Martyris Dialogus cum Tryphone*
(Patristische Texte und Studien 47; Berlin/New York: de Gruyter, 1994). On the
dates of composition, see Skarsaune, *Prophecy*, 9; Eric Francis Osborn, *Justin Martyr*
(BHT 47; Tübingen: Mohr-Siebeck, 1973) 8.

(μαρτύρια) concerning him published before He came and was born as man, and unless we had seen that things had happened accordingly. (*1 Apol.* 53.2)

For Justin, then, proof consists in the accurate prediction by the prophets of events that then took place in the life of Jesus and subsequent history. The μαρτύρια of the scriptures is in turn based on the absolute reliability of the prophets, who are themselves μάρτυρες of the truth:

> In their [i.e., the prophets'] writings they gave no proof (ἀπόδειξις) at that time of their statements, for as reliable witnesses (μάρτυρες) of the truth, they were beyond proof; but the happenings that have taken place and are now taking place force you to believe their words. (*Dial.* 7.2)

Scripture, however, does need proper interpretation. The true meaning of scripture remained closed until Christ disclosed it to his disciples; they in turn taught these things in the world (*Dial.* 53.5; 76.6). In his work of handing on the proper scriptural interpretations in his TCs, Justin understood himself as continuing this apostolic tradition.[22]

Who is the intended audience of the *Dialogue?* Jon Nilson makes a plausible case that the actual audience is not Jews, but rather Roman gentiles who are favorably disposed to both Judaism and Christianity.[23] The purpose of the *Dialogue*, then, would be to demonstrate the superiority of Christianity over Judaism to this audience. Nilson's strongest argument is his consideration of *Dialogue* 1–9. In these introductory chapters, Justin presents Christianity as the fulfillment of his search for the true philosophy; this way of framing the work seems to be intended to impress a gentile audience.[24] A further consideration is that the portrayal of Trypho is flat and stereotypical. Trypho shows little real knowledge of the Judaism of his time, and serves essentially as a foil for Justin's presentation.

(b) *Evidence of Written* Testimonia *Sources*

LXX-divergent texts are frequent in Justin, especially in the *Apology*. Oskar Skarsaune shows that the apologist uses two general quarries

---

[22] See Skarsaune, *Prophecy*, 11–13.

[23] Nilson, "To Whom is Justin's *Dialogue with Trypho* Addressed?" *TS* 38 (1977) 538–46.

[24] Ibid., 540. Skarsaune (*Prophecy*, 258–59) also envisions an audience of God-fearing gentiles.

for his quotations: written Christian *testimonia* sources and full biblical manuscripts.[25] Skarsaune's most compelling evidence is drawn
from the comparison of different versions of the same scriptural quotations on which Justin himself comments.[26] In general, Justin offers
short, non-LXX versions in the *Apology* and longer, LXX quotations
in the *Dialogue*. The *Apology* versions betray multiple indications of
derivation from TCs: Justin shows no awareness of the quotations'
biblical context; conflated texts have close parallels in independent
authors; "Christianized" additions and changes from the LXX are
evident. In the *Dialogue*, many of these versions are corrected toward
the LXX, indicating that Justin himself has looked up the quotations in an LXX scroll.[27]

False attributions abound in both works:[28]

(1) Zephaniah for Zechariah (*1 Apol.* 35.10; correctly in *Dial.* 53.5)
(2) Jeremiah for Daniel (*1 Apol.* 51.8; correctly in *Dial.* 76.1)
(3) Isaiah for Jeremiah (*1 Apol.* 53.10)
(4) Jeremiah for Isaiah (*Dial.* 12.2)
(5) Hosea for Zechariah (*Dial.* 14.8)
(6) Zechariah for Malachi (*Dial.* 49.2)
(7) Isaiah for Numbers (*1 Apol.* 32.12)

In some cases Justin bases his exegetical comments on a peculiar
non-LXX reading witnessed in the *Apology*, and maintains this exegetical reading even when (in the *Dialogue*) he uses the LXX text![29] This
phenomenon shows the strong authority that these *testimonia* sources

---

[25] Ibid., 8.

[26] Ibid., 25–92.

[27] Skarsaune convincingly refutes suggestions that scriptural quotations in the
Dialogue were corrected towards the LXX by a later hand (pp. 17–20). Joost Smit
Sibinga (*The Old Testament Text of Justin Martyr I: The Pentateuch* [Leiden: Brill, 1963]
149–50) also rejects the plausibility of a scribal reworking of Justin's quotations,
showing that many of these long quotations derive from ancient hebraizing recensions such as are preserved in Barthélemy's καίγε text. Barthélemy himself argued
that Justin's text of the Twelve Prophets is taken from the καίγε recension ("Redécouverte d'un chaînon manquant de l'histoire de la Septante," *RB* 60 [1953] 18–29;
repr. in Cross and Talmon, *Biblical Text*, 130; Barthélemy, *Devanciers*, 203–12). More
recently, Robert M. Grant judges that "[Skarsaune] begins with the texts of the
Greek Old Testament in the *Apology* and the *Dialogue* and explains exactly how and
why they are different, showing that we have reliable copies of both works" (Review
of Skarsaune, *Prophecy*, in *CH* 57 [1988] 216).

[28] The first six of these are listed in Osborn, *Justin*, 114. Osborn devotes a valuable chapter to Justin and *testimonia* (pp. 111–19).

[29] *Dial.* 54.1–2 (see *Prophecy*, 28); *Dial.* 81.1–3 (ibid., 67); *Dial.* 31.1 (ibid., 88–90).

(with their exegetical comments) had for Justin. Indeed, Justin insists
that his *testimonia* passages represent the true text of "the seventy";
he labels the longer, LXX-type quotations as "Jewish," and indicates
that he uses this text in the *Dialogue* merely as a concession to his
Jewish opponent.[30] Justin occasionally accuses the Jews of deliberately altering the "true LXX" in their versions of the scriptures.[31]

The evidence suggests that Justin's "Jewish" texts were scroll manuscripts to which he had access through synagogues or other Jewish
sources, and which reflect an LXX or revised LXX text.[32] His strongly
non-LXX Christian proof-texts, then, would have derived from TCs
which Justin regarded as authentic scripture. Justin's occupation as
a Christian teacher places him in a pedagogical setting conducive to
the production and transmission of excerpted material (Bousset's
"tractates"), and his activity as an apologist makes the practical arguments for the Christian use of codex collections (less expense, ease
of transport and reference, the codex as a natural medium for note-
taking and reference material) especially applicable to him.

(c) *Original Form and Setting of Justin's* Testimonia *Sources*

The proof-texts in Justin's TCs were apparently accompanied by
interpretation and arguments.[33] In at least one case (*1 Apology* 60),
Justin's source seems to have included Platonic as well as OT citations.[34] The overwhelming emphasis, of course, is on scriptural proofs:
the quotations show knowledge of Hebrew,[35] and are sometimes built
up around catch-words.[36]

Skarsaune identifies two main blocks of *testimonia* material: a
"kerygma" source and a "recapitulation" source.[37] The kerygma source
combined anti-cultic material with messianic proof-texts grouped into

---

[30] *Dial.* 120.4; 131.1; 137. The "seventy" refers of course to the famous legend
of the seventy scribes who first produced the LXX translation.

[31] *Dial.* 43.5. Perhaps the most famous case is *Dial.* 72.1 where he lists several
passages which he claims the Jews have intentionally omitted in their copies of
scripture.

[32] Christian scriptural manuscripts were only beginning to be produced in Justin's
time (sect. 3.2 above).

[33] Skarsaune, *Prophecy*, 91.

[34] Ibid., 53. Skarsaune argues that the harmonized nature of both OT and Platonic
quotations here show that they were not composed by Justin.

[35] E.g., *1 Apol.* 50.2 (see Skarsaune, *Prophecy*, 63); *Dial.* 85.1 (ibid., 84).

[36] E.g., *Dialogue* 121 and *1 Apology* 32 are collections based on the catch word
ἀνατέλλω (Skarsaune, *Prophecy*, 84).

[37] Ibid., 226–27, for a summary description of these sources.

a "creedal" sequence (*1 Apology* 31–35, 48, 50–53). This source is based on a two advent pattern: Jesus fulfills both the prophecies of suffering in his first advent (earthly ministry) and the prophecies of glory in his second advent. The *testimonia* in the messianic proof-texts feature a common structure:

(1) the scriptural citation is introduced by τὸ δέ ("and the")
(2) a short exegesis of the scripture passage, introduced by words such as σημαίνει (it signifies), follows;
(3) a short historical narrative shows the fulfillment of the prophecy.[38]

These *testimonia* are then presented according to the following "creedal" scheme:

(1) the coming of the Messiah
(2) the virgin birth of the Messiah
(3) the hidden growing up of the Messiah
(4) the healings of the Messiah
(5) the passion of the Messiah
(6) the ascension and glorious return of the Messiah; universal resurrection
(7) the belief of the gentiles rather than of the Jews.[39]

While it is possible that this kerygma source was a single written work, Skarsaune inclines more to Bousset's model: "a connected series of tracts circulating within a 'school' tradition." Especially indicative of a school setting are (1) Justin's great familiarity with the exegetical traditions of the *testimonia* (even when he is working with LXX texts) and (2) the sheer complexity of Justin's material, which makes any suggestion of his dependence on a single source (or even two sources) unlikely.[40]

Skarsaune's proposed "recapitulation" source (found in *Dialogue* 48–108) features a debate in which Justin argues that certain messianic

---

[38] Ibid., 140.
[39] Ibid., 139. A related phenomenon are the several "semi-formal creeds" which lack *testimonia*. J.N.D. Kelly (*Early Christian Creeds* [3d ed.; New York: Longman, 1972] 70–76) identifies trinitarian sequences associated with baptismal confessions and confessions with expanded christological sequences (e.g., *1 Apol.* 21.1; 31.7; 42.4; 46.5; *Dial.* 63.1; 85.2; 126.1). One of these latter—*1 Apol.* 31.7—is understood by Skarsaune as an "anticipatory summary" of the kerygma source *testimonia* collection (*Prophecy*, 139).
[40] Ibid., 228; 234.

texts apply to Jesus rather than (as his Jewish opponent claims) to Solomon or Hezekiah. We see here the two-stage pattern identified by William Kurz in Luke/Acts: in many cases Trypho agrees with Justin that a certain passage has messianic significance; the real argument is over to whom these passages should apply.[41]

3.4.2   Epistle of Barnabas: *Anti-Jewish School* Testimonia

The *Epistle of Barnabas* is a strongly anti-Jewish document written, possibly in Alexandria, between 70 and 130. Originally anonymous, the work was attributed to the apostle Barnabas by later manuscripts and by Clement of Alexandria.[42]

The heart of *Barnabas*, chapters 2–16, consists of various moral, christological, and polemical teachings, accompanied by often extensive series of quotations from the Jewish scriptures. The author makes it clear that he is passing on traditional teachings: he wishes "to communicate (μεταδοῦναι) somewhat of that which I received" (ἀφ'οῦ ἔλαβον).[43] Though the author denies that he is a teacher (διδάσκολος; 1.8; 4.9a), *Barnabas* is best understood as a product of a Christian "school" whose teachings were based on interpretations of scripture.[44]

---

[41] For Trypho's admission that scripture predicts these things about the messiah, see *Dial.* 36.1; 39.7; 89.1; 110.1. Justin refutes suggestions that the quoted prophecies apply to Solomon (*Dialogue* 34; 36) or to Hezekiah (*Dialogue* 33; 68; 71; 77; 83; 85). See Kurz, "Christological Proof," 159; 162–67; see below, sect. 4.4.4 for details.

[42] Greek text in Pierre Prigent and Robert A. Kraft, eds., *Epître de Barnabé* (SC 172; Paris: Cerf, 1971); ET based on Kirsopp Lake, ed., *The Apostolic Fathers* (LCL; 2 vols.; London: Heinemann; New York: Macmillan, 1912) 1. 340–409. See Carleton Paget, *Barnabas*, 3–42, for the most recent discussion of these issues, esp. p. 30 n. 143 for a list of Clement's reference to, and quotations of, *Barnabas*.

[43] *Barn.* 1:5. With Klaus Wengst and others, I understand μεταδίδωμι and λαμβάνω as technical terms for the receiving and passing on of a tradition (*Tradition und Theologie des Barnabasbriefes* [Arbeiten zur Kirchengeschichte 42; Berlin/New York: de Gruyter, 1971] 10). On the use of παραλαμβάνω as a technical term for the passing of knowledge from teacher to student in Plato and Aristotle, esoteric knowledge in the mystery religions, and tradition in the NT (e.g., 1 Cor 11:23; 15:3) see Gerhard Delling, "παραλαμβάνω," *TDNT* 4. 11–14; also Friedrich Büchsel, "παραδίδωμι," *TDNT* 2. 169–73.

[44] See 18:1: Μεταβῶμεν δὲ καὶ ἐπὶ ἑτέραν γνῶσιν καὶ διδαχήν. I understand the "school" as a scribal setting in which relatively sophisticated scriptural interpretations are produced and taught. See Bousset (*Schulbetrieb*, 312); Köster (*Überlieferung*, 152); and Kraft ("Isaiah," 350) for a similar understanding of this life-setting. The "school" which produced the epistle was familiar with a variety of interpretive techniques (including allegorical interpretations and text conflations) and used them to produce anti-cultic TCs and typological reflections. In addition, *Barn.* 10.1–8 contains information (albeit inaccurate) on habits of various animals (synthesized with allegorical interpretations of the Mosaic food laws), which further demonstrates the author's access to school traditions (see the parallels in Philo and Ps.-Aristeas in

In addition to his various scriptural teachings, the author also passes on the "Two Ways" tradition (chaps. 18–20).[45]

(a) *Function of the* Testimonia

Barnabas does not call his proof-texts μαρτύρια; indeed, he applies none of the classical rhetorical language of proof to them. Nevertheless, proof-texts are occasionally employed as forensic argument: Ps 22 (21):40, Ps 119 (118):20, and Isa 50:6–7 "prove" that it was necessary (ἔδει) for Jesus to suffer on a tree (5:13–14); Ps 110 (109):1 and Isa 45:1 witness to Jesus' status as son of God, not son of David (12:10–11); and adapted scriptural narratives (Genesis 21–25 and Exodus 31–32) show that the covenant belongs to Christians and not Jews (chaps. 13–14).[46]

The primary function of the *testimonia* for *Barnabas*, however, is deliberative and didactic. For the Christian audience, the proof-texts function as moral exhortation[47] and more generally as simple instruction.[48] There is no real attempt to communicate with, much less persuade, Jews. The anti-Jewish polemic is actually addressed to Christians as a negative example: Do not be like the Jews! (3.6; 4.14). The teaching and TCs of *Barnabas* are clearly not intended for a Jewish audience.

(b) *Evidence of Written* Testimonia *Sources*

Barnabas has approximately ninety-eight scriptural quotations.[49] Eight follow the LXX exactly; twenty others deviate only slightly.[50] One

---

Robert A. Kraft, "The Epistle of Barnabas: Its Quotations and their Sources" [Ph.D. diss., Harvard University, 1961] 197–98). Finally, *Barnabas* itself presents material in a didactic style, involving the heavy use of imperatives and questions (see Wengst, *Tradition*, 55).

[45] For the scholarly consensus that *Barnabas* here makes use of a source which is also witnessed in *Did.* 1:1–6:1, see Carleton Paget, *Barnabas*, 80–82.

[46] See Kurz on this covenant argument in Luke-Acts ("Christological Proof," 107, 113).

[47] See esp. 2:10 and 3:6–4:2, which draw out the moral implications of anti-Jewish TCs. Chap. 4 is also noteworthy in its juxtaposition of moral exhortation and biblical quotation.

[48] E.g., the midrashic teachings on the allegorical meaning of the promised land (6:8–19); the scapegoat ritual (chap. 7); the sacrifice of the red heifer (chap. 8); food laws (chap. 10); and scriptural types of baptism and the cross (11:1–12:5).

[49] Carleton Paget, *Barnabas*, 86. *Barnabas*'s knowledge of NT writings (esp. of Matthew) remains an open question: Köster argues for independence (*Überlieferung*, 156–58); Massaux for dependence (*Influence*, 59–82); Köhler more cautiously for probable dependence in *Barn.* 4:14 (*Rezeption*, 111–23).

[50] Kraft, "Barnabas," 54–55.

quarter of its quotations are from Isaiah; the close conformity of these quotations with the LXX indicates that *Barnabas* may have had direct access to an Isaiah scroll.[51] Quotations of and allusions to the historical books of scripture, in contrast, are completely lacking.[52] Numerous conflated and LXX-deviant texts are found in *Barnabas* 2–16. The author rarely indicates the specific provenance of his quotations; he prefers such general citation formulas as λέγει ἡ γράφη, λέγει κύριος, or γέγραπται.[53] The LXX-deviant and conflated readings, the use of only certain parts of the Jewish scriptures, and the vague citation formulas all indicate that *Barnabas* does not have direct access to the entire LXX itself.

As an example of the TCs in *Barnabas*, I present below a selection from its *testimonia* on the passion (chap. 5).[54]

Barnabas 5	Function	Parallels/Sources
5:2: Isa 53:5, 7	The Lord suffered for our sanctification and remission of sins	Melito *Hom.* 64; *Acts of Philip* 78[55]
5:12: Zech 13:7	The Jews killed Christ, and in turn were destroyed	Mark 14:27/Matt 26:31; Justin *Dial.* 53.6; Irenaeus *Proof* 76[56]
5:13: Ps 22:21/Ps 119:120/Ps 22: 17/Ps 85:14[57]	It was necessary (ἔδει) that Christ should suffer on a tree	Irenaeus *Proof* 79[58]
5:14: Isa 50:6,7	Same as above	*Odes Sol.* 31.11 (A)
6:1: Isa 50:8–9	Obscure	Irenaeus *Proof* 88; *A.H.* 4.33.13[59]

[51] Kraft, "Isaiah," 337; 350.

[52] Kraft, "Barnabas," 66.

[53] See the detailed references in Carleton Paget, *Barnabas*, 87–88.

[54] See also sect. 3.10 below for evidence of an anti-cultic *testimonia* source in *Barn.* 2.4–3.6.

[55] Both Melito and *Acts of Philip* cite this passage as part of larger TCs; see Kraft, "*Paschal Homily*," 372–73. Kraft argues that the precise verbal parallels indicate a common written source:

Barn./Melito/Acts of Philip	*Isa 53:7b LXX*
ὡς πρόβατον ἐπὶ σφαγὴν ἤχθη	same
καὶ ὡς ἀμνὸς ἄφωνος	καὶ ὡς ἀμνὸς
ἐναντίον τοῦ κείραντος αὐτόν	ἐναντίον τοῦ κείραντος αὐτὸν ἄφωνος

3.4.3 Dialogue of Jason and Papiscus: *A* Testimonia *Source for* Justin, Irenaeus, and the Latin Testimonia *Tradition?*

The philosopher Celsus ridicules this no longer extant work as deserving "pity and hatred."[60] Origen summarizes the book thus: "a Christian is described as disputing with a Jew from the Jewish scriptures and as showing that the prophecies about the Messiah fit Jesus."[61] It has been attributed to Ariston of Pella, and was composed before 178.[62] The work was translated into Latin by the end of the third century, and seems to have been quite influential in the Latin African *testimonia* tradition.[63]

From various fragmentary statements, we know the following of the dialogue's content:

(1) It interprets "In the beginning" (Gen 1:1) as "in the son."[64] Irenaeus *Proof* 43 may preserve this reading in the context of a TC

---

[56] An LXX-deviant form of Zech 13:7 occurs in the canonical Gospels; Stendahl considered it "a testimony which had an independent existence" already in NT times (*School*, 80–83). Justin paraphrases Matthew (Skarsaune, *Prophecy*, 121); Irenaeus follows Justin (see Joseph P. Smith, *Proof of the Apostolic Preaching* [ACW 16; Westminster, MD: Newman; London: Longmans, Green, 1952] 206 n. 307). *Barnabas*'s text differs radically from these parallels in form and function.

[57] See Prigent for an analysis of this conflation (*Testimonia*, 166). The verse is attributed only to "the prophet." Hatch cited this as an example of a possible composite psalm ("Composite Quotations," 208).

[58] With a slight emendation, the Armenian text of the *Proof* is nearly an exact parallel to *Barnabas*. Léon-Marie Froidevaux concludes from this that Irenaeus depends on *Barnabas* ("Sur trois textes cités par Saint Irénée [*Adv. Haer.* IV,29,3 et 55:4; *Démonstration* 79 et 88]," *RSR* 44 [1956] 408–21). While this position is certainly plausible, Irenaeus's different context, together with our uncertainty that he knew *Barnabas*, points towards use of a common source (so Prigent and Kraft, *Epître*, 113–14).

[59] The text deviates strongly from the LXX. Irenaeus *Proof* 88 and *A.H.* 4.33.13 parallel *Barnabas*'s quotation, including the non-LXX addition of the phrase "servant of the Lord." Irenaeus is almost certainly independent of *Barnabas*, however, as his two quotations occur within a series of resurrection/glorification proof-texts, none of which occurs in *Barnabas*. See Kraft ("Isaiah," 346), *pace* Froidevaux ("Trois textes," 414–17).

[60] Greek fragments in PG 5. 1277–86; ET in ANF 8. 749–50. For further information and bibliography, see Williams, *Judaeos*, 28–30.

[61] *Against Celsus* 4.52. I quote from Henry Chadwick, ed., *Origen: Contra Celsum* (Cambridge: Cambridge University Press, 1953).

[62] Attribution by Maximus Confessor (7th cent.) (PG 4. 421). Celsus's *True Account*, which refers to the work, was composed ca. 178 (see Williams, *Judaeos*, 29).

[63] See Pierre Monat, *Lactance et la Bible: Une propédeutique latine à la lecture de la Bible dans l'Occident constantinien* (2 vols.; Paris: Etudes Augustiniennes, 1982) 1. 272–73, esp. n. 25. A cover letter, *To Bishop Vigilius concerning Jewish Unbelief*, accompanying a translation of *Jason* by a certain Celsus to a Bishop Vigilius (late 3d cent.?), is included in an appendix to Cyprian's works (CSEL 3. 119–32); see summary in Williams, *Judaeos*, 64–65; Chadwick, *Contra Celsum*, 227 n. 1.

[64] Jerome, *Quest. Heb. on Gen. 1.1* (PL 23. 985–87).

on the pre-existence of the son: the transliterated Hebrew of Gen
1:1 is translated, "A son was in the beginning; then God created
the heavens and the earth."[65]

(2) *Jason* refers to seven heavens.[66] Again we have a parallel in
Irenaeus *Proof* 9: "But the earth is encompassed by seven heavens
in which dwell Powers and Angels and Archangels." The text goes
on to identify the seven heavens with the seven "charismata" of
Isa 11:2.

(3) *Jason* quotes Deut 21:23 in the form: "Cursed before God is
the one who hangs" (λοιδορία θεοῦ ὁ κρεμάμενος).[67]

Finding connections between all three of these fragments and material in Justin's "recapitulation" source, Skarsaune ventures the claim
that this source and *Jason* are in fact identical.[68] Pierre Nautin[69] and
Pierre Monat[70] similarly argue that *Jason* is a source not only for
Justin and Irenaeus's *Proof*, but also for the *testimonia* material in the
Latin writers Lactantius and Evagrius. Given the extremely fragmentary nature of *Jason*, these claims must remain somewhat speculative. Nevertheless, the evidence does show a widespread circulation
of *testimonia* texts and exegetical traditions found in the dialogue.

3.4.4   *Melito of Sardis* Paschal Homily *and* Selections: *Passion* Testimonia *and the First Explicit Reference to a* Testimonia *Collection*

Melito, bishop of Sardis in the latter half of the second century,
wrote his *Selections* (ἔκλογαι) in response to a request by a certain
Onesimus for biblical extracts "from both the law and the prophets

---

[65] This is my translation of the French in Adelin Rousseau, ed., *Démonstration de la Prédication Apostolique* (SC 406; Paris: Cerf, 1995) 145–47.

[66] Maximus Confessor (PG 4. 422).

[67] Jerome *Comm. on Gal 3:13* (PL 26. 387).

[68] Skarsaune, *Prophecy*, 242. Skarsaune's case is built on (1) parallels between allusions in Justin and a TC in Irenaeus *Proof* 43, which includes the Christianized
quotation of Gen 1:1 (pp. 235–36); (2) parallels between *Jason* and Justin's use of
Isa 11:2 and the doctrine of the angels and powers (237–38); and (3) parallels
between *Jason*'s reading of Deut 21:23 and Justin's "recapitulation" source, particularly the material concerned with interpretation of the story of the bronze serpent
(*Dial.* 91/94; p. 238). Skarsaune also refers to evidence elsewhere in his proposed
recapitulation source indicating that it was originally written in dialogue form (pp.
240–42).

[69] Nautin, "C.r. de la conférence annuelle," in *Annuaire de l'EPHE*, Vᵉ sect., Sc.
Rel. 1967/68 (Paris) 162–67.

[70] Monat, *Lactance* 1. 273.

concerning the Saviour and our faith," and for information on the number and arrangement of the scriptural books.[71] Melito relates that he traveled "back to the east and reaching the place where it was proclaimed and done [i.e., Palestine] I got precise information about the books of the Old Covenant." Melito lists these books and concludes, "From these I have also made the extracts, dividing them into six books."

Two observations can be made on this invaluable passage: (1) Christians in Sardis were explicitly interested in TCs as opposed to entire scrolls, and (2) even a bishop in a major Asian city lacked ready access to a complete collection of scriptural manuscripts.[72] Melito's *Selections* is our earliest explicit witness for the composition of a scriptural TC.

In his *Paschal Homily*, written between 160 and 170, Melito works out an elaborate typology depicting Christ as the fulfillment of the passover lamb.[73] Melito employs scriptural TCs to serve as proofs that Christ's suffering was divinely ordained. In contrast to other writers who attribute Christ's passion to God's will recorded in scripture,[74] Melito proclaims that *Christ* preordained his own sufferings in the patriarchs, prophets, and the whole people (*Homily* 57, lines 398–400). A noteworthy TC is Melito's list of select scriptural figures who serve as types of Christ's passion: Christ is like Abel slain, like Isaac bound, like Joseph sold, like Moses exposed, like David persecuted (*Homily* 59, 69).[75] The list has a family resemblance to the genre of the scriptural lists of moral *exempla* discussed above (2.6.3).

Following is a sample from the *Homily*. All texts, except Ps 2:1–2, are non-LXX.

---

[71] Apud Eusebius *H.E.* 4.26.12–14; Greek text and ET in Stuart George Hall, ed., *Melito of Sardis: On Pascha and Fragments* (Oxford Early Christian Texts; Oxford: Clarendon, 1979), 64–67 (frag. 3).

[72] Arthur Darby Nock dismisses Melito's visit as merely "proem style," since "it was hardly necessary to go to Palestine to get the facts" ("The Apocryphal Gospels," *JTS* n.s. 11 [1960] 63–64 n. 4). Nock's view is rightly challenged by Hall, who argues that Nock underestimates difficulties that Christians would have with obtaining scriptures from local Jews (Hall, *Melito*, 66–67 n. 10).

[73] Greek text and ET in Hall, ed., *Pascha*; p. xxii for the date.

[74] E.g., Justin *Dialogue* 41; Irenaeus *Proof* 75; *Barn.* 5:13; Tertullian *A.J.* 10.4.

[75] For a similar sequence of OT types, see Ps.-Cyprian (sect. 3.5.3 below) and Tertullian *Against the Jews* 10 (sect. 3.5.4 below).

Melito *Homily*	Function	Parallels/Sources
61: Deut 28:66	The mystery of the Lord's death is announced by the voice of the prophets	Irenaeus *Proof* 79[76]
62: Ps 2:1–2	same	*Proof* 74[77]
63: Jer 11:19	same	Justin *Dial.* 72.2[78]
64: Isa 53:7–8	same	Acts 8:32; *Barn.* 5.2[79]

3.4.5 *Irenaeus* Against Heresies

The composition of the five books of *Against Heresies* cannot be dated with precision; they were likely written over a period of many years in the last quarter of the second century.[80] The work seeks to refute the beliefs of Irenaeus's gnostic opponents (especially the Valentinians) by (1) carefully analyzing their errors, and (2) presenting a positive account of the orthodox faith.[81] Books Three and Four make particular use of both Jewish and NT scriptural proofs for orthodox positions; the NT passages predominate. The preface to Book Three has an explicit statement of Irenaeus's purpose:

> But in this, the third book, I shall adduce proofs (*ostensiones*) from the Scriptures, so that . . . you may receive from me the means of combating and vanquishing those who, in whatever manner, are propagating falsehood.

---

[76] See Daniélou, "La vie suspendue au bois (Deut, 28, 66)," in idem, *Etudes*, 53–75, for the widespread use of this *testimonium*.

[77] See Crossan's study of the application of Ps 2:1–2 to the roles of Herod and Pilate in Christ's passion in Acts, Justin, Irenaeus, Melito, Tertullian, and the *Teaching of the Apostles* (*Cross*, 61–75).

[78] Also found in Tertullian *A.J.* 10.12; *Marc.* 3.19.3; 4.40.3; Cyprian *Quir.* 2.20; and Origen *Homily on Jeremiah* 10.2.

[79] For further quotations, among them Justin *Dial.* 72.3; Irenaeus *Proof* 69; Cyprian *Quir.* 2.15; see Othmar Perler, ed., *Méliton de Sardes: Sur la Pâque et Fragments* (SC 123; Paris: Cerf, 1966) 169; also Kraft, "Melito."

[80] For bibliographical information on the critical text in the *Sources Chrétiennes* series, see Dominic J. Unger and John J. Dillon, eds., *St. Irenaeus of Lyons: Against the Heresies*, vol. 1 (ACW 55; New York/Mahwah, NJ: Paulist, 1992) 17; ET in ANF 1. 315–567. *Against Heresies* is preserved in its entirety only in a Latin translation, which fortunately (as shown by comparison with Greek fragments) follows the Greek closely.

[81] Unger and Dillon, *Heresies*, 3–9.

Against Heresies makes occasional use of TCs from the Jewish scriptures that have a number of parallels with other Christian authors. To bolster his argument that the cultic law was a temporary measure that is now abrogated, Irenaeus presents an anti-cultic TC (4.17.1–4) showing extensive parallels with *Barnabas*, Clement of Alexandria, Cyprian, and Tertullian (see sect. 3.9 below). Robert A. Kraft refers to two other passages where LXX-deviant parallels with *Barnabas* suggest common use of a TC.[82] B. Hemmerdinger, arguing from the criterion of false attribution, also holds that Irenaeus used "florilèges scripturaires."[83] Alfred Byron Starratt has provided the most systematic attempt to show that Irenaeus made use of TCs in *Against Heresies*.[84]

Prigent discusses three scriptural sequences (in *A.H.* 3.19.2; 4.33.1; and 4.33.11–12) which follow essentially the same creedal pattern that Skarsaune has identified in Justin's "kerygma" source.[85] The proof-texts witness to Christ's virgin birth, his passion, resurrection and glorification, all according to a two advents schema (one in suffering, one in glory). Prigent argues that Irenaeus drew from a large stock of traditional *testimonia* to compose three different creedal *testimonia* sequences.

In addition to this creedal *testimonia* form, Irenaeus also presents shorter creedal statements, trinitarian in form, which lack scriptural proofs. Perhaps the most well known example is *A.H.* 1.10.1: the church has received the faith in a single God, in a single Jesus Christ, and in a Holy Spirit who has revealed through the prophets Christ's economies and comings, virgin birth, passion, resurrection, ascension, and his coming in glory to recapitulate all things and resurrect

---

[82] On *A.H.* 4.21.2/*Barn.* 13.2, see Kraft, "Oracle of Rebecca," 318–20; on *A.H.* 4.33.13/*Proof* 88/*Barn.* 6.1 see Kraft, "Isaiah," 346. For the less likely view that Irenaeus depends on *Barnabas*, see Froidevaux, "Trois textes," 408–21.

[83] "Remarques sur l'ecdotique de Saint Irénée," in F.L. Cross, ed., *Studia Patristica*, vol. 3 (TU 78; Berlin: Akadamie, 1961) 70.

[84] Starratt, "The Use of the Septuagint in the Five Books against Heresies by Irenaeus of Lyons," (Ph.D. diss., Harvard University, 1952), esp. 101–7, 114–49. Starratt also argues for the use of TCs by Irenaeus's gnostic opponents (pp. 121–25) and shows the close connection between certain NT *testimonia* and those in Irenaeus (pp. 150–77).

[85] Prigent, *Testimonia*, 183–88. Prigent calls them "prophetic lists." The *testimonia* sequence in Irenaeus's own *Proof of the Apostolic Preaching* is related to these lists; see sect. 3.4.6 below.

all flesh.[86] Irenaeus here places his christological sequence not, as might be expected, with Jesus Christ, but rather with the Holy Spirit, since these events were foretold by the Holy Spirit in the scriptures. The immense importance of the scriptural witness is apparent.[87]

3.4.6 *Irenaeus* Proof of the Apostolic Preaching

(a) *Function of the* Testimonia
The *Proof of the Apostolic Preaching*, extant only in an Armenian translation, was written ca. 200, after the completion of at least some of the books of *Against Heresies*.[88] Eusebius (*H.E.* 5.26) refers to it as (λόγος) εἰς τὴν ἐπίδειξιν τοῦ ἀποστολικοῦ κηρύγματος. The *Proof* is a presentation of the basic beliefs of the Christian faith together with scriptural proofs designed to support that faith (*Proof* 1). Irenaeus has several explicit remarks on the function of scriptural proofs: the prophets of the Jewish scriptures predicted events in the life of Christ and the church so that when they occurred believers might recognize the divine plan (chap. 42B); the prophecies show that Christian belief is well grounded and that the preaching tradition is true (chap. 86); more specifically, they show that it was God's will for Jesus to suffer (chap. 75). The word ἐπίδειξις can have the sense of both proving and showing/demonstrating; perhaps Irenaeus has both senses in mind.

(b) *Evidence of Written* Testimonia *Sources*
The case for Irenaeus's use of written TCs in the *Proof* is argued most forcefully by Joseph P. Smith.[89] Smith employs the standard TC detection criteria: LXX-deviant readings; composite quotations;[90] false

---

[86] See Prigent, *Testimonia*, 189–90.

[87] See Kelly, *Christian Creeds*, 76–81, for a summary of creedal passages in Irenaeus. Paralleling his conclusions from his study of Justin, Kelly finds both trinitarian (connected with baptismal confessions) and "elaborated christological" sequences in Irenaeus.

[88] Armenian text in Karapet Ter Mekerttschian and S.G. Wilson, eds., *The Proof of the Apostolic Preaching with Seven Fragments*, (PO 12/5; Paris: Firmin-Didot, 1919); Latin trans. of Armenian text in Rousseau, *Démonstration*; ET in Smith, *Proof of the Apostolic Preaching*. Irenaeus explicitly mentions *Against Heresies* in *Proof* 99.

[89] Smith, *Proof*, esp. 31–34.

[90] Ibid., 33 n. 92. Chap. 24 (conflation of Genesis texts on Abraham); chap. 29 (Deut 32:49 with influence of Deut 32:52); chap. 43 (conflation of Ps 110 [109]:3 and Ps 72 [71]:17; cf. Justin *Dial.* 76); chap. 79 (conflation of Ps 22 [21]:21 and 119 [118]:120; cf. *Barn.* 5.13); chap. 88 (Isa 50:8–9 and 2:17, LXX-deviant).

attributions;[91] and the same passage quoted in two distinct versions.[92]

The issue of *testimonia* use in the *Proof*, however, is complicated by Irenaeus's probable use of Justin's *testimonia* in some cases.[93] Irenaeus follows Justin's *testimonia* sequences[94] and repeats his exegetical comments.[95] On the other hand, substantial portions (e.g., chaps. 80–83) are independent of Justin and show links with other *testimonia* traditions.[96] Finally, even when Justin's and Irenaeus's *testimonia* overlap, Skarsaune has shown that in at least a few cases Irenaeus depends not on Justin directly but on Justin's source.

This last point is worth examining in detail. I noted above that Justin's exegetical comments often presuppose an LXX-deviant *testimonium* text even when he reads an LXX text. In a few cases, Justin's comments presuppose a text which in fact is preserved only in Irenaeus. In *Dial.* 103.4, for example, Justin quotes Hos 10:6 as a *testimonium* of Pilate sending Jesus bound to Herod:

> Pilate favored him by sending Jesus bound to him (ᾧ καὶ Πιλᾶτος χαριζόμενος δεδεμένον τὸν Ἰησοῦν ἔπεμψε) which God in his foreknowledge foretold in these words, "And they brought him to the Assyrian, a present to the king" (καὶ αὐτὸν εἰς Ἀσσυρίου ἀπήνεγκαν ξένια τῷ βασιλεῖ).[97]

The discrepancy between Justin's narrative and the proof-text is striking: the narrative does not mention "to the Assyrian," and the scriptural text mentions nothing about binding. The fit would be better if Justin read the LXX (καὶ αὐτόν εἰς Ἀσσυρίους δήσαντες ἀπήνεγκαν ξένια τῷ βασιλεῖ) which does mention binding. A perfect match would be achieved by adding the LXX δήσαντες and omitting the reference to Assyria. And in fact this is exactly the text found in

---

[91] Smith, *Proof*, 33 n. 93. Chap. 43 ("Jeremiah" for a composite quotations from Psalms); chap. 65 ("Isaiah" for Zech 9:9; cf. Justin *1 Apol.* 35.11, where the attribution is to Zephaniah); chap. 72 ("Jeremiah" for Isa 57:1–4; cf. Justin *1 Apol.* 48.4); chap. 97 ("Jeremiah" for Bar 3:19–4:1).

[92] Smith, *Proof*, 34 n. 95. Isa 9:6 (9:5) in chaps. 54 and 56.

[93] Irenaeus certainly know of Justin; he refers to the apologist as the author of a treatise against Marcion (*A.H.* 4.6.2).

[94] See Skarsaune, *Prophecy*, 452–53 for the close parallels between the quotation sequences in *1 Apology* 32–35 and *Proof* 53–65.

[95] *Proof* 68, 72.

[96] See the summary table below.

[97] This is an example of Justin's use of the καίγε text. See Barthélemy, *Aquila*, 208. Cyril of Jerusalem has the same *testimonium* in the same context, but reads the LXX (*Cat.* 13.14).

Proof 77: "and they brought him bound as a present to the king."[98]
The evidence suggests that both Justin and Irenaeus drew on the same
testimonia source which combined Hos 10:6 with a narrative of Jesus'
trial; Irenaeus preserves the most original form of this *testimonium*.

We must reckon with Irenaeus's use of a wealth of *testimonia* sources
in the *Proof*. He seems to have drawn on Justin; Justin's sources; possibly *Barnabas*; the NT (John in chap. 80; Matthew in chap. 81);
and some *testimonia* which he himself may have added (chap. 75).

(c) *Original Form and Life-Setting of the* Proof's Testimonia *Sources*
The first part of the work (chaps. 1–42b) summarizes basic Christian
beliefs, following a pattern of the history of redemption: creation,
fall, and the work of Christ; the second part offers scriptural (mostly
OT) witnesses for these beliefs. The material in this second part generally takes the form of a thesis supported by scriptural witnesses,
together with often extensive exegetical comments. The creedal form
of the sequence is at once apparent:

(1) The pre-existence and OT theophanies of Jesus the son of God
    (42b–51)
(2) The human birth and messianic titles of Jesus (52–65)
(3) Summary of *testimonia* to Christ in creedal form (66)
(4) Miracles, passion, and glorification of Jesus (67–85)
(5) Function of the apostolic preaching (86)
(6) The Jews and the Law are replaced by the new people of God
    (87–97)
(7) Conclusions (98–100)

The proofs function essentially as fulfillment of prophecy: all these
events (down to such details as Judas's thirty pieces of silver) were
foretold in the scriptures. The *Proof*, then, is likely a catechetical document designed to strengthen believers in their faith.[99]

Following I present a selection from the passion *testimonia* in Irenaeus
Proof 68–85:

---

[98] See Skarsaune, *Prophecy*, 437. See also his similar arguments for Irenaeus's
LXX-deviant readings of Ps 22 (21):15 (p. 437) and Isa 9:5 (p. 390).

[99] See the discussion in Smith, *Proof*, 19–21. Smith prefers the term "apologetic,"
but admits that it is intended not to persuade outsiders but rather to establish more
firmly the faith of believers.

Irenaeus *Proof*		Function	Parallels/Sources
68:	Isa 52:13–53:5 Ps 73:14 (?) Isa 50:6 Lam 3:30	Christ would be despised, tormented, and killed	Justin *1 Apol.* 50[100] *Barn.* 5.14 *1 Apol.* 51[101]
69–70:	Isa 53:5–8		
71:	Lam 4:20	The "spirit" Christ will suffer in the body	*1 Apol.* 55:4–5[102]
72:	Isa 57:1–2 Ps 21:5	The just one died for the sake of our salvation	*1 Apol.* 48.4; *Dial.* 16.5[103]
73:	Ps 3:5	Resurrection	*1 Apol.* 38.4; *Dial.* 97.1; *1 Clem* 26:2[104]
74:	Ps 2:1–2	Herod and Pilate	Acts 4:24–28; *1 Apol.* 40.6[105]
75:	Ps 89:39–46	The passion is by the Father's will	
76:	Zech 13:7	Arrest and trial of Christ	Matt 26:31 (par.); *Barn.* 5.12;
77:	Hosea 10:6[106]		*Dial.* 53.5–6; *Dial.* 103.4
78:	Unknown quotation attributed to Jeremiah	Christ's descent to hell	*Dial.* 72.4.[107]

[100] *Proof* 68 and *1 Apol.* 36.6 have the same exegetical comment: Isaiah speaks of the sufferings not of David but of Christ.

[101] Justin and Irenaeus share a common exegesis of Isa 53:8 as referring to the indescribable origin of Christ.

[102] Justin's citation is in the context of a chapter on symbols of the cross. Daniélou has shown the importance of Lam 4:20 as a christological *testimonium* in the 2d–4th centuries ("Nous vivrons a son ombre" [Lam., 4, 20.], in idem, *Etudes*, 76–95).

[103] Again Justin and Irenaeus share an exegesis: the passage applies both to the death of Christ *and* those who believe in him (*1 Apol.* 48.4); *Dial.* 110.6 applies Isa 57:1 to persecuted Christians.

[104] Justin quotes this as a passion *testimonium; 1 Clement* applies it to the resurrection of believers.

[105] See chart in sect. 3.4.4 above. In *1 Apology* 40, Justin quotes Psalms 1–2 *in extenso*; it is unlikely that Irenaeus depends on him here.

[106] See the discussion of this text above, sect. 3.4.6b.

[107] Irenaeus preserves four other quotations of this passage: *A.H.* 3.20.4; 4.22.1; 4.33.12; and 5.31.1. Here and in *A.H.* 4.22.1 it is attributed to Jeremiah, in *A.H.* 3.20.4 it is attributed to Isaiah (see Prigent, *Testimonia*, 186). No two of the texts are precisely the same, and Irenaeus's texts have two significant deviations from Justin. The evidence thus points to Irenaeus's independence from Justin; but see Skarsaune (*Prophecy*, 452) for a differing view.

(table cont.)

Irenaeus *Proof*	Function	Parallels/Sources
79: Isa 65:2 Ps 22:17 Ps 22:15b *Psalm conflation*: Ps 22:21 Ps 119:120 Ps 22:17 Ps 86:14 Deut 28:66	The crucifixion	1 *Apol.* 35; 38; and *Dial.* 97;[108] *Barn.* 5.13[109] Melito, *Hom.* 61[110]
80: Ps 22:18	Parting of the garments	John 19:24; *1 Apol.* 35; *Barn.* 6.6[111]
81: Jer/Zech 11, 　　attr. to Jeremiah	Thirty pieces of silver	Matt 27:9–10[112]
82: Ps 69:22	Gall and vinegar	*Barn* 7.3, 5; *Gos. Pet.* 5.16[113]
83: Ps 68:18–19	The ascension	Eph 4:8; *Dial.* 39.4; 87.6[114]
84: Ps 24:7–8, 10	Entry into heaven and future judgment	*1 Apol.* 51:7; *Dial.* 36.3–4; 85.4[115]
85: Ps 110:1 　　Ps 19:7		 *Dial.* 36.5[116]

---

[108] Skarsaune holds that Isa 65:2 and Ps 22 (21):17, 19 formed part of the passion/crucifixion section of Justin's kerygma source (*Prophecy*, 80, 158).

[109] On *Barn.* 5:13, see sect. 3.4.2c above.

[110] For the widespread patristic use of this *testimonium* in the context of Jesus' passion, see Daniélou, "La vie suspendue." Prigent and Daniélou have argued that a lacuna in *Dial.* 74 originally contained a discussion of Deut 28:66 (Prigent, *Justin*, 194, and Daniélou, "La vie suspendue," 59).

[111] See Crossan for a discussion on the theme of casting lots for Jesus' clothing in early Christian literature (*Cross*, 190–97). Irenaeus explains that the coat was woven without a seam, a detail missing from Justin but found in John.

[112] Irenaeus follows the Matthean account and fulfillment quotation in Matt 27:3–10, although his quotation deviates from Matthew's.

[113] In reporting that Jesus was given vinegar mixed with gall to drink, Irenaeus follows the sequence not of the canonical gospels but of *Barn.* 7:5; *Gospel of Peter*, and Tertullian *A.J.* 10:4. See Crossan (*Cross*, 208–18).

[114] Irenaeus's text and exegesis of this passage differ markedly from both the NT and Justin.

[115] Skarsaune has shown that although Irenaeus quotes the LXX text, his exegetical comments depend on Justin's non-LXX *testimonium* reading in *1 Apol.* 51 (*Prophecy*,

3.4.7   *Clement of Alexandria* Stromateis, Hypotyposeis, Prophetic Selections

(a) *Function of the* Testimonia

Clement (150–ca. 220) provides a particularly clear example of his understanding of the proof value of scripture in *Stromateis* 7.95.[117] He maintains that scripture, the "voice of God," is for the believer a first principle (ἀρχή); it stands in no need of proof:[118]

> If, however, it is not enough just simply to state one's opinion, but we are bound to prove (πιστώσασθαι) what is said, then we do not wait for the witness (μαρτυρία) of men but we prove the point in question by the voice of the Lord, which is more to be relied on than any demonstration (ἀπόδειξις), or rather which is the only real demonstration. . . . So too we, obtaining from the scriptures themselves a perfect demonstration concerning the scriptures, derive from faith a conviction which has the force of demonstration.

Clement here uses the term ἀπόδειξις, as compared to Irenaeus's ἐπίδειξις. Aristotle used ἀπόδειξις for a demonstrative proof,[119] but by hellenistic times its technical meaning had blurred, and we find it used with the same range of meaning as ἐπίδειξις.[120]

(b) *Evidence of Written* Testimonia *Sources*

The tracing of written TCs is difficult in Clement, for although he has an abundance of *testimonia* sequences in common with *1 Clement* and *Barnabas*, it is also clear that Clement knew and used these writings directly. Clement further has the disconcerting habit of copying sequences of scriptural quotations from NT or patristic authors without citing his intermediary source.[121] The test case presented in section 3.9 below, however, indicates that in certain cases Clement's

---

441–42). Skarsaune identifies this text as the *testimonium* for Christ's ascension in Justin's kerygma source (ibid., 139).

[116] For the immense popularity of this *testimonium*, see Hay, *Glory*.

[117] The *Stromateis* was written ca. 200. Greek text and ET for *Strom.* 7 in F.J.A. Hort and Joseph B. Mayor, eds., *Clement of Alexandria: Miscellanies Book VII* (London: Macmillan, 1902; repr. Greek and Roman Philosophy; New York/London: Garland, 1987).

[118] Cf. *Dial.* 7.2, discussed in sect. 3.4.1a.

[119] *Rhet.* 1.1.11.

[120] See BAG, *sub verbis*, and the references there.

[121] Thus he borrows from *1 Clement* in *Strom.* 4.32–33; 105–113; and 118–19; from *Barnabas* in *Strom.* 4.67 and 5.51–52; and from Paul (Romans 10–11) in *Strom.* 2.43.1–2.

parallels can be shown to be independent of other extant authors, suggesting that Clement and the other authors in question share an anonymous written *testimonia* source.[122]

Clement's voluminous writings include two works closely related to the form of TCs. The eight books of the *Hypotyposeis*, no longer extant, were a commentary on *select* passages of NT and other early Christian writings (e.g., *Barnabas, Apocalypse of Peter*).[123] His *Prophetic Selections* (ἐκλογαὶ προφητικαί) follows the same format of commentary on select OT and NT passages.[124]

3.4.8 *Preaching of Peter*

This work, preserved only in fragments, was likely written in Egypt in the first half of the second century.[125] The fragments preserve a polemic against the false worship by both Greeks and Jews. Christ's command to preach to the whole world is emphasized; proof from scripture is central for this apostolic preaching. Peter is made to say:

> But we opened the books of the prophets which we had, which partly in parables, partly in enigmas, partly with certainty and in clear words name Jesus Christ, and found his coming, his death, his crucifixion and all the rest of the tortures which the Jews inflicted on him, his resurrection and his assumption into heaven before the foundation of Jerusalem, how all was written that he had to suffer and what would be after him. Recognizing this, we believed God in consequence of what is written of (in reference to) him. (Frag. 6)

---

[122] See also André Mehat, "L'hypothèse des 'Testimonia' à l'épreuve des Stromates: Remarques sur les citations de l'Ancien Testament chez Clément d'Alexandrie," in André Benoît and Pierre Prigent, eds., *La Bible et les Pères: Colloque de Strasbourg, 1–3 octobre 1969* (Bibliothèque des Centres d'Etudes Supérieures Spécialisés; Paris: Universitaires de France, 1971) 229–42. Mehat proposes three sources for Clement's scriptural quotations: (1) those he collected himself; (2) those he cites from memory; and (3) those he has taken over from other authors or from written/oral TCs.

[123] Eusebius *H.E.* 6.14.1. Greek text of frags. in Otto Stählin, ed., *Clemens Alexandrinus* (GCS 17; Berlin: Akademie, 1960–80) 195–202 (PG 9. 743–50); ET in *ANF* 2. 571–80. See the comments of Johannes Quasten, *Patrology* (3 vols.; Westminster, MD: Newman; Utrecht/Antwerp: Spectrum, 1950–60) 2. 16–17.

[124] Greek text in Stählin, ed., *Clemens* 17. 135–55 (PG 9. 697–728). I am unaware of an ET.

[125] Greek text of frags. in Ernst von Dobschütz, *Das Kerygma Petri kritisch untersucht* (TU 11/1; Leipzig: Hinrichs, 1893); ET in Edgar Hennecke and Wilhelm Schneemelcher, eds., *New Testament Apocrypha*, vol. 2: *Writings Relating to the Apostles, Apocalypses and Related Subjects* (Cambridge: James Clarke; Louisville, KY: Westminster/John Knox, 1991). 37–40. I follow the fragment numbering in Hennecke and Schneemelcher. For the date, see Wilhelm Schneemelcher, "Introduction to the *Preaching of Peter*," in Hennecke and Schneemelcher, *NTApoc* 2. 34.

Here is the same creedal pattern visible in Justin's *testimonia* sources and in Irenaeus's *Proof.*

The *Preaching* shows connections with Justin's *testimonia* sources. After a polemic against Jewish ritual, the *Preaching* (Frag. 2a) cites an LXX-deviant reading of Jer 31 (38):31–32 which is parallel to Justin's reading in *Dial.* 67.9.[126] Skarsaune's investigations have shown a close correspondence between exegetical arguments in Justin and the sections of Clement of Alexandria which quote the *Preaching.*[127]

The *Preaching*, then, is a document associated with early Christian preaching and apologetic which may have presented an extensive TC arranged in creedal fashion. It may have been one of Justin's sources.

3.4.9   *Acts of Peter 24*

The Greek original of this work, preserved in a Latin translation, was likely composed in the decade of the 180s, possibly in Asia Minor.[128] In this chapter, Peter responds to Simon Magus's arguments that Jesus is merely a man, using *testimonia* to prove the supernatural birth of Jesus. The following table shows that many of the *testimonia* originally served other functions.

Acts of Peter 24	Function	Parallels/Sources
Isa 53:8 Isa 53:2	Supernatural Birth	Justin *Dial.* 76.2 Cf. use of Isaiah 53 in NT
Unknown Quotation	same	
Apocr. Ezek. Frag. 3	same	
Isa 7:13–14	same	Matt 1:23
Asc. Isaiah 11.13–14	same	

---

[126] See Skarsaune, *Prophecy*, 72–73.

[127] Ibid., 229–32. Skarsaune sees these texts as part of the "Law out of Zion" section of his proposed kerygma source.

[128] Latin text in Léon Vouaux, *Les Actes de Pierre: Introduction, Textes, Traduction et Commentaire* (Paris: Letouzey et Ané, 1922); ET in *NTApoc* 2. 285–317. For date and provenance, see Wilhelm Schneemelcher, "Introduction to The Acts of Peter," in Hennecke and Schneemelcher, *NTApoc* 2. 283.

(table cont.)

Acts of Peter 24	Function	Parallels/Sources
Unknown Quotation	same	
Dan 2:34	same	*Dial.* 76.1[129]
Ps 118 (117):22		Cf. use of these texts in
Dan 7:13		"stone" collections
		(sect. 5.6 below)

In addition to the numerous parallels in other TCs, the use of vague citation formulas ("another prophet says," "and again"), and the presence of unknown quotations cited as scripture further indicate that the *Acts* has taken over a previous collection here. The presence of stone and passion *testimonia* shows the flexibility of application.

3.4.10   *Dialogue of Timothy and Aquila*

Williams had dated this dialogue to ca. 200 CE, and speculated that it was probably written in Egypt.[130] The most recent editor, Robert Gerald Robertson, however, concludes that the work was composed in sixth-century Alexandria.[131] The introduction presents the Jewish and Christian disputants, who begin by agreeing upon a list of OT and NT books which may be used for the basis of the discussion.[132] The work treats familiar creedal topics: (1) the trinity and the incarnation (Prov 8:27–30; Gen 1:26; Mic 5:2; Isa 53:8; Bar 3:37–38; Isa 7:14); (2) the rejection of the Jews in favor of the gentiles (Jer 31:31–33; Hosea 1–2); (3) Christ's passion (including a "cross" collection: Gen 28:12; Exod 17:12; Deut 21:23), resurrection, and the

---

[129] Already Justin has Dan 7:13, 2:34 and Isa 53:8 as proof-texts for Christ's supernatural birth (*Dial.* 76.1–2). For further examples of these passages in Justin, see Skarsaune, *Prophecy*, 199–203.

[130] Greek text in Robert Gerald Robertson, "The Dialogue of Timothy and Aquila: A Critical Text, Introduction to the Manuscript Evidence, and an Inquiry into the Sources and Literary Relationships" (Ph.D. diss., Harvard University, 1989); on date and provenance, see Williams, *Judaeos*, 67, 71.

[131] See Robertson, "Timothy and Aquila," 345–83 for details. Robertson finds that the work shares considerable material with Epiphanius's *On Weights and Measures* and Cyril of Jerusalem's *Catechetical Lectures*.

[132] Timothy attacks Aquila's recent translation for omission of passages and mistranslation (fols. 117–19). Folio numbers refer to Conybeare's edition (see following note).

future judgment by Christ. Forensic arguments used in Luke-Acts and Justin recur here: Psalm 2 applies to Jesus, not Solomon (fol. 83); Judah's blessing (Gen 49:10) applies to Jesus, not Judah (fol. 113); God's covenant is no longer with the Jews, but with the gentiles (fol. 113). While Robertson may be correct to assign a late date to the work, the dialogue doubtless preserves much earlier material.

3.4.11 *Dialogue of* Athanasius *and* Zacchaeus

Williams dates the extant form of this work to ca. 325 CE, but Conybeare holds that earlier forms were known already in the third century.[133] The following topics are covered in the debate between a Jew and Christian: (1) the pre-existence of Christ; (2) his incarnation, cross and death; (3) Jesus' anointment by the spirit as Christ; (4) rejection of the Jews and election of the gentiles; (5) details of Christ's life; and (6) sacrifices. The *testimonia* are accompanied by extensive exegetical discussion; reflections on Christ as God's wisdom are prominent.[134]

Similarity between quotations in *Athanasius* (sects. 1–21) and those in *Timothy and Aquila* (esp. fols. 76–81) implies either selective borrowing by the author of *Athanasius* or the common use of a *testimonia* source.[135] Conybeare further argues for a connection of *Athanasius* with the *Dialogue of Jason and Papiscus*.[136] Although the theories of direct dependence vary, the undeniable relationships between *Jason*, *Trypho*, *Timothy*, and *Athanasius* in texts used, common sequences, and common exegesis point towards a complex pattern of possible literary dependence and the use of common *testimonia* texts and interpretive traditions. These texts witness to the importance of the dialogue form in transmitting *testimonia* traditions.

---

[133] Greek text in F.C. Conybeare, ed., *The Dialogues of Athanasius and Zacchaeus and of Timothy and Aquila* (Anecdota Oxoniensia; Classical Series Pt. 8; Oxford: Clarendon, 1898); I am unaware of an ET. See the summary in Williams, *Judaeos*, 117–23. On the date, see Williams, *Judaeos*, 117; Conybeare, *Dialogues*, xxxiv.

[134] See Williams, *Judaeos*, 117–19.

[135] Williams raises the *testimonia* hypothesis as a possible explanation (*Judaeos*, 117 n. 2); he also provides a detailed comparison of the texts (pp. 122–23). Robertson's denies any direct literary relationship between the texts and also rejects Conybeare's early date for *Athanasius*, although he does not suggest an alternative ("Timothy and Aquila," 349–50).

[136] See Williams, *Judaeos*, 117 n. 2.

3.4.12   Apocryphon of Ezekiel

This work survives only in quotations found in a variety of patristic sources.[137] Fragment Two, an admonition to repentance, is quoted as scripture by Clement of Rome, Clement of Alexandria, and in the Coptic *Exegesis on the Soul*.[138] Quotations in Clement of Rome and in the *Exegesis* are given in the context of larger TCs on repentance. As direct dependence of these authors on one another is doubtful, Mueller concludes that quotations most likely derive from the *Apocryphon* itself here.[139] Yet given the presence of these quotations in TCs, together with their imprecise citation formulas (all vaguely attributed to God), I judge it far more likely that the authors are drawing from an authoritative TC on repentance.

Fragment Three is preserved in a "short form" (e.g., "she has given birth and has not given birth," *Acts Pet.* 24) and a "long form" (e.g., "Behold, the heifer has given birth and has not given birth," Ps.-Gregory *Test.* 3).[140] The passage is quoted as a scriptural *testimonium* to the virgin birth of Jesus: *Acts of Peter* 24 (in a TC);[141] Clement of Alexandria *Strom.* 7.94; Tertullian *Flesh* 23 (with Isa 7:14); Epiphanius *Pan.* 30.30.3 (with Isa 7:14 and Num 19:2); Ps.-Gregory of Nyssa *Test.* 3 (in a TC).[142] Again, the use of the passage in *testimonia* contexts, together with the lack of specific attribution (except for Tertullian, who attributes it to Ezekiel), strongly suggests common use of a *testimonia* source.

There is little reason to dispute Mueller's conclusion that the fragments which he studied derive ultimately from a lost *Apocryphon of Ezekiel*.[143] The evidence presented above on Fragments Two and Three, however, indicates that these sayings attained their authoritative status (quoted as scripture) due to their transmission in scriptural TCs on repentance and the virgin birth.

---

[137] For surviving fragments in Greek, Latin, Hebrew, Coptic, and Syriac, see James R. Mueller, *The Five Fragments of the Apocryphon of Ezekiel: A Critical Study* (JSPSup 5; Sheffield: Sheffield Academic Press, 1994); ET in *OTP* 1. 491–95. I follow Mueller's fragment numbering. Summary of witnesses in Mueller, *Apocryphon*, 14–16.

[138] *1 Clem.* 8.3; Clement of Alexandria *Teach.* 1.91.2; and *Exeg. Soul* 135.30–136.4; Clement of Alexandria also has a clear allusion to the text (*Rich Man* 39).

[139] Mueller, *Apocryphon*, 113–20. Mueller argues for mutual independence on the basis of differences in wording and citation formulas.

[140] See Mueller for a full discussion of witnesses (ibid., 120–38).

[141] See sect. 3.4.9 above.

[142] For Ps.-Gregory's *testimonia*, see sect. 3.6.5 below.

[143] Mueller, *Apocryphon*, 166–67.

3.5   *The Latin* Testimonia *Tradition*

3.5.1   *Early Latin Scriptural Translations*

The earliest Latin Christian writings were translations of Greek works, particularly of scripture.[144] The translation process itself was influenced by the *testimonia* tradition: to Mark 13:2 (Jesus' prediction that not one stone of the temple would be left upon another) the Old Latin (OL) adds *et post tridum aliut excitabitur sine manibus,* a clear allusion to the popular stone *testimonium* Dan 2:34.[145] Another OL variant reads *alius* to make even clearer that the reference is to a personal "stone" (i.e., Christ) who will take the place of the stones of the temple.[146]

3.5.2   5 Ezra

This work is extant as a Christian addition (two chapters) to the beginning of the apocalypse *4 Ezra.*[147] Dating between the mid-second to the mid-third century,[148] the work relates God's rejection of Israel and his turning to a new people. God speaks directly to Ezra by means of a cento of OT texts (mainly from Exodus and Isaiah) together with some NT texts.

   Graham N. Stanton argues that the work is heavily influenced by the Gospel of Matthew in its portrayal of Christians as the inheritors of God's promises to Israel.[149] Robert A. Kraft, however, is probably correct in his judgment that the author of *5 Ezra* did not necessarily know Matthew; *5 Ezra* in fact may originally have been a Jewish composition that was later "Christianized."[150] This work is quoted in the fifth-century *Concerning the Dispute between the Church and the Synagogue—A Dialogue*—another indication of the continuity of the

---

[144] See Daniélou, *Origins,* 5.

[145] See sect. 5.6 below for Dan 2:34 in the stone *testimonia.*

[146] See Bakker, "Old-Latin Gospels." Bakker attributed this phenomenon to the influence of the "Testimony Book."

[147] Latin text in R.L. Bensly, ed., *The Fourth Book of Ezra, the Latin Version Edited from the MSS* (TextsS 3.2; Cambridge: Cambridge University Press, 1895); ET in *OTP* 1. 525–28.

[148] Graham N. Stanton ("5 Ezra and Matthean Christianity in the Second Century," *JTS* n.s. 28 [1977] 70) argues for the earlier date; Bruce M. Metzger ("Introduction to The Fourth Book of Ezra," in *OTP* 1. 520) for the later.

[149] Stanton, "5 Ezra."

[150] Kraft, "Towards Assessing the Latin Text of '5 Ezra': The 'Christian' Connection," *HTR* 79 (1986) 164–66. Kraft's article deals extensively with text-critical issues.

testimonia tradition.[151] *5 Ezra* is a witness to the role of the *testimonia* in the emerging Christian consciousness as the new people of God.

3.5.3 *Ps.-Cyprian* Against the Jews

Ps.-Cyprian's *Against the Jews*, a Latin homily written at the end of the second century, seeks to demonstrate God's rejection of the Jews largely through the use of *testimonia*.[152] The biblical text is eclectic: there are connections with the OL, Vulgate, and other witnesses.[153] Of particular interest is a tendentious reading of Isa 1:15 (*A.J.* 71) which modifies the passage into a prediction of the crucifixion: "Because you have stretched out his hands, you may lengthen your prayer, he does not listen, for your hands are full of blood."[154] Ps.-Cyprian shares many exegetical traditions with Melito's *Homily on the Passion*, including a list of prophets who witness to Christ.[155] The work also shares many scriptural traditions with Irenaeus *Proof* 11–29, leading Dirk van Damme to speculate that a now lost biblical "salvation history" source was drawn on by both authors.[156] *Against the Jews* is an important witness to the incorporation of some Greek anti-Jewish scriptural traditions into Latin Christian literature.

3.5.4 *Tertullian* Against the Jews, Against Marcion, Against Praxeas

Extensive clusters of OT *testimonia* occur in Tertullian's *Against the Jews* 9–14 (written ca. 200) and *Against Marcion* Book 3, especially chapters 6–7 and 12–24 (written ca. 207–8).[157] Much of the material

---

[151] See the discussion in Kraft, "5 Ezra," 162–63. On the *Dialogue*, see sect. 3.5.10 below.

[152] Latin text in Dirk van Damme, ed., *Pseudo-Cyprian Adversus Judaeos. Gegen die Judenchristen: Die älteste lateinische Predigt* (Paradosis 22; Freiburg, Switzerland: Universitätsverlag, 1969); see also Gerard Frederick Diercks, ed., *Novatiani Opera* (CChr Series Latina 4; Turnhout: Brepols, 1972) 265–88. I am unaware of an ET. On this work as a homily, see van Damme, *Judaeos*, 7–10.

[153] Ibid., 45.

[154] See ibid., 41.

[155] See ibid., 50–62, esp. 53–56. Van Damme argues that *A.J.* 24–25 and *Homily* 59 and 69 draw on the same list of OT witnesses inspired by Matt 23:35.

[156] Ibid., 46–50.

[157] *Jews*: Latin text in Hermann Tränkle, ed., *Q.S.F. Tertulliani Adversus Iudaeos: Mit Einleitung und kritischem Kommentar* (Wiesbaden: Steiner, 1964); ET in ANF 3. 151–73. *Marcion*: Latin text in René Braun, ed., *Contre Marcion, Livre III* (SC 399; Paris: Cerf, 1994); ET in ANF 3. 321–44. Dates from Timothy D. Barnes, *Tertullian: A Historical and Literary Study* (Oxford: Clarendon, 1985) 120–21.

in the two works is virtually identical; probably Tertullian has simply borrowed and lightly edited his own earlier work in composing *Against Marcion*.[158] The North African polemicist thus fights both "the Jews" and Marcion with the same *testimonia*; ironically, he constantly accuses the anti-Jewish Marcion of taking his positions from the Jews.[159]

(a) *Function of the* Testimonia

In *Against Praxeas*, Tertullian defends the orthodox understanding of the trinity against the theories of Praxeas.[160] In the course of his presentation, Tertullian argues that the "rule of faith" has been passed down to orthodox believers as a guarantee of truth against the innovations of heretics.[161] Later in his argument, Tertullian further bolsters the orthodox position by citing a long TC which shows the usual signs (use of common texts and sequences, employment of a Christianized reading of Isa 45:1) of deriving from a *testimonia* source (*Prax.* 11.5–8). At the end of the *testimonia* sequence, Tertullian provides one of the clearest statements in patristic literature that he is drawing his texts from a authoritative TC which is arranged under different subject headings:

> Haec pauca de multis, nec enim affectamus uniuersas scripturas euoluere cum et in singulis capitulis plenam maiestatem et auctoritatem contestantes, maiorem congressum in retractatibus habemus.

> These are a few testimonies out of many; for we do not pretend to bring up all the passages of scripture, because we have a tolerably large accumulation of them in the various heads of our subject, as we in our several chapters call them in as our witnesses in the fullness of their dignity and authority. (*Prax.* 11.9)

Tertullian presents *Against the Jews* as the written conclusion to an originally oral debate between a proselyte Jew and a Christian (1.1). The former lawyer uses his TCs as forensic proof in a clearly marked rhetorical argument: "Begin we, therefore, to prove (*probare*) that the

---

[158] So Braun, *Marcion*, 20–21. In contrast, Quasten held *Jews* 9–14 to be "certainly spurious," an addendum taken from *Against Marcion* by a later editor (*Patrology* 2. 269).

[159] See, e.g., *Marcion* 3.7.1; 3.8.1.

[160] Latin text in Giuseppe Scarpat, ed., *Q.S.F. Tertulliano Adversus Praxean: edizione critica con traduzione e note italiane* (Biblioteca Loescheriana; Turin: Loescher, 1959); ET in ANF 3. 597–627.

[161] *Prax.* 2.1–2; on Tertullian's summary of the rule of faith in 2.1 see Kelly, *Creeds*, 86–87.

birth was announced by the prophets" (9.1); "we will prove (*proba-bimus*) that it may suffice that the death of the Christ has been proph-esied" (10:14).[162] As did Luke and Justin, Tertullian seeks to prove that the prophecies apply to Christ and not to another (e.g., Ps 2:7–8 cannot apply to David) (chap. 12). The proof-texts seem often to be in a random order, but a creedal sequence is still visible: the birth of Christ and Christ's name predicted (chap. 9); the passion (chap. 10); Christ as the end of the prophecies (chap. 11); the calling of the gentiles (chap. 12); the destruction of Judea connected with the coming of Christ; a passion collection around the word "wood" (*lignum*) (chap. 13); the two advents of Christ (chap. 14).

Who is the real audience of *Against the Jews*? Timothy D. Barnes argues that Tertullian had only superficial contact with contempo-rary Jews; for Tertullian Judaism was a "fossilized faith," not to be taken seriously. He concludes that *Against the Jews* is really written to convert pagans.[163] Barnes's view on Tertullian's attitude towards Judaism seems essentially correct. As noted above, Tertullian regarded anti-Jewish and anti-Marcion arguments as interchangeable; it thus seems likely that Tertullian's polemic was stylized and not aimed at actual flesh and blood Jews.[164]

(b) *Evidence of Written* Testimonia *Sources*
Numerous signs of a TC are evident in *Against the Jews*: LXX-deviant readings (the famous "wood" additions to Deut 28:66 and Ps 96 [95]:10),[165] false attributions (Deut 28:66 attributed to "Exodus" in 11.9), and use of the same series of *testimonia* texts found in other authors. Most scholars have concluded, however, that Tertullian depends on earlier writers, especially Justin and Irenaeus, for his *tes-timonia*.[166] While there is little reason to doubt that Tertullian made

---

[162] See more examples in Daniélou, *Origins*, 265–66.

[163] Barnes, *Tertullian*, 91–93.

[164] In response to Barnes's position, W.H.C. Frend offers some contemporary archaeological and literary evidence for Jewish influence on North African Chris-tianity in general and Tertullian in particular ("Jews and Christians in Third Cen-tury Carthage," in A. Benoît, M. Philenko, and C. Vogel, eds., *Paganisme, Judaïsme, Christianisme: Influences et affrontements dans le monde antique. Mélanges offerts à Marcel Simon* [Paris: Boccard, 1978] 185–94). While Frend's evidence qualifies Barnes's views, it does not substantially challenge the conclusion that Tertullian shows no real knowl-edge of, nor interest in, actual Jews in *Against the Jews*.

[165] Ps 96 (95):10 is quoted in *Jews* 10:11 (cross typology sequence) and Deut 28:66 in *Jews* 11.9.

[166] See Skarsaune, *Prophecy*, 438–45, for detailed arguments concerning Tertullian's reliance on Justin's scriptural quotations; see also the evidence in Braun, *Marcion*,

use of his predecessors' collections, I find that these scholars sometimes overstate the case.[167] In addition to borrowing from other
authors, we must also consider the likelihood that Tertullian found
his texts in an authoritative TC, used perhaps in a school or liturgical setting.[168] His immense respect for the *testimonia* sources is evident: he retains LXX-deviant quotations despite the fact that he is
intimately familiar with the LXX: his normal method was to translate his biblical texts directly from the LXX Greek himself.[169]

I again present a sample from the passion *testimonia* as Tertullian
knows them (*A.J.* 10.6–16):[170]

Tertullian *A.J.* 10		Function	Parallels/Sources
10.6:	Gen 22 (A) Gen 37 (A)	Isaac and Joseph as types (*figurates*) of Christ	Melito *Hom.* 59/69; Ps.-Cyprian *A.J.* 24–25
10.7–9:	Deut 33:17[171] Gen 49:5–6	Types of horns and bulls advents of Christ, and prefigure cross, two crucifixion	
10.10:	Exod 17:8–13 (A) Num 21:1–9 (A)	Moses' outstretched arms and serpent prefigure cross	Justin *Dial.* 91/94
10.11:	Ps 96:10 Isa 9:6	Christ's reign after passion	Justin *1 Apol.* 35.2
10.12:	Jer 11:19 LXX	"Wood" onto bread prefigures Christ on cross	Justin *Dial.* 72

25–27. Daniélou argues for Tertullian's use of an early Latin *testimonia* tradition
reflected in Ps.-Cyprian (*Origins*, 271–72).

[167] Daniélou, for example, argues for Tertullian's dependence on Irenaeus *A.H.*
4.33.12, but in fact only two quotations match exactly, and Irenaeus includes many
more texts.

[168] Barnes also dismisses Tertullian's use of Justin, instead suggesting Tertullian's
reliance on no longer extant works by Melito, Apollinaris or Miltiades (*Tertullian*,
106–7).

[169] Daniélou, *Origins*, 140.

[170] Skarsaune argues that Tertullian is drawing on different passages in Justin in
this chapter, esp. *1 Apology* 35; *Dialogue* 72; *Dial.* 105.1 (*Prophecy*, 441, 443). Skarsaune's
strongest arguments for dependence involve Tertullian's repetition of Justin's exegetical comments (Ps 22 [21]:16 in *A.J.* 10.13 with *Dial.* 97:4: no Jewish king has
suffered what was predicted); Ps 22 [21]:21 in *A.J.* 10.13 with *Dial.* 105.1 (horns =
cross). But has Tertullian collected all these passages himself or is he employing a
common *testimonia* source?

[171] Falsely attributed to "Joseph's father."

(table cont.)

Tertullian *A.J.* 10	Function	Parallels/Sources
10.13: Ps 22:16 Ps 22:21	Passion predictions not applicable to David	*Dial.* 97.4; 105.1

10.15–16: Isa 53:8–10
           Isa 57:2
           Isa 53:12
	Christ's passion, death
	and burial	

Finally I present an important passage illustrating the two advents (humility and glory) schema (*Marc.* 3.7):

Marcion 3.7	Function	Parallels/Sources
	Introduction: Marcion and "the Jews" both err in not understanding the two advents of Christ	
3.7.1–3: Isa 53:7 Isa 53:2–3	*The advent in humility*	Justin *1 Apol.* 52.3/*Dial.* 14.8[172] Irenaeus *A.H.* 4.33.1; 4.33.12
Isa 8:14/28:16 (A)	Christ as rock of offense and stumbling	Rom 9:33/1 Pet 2:6–8 Irenaeus *A.H.* 4.33.1
Ps 8:6	Christ made lower than angels	Heb 2:7
Ps 22:6	Christ despised	Irenaeus *A.H.* 3.19.2
3.7.4–6: Ps 118:22 (A)	*The advent in glory* "stone" collection	*Dial.* 76.1 (Proofs of miraculous birth) Irenaeus *A.H.* 4.20.11
Zech 4:7 (A) Dan 2:34 (A) Dan 7:13–14		
Ps 45:2–3 Ps 8:5–6	Christ triumphant After being humbled, Christ glorified	*A.H.* 4.33.11

---

[172] Isa 53:3 is the central proof-text for Justin's passages on the humble advent; see Skarsaune, *Prophecy*, 154–55, on the multiple quotations and allusions in the *Dialogue*. It is also the first text in Irenaeus's TCs on Christ's humility. Cf. the application of Isa 53:2 in *Acts of Peter* 24 to Christ's birth.

(table cont.)

Marcion 3.7	Function	Parallels/Sources
Zech 12:10, 12	Christ in glory will be recognized by those not acknowledging his humility	John 19:37; Rev 1:7; Matt 24:30; *Barn.* 7 *1 Apol.* 52.12; *Dial.* 14.2; 32.2; 64.7; 118.1
Jer 17:9 (LXX) Isa 53:8	Unrecognizability of Christ	*A.H.* 4.33.11[173]
3.7.6: Zech 3:1–5	High Priest Joshua a type of two advents of Christ	*A.H.* 3.19.2 *Dial. 115;* *Barn.* 7[174]
3.7.7: Scapegoat Ritual (Lev 16:7–10 and mishnaic traditions)	Ritual prefigures two advents of Christ	*Barn.* 7; *Dial.* 40.4–5[175]

3.5.5 *Dream of Nero*

This text is found only as an addition to some manuscripts of the *Gospel of Nicodemus*.[176] The work describes a dream of Nero, the predicted destruction of Jerusalem and the rejection of the Jews, and the restoration by Christ.[177] The *Dream* makes use of Rufinus's translation of Eusebius's *Ecclesiastical History*, thus giving us a *post quem* of the latter 300s for its composition.

The text has thirty-two scriptural quotations, predominantly from the Jewish scriptures (though some of these are presented as spoken through Christ, e.g., *Christus dominus contestans per ora prophetarum dixit per Esaiam*) (chap. 6). Most occur in groups of four or more and are joined by a simple *et*. The quotations function as predictions.

---

[173] In *Dial.* 14:8, Justin reads the Zech 12:10 quotation with Dan 7:13, and ascribes the Zechariah passage to Hosea!

[174] Justin's interpretation does not discuss two advents, but cf. the allusion in *Barnabas* 7.

[175] See Crossan, *Cross*, 114–59, esp. 118–37, for an important discussion of the relationship of these texts to the passion narratives in the *Gospel of Peter* and the canonical gospels.

[176] Latin text in Ernst von Dobschütz, ed., "A Collection of Old Latin Bible Quotations: *Somnium Neronis*," *JTS* 16 (1914–15) 12–27. I am unaware of an ET.

[177] For a summary, see ibid., 7.

The texts bear telltale signs of deriving from a TC: false attribution;[178] edited readings;[179] and different versions of the same verse.[180] A few of the passages are well known in the *testimonia* literature: Num 24:17 in chap. 8; Gen 49:10 in chap. 9; Isa 28:16 in chap. 10. The author is especially fond of quoting a series of *testimonia* from the same biblical book. The text is from the OL, with a few Vulgate readings, and has a "polished and Christianized text for Psalms and Canticles."[181]

3.5.6 *Cyprian* To Quirinus

Under the influence of Harris's writings, the topically arranged proof-texts of the first two books of Cyprian's *To Quirinus* (written in 248 when Cyprian was bishop of Carthage) became the model for *testimonia* collections.[182] Cyprian's work is actually composed of three books: the last is a TC of scriptural (mostly NT) moral admonitions under 120 headings.[183] In the preface to this third book, Cyprian refers to his collection as a summary, designed to facilitate memorization, so that Quirinus might not be wearied with long and numerous books. The preface to the first book echoes some of these concerns: at Quirinus's request, Cyprian has gathered texts which form not so much a treatise on a particular subject, but rather "material for others to treat it." His two books are to help Quirinus in "forming the first lineaments of your faith," and should lead ultimately to the reading of scripture itself. Cyprian's purpose is quite practical.

The anti-Jewish polemic has become stereotyped by Cyprian's

---

[178] Hos 3:4 is attributed to Joel (*Dream* 7.7).

[179] 2 Sam 7:5, 12–14, 16 (*Dream* 11.2) is witnessed also in Cyprian *Quir.* 2.11; Lactantius *D.I.* 4.13.22.

[180] Hos 3:4 in *Dream* 7.7 and 9; Hos 4:6 in *Dream* 7.1 and 12.2.

[181] von Dobschütz, "Collection," 11.

[182] Latin text in R. Weber, ed. (CC 3/1; Turnhout: Brepols, 1972); ET in ANF 5. 507–57. The original title was simply *To Quirinus*, the sub-titles *Liber Testimoniorum Tres* and *Adversus Iudaeos* being later additions; see Pierre Monat, "Les *testimonia* bibliques de Cyprien à Lactance," in Jacques Fontaine and Charles Pietri, eds., *Le monde latin antique et la Bible* (Paris: Beauchesne, 1985) 501. Monat points out that Cyprian himself does not use the term *testimonia*.

[183] This may be compared to Cyprian's *To Fortunatus* (ANF 5. 496–507), a collection of OT and NT texts thematically arranged to serve as moral exhortations to Christians in a time of persecution (so Victor Saxer, "La Bible chez les Pères latins du IIIe siècle," in Fontaine and Pietri, *Monde latin*, 349). Ps.-Cyprian's *Exhortation to Repentance*, an extensive TC proving "that all sins may be forgiven him who has turned to God with his whole heart" (ANF 5. 592–95) should also be mentioned here.

time. The author is not addressing a Jewish audience; rather he means to give a fellow believer a convenient summary of scripture. The life-setting is pedagogical, and Cyprian's interest in memorization reminds us of the notebooks and memory-aides of the classical schools. Daniélou plausibly sees here a catechetical intention.[184]

The first book of *To Quirinus* consists of twenty-four headings designed to show that the Jews, with their ritual practices, have lost God's favor; Christians with their new sacraments have taken their place. Book Two has thirty headings on christological topics (titles of Christ, his incarnation, life, death and resurrection; the creedal sequence is again apparent).

It is almost certain that Cyprian did not compose this entire collection himself. In his prologue, he says that the discourse has "been arranged" and "ordered" by him "as far as my poor memory suggested." Only twenty-two of the three hundred four texts appearing in *Quirinus* 1–2 are used elsewhere in Cyprian's work,[185] while he employs the quotations in the third book and in *To Fortunatus* more widely. The first two books share numerous texts with previous *testimonia* traditions: Justin, *Barnabas*, Irenaeus, and the North African tradition (Ps.-Cyprian, *5 Ezra*, Tertullian).[186] In *Quirinus* 1–2, then, Cyprian seems to have taken over earlier collections, probably re-ordering material, adding quotations, and conforming the quotations to the current Latin biblical text. The scriptural collections in *Quirinus* 3 and *To Fortunatus*, though undoubtedly traditional to some extent, are more reflective of Cyprian's own concerns and interests.[187]

3.5.7 *Lactantius* Divine Institutes *4*

Lactantius, known as the "Christian Cicero" for his rhetorical skill, composed the seven books of the *Divine Institutes* between 304 and 314.[188] It has been called the "first attempt at a Latin *summa* of Christian thought."[189] Book Four, arguing that Christ brought true wisdom and religion to humans, presents extensive TCs arranged in

---

[184] Daniélou, *Origins*, 293.
[185] Monat, "Testimonia," 503 n. 15.
[186] Saxer, "Pères latins," 350.
[187] Ibid., 350–52; Daniélou, *Origins*, 288–95.
[188] Latin text in Pierre Monat, ed., *Lactance: Institutions Divines, Livre IV* (SC 377; Paris: Cerf, 1992); ET in ANF 7. 9–223. Lactantius also wrote an epitome of his work (ANF 7. 224–55).
[189] Quasten, *Patrology* 2. 396–97.

a creedal pattern. In addition to many of the traditional christological and anti-Jewish texts, Lactantius cites the *Sibylline Oracles* and the
Corpus Hermeticum. Pierre Monat has analyzed Book Four as a formal *disputatio*: the *testimonia* function as the *confirmatio* to the creedal
events of the *narratio*, the *regula fidei*.[190] Lactantius's collection of scriptural oracles would serve as *auctores* and *testes* to a pagan Latin unfamiliar with scripture.

Many of the *testimonia* in Book Four parallel those of Cyprian
Quirinus 1–2.[191] Past scholars were convinced of Lactantius's dependence on Cyprian; indeed S. Brandt (1897) edited the text of the
Institutions on the basis of the text established for Cyprian.[192] Recent
studies, however, reveal a more complex picture. Paul McGuckin
finds ninety-nine references to the Jewish scriptures in the *Institutions*,
with forty-four clearly independent of Cyprian; of the eighty-five passages in Book Four, thirty-two are independent of Cyprian.[193] Within
these common quotations, however, textual differences are evident
which suggest Lactantius's use of a different textual tradition.[194] After
a detailed analysis of the "non-Cyprianic" quotations, McGuckin concludes that, in addition to his Cyprianic material, Lactantius also
made use of an anonymous eastern anti-Jewish TC.[195]

Pierre Monat goes a step further in arguing that Lactantius is not
directly dependent on Cyprian's collection at all. Rather, Lactantius,
Cyprian, and other Latin works—notably three 5th-century dialogues:
Evagrius's "The Discussion concerning the Law between Simon a
Jew and Theophilus a Christian; Ps.-Augustine, "Concerning the
Dispute between the Church and the Synagogue—A Dialogue"; and

---

[190] Monat, *Institutions*, 11–19.

[191] For a brief summary of this relationship, see Monat, *Lactance et la Bible*
1. 95–96.

[192] See Paul McGuckin, "The Non-Cyprianic Scripture Texts in Lactantius's *Divine
Institutes*," *VC* 36 (1982) 145. Brandt relied on the critical edition of Hartel (1868)
which was substantially revised by R. Weber (1972).

[193] McGuckin, "Non-Cyprianic Scripture," 146. McGuckin includes both allusions and direct quotations, though he does not discuss his criteria for establishing
allusions. See his convenient lists of non-Cyprianic passages (p. 151) and of all references to the Jewish scriptures in the *Institutions* (pp. 161–63).

[194] Ibid., 147. Where the LXX has different traditions for the same passage,
Lactantius follows one strand and Cyprian the other. See also Monat, *Lactance*, 95.

[195] McGuckin, "Scripture," 152–55. He offers the following arguments for
Lactantius's use of an *eastern* source: (1) use of the Theodotion version of Daniel
(LXX was standard in the west); (2) the *Odes of Solomon* is considered scriptural (*D.I.*
4.12.3; the African canon considered them apocryphal); (3) the same exegesis of
Zech 3:1–8 is given by Eusebius (p. 160 n. 78).

Ps.-Firmicus, "The Discussion of Zaccheus the Christian and Apollonius the Philosopher"—all share a common tradition which derives ultimately from the *Dialogue of Jason and Papiscus*.[196] Lactantius's *Institutions*, with its creedal structure, is a more faithful witness to this original source than Cyprian, who systematized and arranged the source for his own purposes.[197]

Below I reproduce the evidence, so well summarized by Monat, for a common passion tradition shared by Lactantius, Cyprian, the Latin dialogues, and Justin and Irenaeus. Lactantius includes several additional quotations from the *Sybilline Oracles* which Monat does not note.[198]

Scripture	Iren. *Proof*	Just. *Dial.*	Cypr. *Quir.*	Lact. *Inst.* Book 4	Simon and Theoph	Church and Syn.	Zacc. and Appol.
Isa 50: 5–6	86		2.13	18.13	33.10		1116 A
Ps 35: 15–16				18.14			
Isa 53:7		72.3	2.15	18.16	33.1		
Ps 69:22	82			18.18			
Ps-Esdras		72.1		18.22			
Isa 53: 8–9; 12				18.24			
Ps 94: 21–22				18.26	28.6		
Jer 11: 18–19		72.2	2.15 2.20	18.27	28.6	1135	
Deut 28:66			2.20	18.29	28.10	1135	
Num 23:19	79		2.20	18.29	29.3	1135	
Zech 12:10		64.8	2.20	18.29	28.16		1117

---

[196] Monat, *Lactance* 1. 106–8. For bibliographical information on these works, see below sect. 3.5.10.

[197] Ibid., 1. 273.

[198] Ibid., 1. 283.

(table cont.)

Scripture	Iren. Proof	Just. Dial.	Cypr. Quir.	Lact. Inst. Book 4	Simon and Theoph	Church and Syn.	Zacc. and Appol.
Ps 22: 17, 19	79	97.3	2.20	18.30	27.12		1117
1 Kgs 9:6–9				18.32			
Isa 65:2		97.2	2.20		28.6		
Amos 8:9–10			2.23	19.3	39.7		
Jer 15:9			2.23	19.4	39.10		
Ps 16:10			2.24	19.8	38.1	1136	
Ps 3:6			2.24	19.8	38.6	1136	
Hos 13: 13–14				19.9			
Hos 6:2			2.24	19.9	38.8	1136	

Further parallels to these *testimonia* could of course be multiplied. For the present, however, it is important only to note the continuity of the Latin tradition with Justin and Irenaeus (and/or the sources of Justin and Irenaeus). While *Jason and Papiscus* was surely one of the important sources, as Skarsaune also recognizes, there is no need to identify it with Monat as the *fons et origo* of the entire *testimonia* tradition.

3.5.8 *Commodian* Apologetical Song

Commodian's *Apologetical Song* was written between 220 and 240.[199] The second part (lines 265–494) is essentially a christological TC. The *testimonia* function to show that the Jews erred in not recognizing Christ as the messiah. The relationship with Cyprian *To Quirinus* 1–2 is obvious: fifty-four of Commodian's sixty *testimonia* can be found in Cyprian's work. Scholars had long judged Commodian's TC to depend on Cyprian's, but Daniélou and others have marshaled convincing evidence that in fact Commodian's work is earlier than *To*

---

[199] Latin text in Joseph Martin, ed., *Commodiani Carmina, Claudii Marii Victorii Alethia* (CChr Series Latina 128; Turnhout: Brepols, 1960) 73–113; on the date, see Daniélou, *Origins*, 100.

Quirinus and draws on previous collections of Latin *testimonia*. Daniélou argues as follows: (1) Texts common to both Commodian and Cyprian represent only limited portions of *To Quirinus* (1.17–21 and 2.6–26). Both authors may then have been working from an earlier common source. (2) Where Cyprian typically quotes a *testimonium* in its full, LXX form, Commodian frequently quotes partial, LXX-deviant texts. These partial quotations are parallel with traditions in Justin (e.g., Jer 11:19 in *Song* 274; cf. *Dial.* 72:2); *Barnabas* (e.g., Ps 22 (21):16/Ps 119 (118):20 in *Song* 269; cf. *Barn.* 5:13; Irenaeus *Proof* 79); and the widespread tradition of quoting a modified Deut 28:66 (*Song* 276; Melito, Tertullian, Novatian).[200] A composite messianic text (Num 24:17/Isa 11:1, 10) echoes *Dial.* 22.12–13.[201]

Differences in textual forms also rule out Commodian's dependence on Tertullian's collections, though Daniélou allows that Commodian may have drawn on Tertullian for his exegesis.[202]

3.5.9 *Novatian* On the Trinity

The works of the Roman presbyter Novatian make little use of the Jewish scriptures, with the single exception of his *On the Trinity*, written between 240 and 250.[203] In addition to extensive use of NT quotations (especially John), *Trinity* also contains several thematic TCs drawn from Jewish scriptures: on the nature of God (chap. 3); on biblical anthropomorphisms (chap. 6); and a traditional, creedal sequence on the coming of Christ, his birth, healings, passion, resurrection, and role as future judge (chap. 9). The *testimonia* groupings follow the order of the Jewish canon: Pentateuch, Prophets, Psalms. The sequence in chapter nine follows an explicitly trinitarian framework, and is presented as part of the "rule of faith." Victor Saxer reasonably concludes that Novatian is using a TC which made up part of a Roman catechism.[204]

Most of the texts in Novatian's collection are well-established *testimonia* (Gen 49:10; Deut 28:66; Isa 7:13; Isa 53:7 and other servant passages; Isa 11:10; Ps 110:1). Several non-standard texts with

---

[200] On the Deut 28:66 tradition, see Daniélou, "La vie suspendue."

[201] Daniélou provides many more examples (*Origins*, 273–84).

[202] Ibid., 284–87. See also Daniélou, "Testimonia de Commodien."

[203] Latin text in Gerard Frederick Diercks, ed., *Novatiani Opera* (CChr Series Latina 4; Turnhout: Brepols, 1972) 11–78; ET in ANF 5. 611–44. On the date, see Diercks, *Novatiani Opera*, xii.

[204] Saxer, "Pères latins," 354. See also Daniélou, *Origins*, 329.

parallels in other authors demonstrate Novatian's contact with *testimonia* tradition.[205]

3.5.10   Testimonia *Traditions in Latin Dialogues*

The Latin *testimonia* tradition continued in three fifth-century Latin dialogues: Evagrius's *The Dialogue on the Law between Simon a Jew and Theophilus a Christian*, Ps.-Augustine's *Concerning the Dispute between the Church and the Synagogue—A Dialogue*, Ps.-Firmicus's *The Discussions of Zacchaeus the Christian and Apollonius the Philosopher*.[206] All three dialogues end with the conversion of the Jew to Christianity. In his study of Lactantius, Monat discusses at length the complex relationship between the *testimonia* in these three dialogues with *testimonia* in Cyprian, Lactantius, Justin and Irenaeus. These relationships, involving an intricate pattern of non-standard readings, conflated texts, and common groupings, defies any explanation of direct borrowing.[207] The dialogues, while technically out of the scope of our study of the *testimonia* of the first three centuries CE, are important witnesses to earlier collections. In addition to the possible use of the lost *Jason and Papiscus*,[208] the involved patterns of literary dependence and independence evident in the dialogues point once again to a school life-setting in which small-scale TCs were passed down.

---

[205] Novatian has a variant of the well-known Deut 28:66 (*Trin.* 9.5). Edmondo Lupieri notes that a non-standard text of Isa 40:12 (*Trin.* 3:1 and 30.11) is read in *Barn.* 16:2. This passage in *Barnabas* is part of an extensive *testimonia* tradition that reads Isa 40:12 with Isa 66:1 (including Irenaeus, Clement of Alexandria, Hilary, Jerome, Augustine, John Cassian, Gregory of Elvira, and Gregory the Great). While Novatian does not combine the passages, he does read elsewhere a non-standard form of Isa 66:1 parallel to *Barn.* 16.2 (*Trin.* 3.4). Novatian also reads the famous non-LXX *testimonium* Isa 45:1 (*Trin.* 26.7; for the extensive patristic witnesses, see Kraft, "Isaiah," 342). See Lupieri, "Novatien et les *Testimonia* d'Isaïe," in Elizabeth A. Livingstone, ed., *Studia Patristica*, vol. 17/2 (Oxford/New York: Pergamon, 1982) 803; see also Lupieri's fuller study, *Il cielo è il mio trono. Is. 40,12 e 66,1 nella tradizione testimoniara* (Temi e testi 28; Rome: Edizioni di storia e letteratura, 1980).

[206] *Simon and Theophilus* in Edward Bratke, ed., *Evagrii Altercatio Legis inter Simonem Iudaeum et Theophilum Christianum* (CSEL 45; Scriptores Eclesiastici Minores Saec IV V VI; Vindobona: Tempsky; Lipsia: Freytag, 1904); summary in Williams, *Judaeos*, 298–305. *Church and Synagogue* in PL 42. 1131–40; summary in Williams, *Judaeos*, 326–338; *Zacchaeus and Apollonius* in PL 20. 1071–1182 (attributed to Ps.-Firmicus); summary in Williams, *Judaeos*, 295–97.

[207] See Monat's valuable summary tables (*Lactance* 1. 281–83); discussion on general textual relationships (pp. 1. 98–99); and Monat's indices under the names of the individual dialogues for detailed information.

[208] See the discussion of the arguments of Nautin and Monat in sect. 3.4.3 above.

3.6 *Later Greek Tradition (200–400)*

3.6.1 *Papyrus Rylands Greek 460*

This fragmentary Greek papyrus codex dates from the early fourth century, probably from the Fayyum.[209] The contents are as follows:

> Folio 1 recto:
>   Isa 42:3–4
>   Isa 66:18–19
> Folio 1 verso:
>   Isa 52:15
>   Isa 53:1–3
> Folio 2 verso:
>   Isa 53:6–7; 11–12
> Folio 2 recto:
>   Unidentified verse
>   Gen 26:13–14
>   2 Chr 1:12
>   Deut 29:8, 11

Its physical characteristics (small size: 11 cm. wide; a full line of text would be only 5 cm.!; a "crude and irregular hand") indicate a personal anthology.[210] Although generally drawn from an LXX text, some LXX-deviant readings are witnessed.[211] Roberts considers it a general Christian TC with no anti-Jewish intent.[212] Lucien Cerfaux, in contrast, finds the text more closely linked to previous anti-Jewish literature, in particular with Cyprian's *Quirinus* collection.[213] Given the lack of exegetical comments, a precise determination of function and life-setting must remain elusive. Nevertheless, one can conclude with Joseph Fitzmyer that this concrete example of a TC "lends some support to the hypothesis of the *testimonia*, which cannot be lightly dismissed."[214]

---

[209] Published in C.H. Roberts, "Two Biblical Papyri in the John Rylands Library, Manchester," *BJRL* 20 (1936) 241–44. For date and provenance, see ibid., 240. Roberts called the papyrus a "fragment of a testimony book."

[210] See sects. 2.3.6 and 2.8 on personal collections; cf. 4QTestimonia (sect. 2.7.5) and 4QTanhumim (2.7.6) as two other possible personal collections.

[211] Isa 42:3 (cf. Justin *Dialogue* 135) and Isa 53:6–7 (cf. *Quir.* 2.13). Lucien Cerfaux ("Un chapitre du Livre des 'Testimonia' [P. Ry. Gr. 460]," *ETL* 14 [1937] 69–74; repr. in idem, *Recueil Cerfaux* 2. 222, 225 n. 5) sees this as evidence that the texts were drawn from previous TCs; this is possible.

[212] Roberts, "Biblical Papyri," 238–41.

[213] Cerfaux, "Livre," 219–26.

[214] Fitzmyer, "4QTestimonia," 76–79.

3.6.2 *Ps.-Epiphanius* Testimonies

The work in its present form is attributed by its editor to Asia Minor
in "the fourth century or slightly later"; its association with Epiphanius
(lived 315–403 in Palestine and Cyprus) should also be taken seriously as a clue to date and provenance.[215] It consists of one hundred and two short chapters: each has a heading beginning with ὅτι
followed by carefully attributed proof-texts. The TCs follow a creedal
sequence: Christ's pre-existence, incarnation, virgin birth, ministry,
passion, resurrection and glorification; eschatological predictions complete the work. Hotchkiss makes the reasonable proposal that the
document served as a preparation for, or explanation of, Christian
baptism.[216] The document is remarkable in the *testimonia* literature
for its relative lack of anti-Jewish rhetoric: there is no anti-cultic
sequence and only one anti-Jewish collection (*Testimonies* 35: "That
the Jews would be disbelieving").

The texts are for the most part LXX (Daniel is Theodotion); a
significant exception is its use of the famous ἐπὶ ξύλου addition to
Deut 28:66 (*Test.* 57.1). No NT texts are quoted explicitly, though
the author clearly uses the NT occasionally as a source for OT
quotations.[217] It is also apparent that Ps.-Epiphanius knows at least
Matthew's narrative: many *testimonia* witness to details of the Gospel's
infancy narrative, description of Christ's miracles, and passion narrative. Many of the chapters parallel widely attested *testimonia* and
testimonia sequences (e.g., *Testimonies* 51 on the crucifixion: Jer 11:19,
Isa 53:7, Wis 2:20, Ps 22:17); other proof-texts are idiosyncratic (e.g.,
three citations of Song of Songs in *Testimonies* 53, to prove "that they
would give him vinegar and gall to drink"). The author has constructed a comprehensive *testimonia* book from his own knowledge of
the NT, *testimonia* traditions, and his own artistry.

---

[215] Greek text and ET in Robert V. Hotchkiss, ed., *A Pseudo-Epiphanius Testimony
Book* (SBLTT 4; Early Christian Literature Series 1; Missoula, MT: SBL/Scholars
Press, 1974).

[216] Ibid., 5. Hotchkiss argues from editorial remarks and chaps. 90 ("That we
would be called Christians"); 91 ("That even the mark on the forehead was foretold"); and 92 ("That baptism in Christ was foretold").

[217] *Test.* 45.2 is virtually identical to Matthew's conflation of Jeremiah and Zechariah
(Matt 27:9–10); *Test.* 13b quotes exactly Paul's conflation of Isa 8:14 and 28:16
(Rom 9:33). Noteworthy also is the author's exact citation of Matt 24:35 and his
attribution of it to "Isaiah" (96.3).

3.6.3   *Eusebius* Prophetic Selections *and* Proof of the Gospel

The *Prophetic Selections* (ἐκλογαὶ προφητικαί) comprise books six through nine of Eusebius's *General Elementary Introduction*; the *Selections* consists of brief comments on select *testimonia* from the Jewish scriptures.[218] It is an early work, written sometime between 303 and 313, before Eusebius became bishop of Caesaria.[219] The four books follow the order of the Christian canon: historical books; Psalms; poetic books and prophets; and Isaiah (contrast Novatian's *testimonia* sequence, which follows the Jewish canon). We see here how a TC with commentary formed an important part of beginning instruction in the Christian faith:

> I think that my enterprise will be especially suitable to them [i.e., those who are at a lower level and are just approaching the divine word for the first time], so that they may be able thereby to understand thoroughly the truth of matters about which they have been informed [Luke 1:4]. Pure and simple faith possesses the firm force of conviction all the more when a man uses his reason and first lays foundations by demonstration and then receives elementary instruction in the certain apprehension and knowledge of what must be accepted on faith. . . .[220]

The *Proof of the Gospel* (ἀπόδειξις τοῦ εὐαγγελίου), composed between 314 and 319, presents twenty books (ten are extant) based explicitly on "the prophecies extant from the Hebrews from the earliest times" (*Proof*, Book 1, introduction).[221] Eusebius employs TCs arranged under familiar anti-Jewish (e.g., the downfall of Israel and the calling of the gentiles) and christological headings (e.g., prophecies showing Christ's pre-existence, earthly career, and passion). The author insists that the work is not an attack on the Jews, rather it is simply a demonstration that Christianity is established upon the Hebrew scriptures (1.1.9). As was the case with Tertullian, it is unlikely that Eusebius'

---

[218] Greek text in Thomas Gaisford, ed., *Eusebius: Eclogae Propheticae* (Oxford: Academic, 1842) (PG 22. 1021–1262). Timothy D. Barnes provides bibliography for some improvements of certain passages of the text (*Constantine and Eusebius* [Cambridge, MA/London: Harvard University Press, 1981] 360 n. 18). I am unaware of an ET.

[219] See Quasten, *Patrology* 3. 328–29; Barnes, *Constantine*, 168–70.

[220] Prophetic Selections 1.2; ET in Barnes, *Constantine*, 170.

[221] Greek text in Ivar A. Heikel, ed., *Eusebius Werke 6: De Demonstratio Evangelica* (GCS 23; Berlin: Hinrichs, 1913); ET in W.J. Ferrar, ed., *The Proof of the Gospel* (2 vols.; Translations of Christian Literature Series 1; New York: Macmillan; London: SPCK, 1920; repr. Grand Rapids: Baker, 1981).

intended audience were Jews. Rather this work, together with the *Preparation for the Gospel*, were likely intended as a refutation of Porphyry's *Against the Christians*, and as an appeal to sympathetic pagans showing the superiority of Christianity to both the pagan and Jewish religions.[222] Eusebius's achievement was to collect and systematize earlier Christian *testimonia* traditions, at the same time no doubt adding his own material.[223]

3.6.4 *Athanasius* On the Incarnation

Athanasius likely composed *On the Incarnation* around 335–37.[224] In the course of his treatise on the divine necessity of Christ's incarnation, crucifixion, and resurrection, Athanasius suddenly launches into a refutation of Jewish objections (chaps. 33–40). The argument takes the form of an extensive three-part TC: (1) on the incarnation of the Word (chap. 33); (2) on the passion and death of Christ (chaps. 34–37); and (3) on the recognition of the messiah (chaps. 38–40). The texts employed and certain sequences parallel TCs in Eusebius, Cyprian, Tertullian, Novatian, Irenaeus and Justin, demonstrating Athanasius's contact with different *testimonia* traditions.[225] With Eusebius, Athanasius is a witness to the continuing vitality and authority of the traditional *testimonia* in the fourth century.

3.6.5 *Ps.-Gregory of Nyssa* Selected Testimonies from the Old Testament against the Jews

This work, written around 400 CE, begins with long TCs on the trinity (thirty-six quotations) and the incarnation (forty-three quotations), followed by twenty shorter groupings.[226] Each collection (except

---

[222] Quasten, *Patrology*, 3. 331; Barnes, *Constantine*, 175, 178.

[223] See Ferrar, *Proof*, xiv, for the relationship between the quotations in the *Proof* and those in Justin and Origen. On the relationship with the collection in Athanasius's *On the Incarnation*, see Charles Kannengieser, ed., *Sur l'Incarnation du Verbe* (SC 199; Paris: Cerf, 1973) 143–47.

[224] Greek text in Kannengieser, *Sur l'Incarnation* (see previous note); ET in NPNF 2d ser. 4. 31–67. On the date, see Charles Kannengieser, "Le témoignage des *lettres festales* de Saint Athanase sur la date de l'Apologie *Contre les paines—Sur l'incarnation du Verbe*," *RSR* 52 (1964) 100; repr. in idem, *Arius and Athanasius: Two Alexandrian Theologians* (Hampshire: Variorum, 1991).

[225] For details, see Charles Kannengieser, "Les citations bibliques du traité athanasien 'Sur l'incarnation du Verbe' et les testimonia," in Benoît and Prigent, *Bible*, 135–60.

[226] Greek text in PG 46. 194–234. To my knowledge, no critical text nor ET has been produced. For a summary of this work, see Williams, *Judaeos*, 124–31.

the first) are grouped under a heading beginning with περί or ὅτι. While Jewish scriptural texts predominate, occasionally NT texts are also employed. The first half of the collection follows a creedal sequence: trinity, incarnation, virgin birth, Christ's miracles, passion, resurrection, ascension, glory of the church. We then find a series of anti-cultic TCs (circumcision, sacrifices, sabbath) followed by a TC on Christian sealing (περὶ τοῦ κατασφραγίζεσθαι).[227] *Testimonia* on Christian life follow: on the gospel, on the church of the gentiles (and unbelief of the Jews), that Elijah will come before the second appearance, and "that we shall be called Christians." The final *testimonia* are miscellaneous groupings which Williams holds to be a later addition.[228]

The collection gives every indication of drawing on previous TCs rather than the biblical text itself: numerous LXX-deviant readings, text forms and sequences mirrored in other authors (especially Justin, Irenaeus, Tertullian, and Cyprian), and false attributions. I present a few examples from chapter seven.

Ps.-Greg *Test.* 7	Function	Parallels/Sources
Deut 28:66–7	"On the cross, and the accompanying darkness"	see Daniélou, "Vie suspendue"
Amos 8:9	same	*Gos. Pet.* 15 (A); Irenaeus *A.H.* 4.33.12; Tertullian *A.J.* 10.17, 19[229]
Jer 15:9	same	Irenaeus *A.H.* 4.33.12
Isa 65:2	same	*1 Apol* 35.3; *Barn.* 12.4[230]
Isa 62:10	same	
Unknown quotation. attr. to Isaiah[231]	same	*Barn.* 12.1
Zech 14:6–7	same	

---

[227] The passages in this "sealing" group are connected by the catch-word σημεῖον.

[228] See Williams, *Judaeos*, 125.

[229] Crossan argues plausibly that the text of Amos 8:9–10 (darkness at midday) is behind the passion narrative accounts of darkness at Jesus' crucifixion (*Cross*, 198–200; *Jesus*, 1–4). Tertullian quotes Amos 8:9–10 in several of his works.

[230] Isa 65:2 formed part of Skarsaune's proposed passion section of the kerygma source (*Prophecy*, 146); see also Irenaeus *Proof* 79; Tertullian *A.J.* 13:10.

[231] The text reads, "And then these things will be accomplished, says the Lord,

Ps.-Gregory fits in the "mainstream" of the *testimonia* tradition both in terms of texts and topics. Nevertheless, given our complete ignorance of the author and the lack of his own exegetical comments, we can say little about the specific function and life-setting of this collection. We do have some clues, however. The author is strongly interested in the trinity and the incarnation, and the work has noteworthy parallels with Ps.-Epiphanius *Testimonies* on two topics: (1) sealing/signing (Ps.-Gregory *Testimonies* 14; Ps.-Epiphanius *Testimonies* 91) and (2) on the name "Christians" (Ps.-Gregory *Testimonies* 18; Ps.-Epiphanius *Testimonies* 90).

3.7   A "Gnostic" Testimonia Collection: The Exegesis on the Soul

This short account relates the gnostic myth of the soul's fall to the earth, her repentance, rescue, and return to heaven.[232] Woven into the narrative are quotations from Homer as well as both OT and NT quotations.[233] The texts serve a variety of functions: (1) prophesying the prostitution of the soul (*Exeg. Soul* 129–30: Jer 3:1–4; Hos 2:4–9; Ezek 16:23–26; and several NT texts are linked with the catch-word *pornia* [πορνεία]); (2) prophesying the return to the Father's house (*Exeg. Soul* 133: Ps 45 [44]:11–12 and Gen 12:1 are linked with the catch-phrase *peei empeeiot* [οἶκος τοῦ πατρός]); and (3) demonstrating the goodness and love of the Father that offers a chance for repentance (*Exeg. Soul* 135–36: *Apocr. Ezek.* 3; Isa 30:15; Isa 30:19–20 are linked with the catch-words *metanoei* and *kote* [μετανοέω; ἐπιστρέφω]).[234]

As noted above, the *Exegesis*'s probable quotation of a widely-

---

when the tree of trees is bent, and rises, and when blood will drip from the tree" (my translation). *Barnabas* 12.1 preserves a version of this text: "When the tree shall fall and rise, and when blood shall flow from the tree."

[232] Coptic text in Jean-Marie Sevrin, ed., *L'Exégèse de l'Ame (NH II, 6)* (Bibliothèque Copte de Nag Hammadi, Section "Textes" 9; Québec: Presses de l'Université Laval, 1983); ET in James M. Robinson, ed., *The Nag Hammadi Library* (3d ed.; San Francisco: HarperSanFrancisco, 1990) 192–98.

[233] Although some scholars have concluded that the quotations are a later addition to the basic narrative, Robert McL. Wilson ("Old Testament Exegesis in the Gnostic Exegesis on the Soul," in Martin Krause, ed., *Essays on the Nag Hammadi Texts in Honour of Pahor Labib* [NHS 6; Leiden: Brill, 1975] 217–24) argues persuasively that the quotations form an integral part of the narrative.

[234] For an argument that these groupings are derived from TCs, see Maddela Scopello, "Les 'Testimonia' dans le traité de 'L'exégèse de l'âme' (Nag Hammadi, II, 6)," *RHR* 191 (1977) 159–71.

attested fragment from the *Apocryphon of Ezekiel* is a hint that the gnostic work made use of a TC on repentance that contained this fragment.[235] After the quotation of the Apocryphon (attributed vaguely as the Father's word to "the prophet"), the *Exegesis*'s repentance TC goes on to cite Isa 30:15 and Isa 30:19–20, introducing both quotations with the vague "again in another place." This apparent lack of awareness of the biblical context is another indication that a TC is in use here.[236]

The two quotations from the *Odyssey* can also safely be attributed to an anthology.[237] Scopello's concludes, based on catch-word connections between the Homeric and the scriptural quotations, that both sets of quotations derive from the same source. Such a mixed collection is not unknown within gnostic circles: Hippolytus knows of a Naasene collection that quotes the *Odyssey*, Empedocles, and both the Jewish scriptures and the NT.[238] Scopello's proposal should also be compared with Skarsaune's conclusion that Justin's source in *1 Apol.* 60.9 contained both scriptural citations and harmonized readings from Plato.[239]

Closely related to the anthology or TC, the cento genre is often associated with gnostic writings by the early Christian fathers. After an extended discussion of how gnostics misinterpret scripture, Irenaeus cites a Homeric cento as a parallel example (*A.H.* 1.9.4).[240] Tertullian

---

[235] See sect. 3.4.12. For detailed arguments, see Sevrin, *L'Exégèse*, 13; Scopello, "Les 'Testimonia,'" 167–70.

[236] Scopello offers further parallels (in Origen and Clement of Alexandria) to the "prostitution" grouping (pp. 162–64) as well as parallels to the "return to the Father's house" grouping in Origen, John Chrysostom, and Philo (pp. 165–67). This evidence is less convincing. See Scopello's detailed analysis of quotation sources in idem, *L'Exégèse de l'Ame (Nag Hammadi Codex II, 6): Introduction, Traduction et Commentaire* (NHS 25; Leiden: Brill, 1985) 17–44.

[237] Ibid., 30–32. Scopello's conclusion is based on catch-word links between the two quotations, and the citation of the same passages in other authors.

[238] Hippolytus *Ref.* 5.7.30–33 (the passage is found in *Ref.* 5.2 in the ANF edition (5. 51); see ibid., 33–34.

[239] Skarsaune, *Prophecy*, 53; see also Smit Sibinga, *Old Testament Text*, 100.

[240] Cf. Irenaeus's remark shortly before the cento discussion: "They disregard the order and sequence of the scriptures, and in so far as they are able they dismember the truth. They transform and re-make passages, making one thing out of another" (*A.H.* 1.8.1). See the discussion in Robert L. Wilken, "The Homeric Cento in Irenaeus, 'Adversus Haereses,' I, 9, 4," *VC* 21 (1967) 25–33. Wilken provides an ET of the cento together with the passages in the *Iliad* or *Odyssey* from which each passage is drawn (p. 26). Daniélou had argued that the cento was actually composed by Valentinus, but Wilken is probably correct to maintain that Irenaeus employs it merely to point out the parallel techniques used in the cento and by

mirrors Irenaeus's concerns: just as contemporary authors create centos from Vergil and Homer, so the heretics (Marcion and Valentinus
had been mentioned in the previous chapter) corrupt the meaning
of scripture (*Prescr.* 39.3–6).[241] Clement of Alexandria, too, complains
about the heretics' use of scripture: they do not use all scriptures;
those they do employ are not used in their entirety; they select ambiguous phrases and pervert the sense of these selections (ἐκλογαί).[242]
In light of Clement's own clear use of TCs, his remark is, to say
the least, slightly ironic.[243]

3.8   *Syriac Writers: Aphrahat and Bar Salibi*

In his *Testimonies*, Harris used the treatise *Against the Jews* of Bar Salibi
(bishop of Amid, near Edessa; d. 1171) as one of the extant paradigms for the shape of the Testimony Book.[244] The treatise contains
much material reflective of *testimonia* passages and topics presented
in this chapter, though it is hardly safe to follow Harris in using Bar
Salibi to reconstruct early Christian TCs.

Testimonia traditions are also found in the *Demonstrations* (or *Homilies*)
of Aphrahat, bishop of Mar Mattai (in what is now Iraq), which
he composed during the years 336–45.[245] Aphrahat answers Jewish
objections to Christian claims that Jesus is messiah and son of God
with traditional *testimonia* (using Ps 2:7; Ps 110 (109):3; Isa 9:6; 7:14)

---

the gnostics (cf. Daniélou, *Evangelical Message and Hellenistic Culture* [A History of Early
Christian Doctrine before the Council of Nicaea 2; London: Darton, Longman &
Todd; Philadelphia: Westminster, 1973] 85).

[241] Almost two centuries later, Jerome also explicitly links false interpretations of
scripture with the method of the cento (*Letters*, 53.7).

[242] *Strom.* 7.96.

[243] Starratt presents good evidence from Irenaeus (*A.H.* 1.3.4–5 [on the Valentinians]
and *A.H.* 1.18 [on the Marcosians]) that these gnostic groups composed NT and
OT TCs (respectively) to support their beliefs ("Five Books," 121–25). He concludes
that, despite the protestations of Irenaeus, there is no essential difference between
the exegetical techniques of Irenaeus and those of his gnostic opponents (ibid.,
37–60, 180–84).

[244] Harris, *Testimonies* 1. 7, 57–59. For a summary of Bar Salibi's work, see
Williams, *Judaeos*, 109–12. Williams notes that the Syriac manuscript was edited by
J. De Zwaan (Leiden, 1906).

[245] Syriac text in J. Parisot, ed., *Aphraatis Sapientis Persae Demonstrationes* (Patrologia
Syriaca 1–2; Paris: Firmin-Didot, 1894, 1907); critical ed. and French translation
of the *Demonstrations* in Marie-Joseph Pierre, *Aphraate le Sage Persan: Les Exposés*
(2 vols.; SC 349, 359; Paris: Cerf, 1988); ET of select *Demonstrations* in NPNF 2d ser.
13/2. 345–412. On the dates, see Pierre, *Aphraate*, 38.

(*Dem.* 17). Contact with ancient messianic tradition is evident in a reading of Gen 49:10 that is reflected in Justin and indeed already at Qumran.[246] The traditional *testimonia* theme of the replacement of Israel by the gentiles is also prevalent; *Demonstration* 16 has a TC of about fifty quotations![247] Aphrahat also presents extensive scriptural *exempla* collections: on examples of prayer (*Dem.* 4); of virtue (e.g., *Dem.* 1 on faith), negative examples of those led into sin (*Dem.* 6.3); reversals of fortune (*Dem.* 14.27); the righteous who were persecuted (*Dem.* 21); and lists of extended comparisons (*Dem.* 6.13).[248] Aphrahat's collection on faith reflects a formal creedal genre in which a list of scriptural events forms an essential part of the articles of belief.[249]

Jacob Neusner's *Aphrahat and Judaism* contains a detailed and valuable section comparing Aphrahat's *testimonia* with texts from the NT and the early church fathers.[250] Neusner concludes that while Aphrahat does follow the general pattern of NT *testimonia* (especially christological passages), his *testimonia* do not show dependence on any one church father. Rather, his selection of texts and above all his interpretations show original thinking. For Neusner, Aphrahat, almost alone among the church fathers, has real knowledge of Jewish traditions and employs it in a serious debate based on scriptural texts.[251]

While Neusner is correct to note Aphrahat's lack of dependence on any one church father, he overemphasizes Aphrahat's independence from more general *testimonia* traditions. We have some indications (false attributions and composite texts paralleled in other Syriac

---

[246] See Robert Murray, *Symbols of Church and Kingdom: A Study in Early Syriac Tradition* (Cambridge: Cambridge University Press, 1975) 282–84.

[247] Ibid., 42–43. Murray (pp. 350–51) provides a summary table showing a common *testimonia* tradition involving Gen 49:10 that links *Barnabas*, Justin, Irenaeus, Tertullian, Cyprian, Eusebius, and Ps.-Gregory with the Syriac writers Aphrahat and Ephrem.

[248] The categories are those of Robert Murray ("Some Rhetorical Patterns in Early Syriac Literature," in Robert H. Fischer, ed., *A Tribute to Arthur Vööbus: Studies in Early Christian Literature and Its Environment, Primarily in the Syrian East* [Chicago: Lutheran School of Theology at Chicago, 1977] 109–31). In addition to his overview of *exempla* lists in Aphrahat, Murray also sketches this genre in Ephrem and in a broad range of Jewish and Christian literature and art; see also Pierre, *Aphraate*, 68–70.

[249] See the discussion in Pierre, *Aphraate*, 144–56; esp. 148–49, which presents a synoptic comparison of a creedal sequence in Aphrahat with Irenaeus *A.H.* 3.3.3, *Apostolic Constitutions* 8.12, and the Syriac version of the *Acts of Philip*.

[250] Neusner, *Aphrahat and Judaism: The Christian-Jewish Argument in Fourth-Century Iran* (SPB 19; Leiden: Brill, 1971) 196–244, including convenient synoptic tables (pp. 201–13 on NT and pp. 233–42 on patristic authors).

[251] Ibid., 232–33, 242–44.

authors) of his use of oral or written TCs.[252] His use of a classic stone TC[253] is part of an extensive Syriac stone *testimonia* tradition, in which stone texts were applied to Christ, Simon Peter (esp. in relation to Matt 16:16–18), and the temple/church as the building on the rock.[254] Aphrahat's contact with christological and replacement-of-Israel *testimonia* was noted above. If we can trace no direct line of *testimonia*, Aphrahat nevertheless stands within a wider NT and early Christian *testimonia* tradition which he adjusted to fit particular local situations.

3.9 *Case Study: An Anti-Cultic* Testimonia *Collection*

Standing back from analysis of particular authors, I now present a detailed case study which demonstrates use of an anonymous anti-cultic TC by *Barnabas*, Irenaeus, Clement of Alexandria, and Ps.-Gregory.

3.9.1 *Evidence of a Written TC*

The author of *Barnabas* introduces his first scriptural teaching thus: "For he [the Lord] has made plain to us through all the prophets that he needs neither sacrifices nor burnt-offerings nor oblations" (2.4). This assertion can be considered the "heading" of the following TC (2.4–3.6).[255] A consensus of scholars accept that the author has taken over this TC from a source rather than composing it himself.[256] The TC has two strings of thematically linked scripture cita-

---

[252] See Pierre, *Aphraate*, 68, 213 n. 13, 221 n. 26, and esp. 138.

[253] Aphrahat, *Dem.* 1.16–21 (1.6–9): Ps 118:22; Isa 28:16; Luke 20:18; Dan 2:34–44; Zech 4:7; Zech 3:9 are used with extensive exegetical comments. A stone TC also appears in the Syriac *Acts of the Eastern Martyrs* (see Murray, *Church and Kingdom*, 206–8).

[254] See ibid., 205–38, 295–97, and Murray's summary table (p. 353). The stone *testimonia* are reflected in Ephrem's writings not in direct quotations but rather in typological images (pp. 208–12).

[255] See Prigent, *Testimonia*, 31. Prigent shows that the theme of God's self-sufficiency obviating any need for sacrifice was a common one in contemporary Jewish (Philo *Spec. Laws* 1.271; Josephus *Ant.* 8.111) and early Christian (e.g., Athenagoras *Leg.* 13.1; Justin *Dial.* 22.1) literature (ibid., 31–33).

[256] Klaus Wengst is representative. In comparing the TC with "frame" passages representative of *Barnabas*'s author (chaps. 1, 17, 21), he finds that (1) the collection can be read independently of its context; (2) it twice uses the key word νόμος (2.6; 3.6), found nowhere else in the epistle; (3) it features a thematic sequence (wor-

tions: the first (2.5–10a) rejects sacrifices to God in favor of concern for neighbor; the second (3.1–6) rejects fasting in favor of concern for the poor and oppressed. Both series are interspersed with redactional comments. Nowhere in the TC is a specific attribution given to a passage.[257]

The collection begins with a quotation of Isa 1:11–13 in a text almost identical to the LXX:[258]

> "What is the multitude of your sacrifices to me?" says the Lord. "I am full of burnt offerings and desire not the fat of lambs and the blood of bulls and goats, not even when you come to appear before me. For who has required these things at your hands? Henceforth shall you tread my courts no more. If you bring flour, it is vain. Incense is an abomination to me. I cannot put up with your new moons and sabbaths."

An editorial remark (2.6) claims that these things have been abolished (καταργέω) in order that the new law of Christ take their place.

Next a conflation of Jeremiah and Zechariah is presented (λέγει δὲ πάλιν) as a single source (2.7–8). In the following, I present the passages from *Barnabas*, together with their probable scriptural sources. Solid underlining indicates *Barnabas*'s exact quotation of scripture; dotted underlining indicates parallels in sense if not in precise wording.

> *Barn. 2.7–8:* Μὴ ἐγὼ ἐνετειλάμην τοῖς πατράσιν ὑμῶν ἐκπορευομένοις ἐκ γῆς Αἰγύπτου, προσενέγκαι μοι ὁλοκαυτώματα καὶ θυσίας; ἀλλ᾽ ἢ τοῦτο ἐνετειλάμην αὐτοῖς. ἕκαστος ὑμῶν κατὰ τοῦ πλησίον ἐν τῇ καρδίᾳ ἑαυτοῦ κακίαν μὴ μνησικακείτω, καὶ ὅρκον ψευδῆ μὴ ἀγαπάτω.

> Did I command your fathers when they came out of the land of Egypt to offer me burnt offerings and sacrifices? No, but rather did I command them this: Let none of you cherish any evil in his heart against his neighbor, and love not a false oath.

> *Jer 7:22–23:* ὅτι οὐκ ἐλάλησα πρὸς τοὺς πατέρας ὑμῶν καὶ οὐκ ἐνετειλάμην αὐτοῖς ἐν ἡμέρᾳ, ᾗ ἀνήγαγον αὐτοὺς ἐκ γῆς Αἰγύπτου, περὶ ὁλοκαυτωμάτων καὶ θυσίας· ἀλλ᾽ ἢ τὸ ῥῆμα τοῦτο ἐνετειλάμην αὐτοῖς λέγων Ἀκούσατε τῆς φωνῆς μου . . .

---

ship of God closely connected with love of neighbor) not found elsewhere in *Barnabas* (*Tradition*, 18).

[257] Thus διὰ πάντων τῶν προφητῶν (2:4), λέγει δὲ πάλιν πρὸς αὐτούς (2.7), ἡμῖν οὖν οὕτως λέγει (2.10); see also 3.1, 3.3.

[258] The only significant change is that *Barnabas* drops "the great day" from the list of things which the Lord cannot bear.

Zech 8:17: καὶ ἕκαστος τὴν κακίαν τοῦ πλησίον αὐτοῦ μὴ λογίζεσθε ἐν ταῖς καρδίαις ὑμῶν καὶ ὅρκον ψευδῆ μὴ ἀγαπῶτε, διότι ταῦτα πάντα ἐμίσησα, λέγει κύριος παντοκράτωρ.

Zech 7:10: καὶ χήραν καὶ ὀρφανὸν καὶ προσήλυτον καὶ πένητα μὴ κατα δυναστεύετε, καὶ κακίαν ἕκαστος τοῦ ἀδελφοῦ αὐτοῦ μὴ μνησικακείτω ἐν ταῖς καρδίαις ὑμῶν.

As can be seen, *Barnabas* deviates from Jer 7:22–23a, but retains its sense. The quotation of Zech 8:17 is apparently influenced by a phrase from Zech 7:10.[259]

The next quotation is perhaps the most intriguing:

Barn. 2.10a: Θυσία τῷ θεῷ καρδία συντετριμμένη[260]
ὀσμὴ εὐωδίας τῷ κυρίῳ καρδία δοξάζουσα τὸν πεπλακότα αὐτήν.

Sacrifice to God is a broken heart;
a smell of sweet savor to the Lord is a heart
that glorifies him that made it.

Ps 50:19 (LXX): Θυσία τῷ θεῷ πνεῦμα συντετριμμένον
καρδίαν συντετριμμένην καὶ τεταπεινωμένην
ὁ θεὸς οὐκ ἐξουθενώσει

The first part of this quotation seems to be an adaptation of Ps 51 (50):19; the second part has not been identified from any extant writing.[261] Considering the parallelism of the two parts (τῷ θεῷ καρδία matches τῷ κυρίῳ καρδία and Θυσία parallels ὀσμὴ εὐωδίας), together with the widespread understanding of ὀσμὴ εὐωδίας as a term for the Christian eucharist (Eph 5:2; *Test. Levi* 3.5), this may be a phrase borrowed from Christian liturgy.[262]

The TC continues in chapter three with a new emphasis: fasting is rejected in favor of concern for the poor and oppressed. This argument is based on a quotation of Isa 58:4b–10a in a text quite close to the LXX.

---

[259] So Prigent and Kraft, *Epître*, 84 n. 2.

[260] Codex Sinaiticus reads τῷ κυρίῳ in this verse; Lake's edition adopts this reading, but I follow Prigent and Kraft.

[261] A marginal note in manuscript H identifies it as from the *Apocalypse of Adam*, but this passage has not been identified in the extant "Adamic" literature (see Prigent and Kraft, *Epître*, 86–87 n. 1).

[262] So Daniélou, *Theology*, 90. Cf. also Hatch's speculation that this passage was taken from adapted Greek psalms known to *Barnabas* ("Early Quotations," 181). I will designate this quotation UQ (unknown quotation).

All the texts cited in this TC are also found extensively in other Christian anti-cultic arguments.[263] The fact that many of these texts are found *grouped together* in independent authors argues that they draw on a common *testimonia* source. The following synopsis shows parallels between the *Barnabas* TC and texts from Clement of Alexandria, Irenaeus, and Ps.-Gregory of Nyssa.[264]

Barn. 2.4–3:5	Clem. *Teach.* 3.89–91	Irenaeus *A.H.* 4.17.1–4	Ps.-Greg. *Test. 12*
Isa 1:11–13	*Isa 58:7b–8*	1 Sam 15:22	*Jer 7:22*
Jer 7:22–23	*Isa 58:9a*	Ps 40:7	*Jer 7:22*
Zech 8:17/7:10	*Isa 58:4b–5*	*Ps 51:18–19*	*Isa 1:11–14a*
Ps 51:19	*Isa 58:6–7a*	Ps 50:9–13	Isa 1:16
UQ	*Isa 1:11–13*	Ps 50:14–15	Ps 49:13–14
Isa 58:4b–10a	*Ps 51:19a*	*Isa 1:11a*	Ps 49:9
	UQ	Isa 1:16–18	Ps 49:14
	Luke 18:3	*UQ*	Amos 5:21–23
	Prov 13:11	Jer 6:20	Mal 1:10
	2 NT texts	Jer 7:2–4	
	Jer 7:22–23	*Jer 7:21–25*	
	Zech 7:10/8:17	Jer 9:24	
		Isa 43:23/66:2+	
		Jer 11:15+ *Isa 58:6–9*	
		Zech 7:9–10	
		Zech 8:16–17	
		Ps 34:13–15 (continues with other NT and prophetic texts)	

Clement of Alexandria Teacher *3.89–91*[265]

While Clement knows and quotes from *Barnabas*, several considerations argue against his direct use of the epistle here. (1) In contrast

---

[263] Examples can be found in Tertullian, *Epistle to Diognetus*, Evagrius, Cyprian, and Aphrahat, all of who use texts from Isa 1:11–15 in an anti-cultic context (see Prigent, *Testimonia*, 33–34; Kraft, "Barnabas," 109–10). For further references see the parallels below.

[264] For a detailed discussion of these parallels see Kraft ("Barnabas," 95–117) to whom I am indebted for these references.

[265] Greek text in C. Mondésert, C. Matray, and H.-I. Marrou, *Le Pédagogue*, vol. 3 (SC 158; Paris: Cerf, 1970); ET in ANF 2. 207–96.

to *Barnabas*'s polemical intent to show that God has no need of sacrifice, Clement's quotations are given in a much broader, non-polemical context (chaps. 11–12) discussing Christian life and morals. (2) Common texts are given in a different order,[266] and NT quotations are added in Clement. (3) Clement's texts show a pattern of both agreement with *Barnabas* over against the LXX and agreement with the LXX over against *Barnabas*, a pattern defying a simple explanation of direct borrowing.[267] Finally, Clement shows a similar sequence of texts, including the UQ, elsewhere (*Strom.* 2.79.1).[268]

Irenaeus A.H. 4.17.1–4

Irenaeus echoes the "thesis statement" of *Barnabas*'s TC (3.4) as he introduces his collection against ritual observance:

> Moreover, the prophets indicate in the fullest manner that God stood in no need of their slavish obedience, but that it was upon their own account that he enjoined certain observances in the law. And again, that God needed not their oblation. . . .

Unlike *Barnabas*, Irenaeus is careful to give the sources of his quotations, even indicating the precise number of the 49th and 50th psalms. It is all the more suggestive of his use of a non-scriptural collection, then, when he includes the UQ (introduced vaguely with "as he elsewhere declares") (4.17.2) and attributes a conflation of Isa 43:23; 66:2; Jer 11:15 and Isa 58:6–9 only to Isaiah (4.17.3). The texts cited do not appear elsewhere in Irenaeus (with the exception of *A.H.* 4.36.2; itself a scriptural EC!). The fact that the quotations follow the order of the Hebrew scriptures rather than the LXX is a further indication of a non-LXX source for the collection.[269] Irenaeus

---

[266] Especially striking is the contrast between *Barnabas*'s full quotation of Isa 58:4b–10a and Clement's piecemeal quotation (58:7b–8; 58:9a; 58:4b–5; 58:6–7a) which does not include 58:9b–10a.

[267] See the detailed comparison in Kraft, "Barnabas," 103–5. Carleton Paget cites the example of Isa 1:11–13: both *Barnabas* and Clement agree in leaving out the LXX ἡμέραν μεγάλην (v 13), yet *Barnabas* and the LXX agree against Clement in reading τράγων in v 11 (Clement has ἐρίφων), while Clement agrees with the LXX against *Barnabas* (S) in reading κριῶν (v 11).(*Barnabas*, 104 n. 16).

[268] Proverbs 15:8; 16:7; Isa 1:11; Isa 58:6 *conflated* with the UQ.

[269] See these arguments in A. Benoît, "Irénée *Adversus haereses* IV 17, 1–5 et les Testimonia," in F.L. Cross, ed., *Studia Patristica*, vol. 4/2 (TU 79; Berlin: Akademie, 1961) 20–27. Benoît cites further connections between Irenaeus's collection and anti-cultic collections in Tertullian *Against the Jews* 5 and Cyprian *Quir.* 1.16.

does not depend on *Barnabas*,[270] but the many points of contact between the two TCs point towards some sort of indirect relationship.

Ps.-Gregory Selected Testimonies *Against the Jews* 12

The twelfth chapter of Ps.-Gregory's *Testimonies* is entitled "On Sacrifices" (περὶ θυσιῶν). The chapter begins with an LXX-deviant quotation of Jer 7:22, followed immediately with another quotation of Jer 7:22, this time in a text form paralleling *Barn.* 2.7, but attributed to Isaiah! The non-LXX parallel with *Barnabas*, together with Ps.-Gregory's apparently complete ignorance of the original biblical context, again indicates the use of a TC.

Several conclusions can be drawn from the above discussion: (1) Each author, considered individually, gives some indication of the use of a TC (vague or false citations, conflations presented as a single text, non-LXX readings). (2) While the four works are apparently independent of one another, we must posit some sort of common source or tradition to account for the use of the same texts. A common *written* source seems to be demanded by the use of the UQ in three of the authors, the close non-LXX agreement of *Barnabas* and Ps.-Gregory in the quotation of Jer 7:22, and the close agreements of *Barnabas* and Clement. The presence of the UQ in these authors argues that the *testimonia* source was accepted with the same authority as the original scripture from which it was excerpted. (3) At the same time, a *single* written source cannot be posited: striking differences in the actual texts used, the textual form, and the sequence of texts militate against this. If we can speak of a common written source, it is a *flexible* common source in which texts (perhaps in the form of tractates or note sheets) were collected around a theme, but apparently quotations could be added or deleted from the collection as needed. Some kind of "school" activity is the most adequate explanation for these facts. Kraft's model of "testimony note sheets" circulating at the local level helps to explain the combination of precise textual parallels and the general flexibility evidenced in the above analysis.[271]

---

[270] Some obvious general differences are these: Irenaeus has a much greater number of texts, a different sequence, and is closer to the LXX. One detailed example will suffice: Irenaeus agrees with *Barnabas* in citing Jer 7:22–23, Zech 7:9–10 and Zech 8:16–17, but in contrast to *Barnabas* gives them in LXX and unconflated forms.

[271] Kraft, "Isaiah," 350.

3.9.2   *Original Form and Life-Setting of the* Testimonia *Source*

Skarsaune argues that anti-cultic TCs such as the one just analyzed were in fact part of a larger source (or common tradition) that combined attacks on the cult with *testimonia* which read cultic rituals as types of Jesus and the Christian sacraments.[272] This combination is in fact already evident in the *Barnabas* TC itself: the fierce polemic of Isa 1:11–13 and the Jeremiah/Zechariah conflation are immediately followed by the positive typology of the UQ (sacrifice is a broken heart) and the "true fast" of giving help to the needy.[273] The conclusion to *Barnabas*'s full TC, Skarsaune argues, occurs in *Barn.* 5.1: "For it was for this reason that the Lord endured to deliver up his flesh to corruption, that we should be sanctified by the remission of sins, that is, by his sprinkled blood."[274] The overall movement of thought runs thus: the ritual cult is done away with, replaced by the blood of Christ in baptism.[275] In 5.2, *Barnabas*'s quotation of Isa 53:5, 7 picks up the image of Christ as the sacrificial paschal lamb.

Justin has several TCs which follow the same polemic/typology sequence seen in *Barnabas* and employs many of the same passages: *1 Apol.* 37.5–8;[276] *Dial.* 12.3–15.6; and *Dialogue* 40–42.[277] The *testimonia* sequences in both Justin and *Barnabas* interpret Christ's death and the Christian sacraments as replacements of the Jewish cult; the connection with baptism is especially strong.[278] We can conclude,

---

[272] Skarsaune, *Prophecy*, 295–98.

[273] See ibid., 296–97. Stegemann had in some ways anticipated Skarsaune's work by rejecting Prigent's sharp distinction between *Barnabas*'s anti-cultic *testimonia* and "midrashic," typological sources (Stegemann, Review of Prigent, 144, 147).

[274] Skarsaune considers *Barnabas* 4 the author's own interruption of the *testimonia* source with a reflection on the one covenant.

[275] Skarsaune, *Prophecy*, 297, 301. For the connection of "remission of sins" with baptism see *Barn.* 6.11–12, 11.2, 16.8b, and the accompanying notes in Prigent and Kraft, *Epître*. For the connection of "sprinkling," remission of sins, and a typology of the red heifer as the slain Jesus see *Barnabas* 8.

[276] See Skarsaune, *Prophecy*, 55–57 for a detailed analysis of this quotation.

[277] In this sequence, Justin begins by arguing that the sacrifice of the passover lamb is a type of the death of Christ and that Christ's sacrificial death means the end of Jewish sacrifice (40.1–2). Justin understands the sacrifices as types of Christian realities: the two goats offered on the Day of Atonement prefigure the two appearances of Christ, the offering of fine flour is a type of the eucharist, and circumcision typifies the Christian's true spiritual circumcision (see Skarsaune, *Prophecy*, 177–80).

[278] See, e.g., *Dial.* 13.1 and 14.1. Also worth mentioning here is the connection between *Barnabas* 11 (types of baptism and the cross) and *Dialogue* 114 (types of the

then, that Justin and *Barnabas* draw independently on a common *testimonia* source which combined anti-cultic and typological *testimonia*. Skarsaune refers to a passage from the Ps.-Clementine literature as a concise summary of this early Christian train of thought:

> Lest they (the Jews) might suppose that on the cessation of sacrifice there was no remission of sins for them, he (Christ) instituted baptism by water among them, in which they might be absolved from all their sins on the invocation of his name. (Ps-Clem. *Rec.* 1.39.2)[279]

3.10   *Excursus: Wood/Tree/Cross Collections in Patristic Literature*

I now present briefly an example of a patristic collection based on catch-words.

In a manner analagous to the stone *testimonia* (see sect. 5.6 below), early Christians gathered texts which were centered on vocabulary or images involving wood, a tree, or other images of the cross.[280] The "wood" *testimonia* are rightly understood as part of the passion apologetic for the crucifixion of Jesus: the collections function to prove that this suffering was prophesied in scripture. Paul's use of Deut 21:23 ("Cursed is everyone who hangs on a tree [ξύλον]") in Gal 3:13, the description of Jesus' death on a tree in the speeches in Acts (5:30; 10:39; and 13:29), and the formulaic ἔδει γάρ, ἵνα ἐπὶ ξύλου πάθη ("for it was necessary that he suffer on a tree") (*Barn.* 5:13) are indications that "tree" language and imagery, the death of Jesus, and scriptural *testimonia* were connected at a very early stage.[281]

Limited space precludes a detailed discussion of this important

---

passion connected with a discussion of living water). The shared non-LXX conflation of Jer 2:13/Isa 16:1 (*Barn.* 11.2–3 and *Dial.* 114.5) is convincing evidence that both passages rely on a common source (see the discussion in Skarsaune, *Prophecy*, 69–70; Kraft, "Isaiah," 346–48).

[279] Skarsaune, *Prophecy*, 297; Greek text in Bernhard Rehm and Georg Strecker, eds., *Die Pseudoklementinen*, vol. 1 (GCS; Berlin: Akademie, 1992); ET of the Ps.-Clementine *Recognitions* in ANF 8. 75–211.

[280] For a detailed discussion of these *testimonia*, see Prigent, *Justin et l'Ancien Testament*, 174–94; Daniélou, "Vie suspendue"; and esp. G.Q. Reijners, *The Terminology of the Holy Cross in Early Christian Literature as Based upon Old Testament Typology* (Graecitas Christianorum Primaeva Fascicle 2; Nijmegen: Dekker & Van de Vegt, 1965).

[281] See the comment of Reijners on *Barn.* 5:13: "It is impossible to escape the impression that ἔδει γάρ, ἵνα ἐπὶ ξύλου πάθη was one of the themes both in the early catechesis and in the debates with the Jews; and on this plane the use of the term ξύλον in recalling *testimonia* from the Old Testament is easily understood" (*Holy Cross*, 25).

group of *testimonia*, but a few comments can be made. Two remarkable "wood" additions to biblical quotations are witnessed: ἀπὸ τοῦ ξύλου ("from the tree") is added to Ps 96 (95):10 and *in ligno* (on the wood) is added to Deut 28:66. Though widely attested in Christian writers, there is no evidence that these additions were ever part of a scriptural manuscript tradition.[282] In *Dialogue* 71–72 Justin accuses the Jews of having excised certain passages from scripture: one of his examples is Ps 96:10; Daniélou and Prigent argue that in Justin's original text Deut 28:66 was given as another example.[283] The addition to Ps 96:10 is reflected in *Barn.* 8:5 and quoted in Tertullian *Marc.* 3.19.1 (also *A.J.* 10.11; 13.11). The Latin liturgical tradition maintained the reading in the Roman Psalter, Venantius Fortunatus's hymn *Vexilla Regis*, and even in the Roman liturgy of the Mass.[284] Similarly, the addition *in ligno* to Deut 28:66 is witnessed in Tertullian, Commodian, Hilary, Asterius (d. after 341), Chromatius (d. 407), Ps.-Athanasius, Faustus (late 4th cent.), and Augustine.[285] These examples demonstrate the authority of *testimonia* readings: they continued to be employed by Christians long after they were recognized as no part of original Jewish scripture.[286]

Extensive wood/cross collections are found in Justin *Dialogue* 86; Irenaeus *Proof* 79; Tertullian *Marc.* 3.18–19; and Cyprian *Quir.* 2.20–22.[287] In addition to use of the catch-word ξύλον as a means of collecting texts, texts with images of crosses were also gathered: Justin *Dialogue* 90–94; *Barnabas* 12; and Tertullian *Marc.* 3.18 (cf. *A.J.* 10; 13). In these collections, Isaac, Joseph, the horns of a bull, Moses praying, and the bronze serpent are all considered types of Christ.

---

[282] The Ps 96 (95):10 reading is found in some streams of the LXX ("western" and upper southern Egyptian texts), but this is due to Christian influence (see Alfred Rahlfs, *Psalmi cum Odis*, vol. 10, *Septuaginta: Vetus Testamentum Graecum* [Academia Litterarum Gottingensis; 2d ed.; Göttingen: Vandenhoeck & Ruprecht] 31).

[283] Daniélou, "Vie suspendue," 59; Prigent, *Justin*, 189–94. There is a lacuna in Justin's text after *Dialogue* 74.

[284] See Reijners, *Holy Cross*, 37.

[285] See Daniélou, "Vie suspendue," 68.

[286] The text was still controversial in Augustine's time: Faustus rejects its legitimacy, holding it to be a Christian addition; in reply Augustine does not defend its textual accuracy, but argues that its christological exegesis remains valid (ibid., 73–74).

[287] The titles of Cyprian's collections are as follows: *Quir.* 2.20: "That the Jews would fasten Christ to the cross"; 2.21: "That in the passion and the sign of the cross is all virtue and power"; 2.22: "That in this sign of the cross is salvation for all people who are marked on their foreheads."

The connection of the cross with the tree of life is also an important Christian emphasis.[288] A hint of the original life-setting of these collections is the explicit connection with the water of baptism made in Justin *Dialogue* 86, *Barnabas* 11, and Tertullian *A.J.* 13:12, 17–19.[289]

3.11   *Conclusions*

(1) The detailed presentation of TCs in this chapter has demonstrated the intricate relationship between these collections in terms of both texts used and textual forms. The parallels between authors are too complex to be accounted for simply by a hypothesis of direct borrowing; at the same time, the notion of a common general or oral tradition is inadequate to explain the close verbal parallels which often exist between these witnesses. The evidence points towards an independent "school" tradition which produced and transmitted these collections.

(2) This common *testimonia* tradition is widely spread: expressed in Greek, Latin, Coptic, and Syriac, it is witnessed in Alexandria, Carthage, Rome, Asia Minor, and Palestine. There is evidence in some early collections of a knowledge of Hebrew. A stable, if flexible, tradition can be traced from the mid-second century through the fourth century and indeed well beyond.

(3) This chapter has uncovered a variety of forms in which the *testimonia* circulated. Christians drew their proof-texts from the NT, other Christian writers, and anonymous *testimonia* sources. These *testimonia* sources may have taken the form of dialogues, texts and commentary, proofs accompanying a narrative of the life of Jesus, or simple lists of texts. The dialogue form (especially *Jason and Papiscus; Dialogue with Trypho*) was quite influential.

(4) The two main categories of the collections are anti-Jewish (often anti-cultic) and christological proof-texts. Some of the earliest collections (sources used by *Barnabas* and Justin) seem to have combined

---

[288] See Ignatius *Trall.* 11.2; Justin *Dial.* 86.1; Irenaeus *Proof* 34 (cross and tree of knowledge). Skarsaune points out Jewish texts which link the righteous man with the tree of life and the tree of Ps 1:3 (*Prophecy*, 378).

[289] *Dial.* 86.6: "even as our Christ, by being crucified on a tree, and by purifying [us] with water"; *Barn.* 11.1: "But let us inquire if the Lord took pains to foretell the water of baptism and the cross"; *A.J.* 13.12: "drinking, 'by the faith which is on Him,' the baptismal water of the 'tree' of the passion of Christ."

anti-cultic sequences with typological (especially christological) interpretations of the cult. Evidence points to Christian sacraments, in
particular baptism, as the life-setting for these early sources.

(5) The christological proof-texts often take a creedal pattern, witnessing to Christ's pre-existence, incarnation/virgin birth, healings,
his passion, death, resurrection and glorification. Tertullian and Novatian are explicit in linking his *testimonia* collections with the "rule of
faith."

(6) The precise force of the proof varied. For Justin, it is clear
that the proof-texts function as predictions: the prophets are trustworthy witnesses (μάρτυρες) whose predictions have in fact taken
place. This forensic understanding is also explicit in comments made
by Clement of Alexandria, Tertullian, and Lactantius. A distinct
stream of the *testimonia*, however, understands the Christ-events not
so much as fulfillments of specific predictions, but as the consummation of larger scriptural patterns. This pattern is apparent in *exempla* passages in Melito *Homily* 59, 69; Ps.-Cyprian *A.J.* 24–25; and
Tertullian *A.J.* 10.6.

Yet this distinction should not be overdrawn. Given the heavy
emphasis on creedal patterns, it is likely that no *testimonium* was read
as an isolated proof-text: it is always understood as either part of (1)
a larger creedal narrative or (2) a larger scriptural pattern.

(7) These collections enjoyed a great authority. The simple presentation of a TC is enough to "prove" a point without further argument. Their authority was such that the non-standard scriptural
readings which they preserve (e.g., "wood" additions to Ps 96 (95):10
and Deut 28:66 and the tendentious reading of Isa 45:1) were treated
as scripture even when it was known that they were not part of
scriptural manuscripts.

(8) This patristic survey has uncovered *no* indisputable evidence
that the *testimonia* were used in actual debate with Jews. Already in
the *Dialogue with Trypho*, the form of the dialogue between a Jew and
a Christian seems to be a literary fiction; the aim was to instruct
Christians or persuade a pagan audience. The overwhelming evidence points towards the development of these *testimonia* collections
in a catechetical life-setting. The texts, read as proof of basic creedal
beliefs, were evidently part of the basic instruction of many Christian
groups.

CHAPTER FOUR

TESTIMONIA IN THE NEW TESTAMENT:
PAUL'S WRITINGS; MATTHEW'S FORMULA CITATIONS;
SPEECHES IN ACTS; AND HEBREWS 1–2

4.1 *Overview of the Chapter*

I shall now present arguments for the use of oral *testimonia* traditions and written *testimonia* collections in the NT itself. I shall employ the criteria for detecting *testimonia* use which were discussed in the first three chapters. As with the collections studied in chapter three, I will (1) discuss the function of the scriptural quotation or allusion within the NT work; (2) provide evidence that the NT work draws on a previous oral or written *testimonia* source (whether Jewish or Christian); and (3) determine as far as possible the original form and function of that *testimonia* source. In step two, in addition to surveying the use of the particular quotation within Second Temple Jewish literature (to determine if the NT takes over Jewish *testimonia*) I will also examine Christian literature outside the NT to determine what light these traditions can shed on the NT passages.

In this chapter I will examine discrete sections of the NT: Paul's writings; the formula citations in Matthew; the speeches in Acts; and Heb 1:5–2:8, leaving for chapter five the study of broader *testimonia* traditions which are found in various strands of the NT.

4.2 *Paul and* Testimonia

4.2.1 *Evidence for Paul's Use of* Testimonia *Collections and Traditions*

(a) *D.A. Koch and Christopher Stanley: Paul's Personal Anthology*
Dietrich-Alex Koch and Christopher D. Stanley offer an intriguing variant of the *testimonia* hypothesis, arguing that Paul worked from his own personal anthology of scriptural citations. They posit that while studying scripture during his far-flung travels, Paul collected biblical extracts on various topics into a working anthology which he later used in letters or sermons. This hypothesis has several advantages:

(1) it provides a more plausible model for Paul's method of quotation than alternative suggestions that Paul looked up individual quotations in bulky and expensive scrolls in the course of composing his letters; (2) it explains the great textual variety evident in Paul's quotations by proposing that Paul collected texts at different travel stops;[1] and (3) it explains such phenomena as Paul's use of a passage in a sense foreign to its original context.[2] Stanley further points to Greek and Roman authors (including Plutarch, Cicero, and Pliny the Elder) who explicitly refer to their own use of such personal anthologies as an aid to composition.[3]

While Koch's and Stanley's arguments are sound, they do not provide adequate criteria to distinguish between Paul's use of a personal anthology and his appropriation of a previously compiled EC. I argue below that Paul does in fact make use of these previously established collections, originally composed in both Jewish and Christian life-settings.

(b) *1 Cor 15:3–4: The Meaning of* κατὰ τὰς γραφάς
Toward the end of his first letter to the Corinthians, Paul reminds his readers of the tradition that he has passed on to them:

> For I handed on to you as of first importance what I in turn had received: that Christ died for our sins in accordance with the scriptures (κατὰ τὰς γραφάς), and that he was buried, and that he was raised on the third day in accordance with the scriptures (κατὰ τὰς γραφάς). (1 Cor 15:3–4)

Important for our purposes is the twice repeated κατὰ τὰς γραφάς: the first linked to "that Christ died for our sins," the second to "that he was raised on the third day." For our study of the form and function of *testimonia*, two questions are central: (1) Does this formulation have specific scriptures in view, and if so, which ones? and

---

[1] Arguing against the suggestion that Paul worked from a single scroll in composing his letters, Stanley notes that even Paul's use of a single book (Isaiah) in a single letter (Romans) shows an extensive variety of textual traditions. Thus Paul's Isaiah quotations in Romans agree with a unified LXX tradition (e.g., 9:29); with diverse strands of a divided LXX tradition (e.g., 2:24); with a "Hebraizing" revision of the Old Greek text (e.g., 10:15); and with a "Christianized" text (9:33). In addition, Stanley judges the source of certain quotations "wholly uncertain" (1:17; 10:20) (*Language of Scripture*, 255 n. 12).

[2] Ibid., 73–78. Stanley notes that he follows the lead of Koch (*Schrift als Zeuge*, 99) in proposing Paul's use of a personal anthology.

[3] Stanley, *Language of Scripture*, 74–76; cf. sect. 2.3.6 above.

(2) What is the precise force of κατὰ τὰς γραφάς? Does it intend a forensic proof (e.g., a proof from prophecy) or a more general agreement with broader patterns of scripture (e.g., Jesus died but was vindicated by God, just as so many righteous scriptural figures suffered but were ultimately vindicated)?

Some scholars have argued that the phrase intends specific texts: Isaiah 53 is often proposed as the reference for the first κατὰ τὰς γραφάς;[4] Hos 6:2 has been proposed as the referent of the second.[5] Against this conclusion, however, it should be noted: (1) The phrase κατὰ τὰς γραφάς itself is as general as possible, more so than even the vague attribution to "the prophets" often seen in the *testimonia* literature; (2) the structure of the phrases themselves is essentially an event followed by two adverbial clauses:

Χριστὸς ἀπέθανεν	ὑπὲρ τῶν ἁμαρτιῶν ἡμῶν	κατὰ τὰς γραφάς
ἐγήγερται	τῇ ἡμέρᾳ τῇ τρίτῃ	κατὰ τὰς γραφάς

In this sense, the κατὰ τὰς γραφάς can be translated as an adverb: "according to the pattern of scripture as a whole" or simply "scripturally."[6]

Important studies have made clear that early Christian and contemporary Jewish literature often referred to a general pattern in scripture in which God's chosen and/or a righteous one suffers, but is ultimately vindicated.[7] Liebers is a recent advocate of this position, identifying 1 Cor 15:3b–5, together with Mark 9:11–13; 14:21; and 14:48–49 as references to scripture as a whole without specification of a particular quotation or allusion.[8] These texts, Liebers contends, show a general scriptural *pattern* of the fate (*Geschick*) of a righteous person, one who suffers, dies, but is eventually glorified by resurrection. He discusses several texts which exemplify this pattern (including different combinations of the following elements: death; atonement for sins; and resurrection): Isaiah 53; Daniel 11–12; Wisdom 2–5; 2 Maccabees 7; and 4 Maccabees (esp. 6:27–28; 17:21–22; 18); and

---

[4] See Conzelmann, *1 Corinthians*, 255; Lindars, *Apologetic*, 60.

[5] See Lindars, *Apologetic*, 60–66.

[6] The German "schriftgemäß" ("according to the measure of scripture") captures this sense of κατὰ τὰς γραφάς even more precisely.

[7] See Hooker, *Servant*, 159–63; George W.E. Nickelsburg, *Resurrection, Immortality, and Eternal Life in Intertestamental Judaism* (HTS 26; Cambridge, MA: Harvard University Press, 1972).

[8] Liebers, *Wie Geschrieben*.

Test. Ben. 3.8.[9] In this sense, κατὰ τὰς γραφάς can be understood as parallel to the δεῖ concept seen often in *testimonia* literature: it is a general principle which applies to scripture as a whole.

If this general reference to the scriptural pattern of righteous suffering and vindication in 1 Cor 15:3b–5 is not to be gainsaid, nevertheless, the close connection between the first κατὰ τὰς γραφάς and ὑπὲρ τῶν ἁμαρτιῶν ἡμῶν almost certainly *also* intends a more specific reference to Isaiah 53. Especially close are the parallels between ὑπὲρ τῶν ἁμαρτιῶν ἡμῶν and τὰς ἁμαρτίας ἡμῶν φέρει (53:4), διὰ τὰς ἀνομίας ἡμῶν (53:5), and κύριος παρέδωκεν αὐτὸν ταῖς ἁμαρτίαις ἡμῶν (53:6b). Significantly, Liebers's other examples of texts which connect the death of a righteous one with forgiveness of sins are all influenced by Isaiah 53 to a greater or lesser extent: Wisdom 2–5 can be understood as a reworking of Isaiah 53;[10] Isaiah 53 has influenced 2 Maccabees 7;[11] and 4 Maccabees is itself a reworking of 2 Maccabees.[12]

Many of the above texts would also have supported the second κατὰ τὰς γραφάς, referring to the resurrection on the third day. In addition, Liebers adduces other texts that present the "third day" as the paradigmatic day of God's salvation:[13]

> *Gen 22:4*: Abraham reaches the place of the sacrifice of Isaac on the third day.
>
> *Gen 40:20*: Pharaoh's cupbearer is vindicated, his baker hanged on the third day.
>
> *Exod 19:11*: "and prepare for the third day, because on the third day the Lord will come down upon Mount Sinai in the sight of all the people."
>
> *2 Kgs 20:5*: Isaiah's prophecy to Hezekiah: "Thus says the Lord, the God of your ancestor David: I have heard your prayer, I have seen your tears; indeed I will heal you, on the third day you shall go up to the house of the Lord."

---

[9] Ibid., 349–64. Liebers sees the story of Joseph as an influence on these accounts.

[10] Nickelsburg, *Resurrection*, 62–66; Liebers, *Wie Geschrieben*, 344–45.

[11] Nickelsburg, *Resurrection*, 103; Liebers, *Wie Geschrieben*, 356.

[12] Liebers, *Wie Geschrieben*, 357. Liebers holds for the independence of *Test. Ben.* 3.8 from Isaiah 53, although many other scholars (Jeremias, Kleinknecht, Rese) argue for dependence (see ibid., pp. 361–63, esp. n. 45, and the references there).

[13] Ibid., 364–66. Liebers further refers to Gen 42:18 (the figure of Joseph as a suffering righteous one); 1 Sam 30:1; 1 Kgs 12:12 (= 2 Chr 10:12), and rabbinic passages. "Third day" TCs are found in Tertullian *A.J.* 13:23 (with Hos 6:2); Cyprian *Quir.* 2.25 (with Hos 6:2; Exod 19:10–11; Matt 12:39–40 = Sign of Jonah).

Esth 5:1: Queen Esther intercedes for her people with the king "on the third day."

Hos 6:2: "After two days he will revive us; on the third day he will raise us up, that we may live before him."

Such texts may have been used to support the specific reference to the third day; it is perhaps more likely, however, that "on the third day" is a general reference to a short time, and that this phrase, together with the second κατὰ τὰς γραφάς, should be seen as references to the general pattern of scripture.

It is probably a mistake, however, to consider intended references to scriptural patterns on the one hand and references to specific texts on the other as mutually exclusive options. References to scripture as a whole do not preclude references to particular passages, or a collection of particular passages, as concrete examples of a given scriptural pattern.

In 4 Maccabees, for example, the genre of the *exempla* list is employed in the last speech of the mother of the seven martyrs. She reminds her sons of their father:

> He, while he was still with you, taught you the Law and the Prophets. He read to you of Abel, slain by Cain, of Isaac, offered as a burnt offering, and of Joseph, in prison. He spoke to you of the zeal of Phineas, and taught you about Hananiah, Azariah, and Mishael in the fire. He sang the praises of Daniel in the lion's den and called him blessed. (18:10–13)

We have seen this genre occur numerous times in the *testimonia* literature (Melito, Ps.-Cyprian, Tertullian, Aphrahat),[14] in the scriptures themselves,[15] and in Greco-Roman literature.[16] It takes only a small leap of the historical imagination, then, to suggest that a similar list of righteous sufferers vindicated would have accompanied the tradition to which Paul refers, perhaps in a didactic or catechetical life-setting. This putative list, in addition to brief allusions (as in the example above), may well have included direct quotations from scripture (e.g., examples from psalms). This "mixed" form is in fact what we find in the 4 Maccabees example, as the passage continues:

---

[14] Sects. 3.4.4; 3.5.3; 3.5.4, and 3.8 respectively.
[15] Sect. 2.6.3.
[16] Sect. 2.2 and 2.3.2d.

He reminded you of the scripture of Isaiah which says, "Even though you walk through the fire, the flame shall not burn you" [Isa 43:3]. He sang to you the psalm of David which says, "Many are the afflictions of the righteous"[Ps 34:19]. He recited the proverb of Solomon which says, "He is a tree of life to those who do his will" [Prov 3:18]. He affirmed the word of Ezekiel, "Shall these dry bone live?" [Ezek 37:3]. Nor did he forget the song that Moses taught which says, "I kill and I make alive," for this is your life and the length of your days." (4 Macc 18:14–19)

If we have identified some likely forms for the referent of τὰς γραφάς, it remains to ask what function the phrase κατὰ τὰς γραφάς would have served. Liebers's conclusion is clear: these texts are not to be thought of under the rubric of prophecy/promise and fulfillment; rather the scriptural pattern sheds light on each individual manifestation of that pattern. In other words, Liebers denies that this exegesis is "christological": Jesus Christ is not found in the scriptures, rather the (pre-Christian) scriptural pattern of the righteous sufferer is applied to Jesus.[17]

Liebers ties his conclusions on function closely to his conclusions on form: he identifies a prophecy-fulfillment schema with *testimonia* collections, and thus argues that an understanding of a general scriptural pattern obviates the need for a TC.[18] Liebers's reasoning may be critiqued on two points: I showed above that a "pattern" understanding of scripture does not rule out use of a written *exempla* collection to exemplify this pattern; (2) Liebers draws wide-ranging conclusions about early Christian scriptural exegesis on the basis of what he himself recognizes is only one specific (albeit early) type of exegesis.

Liebers's major point, however, is important. Modern scholars must not force all early Christian exegesis to fit the Procrustean bed of "prophecy and fulfillment": we should recognize that while Matthew's formula citations certainly fit this category, the texts studied by Liebers do not. Liebers's point is a reminder of the parallel discussion in classical rhetoric on the force of *exempla*, where the debate concerned whether *exempla* carried at least some kind of forensic force (so Aristotle, Cicero, and Quintilian) or whether their role was simply to clarify rather than confirm or bear witness (so the *Rhetorica ad Herennium*).[19]

---

[17] Liebers, *Wie Geschrieben*, 392–93.
[18] Ibid., 393, esp. n. 7, where he cites with approval Koch's rejection of TCs in the earliest Christian literature.
[19] Sect. 2.1 above.

(c) *Traditional Scriptural Formulas in Romans (Rom 1:3–4; 3:24–26; 4:25; 11:25–27; 15:12)*

As is well known, Paul makes use of specific traditions and creedal formulas (expressed as confessions and hymns) which he had received.[20] In this section I will examine a number of these traditions in Romans that have a more or less clearly identifiable scriptural background. I will discuss a further example of the use of a pre-Pauline scriptural tradition in 1 Cor 15:25–27 below (5.3.3a).

In the opening of his letter to the Romans, Paul describes Christ as he "who was descended from David according to the flesh and was declared to be Son of God with power according to the spirit of holiness by resurrection from the dead, Jesus Christ our Lord" (Rom 1:3–4). This is a traditional formula, which Paul assumes will be familiar to the Roman Christians, and which he cites at least in part to assure his audience that they share a common faith.[21] That the formula is closely tied to scripture is evident from the references to David and from the description of the gospel in the immediately preceding verse, "which he promised beforehand through his prophets in the holy scriptures" (Rom 1:2). It is unclear if specific *testimonia* are in mind; what is beyond doubt is that Paul takes over an authoritative scriptural reflection on the events of the gospel.

Scholars agree that Romans 3:24–26 contains a pre-Pauline formula; the debate concerns the extent to which Paul has redacted this formula.[22] The background of this traditional formula is complex, but certainly has to do with identifying the death of Jesus with Jewish concepts of atoning sacrifice; the ritual of the Day of Atonement seems particularly to be in view.[23] Parallel understandings of the death of Jesus as a sacrifice are standard in the *testimonia* literature.[24]

---

[20] This is especially clear when Paul uses the technical terms παραδίδωμι, παραλαμβάνω, παράδοσις: 2 Thess 2:15; 3:6; 1 Cor 11:2, 23; 15:3. See the discussion of this language in a didactic life-setting in sect. 3.3.2 above.

[21] On the evidence for a pre-Pauline formula and a similar interpretation of its function, see James D.G. Dunn, *Romans* (WBC 38; 2 vols.; Dallas, TX: Word, 1988) 1. 5.

[22] See Dunn, *Romans* 1. 163–64, for discussion. See also Ben F. Meyer, "The Pre-Pauline Formula in Rom 3:25–26a," *NTS* 29 (1983) 206. Meyer holds that the formula derived from a christological hymn whose likely life-setting was the baptismal liturgy of the ἑλληνισταί (the "Hellenists" referred to in Acts 6:1–6).

[23] Dunn (*Romans* 1. 172) refers in particular to Lev 16:21, the Day of Atonement ritual, in which the sins of the people are laid on the head of the goat.

[24] See sect. 3.9.2 above for the understanding of Jesus as the fulfillment of cultic

The first part of the expression, "who was handed over to death for our trespasses," (Rom 4:25) is a "variation of quite a well established formulation in earliest Christianity."[25] The formula depends on Isa 53:12:[26]

Rom 4:25a: ὃς παρεδόθη διὰ τὰ παραπτώματα ἡμῶν
Isa 53:12: καὶ διὰ τὰς ἁμαρτίας αὐτῶν παρεδόθη

This formulation, then, indicates reflection on Jesus' death in light of Isaiah 53. The extent of the influence of Isaiah 53 has no doubt been exaggerated in the past, but this is hardly a reason to deny its influence in this particular case.

The conflation of Isa 59:20–21 and Isa 27:9 (Rom 11:25–27) functions as the climax to Paul's reflection on Israel's fate in the scripturally saturated Romans 9–11. More specifically, it is linked to Paul's conclusion:

> And so all Israel will be saved; as it is written, "Out of Zion will come the Deliverer; he will banish ungodliness from Jacob. And this is my covenant with them, when I take away their sins." (Rom 11:26–27)

With Stanley and Koch, I find this quotation hard to attribute to Paul himself. There is no reason for Paul to refer to Zion in this context; it is in fact a term he almost never uses.[27] The vocabulary (especially replacing LXX ἕνεκεν Σιών with ἐκ Σιών) and stylistic (e.g., changing the singular ἁμαρτία of Isa 27:9 to plural) changes are not readily attributable to Paul's concerns.[28] Koch attributes this quota-

---

types; also sect. 4.4.2b below for the argument that a TC including Day of Atonement imagery underlies Acts 3:22–25.

[25] Dunn, *Romans* 1. 224.

[26] The allusion to Isa 53:12 is guaranteed by the common use of the passive παρεδόθη and the use of διά instead of the usual ὑπέρ. Koch (*Schrift als Zeuge*, 237–38) denies a reference to Isa 53:12 here: Romans uses a different word for "sin"; the passive παρεδόθη is used to balance the passive ἠγέρθη in 4:25b; and the use of διά has a parallel in 2 Macc 7:32. Yet it is precisely the combination of *both* the employment of the passive and of the unusual διά that supports an allusion to Isa 53:12.

[27] The one exception is Rom 9:33, but this is itself a quotation that Paul has taken over from previous Christian tradition (see sect. 5.4.3 below).

[28] See Stanley, *Language of Scripture*, 166–71; idem, "The Redeemer Will Come ἐκ Σιών: Romans 11.26–27 Revisited," in Craig A. Evans and James A. Sanders, eds., *Paul and the Scriptures of Israel* (JSNT 83; Studies in Scripture in Early Judaism and Christianity 1; Sheffield: JSOT, 1993) 121–24; Koch, "Beobachtungen zum christologischen Schriftgebrauch in den vorpaulinischen Gemeinden," *ZNW* 71 (1980) 188–89.

tion to the pre-Pauline Christian community; Stanley holds rather that Paul draws on a Jewish tradition here.[29] In this Jewish tradition, Yahweh himself marches out of Zion on the eschatological day in order to subdue the nations and redeem Israel.[30] Stanley concludes that Paul, in his use of this Jewish *testimonium*, considers the Redeemer to be God, rather than Christ specifically.[31] While Stanley marshals some strong arguments, I find it at least equally possible that the Rom 11:26–27 quotation is drawn from the Christian "Law out of Zion" *testimonia* tradition identified by Skarsaune, and thus that "the Deliverer" is Christ.[32]

In Rom 15:12, Paul quotes Isa 11:10 in the context of a larger TC (Ps 18:49 [17:50]; Deut 32:43; Ps 117 [116]:1; Isa 11:10) that demonstrates that "the Gentiles might glorify God for his mercy" (15:9). I will show below that this text was part of a complex of messianic *testimonia* in pre-Christian Jewish as well as early Christian circles.[33] Koch rightly concludes that Paul has taken this use of Isa 11:10 (with its focus on the "root of Jesse") from previous Christian tradition: Paul elsewhere shows no interest in the son of David christology inherent in this title,[34] and the purpose of his current TC is not served by including this title.[35]

This brief survey of Romans reminds us that Paul, for all his brilliant originality, is not the first Christian to apply the scriptures to an understanding of Christ. Certain scriptural passages have already

---

[29] Stanley, "Redeemer," 125–26. Stanley argues: (1) there are no exclusively Christian concepts in the conflation; (2) there is no other early Christian use of Isa 59:20 as a *testimonium*; (3) the self-designation of a Christian community as "Jacob" would be ambiguous; and (4) there is no extant Christian parallel to the concept that Christ would come "out of Zion." This last point should be qualified in light of evidence (in Justin's "kerygma" *testimonia* source) for a christological reading of Isa 2:3 which understood Christ as the new law going out from Zion (see Skarsaune, *Prophecy*, 158–60, 360–63).

[30] The image is found in Isaiah (esp. chaps. 59–63) and developed in various intertestamental texts (see Stanley, "Redeemer," 126–32).

[31] Ibid., 137. The connection between Paul's πᾶς Ἰσραήλ (Rom 11:25) and the τὰ πάντα of 1 Cor 15:28 (both in contexts of God's decisive action in the end times) would be worth exploring.

[32] Skarsaune, *Prophecy*, 158–60, 360–63.

[33] On patristic and Jewish use of Isa 11:1, 10; Num 24:17; and Gen 49:10 see sect. 5.2 above.

[34] The only exception is Rom 1:3, which itself (as discussed above) is a pre-Pauline tradition.

[35] Paul's interest is in the second half of the verse: "in him the Gentiles shall hope." See Koch, "Schriftgebrauch," 185–86. See also sect. 5.2.2 below on allusions to Isa 11:1, 10 in Rev 5:5 and 22:16.

been invested with a Christian interpretation and have been fixed into authoritative formulas which Paul has taken over.

(d) *Parenetic Use of Scripture (Rom 12:19; 13:9; 2 Cor 13:1)*
As part of his extended *parenesis* in Romans 12, Paul urges his readers: "Beloved, never avenge yourselves, but leave room for the wrath of God; for it is written, 'Vengeance is mine, I will repay,' says the Lord" (12:19). The scriptural quotation in paralleled exactly in Heb 10:30:

> *Rom 12:19:* Ἐμοὶ ἐκδίκησις, ἐγὼ ἀνταποδώσω, λέγει κύριος
> *Heb 10:30:* Ἐμοὶ ἐκδίκησις, ἐγὼ ἀνταποδώσω[36]
> *Deut 32:35a:* Ἐν ἡμέρᾳ ἐκδικήσεως ἀνταποδώσω
> *MT Deut 32:35a:* לי נקם ושלם
> Vengeance is mine, and recompense
> *Frg. Tg.:* דידי היא נקמתא ואנא הוא די משלים[37]
> Mine is vengeance, it is I who will requite.
> *Tg. Onq.:* קדמי פורענותא ואנא אשלים[38]
> Before me is the punishment, I will repay.

The Hebrews/Romans reading thus deviates from the LXX and MT; it is closest to the readings of the targums. Stanley concludes from this that Paul was simply using a Hebraizing Greek translation, but he does not account adequately for the precise parallel in Hebrews.[39] Various alternative proposals have been put forth. Westcott attributes this common reading to a written source, referring to Hatch's proposals.[40] For Ellis, this form was one example of a special group of pronouncements by early Christian prophets: the λέγει κύριος quotations.[41] Koch and Simon Kistemaker attribute this form to oral tradition.[42]

---

[36] ℵ² A D² add λέγει κύριος.

[37] Aramaic text and ET in Michael L. Klein, *The Fragment-Targums of the Pentateuch According to their Extant Sources* (2 vols.; AnBib 76; Rome: Biblical Institute, 1980).

[38] Aramaic text in Alexander Sperber, ed., *The Bible in Aramaic*, vol. 1: *The Pentateuch according to Targum Onkelos* (Leiden/New York/Cologne: Brill, 1992).

[39] Stanley, *Language of Scripture*, 172–73. He holds that the Hebrews quotations could reflect familiarity with Romans (not generally accepted) or use of an identical *Vorlage* (ibid., n. 305). But how likely is it that two authors who generally quote from the LXX would independently use another translation in this particular case?

[40] Westcott, *Hebrews*, 477.

[41] Ellis, *Paul's Use of Scripture* (Edinburgh: Oliver & Boyd, 1957; repr. Grand Rapids: Baker, 1981) 107–12; also idem, "Λέγει κύριος Quotations in the New Testament" *EvQ* 29 (1957) 23–28; repr. in idem, *Prophecy and Hermeneutic*, 182–87. Ellis sees this group of quotations as closely related to *testimonia* collections.

[42] Koch, *Schrift als Zeuge*, 77–78; Kistemaker, *The Psalm Citations in the Epistle to the Hebrews* (Amsterdam: Van Soest, 1961) 46.

Ellis's thesis has not received much support.[43] The oral tradition proposal is also problematic. Both Paul and Hebrews clearly present the passages as written scripture: Paul introduces the quotation with γέγραπται, and Hebrews follows the quotation with καὶ πάλιν and another quotation (classic indications of a written TC). A more fruitful path is indicated in F.F. Bruce's observation that the quotation derives from the Song of Moses (Deut 32:1–43), a section of scripture that "furnished the early Christians with a remarkable number of *testimonia*—largely, but not exclusively, on the subject of Jewish unbelief."[44] Given that both Hebrews and Paul employ the quotation in a parenetic context, it is unlikely that we have to do with an anti-Jewish TC. Although conclusions must be tentative, the evidence suggests that Hebrews and Paul are here drawing on a common Christian parenetic EC, analogous to that preserved in Cyprian *Quirinus* 3. The numerous contemporary Greco-Roman moral ECs further enhance the plausibility of this suggestion.[45]

Continuing his parenesis in Romans 13, Paul urges that the Roman Christians "owe no one anything, except to love one another; for the one who loves another has fulfilled the law" (13:8). Paul then quotes several commandments, "You shall not commit adultery; You shall not murder; You shall not steal; You shall not covet"; and concludes that these and "any other commandment are summed up in this word, 'Love your neighbor as yourself'" (Rom 13:9–10). Several observations can be made:

(1) The order of Paul's quotation of the commandments from the Decalogue differs from the MT of both Exod 20:13–17 and Deut 5:17–21, but agrees with LXX B of Deuteronomy 5; the Nash papyrus;[46] Luke 18:20; Jas 2:11; and several passages of Philo.[47] Dunn concludes that this "strongly suggests that this was the order in which

---

[43] See, e.g., Stanley's criticism (*Language of Scripture*, 173 n. 307).

[44] Bruce, *The Epistle to the Hebrews* (NICNT; rev. ed.; Grand Rapids: Eerdmans, 1990) 264. Bruce refers to Rom 10:19 (32:21), 15:10 (32:43); 1 Cor 10:20, 22 (allusion to 32:17, 21); Phil 2:15 (32:5 allusion); and Heb 1:6 (32:43). Various passages from the Song are employed heavily by Justin, Irenaeus, and Tertullian in their TCs (e.g., Irenaeus *Proof* 95, where a quotation from the Song "proves" that the Jews have abandoned God and been replaced by the gentiles).

[45] See sects. 2.3.1 and 2.3.3b above.

[46] See sect. 2.7.2 above.

[47] Philo *Decal.* 36, 51, 121–37, 168–71; *Spec. Laws* 3.8; for these and further references see Dunn, *Romans* 2. 777.

the commandments were widely known in the diaspora";[48] Stendahl finds that the "variety [of order] is certainly due to the fact the different forms of catechism have made their way into the wording of the Decalogue."[49]

(2) Paul's choice of his examples from the Decalogue is hardly random. On the contrary, he selects the more "universal" moral standards and avoids the more distinctively Jewish commandments (e.g., observation of the sabbath). Here Paul follows a practice which we have already observed in the collections of Ps.-Phocylides and the "summaries of the law" found in Philo and Josephus.[50]

(3) Parallels with NT passages (Jas 2:8–13; Mark 12:28–34 par.; see also Gal 5:14) show that discussion on the essence of the law was common in early Christian literature as well.[51] In Rom 13:8–10, then, Paul draws on either Jewish or Christian catechetical scriptural reflection to form the basis of his parenesis.

In 2 Cor 13:1, Paul quotes from Deut 19:15 in the context of warning the Corinthians of his coming visit:

> *2 Cor 13:1*: ἐπὶ στόματος δύο μαρτύρων καὶ τριῶν σταθήσεται πᾶν ῥῆμα
> Any charge must be sustained by the evidence of two or three witnesses.
> *Deut 19:15*: ἐπὶ στόματος δύο μαρτύρων καὶ ἐπὶ στόματος τριῶν στήσεται πᾶν ῥῆμα
> *Matt 18:16*: (ἵνα) ἐπὶ στόματος δύο μαρτύρων ἢ τριῶν σταθῇ πᾶν ῥῆμα
> *1 Tim 5:19*: ἐκτὸς εἰ μὴ ἐπὶ δύο ἢ τριῶν μαρτύρων

This passage may reveal a further aspect of the didactic tradition which Paul had received; parallels appear in Matt 18:16 and 1 Tim 5:19.[52] The context in Matthew and 1 Timothy is explicitly that of instructions for church order; there can be little doubt that the Pauline churches also included this passage as part of their disciplinary guidelines. This passage likely formed part of an early Christian collection—written or oral—of rules for church order.[53]

---

[48] Ibid.

[49] Stendahl, *School*, 62.

[50] See sect. 2.6.2 above. For references to rabbinic discussions of a scriptural phrase that sums up the whole of the law, see Dunn, *Romans* 2. 778–79.

[51] See ibid., 2. 778.

[52] "Both in the synagogue and in the early church this was a basic statement for church discipline" (Stendahl, *School*, 138).

[53] Koch, *Schrift als Zeuge*, 117–18, plausibly attributes this to a common oral tradition; but comparison should also be made to written Qumran halakhic collections (see sect. 2.7.4).

(e) *Paul's Use of a Jewish Psalms Collection (Rom 3:10–18)*
In the course of his reflections on the advantages of the Jews, Paul exclaims, "What then: Are we any better off? No, not at all; for we have already charged that all, both Jews and Greeks, are under the power of sin" (Rom 3:9). As a demonstration of this charge, Paul presents a catena of scriptural quotations—five texts from Psalms and one from Isaiah—that detail the sins in which all people are engaged. Following is the Rom 3:10–18 catena, together with its probable LXX sources:[54]

<blockquote>

[10]Οὐκ ἔστιν δίκαιος οὐδὲ εἷς
There is not one who is righteous, not even one
Ps 13:1c: οὐκ ἔστιν ποιῶν χρηστότητα, οὐκ ἔστιν ἕως ἑνός.
Cf. *Eccl 7:20a*: ὅτι ἄνθρωπος οὐκ ἔστιν δίκαιος ἐν τῇ γῇ

[11]οὐκ ἔστιν ὁ συνίων, οὐκ ἔστιν ὁ ἐκζητῶν τὸν θεόν.
there is no one who has understanding,
there is no one who seeks God.
Ps 13:2b: τοῦ ἰδεῖν εἰ ἔστιν συνίων ἢ ἐκζητῶν τὸν θεόν.

[12]πάντες ἐξέκλιναν ἅμα ἠχρεώθησαν·
οὐκ ἔστιν ὁ ποιῶν χρηστότητα, [οὐκ ἔστιν] ἕως ἑνός.
All have turned aside, together they have become worthless; there is not one who shows kindness, there is not even one.
Ps 13:3: πάντες ἐξέκλιναν ἅμα ἠχρεώθησαν·
οὐκ ἔστιν ποιῶν χρηστότητα, οὐκ ἔστιν ἕως ἑνός.

[13]τάφος ἀνεῳγμένος ὁ λάρυγξ αὐτῶν,
ταῖς γλώσσαις αὐτῶν ἐδολιοῦσαν,
ἰὸς ἀσπίδων ὑπὸ τὰ χείλη αὐτῶν·
Their throats are opened graves;
they use their tongues to deceive;
The venom of vipers is under their lips.
Ps 5:10b: τάφος ἀνεῳγμένος ὁ λάρυγξ αὐτῶν,
ταῖς γλώσσαις αὐτῶν ἐδολιοῦσαν,
Ps 139:4: ἰὸς ἀσπίδων ὑπὸ τὰ χείλη αὐτῶν·

[14]ὧν τὸ στόμα ἀρᾶς καὶ πικρίας γέμει,
Their mouths are full of cursing and bitterness.
Ps 9:28a: οὗ ἀρᾶς τὸ στόμα αὐτοῦ γέμει καὶ πικρίας καὶ δόλου

[15]ὀξεῖς οἱ πόδες αὐτῶν ἐκχέαι αἷμα,
Their feet are swift to shed blood
Isa 59:7a: οἱ δὲ πόδες αὐτῶν ἐπὶ πονηρίαν τρέχουσι ταχινοὶ ἐκχέαι αἷμα
Cf. *Prov 1:16*: οἱ γὰρ πόδες αὐτῶν εἰς κακίαν τρέχουσιν
καὶ ταχινοὶ τοῦ ἐκχέαι αἷμα

</blockquote>

---

[54] This analysis makes use of the following discussions: Stanley, *Language of Scripture*, 87–99; Koch, *Schrift als Zeuge*, 118–19, 145, 179–84; Joseph A. Fitzmyer, *Romans: A New Translation with Introduction* (AB 33; New York/London: Doubleday, 1993) 333–39; Dunn, *Romans* 1. 144–57.

¹⁶σύντριμμα καὶ ταλαιπωρία ἐν ταῖς ὁδοῖς αὐτῶν
    ruin and misery are in their paths
    Isa 59:7c: σύντριμμα καὶ ταλαιπωρία ἐν ταῖς ὁδοῖς αὐτῶν
¹⁷καὶ ὁδὸν εἰρήνης οὐκ ἔγνωσαν.
    and the way of peace they have not known ˀ
    Isa 59:8a: καὶ ὁδὸν εἰρήνης οὐκ οἴδασι
¹⁸οὐκ ἔστιν φόβος θεοῦ ἀπέναντι τῶν ὀφθαλμῶν αὐτῶν
    There is no fear of God before their eyes
    Ps 35:2: οὐκ ἔστιν φόβος θεοῦ ἀπέναντι τῶν ὀφθαλμῶν αὐτοῦ

Unlike so many of the *testimonia* passages which we have studied, there is no need to posit a non-LXX source here. Besides the exact quotations (vv 12, 13, 16), deviations from the LXX are explicable as stylistic adaptations of an LXX *Vorlage*: singular pronouns are changes to plurals to emphasize the participation of *all* people in these wicked deeds (vv 14, 18); extraneous material is deleted and texts are shortened (vv 14, 15) to maintain a tight focus on the image of *complete* unrighteousness; some vocabulary is changed (10, 15, 17). The texts are drawn from LXX Psalms and from Isaiah 59 on the basis of thematic and vocabulary links. The image of the entire body engaged in sin is found in every text, both in the quoted material and in the wider contexts:

> *Psalm 5*: mouth, heart, throat, tongue (v 10)
> *Psalm 9*: mouth, tongue (v 28)
> *Psalm 13*: heart (v 1)
> *Psalm 35*: eyes, mouth, foot and hand (vv 2–4, 12)
> *Psalm 139*: tongue, lips, hands (vv 4, 5, 10)
> *Isaiah 59*: hands, lips, tongue, feet (vv 3, 7)

The concept of righteousness also connects these sources: the words δίκαιος, δίκη, and δικαιοσύνη occur at least once in the wider context of every Psalm and several times in Isaiah 59: Ps 5:9, 13; Ps 9:5, 9; Ps 13:5; Ps 35:7, 11; Ps 139:13, 14; and Isa 59:4, 9, 14, 17.

The evident complexity of the catena shows that Paul did not compose this *ad hoc* as he dictated Romans: he either composed it himself beforehand, or he is drawing on another written source.[55] Several factors favor the second option.

(1) *Style, Selection of Texts, and Vocabulary.* Although Paul certainly did put together composite quotations, this particular quotation is

---

[55] Stanley (*Language of Scripture*, 87–99) and Koch (*Schrift als Zeuge*, 179–84, 241) opt for previous composition by Paul.

unusually long for him.[56] Leaving aside the probably non-Pauline 2 Cor 6:16–7:1, Paul's other composite quotations use no more than two texts without an intervening remark.[57] Similarly, Paul does quote extensively from the Psalter elsewhere, but does not quote these particular texts anywhere outside this catena. He cites the larger context of Isaiah 59 only once (Isa 59:20–21 in Rom 11:26–27).[58] Vocabulary changes in the catena are also not particularly typical of Paul.[59]

(2) *Independence from context.* While thematic connections can be made with Paul's previous argument up to this point in Romans (most obviously the thesis that no one is righteous), few vocabulary links are evident, and the body imagery, so central to the catena, is wholly missing in the earlier part of the letter. The catena itself is structurally independent: it makes complete stylistic and thematic sense as it stands.

(3) *Textual Evidence.* The catena as quoted in Rom 3:13–18 is contained in numerous LXX manuscripts after Ps 13:3. This addition is remarkably well attested: it appears in all three of the oldest Old Greek textual streams of Psalms: the upper Egyptian, the lower Egyptian, and the so-called Western text, as well as in several of the versions.[60] The presence of the catena in these manuscripts is usually

---

[56] Composite quotations with no intervening remarks: Rom 9:25–26; 10:6–8; 11:26–27, 34–35; 14:11 (see Koch, *Schrift als Zeuge*, 172–86). Paul also composed conflated quotations: Rom 9:9, 25, 27, 33; 11:8, 34 (ibid., 160–72) and "chain" quotations separated only by short introductory remarks: Rom 9:12–13, 25–29; 10:5–8, 19–21; 11:8–10; 15:9–12 (see Ellis, *Paul's Use*, 186). I understand composite quotations as two or more discrete passages quoted together and conflated quotations as the insertion of part of one passage within another passage.

[57] On 2 Cor 6:16–7:1, see sect. 4.2.1f below.

[58] This last point raises a serious problem for the Stanley-Koch hypothesis: if Paul drew these texts (which support one of his central theological positions) from his personal anthology, why does he not employ these same quotations in his other writings?

[59] The substitution of ὀξεῖς for ταχινοί in v 15 is not obviously Pauline, for nowhere else does the apostle use ὀξύς. The replacement of οἴδασιν with ἔγνωσαν in v 17 is again not typical; he in fact uses οἶδα more often (16X) than γινώσκω (9X) in Romans. A significant change possibly attributable to Paul is the substitution of δίκαιος for ποιῶν χρηστότητα in 3:10. While the term δίκαιος is of course central for Paul, its widespread currency in contemporary Greco-Roman and Jewish culture does not allow it to be considered a distinctive term of the apostle.

[60] See Robert A. Kraft, "Christian Transmission of Greek Jewish Scriptures: A Methodological Probe," in A. Benoit, et. al., eds., *Paganisme*, 220–21. See the full list of witnesses given in Stanley, *Language of Scripture*, 88 n. 17. The addition is also preserved in the Syriac translation of Lucian's recension, Origen's *Hexapla* (where

explained as an example of Christian influence on the transmission of the LXX,[61] but this conclusion is by no means necessary.[62] The alternative suggestion is that this psalmic composition had reached authoritative status in a Jewish milieu and was considered scripture by Paul. When he quotes the composition in the letter, Paul expects that his Roman audience will accept it as authoritative as well.

Just as there are no compelling reasons to attribute authorship of the catena to Paul, neither are there persuasive reasons to attribute it to any Christian author. Justin knows a modified version of the catena (*Dial.* 27.3), but he is here most likely dependent on Paul.[63] A review of the rest of Justin's corpus, the apostolic fathers, and the NT itself reveals that our catena texts (the Psalms and Isaiah 59) are apparently not cited by early Christian authors outside of Romans and this passage in Justin. This fact, together with the catena's lack of obviously Christian characteristics, suggests an originally Jewish milieu for its composition.

It is possible to explore this suggested original Jewish life-setting in more detail. Formal parallels to this composite psalm are not far to seek. Already in the Hebrew scriptures themselves psalms or sections of psalms are combined to form new literary units. Psalm 70,

---

it is obelized) and the Vulgate. Its absence from codex Alexandrinus and the "Lucianic" recension is probably due to secondary correction (so Koch, *Schrift als Zeuge*, 56).

[61] See Rahlfs, *Psalmi*, 30–31; Koch, *Schrift als Zeuge*, 56; Stanley, *Language of Scripture*, 88.

[62] The following points argue against Christian influence: (1) This putative insertion is extraordinarily long in comparison to other examples of possible Christian influence on the LXX; other cases normally involve only minimal changes in vocabulary. (2) These other examples of potential Christian influence (e.g., the addition "from the tree" [ἀπὸ τοῦ ξύλου] to the phrase "he shall reign" in some mss of Ps 96 [(95):10] are virtually all christologically motivated. Our catena, however, makes no christological point, indeed it has no distinctively "Christian" emphasis to it at all. (3) Kraft has presented some further arguments ("Christian Transmission," 219–20): (a) If Christian scribes took over Paul's composition wholesale, why did the opening of the Romans catena (i.e., the adaptation of Ps 13:1c–2b) not influence the first verses of LXX Psalm 13?; (b) Why have other conflated quotations in Romans had almost no influence on LXX manuscripts?; (c) Given the catena's early and widespread textual witnesses, it is difficult to date a supposed LXX archetype that included the Romans catena *early* enough to have influenced all these far-flung witnesses by the third century, yet *late* enough to have itself been influenced by Romans as an authoritative text. Kraft adds that if one posits *independent* influence of Paul on the different textual streams, then one has difficulty explaining the relative homogeneity of the witnesses (e.g., all show no influence of Romans 3:10–11 on the Psalm).

[63] See Skarsaune, *Prophecy*, 93.

for example, is found in essentially the same form in Ps 40:14–18.[64] Psalm 108 is in fact composed from sections of two other psalms: Ps 57:8–12 and Ps 60:7–14.[65] 1 Chronicles 16:8–36 is a composition drawn from sections of Ps 105:1–15; Psalm 96; and Ps 106:46–48; (perhaps Ps 106:1).[66] The same techniques witnessed in the composition of the Romans catena are used in this latter case: limited selections are quoted, texts are adjusted to their new grammatical context, verses are omitted, and vocabulary is changed.[67] These examples illustrate two points: first, that at some stage in the development of the Hebrew Psalter, there was considerable freedom to compose new psalms from combinations of older material; secondly, that these new compositions could achieve authoritative status.

Texts from Qumran show this same tendency to compose new psalms from old, and this same openness to accepting new compositions as authoritative. A Cave 4 fragment (4QPs[a], frag. g) shows Psalm 38 and Psalm 71 written as a single composition.[68] In the much discussed 11QPsalms[a] (11Q5) scroll, several compositions not found in the MT are included alongside the canonical Hebrew Psalms, and the Psalms themselves are in a different order from the Masoretic sequence.[69] While some scholars hold that this collection is derived from the collection of the 150 Psalms of the MT,[70] James A. Sanders has made a strong case that 11QPsalms[a] is not secondary to the collection of the MT 150 but rather represents an authoritative collection

---

[64] See Marvin E. Tate, *Psalms 51–100* (WBC 20; Dallas: Word, 1990) 204.

[65] See the analysis in Leslie C. Allen, *Psalms 101–150* (WBC 21; Dallas: Word, 1983) 67.

[66] 1 Chronicles 16:34 is often said to reflect Ps 106:1, but its stereotypical language makes a sure identification difficult.

[67] Third person plural to second person plural in adapting Psalm 105; two of the four lines of Ps 96:1–2 are omitted in 1 Chr 16:23; and the "seed of Abraham" in Ps 105 is changed to "seed of Israel" (v 13). See the analysis in Roddy Braun, *1 Chronicles* (WBC 14; Dallas: Word, 1986) 192–93.

[68] See Gerald Henry Wilson, *The Editing of the Hebrew Psalter* (SBLDS 76; Chico, CA: Scholars Press, 1984) 97. There is no blank space or line between the last words of the former and the beginning words of the latter Psalm.

[69] 11Q5 is published in DJD 4; ET of additional psalms in *Scrolls*, 304–10. Wilson provides a description of the Qumran psalms scrolls (*Hebrew Psalter*, 96–116; pp. 124–25 gives a schematic of 11QPs[a]).

[70] M.H. Goshen-Gottstein ("The Psalms Scroll [11QPs[a]]: A Problem of Canon and Text," *Textus* 5 [1966] 22–33) argues that this is a liturgical collection; Patrick W. Skehan ("Qumran and Old Testament Criticism," in M. Delcor, ed., *Qumrân: sa piété, sa théologie et son milieu* [BETL 46; Louvain: Duculot, 1978] 163–82) holds that 11Q[a] is dependent on the Psalter witnessed in the MT.

in its own right.[71] This evidence, then, shows that a psalmic composition could indeed achieve authoritative status as late as the time of the Qumran community: the canon was still open, at least among some Jewish groups.

In discussing Jewish parallels to the catena, most commentators point to texts emphasizing *universal* sin (e.g., 4 Ezra 8:35: "there is no one among those who have been born who has not acted wickedly").[72] However, given the original context of the quoted psalms, in which the righteous speaker is set over against unrighteous enemies, the possibility that the catena originally referred solely to the *enemies* of the speaker should be given first priority. *Psalms of Solomon* 17:15–20 mirrors the universalistic language of the catena, but clearly applies it to a particular enemy, in this case Jews in Jerusalem who cooperated with the invading force of Pompey.[73]

> [15] And the children of the covenant (living) among the gentile rabble adopted these (practices).
> *No one among them in Jerusalem acted (with) mercy or truth.*
> (οὐκ ἦν ἐν αὐτοῖς ὁ ποιῶν ἐν Ιερουσαλημ ἔλεος καὶ ἀλήθειαν)
> [19b–20] *For there was no one among them who practiced righteousness or justice:*
> (ὅτι οὐκ ἦν ἐν αὐτοῖς ὁ ποιῶν δικαιοσύνην καὶ κρίμα.)
> From their leader to the commonest of the people, (they were) in every kind of sin.[74]

---

[71] Sanders, "Cave 11 Surprises and the Question of Canon," in D.N. Freedman and J.C. Greenfield, eds., *New Directions in Biblical Archaeology* (Garden City, NY: Doubleday, 1969) 101–16; idem, "The Qumran Psalms Scroll (11QPs^a) Reviewed," in M. Black and W. Smalley, eds., *On Language, Culture, and Religion: In Honor of Eugene A. Nida* (Approaches to Semiotics 56; The Hague/Paris: Mouton, 1974) 79–99. Sanders shows that 11QPs^b is a copy of 11QPs^a which witnesses to the same order and mixture of "canonical" and "non-canonical" texts.

[72] E.g., Fitzmyer, *Romans*, 333.

[73] ET in *OTP* 2. 651–70. The Psalms were likely composed in Hebrew in the 1st cent. BCE and translated into Greek by the 1st cent. CE (see R.B. Wright, "Introduction to the *Psalms of Solomon*," *OTP* 2. 640–41). The party of the Hasmonean Hyrcanus II had opened the gates of Jerusalem to Pompey, facilitating his conquest (see Emil Schürer; rev. eds., Geza Vermes, Fergus Millar, Matthew Black, Martin Goodman, *The History of the Jewish People in the Age of Jesus Christ (175 B.C.–A.D. 135)* [3 vols.; Edinburgh: T & T Clark, 1973] 3. 193–94).

[74] Leander Keck offers a section of the Damascus Document (CD 5:13–17) as a parallel to the Romans catena in which a string of scriptural texts condemning the wickedness and lack of discernment of sinners is combined with comments identifying the sinners with the Jerusalem priesthood. Keck suggests that this catena against sinners arose in Jewish "apocalyptic circles" ("The Function of Romans 3:10–18. Observations and Suggestions," in Jacob Jervell and Wayne A. Meeks, eds., *God's Christ and his People: Studies in Honor of N.A. Dahl* [Oslo: Universitetsforlaget, 1977] 148–49).

The life-setting in which *Psalm of Solomon* 17 was produced is also the most likely setting for the production of our catena: a group considering themselves righteous polemicizes against sinners, be they gentiles or Jewish supporters of the gentiles. For these "righteous" groups, the catena was accepted as an authoritative addition to scripture.

(f) *A Temple* Testimonia *Collection in 2 Cor 6:16–7:1*
The passage begins with admonitions for the addressees (identified as believers, and associated with righteousness, light, the temple of God, and Christ) to avoid contact with unbelievers (associated with lawlessness, darkness, Beliar, and idols) on the grounds that "we are the temple of the living God." A TC then follows, introduced by "as God says":

> I will live in them and walk among them, and I will be their God, and they shall be my people. (Lev 26:11–12 with Ezek 37:27)
> Therefore come out from them, and be separate from them, says the Lord, and touch nothing unclean; (Isa 52:11)
> then I will welcome you, (Ezek 20:34)
> and I will be your father, and you will be my sons and daughters, says the Lord Almighty. (2 Sam 7:14/7:8)[75]

The texts thus function to portray the community as God's chosen people, separate from all uncleanness. With most scholars, I see this composition as non-Pauline.[76] Several observations lead to this conclusion: (1) The passage interrupts the flow of Paul's argument;[77] (2) the passage itself forms a coherent, self-contained unit; (3) key vocabulary of the passage is not only non-Pauline, but also includes several words that are *hapax legomena* in both the NT and LXX;[78] (4) the theological vision of the unit has more affinity with Qumran sectarian documents than with Paul's usual positions.

We have here a carefully constructed TC which Paul has either taken over, or—more likely—has been interpolated into his Corinthian

---

[75] See the detailed analysis in Stanley, *Language of Scripture*, 217–30.

[76] See Joseph A. Fitzmyer, "Qumran and the Interpolated Paragraph in 2 Cor 6:14–7:1," *CBQ* 23 (1961) 271–80; repr. in idem, *Semitic Background*, 205–17; Victor Paul Furnish (*II Corinthians* [AB 32A; Garden City, NY: Doubleday, 1984] 375–83) provides a thorough discussion of the issues.

[77] In 2 Cor 6:11–13, Paul admonishes the Corinthians to "open their hearts"; 7:2 resumes that theme.

[78] ἑτεροζυγέω; μετοχή; συμφώνησις; συγκατάθεσις; Βελιάρ; μολυσμός; see Fitzmyer, "Interpolated Paragraph," 206–7.

correspondence. Fitzmyer concludes that the passage represents "Qumran ideas and expressions [that] have been reworked in a Christian cast of thought"; Hans Dieter Betz finds in this passage an expression of the theological position of Paul's *opponents* as found in the letter to the Galatians.[79] In any case, we have here another example of a carefully crafted early Christian TC, expressing a position common in the *testimonia* literature: Christians as the chosen people of God.[80]

(g) *Paul and Other NT* Testimonia

For discussion of Paul's participation in wider NT *testimonia* traditions—the use of Ps 110:1 and the "hardening" tradition (based on Isa 6:9–10)—see sections 5.2 and 5.4 below.

4.2.2 *Conclusions*

Already by Paul's time, extensive Christian reflection on scripture had produced *authoritative* scriptural traditions and collections. This is clear in the formula κατὰ τὰς γραφάς in 1 Cor 15:3b–5 and in the scriptural background to authoritative christological formulas (Rom 1:3–4; 3:24–26; 4:25). Scriptural reflection, then, was a central part of the Christian catechetical tradition as it is reflected in Paul.

In addition to these Christian traditions, Paul also has taken over *testimonia* from Jewish sources. Isaiah 11:10 (Rom 15:12) is a well established Jewish messianic *testimonium*; Jewish traditions have been incorporated into Paul's parenesis (Rom 12:19), his versions of the Decalogue (Rom 13:9–10), and his church orders (2 Cor 13:1). Rom 3:10–18 is an extended Jewish reflection on unrighteousness that Paul has likely placed for the first time in a Christian context. While the parenetic material and church orders could conceivably be writ-

---

[79] Ibid., 217; Betz, "2 Cor 6:14–7:1: An Anti-Pauline Fragment?" *JBL* 92 (1973) 88–108; repr. in idem, *Paulinische Studien: Gesammelte Aufsätze III* (Tübingen: Mohr-Siebeck, 1994) 20–45.

[80] Hodgson ("Testimony," 371) notes similarities between this Corinthians passage and Revelation 21: temple imagery (2 Cor 6:16; Rev 21:3, 22); God as παντοκράτωρ (2 Cor 6:18; Rev 21:22); and the common use of Lev 26:12/Ezek 37:27 (allusion in Rev 21:3) and 2 Sam 7:14 (allusion in Rev 21:7). While the connections are not close enough to speak strictly of a common TC, the use of the Leviticus and 2 Samuel quotations may certainly be seen as part of a more general *testimonia* tradition witnessing to beliefs in God's special selection (cf. also the messianic use of 2 Samuel 7 in Christian TCs and its use in 4QEschatological Midrash).

ten or oral, the collections in Rom 3:10–18 and 11:25–27 certainly were known to Paul in written form.

The scriptural traditions behind the κατὰ τὰς γραφάς in 1 Cor 15:3b–5 and behind the christological formulas in Romans were of fundamental importance for early Christians. It seems clear that these phrases were meant to invoke scriptural patterns as a whole, in particular the pattern of the suffering chosen one who is ultimately vindicated by God. Such scriptures would not necessarily have the force of forensic proof-texts or proofs-from-prophecy, rather, they suggest that the Christ events fit into (or indeed consummate) an overall scriptural pattern. At the same time, texts such as Isaiah 53 played an undeniably important role in this early Christian reflection, and we can well imagine that collections of scriptural *exempla* were composed to illustrate the pattern of God's vindication of his righteous one(s).

4.3   *The Formula Citations in Matthew*

Within the Gospel of Matthew's numerous explicit quotations of scripture is a distinct group that has been called "formula citations."[81] These ten to fourteen quotations accompany narratives of events in Jesus' life, and indicate with a relatively fixed formula (ἵνα πληρωθῇ τὸ ῥηθέν) that these events took place to fulfill a scriptural prophecy. The uncertainty about the number is a result of disagreement over how to categorize some quotations with "incomplete" formulas. In addition to their common citation formula, the quotations are characterized by non-standard texts (although often closer to the Hebrew than the LXX) and contact with various Greek, Hebrew, and Aramaic interpretive traditions.[82]

Investigation of the peculiarities of this group of Matthew's quotations was the catalyst for much early *testimonia* scholarship.[83] Their complexity led Stendahl to posit a "school of St. Matthew" that

---

[81] This group is also referred to as "fulfillment" citations; in German they have been called *Reflexionszitate* (alluding to the process of scriptural reflection behind these quotations); see Brown, *The Birth of the Messiah: A Commentary on the Infancy Narratives in the Gospels of Matthew and Luke* (AB Reference Library; updated ed.; New York/London: Doubleday, 1993) 96 n. 1. I follow Brown in the use of the term "formula citation."

[82] See Strecker, *Weg*, 82.

[83] Already Credner, *Urevangelium* (1838).

employed sophisticated scribal techniques (e.g., *pesher* interpretations; collection and selection of useful variants) to produce them.[84] Gundry, rejecting both the *testimonia* and the school model, attributes the scribal sophistication to the evangelist himself.[85]

4.3.1 Overview of the Formula Citations in Matthew

To give a quick overview of the formula quotations and their functions, I present the chart below.[86] The quotations function to show that these events in the life of Jesus occurred in order to fulfill scripture, thus demonstrating that the events of Jesus' life are part of God's preordained plan recorded in scripture.

Matthew	Scripture	Function: Events which fulfill scripture
1:22–23	Isa 7:14	Mary conceived Jesus by the Holy Spirit
2:6	Mic 5:2/2 Sam 5:2	The messiah to be born in Bethlehem
2:15b	Hos 11:1	Child Jesus journeys to Egypt
2:17–18	Jer 31:15 (38:15)	Herod slaughters the infants
2:23b	UQ	Jesus lives in Nazareth
3:3	Isa 40:3	The Baptist preaches in the wilderness
4:14–16	Isa 8:23–9:1	Jesus lives in Zebulun and Naphtali
8:17	Isa 53:4	Jesus heals the sick
12:17–21	Isa 42:1–4	Jesus heals, but orders people not to make him known

[84] See sect. 1.16.3 above.

[85] For Gundry (*Use of the Old Testament*, 172) Matthew "was his own targumist and drew on a knowledge of the Hebrew, Aramaic, and Greek textual traditions of the OT."

[86] I base this on the listing in Brown, *Birth of the Messiah*, 98. Brown marks Matt 2:5b–6; 3:3; 13:14–15; and 26:56 as uncertain examples of formula citations.

(table cont.)

Matthew	Scripture	Function: Events which fulfill scripture
13:14–15	Isa 6:9–10	Listeners will not understand Jesus' parables
13:35	Ps 78:2	Jesus speaks in parables[87]
21:4–5	Isa 62:11/Zech 9:9	Jesus enters Jerusalem on "a donkey and a colt"
26:56 (cf. 26:54)	general reference to the "scriptures of the prophets"	Jesus is arrested[88]
27:9–10	Zech 11:12–13 with references to Jeremiah, to whom it is attributed	The chief priests buy the potter's field with thirty pieces of silver

We can make some general comparisons with the patristic TCs studied in the last chapter. (1) Some of the citation quotations are widespread Christian *testimonia* (Isa 6:9–10; 7:14; Zech 9:9), but more often they are idiosyncratic. Even the quotation of the famous passion *testimonium* Isa 53:4 is not applied to Jesus' passion, but functions as a witness to Jesus' healings. (2) Matthew shows a greater interest in the details of Jesus' life (in particular Jesus' infancy) in contrast to the creedal emphasis (with its particular focus on Jesus' suffering, death, and resurrection) of the wider *testimonia* tradition. (3) Matthew's collection has standard characteristics of a TC: conflated readings, false attributions, an unknown quotation, and (to some extent) parallels in other writers.[89]

---

[87] The quotation is introduced ambiguously διὰ τοῦ προφήτου (א* Θ f¹ f¹³ vgᵐˢ); patristic witnesses read διὰ Ἡσαΐου.

[88] Unlike most of the others, this citation is spoken not by the narrator but by Jesus himself.

[89] The latter criterion is inconclusive: other writers (e.g., Justin) depend on Matthew for at least some of their *testimonia*.

4.3.2 *Evidence for a* Testimonia *Collection Behind Matthew's Formula Citations*

In the following, I will investigate three of the quotations in some detail, with two main questions in mind. First, I will explore the relationship between each formula quotation and its accompanying narrative. Is the quotation the basis from which the narratives was developed, or was the quotation added as proof or illustration of an already existing narrative?[90] Secondly, I will consider whether the evangelist himself selected the quotations or drew upon a source. Answering this second question involves the standard analysis of establishing the source of the quotation, consideration of the Jewish background and early Christian parallels to the passage, and comparing the quotation with the particular theological intentions and literary style of Matthew.

(a) *Matt 2:6 (Mic 5:1/2 Sam 5:2)*

In response to Herod's question concerning where the messiah is to be born, the μάγοι respond with the following conflated text (Matt 2:4–6). This particular form differs from other formula citations in its lack of πληρόω:

> *Matt 2:6*: Καὶ σὺ Βηθλέεμ, γῆ Ἰούδα, οὐδαμῶς ἐλαχίστη εἶ ἐν τοῖς ἡγεμόσιν Ἰούδα·
> ἐκ σοῦ γὰρ ἐξελεύσεται ἡγούμενος, ὅστις ποιμανεῖ τὸν λαόν μου τὸν Ἰσραήλ.
> And you, Bethlehem, in the land of Judah, are by no means least among the rulers of Judah; for from you shall come a ruler who is to shepherd my people Israel.
> *LXX Mic 5:1*: Καὶ σύ, Βηθλεεμ οἶκος τοῦ Εφραθα, ὀλιγοστὸς εἶ τοῦ εἶναι ἐν χιλιάσιν Ιουδα· ἐκ σοῦ μοι ἐξελεύσεται τοῦ εἶναι εἰς ἄρχοντα ἐν τῷ Ισραηλ, καὶ αἱ ἔξοδοι αὐτοῦ ἀπ᾽ ἀρχῆς ἐξ ἡμερῶν αἰῶνος.
> *MT Mic 5:1*: וְאַתָּה בֵּית־לֶחֶם אֶפְרָתָה צָעִיר לִהְיוֹת בְּאַלְפֵי יְהוּדָה מִמְּךָ לִי יֵצֵא לִהְיוֹת מוֹשֵׁל בְּיִשְׂרָאֵל
> But you, O Bethlehem of Ephrathah, who are one of the little clans of Judah, from you shall come forth for me one who is to rule in Israel
> *2 Kingdoms 5:2 (2 Sam 5:2)*: καὶ εἶπεν κύριος πρὸς σέ Σὺ ποιμανεῖς τὸν λαόν μου τὸν Ισραηλ, καὶ σὺ ἔσει εἰς ἡγούμενον ἐπὶ τὸν Ισραηλ.

Matthew's text of Mic 5:1 (5:2 ET) differs strongly from both the MT and the LXX (which essentially follows the MT). Matthew's

---

[90] See Brown, *Birth of the Messiah*, 99, on these alternatives.

reading shortens the text (e.g., by dropping the reference to Ephraim); explicitly denies the plain meaning of the first phrase of the LXX and MT ("you are too small"/"[you are] small" is replaced by "you are by no means the least"); and ἄρχων (מושל) is replaced by ἡγούμενος. The quotation's intent is plain: a tendentious insistence on the importance of *Bethlehem* as the birthplace of the ruler. The addition of a phrase from 2 Sam 5:2 (referring to David's rule over Israel) emphasizes the point that this ruler is to be Davidic.

The most likely life-setting for this quotation is within early Christian apologetical attempts to prove that Jesus is the messiah born in Bethlehem.[91] This scenario is explicitly played out in John 7:40–42, where "the crowd" debates whether the messiah could come from Galilee, when scripture indicates that he must come from Bethlehem. While the current form of the Matthew quotation is most likely due to Christian adaptation, it is possible that our text is originally a Jewish messianic composition.[92]

The accompanying story (Matt 2:1–12) of the visit of the magi can hardly have been developed out of the Micah/2 Samuel composite quotation—the quotation touches only one detail of the narrative.[93] The quotation, then, was put together independently from the narrative. For Brown, this independence indicates that Matthew himself has added the quotation. This may well be true, but we must ask further: where did Matthew get the quotation? If Matthew was simply seeking a proof-text to illustrate the story of the magi, it makes little sense that he would go to the trouble of altering Mic 5:1 and adding 2 Sam 5:2 for good measure.[94] Lindars rightly sees

---

[91] See Brown, *Birth of the Messiah*, 186 (Christian emphasis on Bethlehem); Stendahl, *School*, 100 (Christian change to ἡγούμενος); Lindars, *Apologetic*, 189–94.

[92] Targum Jonathan to the Prophets interprets thus: "from you shall come forth before Me the Messiah, to exercise dominion over Israel, he whose name was mentioned from before, from the days of creation" (see Samson H. Levey, *The Messiah: An Aramaic Interpretation, The Messianic Exegesis of the Targum* [HUCM 2; Cincinnati/New York: Hebrew Union College-Jewish Institute of Religion, 1974] 93).

[93] This is not deny the profound influence of other scriptures on this narrative. Brown (*Birth of the Messiah*, 190–96) holds the plausible position that the story of the magi was developed out of reflection on the Balaam narrative, including the oracle of the star that would rise from Judah (Num 24:17).

[94] Even Brown, who argues for Matthew's creative role in adding the quotations, is willing to entertain the possibility of a pre-Matthean Christianized reading: "One may theorize that the text of Micah 5:1 came to Matthew in a form already fixed by Christian usage—a form different from the standard versions we know" (*Birth of the Messiah*, 186). Brown adds that the hypothesis of a fixed text would explain

this as a product of pre-Matthean apologetic activity, but his model of oral tradition cannot explain the complex conflated text: the likeliest possibility is that Matthew drew on a written *testimonia* source compiled to prove that the messiah would be born in Bethlehem.

The Mic 5:1/2 Sam 5:2 conflation occurs in the later *testimonia* tradition (Justin *1 Apol.* 34.1; *Dial.* 78.1; Irenaeus *Proof* 63). The exact correspondence of these quotations with Matthew's, however, shows that Justin and Irenaeus were simply copying Matthew's text.

(b) *Matt 2:23 (Unknown Quotation)*

On the return of Joseph, Mary, and the infant Jesus from Egypt, Joseph is warned in a dream not to return to Judea; he instead goes to Galilee.

> There he made his home in a town called Nazareth, so that what had been spoken through the prophets might be fulfilled, "He will be called a Nazorean" (Ναζωραῖος κληθήσεται). (Matt 2:23)

The source of this quotation in the Jewish scriptures is not at all clear, and thus the quotation has been the occasion for extensive scholarly speculation.[95] It is possible that the citation intends no one scriptural passage, but rather refers to a group of related passages. Three explanations for the term Ναζωραῖος should be considered: (1) that the name derives from Nazareth; (2) that the name recalls a Nazirite (נזיר), a person consecrated to God by a vow (see Num 6:1–21; Judg 13:5–7 [Sampson]; 1 Sam 1:11 [Samuel]); and (3) that the name recalls the messianic "branch" (נצר) (see Isa 11:1).[96] The second proposal is less likely than the others, as these scriptural passages seem to have been little used by early Christians.[97] Given the messianic interest of the citations formulas, the best conclusion is that the quotation results from an effort to show that Jesus was the messiah by relating נצר to Nazareth, the known hometown of Jesus.

---

the differences between Matthew's reading "Bethlehem of Judea" (2:1, 5a) and "Bethlehem (in the) land of Judah" in the Micah quotation (ibid., 186); see also Strecker, *Weg*, 57, for the judgment that the quotation text is pre-Matthean.

[95] The following discussion draws on Lindars, *Apologetic*, 194–96, and Brown, *Birth of the Messiah*, 207–13, 218–19, 223–25.

[96] On the messianic understanding of Isa 11:1 in Second Temple Judaism and early Christianity, see sect. 5.2 above.

[97] So Lindars, *Apologetic*, 194 n. 2, but Brown (*Birth of the Messiah*, 223–25) argues that the term "Nazarite" played at least some role in the development of Matthew's quotation.

Matthew's citation, then, refers primarily to a messianically under-stood Isa 11:1, but may also refer to related passages.[98]

Again it is unlikely that Matthew is responsible for this citation. His clumsy application of the quotation—in the context, the gram-matical subject of "He shall be called a Nazarene" should be Joseph!—suggests that he is taking over a source. If Matthew had chosen a proof-text himself, one would expect that he would have clearly cited the authoritative scripture from which it came. These considerations lead to the conclusion that Matthew has drawn on a collection of messianic proof-texts that had been applied to Jesus, a collection that he considered to be authoritative scripture.[99]

(c) *Matt 12:18–21 (Isa 42:1–4)*

Full synoptic comparisons of Matt 12:18–21 and Greek, Hebrew, Syriac, and Aramaic versions of Isa 42:1–4 are set out by Stendahl and Gundry.[100] Matthew introduces this long quotation from Isaiah in the following way (Matt 12:15–17):

> When Jesus became aware of this [i.e., the Pharisees' plot to kill him], he departed. Many crowds followed him, and he cured all of them, and he ordered them not to make him known. This was to fulfill that had been spoken through the prophet Isaiah:

> *Matt 12:18a*: Ἰδοὺ <u>ὁ παῖς μου</u> ὃν ᾑρέτισα, ὁ ἀγαπητός μου εἰς ὃν εὐδόκησεν <u>ἡ ψυχή μου·</u>
> Here is my servant, whom I have chosen, my beloved, with whom my soul is well pleased.
> *LXX Isa 42:1a*: Ιακωβ <u>ὁ παῖς μου</u>, ἀντιλήμψομαι αὐτοῦ· Ισραηλ ὁ ἐκλεκτός μου, προσεδέξατο αὐτὸν <u>ἡ ψυχή μου·</u>
> *MT Isa 42:1a*: הן עבדי אתמך־בו בחירי רצתה נפשׁי
> Here is my servant, whom I uphold, my chosen, in whom my soul delights

Matthew's quotation is closer to the Hebrew, deviating strongly from the LXX, which gives a corporate interpretation to the servant figure

---

[98] Brown (*Birth of the Messiah*, 212) notes that the נצר of Isa 11:1 would have evoked other groups of words that carried similar messianic weight, e.g., "shoot" (צמח) (Jer 23:5; 33:15; Zech 3:8; 6:12) and "root" (נזע) (Isa 11:1; cf. Rev 5:5; 22:16); Lindars (*Apologetic*, 195–96) considers Isa 49:6 (נציר) a likely further reference (see Lindars for discussion of the range of meanings of this word).

[99] Again this quotation can hardly have been the basis for the accompanying narrative. The knowledge that Jesus was from Nazareth is primary; this knowledge led to an effort to connect his hometown with scriptural references.

[100] Stendahl, *School*, 107–8; Gundry, *Use of the Old Testament*, 110.

("Israel" and "Jacob"). The designations παῖς (LXX) and ἀγαπητός (LXX-deviant) have wider associations in Christian reflection: παῖς is used in the speeches in Acts (3:13, 26; 4:27, 30) and may be one of the earliest designations for Jesus;[101] ἀγαπητός (not found in any Greek version of Isa 42:1) is found in the accounts of the heavenly voice at Jesus' baptism (Mark 1:11 par.) and transfiguration (Mark 9:7 par.); these NT accounts themselves show the influence of applications of Ps 2:7, Deut 18:15, and Gen 22:2 to the life and work of Jesus.[102] These simple designations already reveal a complex Christian reflection involving Isa 42:1–4; Ps 2:7; Deut 18:15; and Gen 22:2 on Jesus as God's chosen one (i.e., his "messiah").[103]

> *Matt 12:18b*: θήσω τὸ πνεῦμά μου ἐπ' αὐτόν, καὶ κρίσιν τοῖς ἔθνεσιν ἀπαγγελεῖ.
> I will put my spirit upon him, and he will proclaim justice to the Gentiles.
> *LXX Isa 42:1b*: ἔδωκα τὸ πνεῦμά μου ἐπ' αὐτόν, κρίσιν τοῖς ἔθνεσιν ἐξοίσει.
> *MT Isa 42:1b*: נתתי רוחי עליו משפט לגוים יוציא
> I have put my spirit upon him; he will bring forth justice to the nations.
> *Tg. Isa 42:1b*: אתין רוח קודשי עלוהי דיני לעממין ינלי[104]

Matthew's θήσω and ἀπαγγελεῖ. are both closer to the targum's reading than to either the LXX or the MT.[105]

> *Matt 12:19*: οὐκ ἐρίσει οὐδὲ κραυγάσει, οὐδὲ ἀκούσει τις ἐν ταῖς πλατείαις τὴν φωνὴν αὐτοῦ.
> He will not wrangle or cry aloud, nor will anyone hear his voice in the streets.
> *LXX Isa 42:2*: οὐ κεκράξεται οὐδὲ ἀνήσει, οὐδὲ ἀκουσθήσεται ἔξω ἡ φωνὴ αὐτοῦ.
> *MT Isa 42:2*: לא יצעק ולא ישא ולא־ישמיע בחוץ קולו
> He will not cry or lift up his voice, or make it heard in the street

---

[101] See Joachim Jeremias, "παῖς θεοῦ in the New Testament," *TDNT* 5. 700–717.

[102] Psalm 2:7 has influenced the reading "You are my son" in the baptism accounts; the Synoptic accounts of the transfiguration all add αὐτοῦ ἀκούετε, a clear reference to Deut 18:15 (see Lindars, *Apologetic*, 144–47). On pre-Christian Jewish messianic interpretation of Psalm 2 see Collins, *Scepter*, 56; 163–67; on Deut 18:15–19, see ibid., 113. On the influence of Gen 22:2 on the use of ἀγαπητός, see William Richard Stegner, *Narrative Theology in Early Jewish Christianity* (Louisville, KY: Westminster/John Knox, 1989) 17–20.

[103] Luke's version of the transfiguration reads ἐκλελεγμένος (9:35), reflecting the reading of Isa 42:1!

[104] Aramaic text and ET in J.F. Stenning, ed., *The Targum on Isaiah* (Oxford: Clarendon, 1949).

[105] See Gundry, *Use of the Old Testament*, 113.

Stendahl holds that Matthew's ἐρίσει reflects knowledge of an Eastern Syriac rendering found in the OT Peshitta, but this suggestion is unnecessary, as it is also a viable translation of the Hebrew צעק.[106] The second phrase is active, in contrast to the passive construction of both the LXX and the Hebrew.

> *Matt 12:20*: <u>κάλαμον</u> συντετριμμένον οὐ κατεάξει <u>καὶ λίνον</u> τυφόμενον <u>οὐ σβέσει</u>,
> ἕως ἂν ἐκβάλῃ εἰς νῖκος τὴν <u>κρίσιν</u>.
> He will not break a bruised reed or quench a smoldering wick until he brings justice to victory.
> *LXX Isa 42:3*: <u>κάλαμον</u> τεθλασμένον οὐ συντρίψει <u>καὶ λίνον</u> καπνιζόμενον <u>οὐ σβέσει</u>, ἀλλὰ εἰς ἀλήθειαν ἐξοίσει κρίσιν.
> *MT Isa 42:3*: קנה רצוץ לא ישבור ופשתה כהה לא יכבנה לאמת יוציא משפט
> a bruised reed he will not break, and a dimly burning wick he will not quench;
> *MT Hab 1:4*: יצא לנצח משפט

Matthew continues the quotation with a deviant, although essentially synonymous, rendering of LXX Isa 42:3ab, omitting Isa 42:3c: "but he shall bring forth judgment to truth" and v 4a: "He shall shine out and not be discouraged." Matthew's εἰς νῖκος is commonly understood as a translation of לנצח drawn from a similar context in Hab 1:4.[107] If this is so, the catch-word connection was made originally at the level of the Hebrew, as the Greek renderings differ.[108]

> *Matt 12:21*: καὶ τῷ ὀνόματι αὐτοῦ ἔθνη ἐλπιοῦσιν.
> And in his name the Gentiles will hope.
> *LXX Isa 42:4b*: καὶ ἐπὶ τῷ ὀνόματι αὐτοῦ ἔθνη ἐλπιοῦσιν.[109]
> *MT Isa 42:4b*: ולתורתו איים ייחילו
> and the coastlands wait for his teaching.

This last phrase closely follows the LXX, which itself deviates considerably from the Hebrew.

An adequate analysis of this quotation must make use both of Stendahl's "school" model and Lindars's developmental schema. Stendahl's proposal helps account for the sheer complexity of the textual traditions (Greek, Hebrew, Aramaic), together with the variety of scholarly techniques used. The conflation with other scriptural

---

[106] Stendahl, *School*, 111–12; see the criticism in Gundry, *Use of the Old Testament*, 113–14.
[107] So ibid., 114–15; Stendahl, *School*, 113; Lindars, *Apologetic*, 149.
[108] Gundry, *Use of the Old Testament*, 115 n. 1.
[109] Rahlfs (*Psalms*, 277) prints ἐπὶ τῷ νόμῳ, following the MT.

texts, the careful selection of variant translations and (possibly) independent translations of the Hebrew, the careful redaction of vocabulary and syntax—all of these techniques presuppose the work of a
trained scribe or group of scribes. The use of a range of textual traditions suggests access to a library (cf. the Qumran collection), while
the messianic reflections in v 18 presuppose contact with Christian
written or oral teachings.

At the same time, Lindars's view that different stages of theological reflection can be discerned in this passage has much to com-
mend it.[110] While Lindars is more precise in isolating these "stages"
and their "logical" development than the evidence allows, he is profoundly correct in finding evidence for a variety of theological agen-
das in this passage. We have in Matt 12:15–18 no mere quotation,
but creative scriptural reflection using techniques of active adaptation. Lindars discerned four different apologetical goals in the passage: adaptations to illustrate or "prove" Jesus' resurrection ("Behold
my servant"), baptismal designation as messiah (use of "my beloved"),
the quietness or gentleness of Christ's ministry (Isa 42:2 adapted
in Matt 12:19), and an apologetic for the ministry to the gentiles
("and in his name the Gentiles will hope"). While these passages
do not necessarily imply logical or temporal stages, they do indicate
that the quotation was likely reworked at different times for distinct
purposes.

Jerome H. Neyrey also finds multiple theological claims in this
passage, but attributes this variety to Matthew's redactional creativity. He judges the various phrases of the Isa 43:1–4 quotation to be
"major thematic statements in the episodes recorded in the narrative of chaps. 11–13."[111] Neyrey matches each phrase with a central
topic in this section of the Gospel: (1) God's commissioning ("Behold
my servant"); (2) discussion of whose spirit Jesus has ("I shall place
my spirit"); (3) Jesus' address to believers, especially gentiles ("he will
announce judgment to the nations"); (4) Jesus' refusal to give a sign
("he will not wrangle or cry aloud"); (5) opponents (e.g., the scribes
and Pharisees) refusing to hear Jesus; (6) the healing activity of Jesus
("he will not break a bruised reed"); (7) judgment announced against

---

[110] See sect. 1.13 above for further discussion of Lindars's positions.
[111] Neyrey, "The Thematic Use of Isaiah 42, 1–4 in Matthew 12," *Bib* 63 (1982)
471.

unbelievers ("until he brings justice to victory"); (8) God's servant named ("and in his name the Gentiles will hope"). Neyrey ingeniously, if not always convincingly, connects these phrases with pericopes in Matthew 11–13.[112]

Against Neyrey's proposal that the passage reflects Matthew's particular redactional interests, one can note that the "themes" which he isolates reflect more general Christian concerns, rather than particularly Matthean interests. I am more inclined to accept Strecker's view, that the Isaiah quotation represents a "surplus" when compared with Matthew's context in chapter 12, that is, this complex quotation outruns its proof-text value for Matthew's immediate context.[113]

Instead of attributing both this scribal virtuosity and the multiple theological viewpoints to a single super-redactor, we must again have recourse, as often in *testimonia* study, to a "school" life-setting. Isaiah 42:1–4, perhaps as part of a larger scriptural collection, would have been passed down in a school that was reflecting on the connections between scripture and the life of Jesus. The passage would have been reworked by different hands over a period of time.

Justin preserves an important variation on this tradition. In *Dial.* 123.8, Justin quotes a mixed text: Isa 41:1a, 3b–4 are LXX, while vv 1b–3a follow Matthew's reading. Justin has not copied directly from Matthew here: the apologist retains "Jacob" and "Israel" in Isa 41:1a, which Matthew deletes; indeed, Justin's desire to prove that Jesus is also called "Jacob" and "Israel" are his motivation for quoting the passage in the first place. Skarsaune tentatively concludes that Justin here is using a *testimonia* source that has been influenced by Matthew.[114] The passage remained influential in the *testimonia* tradition: both Tertullian *A.J.* 9.30 (par. *Marc.* 4.23) and Cyprian *Quir.* 2.13 use Isa 42:2–4 as a proof-text for Christ's humility.[115]

---

[112] E.g., his view that "he will not break a bruised reed" applies to Jesus' healings seems forced.

[113] Strecker, *Weg*, 69–70, 83.

[114] Skarsaune, *Prophecy*, 60. In *Dial.* 135.2 Justin reads a more strictly LXX text of Isa 42:1–4, although even here there are influences from Matthew that Skarsaune would attribute to textual contaminations (ibid.). Hilgenfeld interpreted the connections between Matthew and *Dial.* 123.8 as evidence for a common source drawn on by both writers ("Citate Justin's," 571).

[115] A passage from Isaiah 53 precedes this quotation in both authors.

4.3.3 *Conclusions*

The above discussion presented evidence that Matthew has taken
over a *testimonia* source that correlated scriptural proof-texts with
events in the life of Jesus. Quotations in Matt 2:6 and 2:23 show a
marked interest in proving messianic claims; the quotation in Matt
12:18–21 seems to serve a more complex function of correlating
Jesus' ministry with scripture. The accompanying narratives have not
been composed on the basis of the quotations; rather the scribe seems
to have known an event in Jesus' life (born in Bethlehem; raised in
Nazareth) and sought scriptural witness for the event.

The complexity of the quotations argues that they derive from a
"school" familiar with scribal techniques. The evidence of the Isa
42:1–4 quotation suggests that it was reworked by scribes over some
period of time before its incorporation in Matthew's Gospel.

4.4   Testimonia *in the Speeches in Acts*

The speeches in Acts 1–15, with their presentation of early Christian
preaching supported by numerous proof-texts, have long been a rich
mine for *testimonia* research.[116] In this section I will first evaluate the
recent work of Traugott Holtz on Luke's use of *testimonia*; I then
turn to two case studies in the Acts speeches where Luke apparently
draws on *testimonia* sources: Peter's speech at Solomon's Portico (Acts
3:11–26) and Paul's discourse at Pisidian Antioch (Acts 13:16b–41).

4.4.1   *Traugott Holtz: Luke's Limited Knowledge of the LXX and Use of* Testimonia

The work of Traugott Holtz is perhaps the most important recent
treatment of the *testimonia* question in Luke-Acts.[117] Setting himself

---

[116] Harris, *Testimonies* 2. 77–83; Lucien Cerfaux, "Citations scripturaires et tradition textuelle dans le Livre des Actes," in *Aux sources de la tradition chretienne: Mélanges
M. Goguel* (Bibliothèque theologique; Neuchâtel: Delachaux & Niestle, 1950) 43–51;
repr. in idem, *Recueil Cerfaux* 2. 93–103, esp. 100–101; F.F. Bruce, *The Acts of the
Apostles: The Greek Text with Introduction and Commentary* (3d ed.; Grand Rapids: Eerdmans;
Leicester: Apollos, 1990) 110–11, 151, 157, 207, 305–6, 310, 436, 504. One intriguing, if ultimately unpersuasive, argument is that Acts 26:23 represents a series of
headings from a messianic TC, used by Paul as a kind of shorthand in his speech
to King Agrippa (Harris, *Testimonies* 1. 19–20; Bruce, *Acts*, 504).

[117] Holtz, *Zitate bei Lukas*.

the task of determining the sources of Luke's scriptural quotations, Holtz concludes that Luke's first-hand knowledge of the LXX was limited to the Twelve Prophets, Isaiah, and Psalms; for his references to the Pentateuch and the historical books he depended on other sources, including quotations in Mark, catechetical traditions,[118] Jewish historical summaries (Acts 7; 13), and messianic *testimonia*.[119] Holtz relies especially on the criteria of LXX-deviant forms, parallel ("traditional") uses of the quotations in contemporary Jewish or early Christian authors, and Luke's apparent lack of awareness of scriptural context.

Holtz's proposal concerning Luke's limited knowledge of the LXX is open to several criticisms: (1) he underestimates Luke's own stylistic or theological adaptation and shaping of quotations; (2) he does not give sufficient consideration to Luke's use of other non-LXX texts (e.g., revisions towards the Hebrew); (3) he makes the unwarranted leap from Luke's *non-use* of a source to the conclusion that Luke *did not know* the source; and (4) he does not take sufficient account of Luke's scriptural allusions.[120] Nevertheless, Holtz's work is of great value in renewing scholarly debate on the precise nature of the sources of Luke's scriptural quotations.

4.4.2 *Evidence for Luke's Use of* Testimonia *Collections in the Speeches of Acts*

(a) *Acts 3:22–25: A* Testimonia *Collection on the Day of Atonement*
In his speech at Solomon's portico (Acts 3:12–26), Peter argues that although "the Israelites" killed "the Author of life," they did so out

---

[118] Luke 10:27 quotes the LXX-deviant conflation of Deut 6:5 and Lev 19:18 (Luke's quotation deviates from the synoptic parallels) with no awareness that two separate texts are involved (ibid., 64–68). Stendahl (*School*, 73–76) explains the LXX-deviant readings of the *shema* in the NT as due to catechetical or liturgical use. Luke 18:20, a partial listing of the decalogue, differs both from the parallel in Mark 10:19 and from the LXX (see Holtz, *Zitate bei Lukas*, 81–82). Stendahl also concludes that this variety is due to the influence of different catechetical traditions (*School*, 62). On the use of such a catechetical tradition in Rom 13:8–10, see above 4.2.1d.

[119] See Holtz's conclusions, *Zitate bei Lukas*, 169–73.

[120] For critiques, see Martin Rese, *Alttestamentliche Motive in der Christologie des Lukas* (SNT 1; Gütersloh: Mohn, 1969) 211–16; Darrell L. Bock, *Proclamation from Prophecy and Pattern: Lucan Old Testament Christology* (JSNTSup 12; Sheffield: JSOT, 1986) 14–16; Wayne Douglas Litke, "Luke's Knowledge of the Septuagint: A Study of the Citations in Luke-Acts" (Ph.D. diss., McMaster University, 1993) 19–20. Rese and Litke assign a much greater role to Luke's creative composition than does Holtz.

of ignorance, thereby fulfilling the scriptural prophecy that God's
messiah would suffer. He urges his audience to repent so that God
might send the messiah Jesus from heaven when the time for universal restoration foretold in the prophets occurs (vv 17–21). Then
the following quotation, attributed to Moses is given (vv 22–23):

> *Acts 3:22–23*: Προφήτην ὑμῖν ἀναστήσει κύριος ὁ θεὸς ὑμῶν ἐκ τῶν ἀδελφῶν
> ὑμῶν ὡς ἐμέ· αὐτοῦ ἀκούσεσθε κατὰ πάντα ὅσα ἂν λαλήσῃ πρὸς ὑμᾶς.
> ἔσται δὲ πᾶσα ψυχὴ ἥτις ἐὰν μὴ ἀκούσῃ τοῦ προφήτου ἐκείνου
> ἐξολεθρευθήσεται ἐκ τοῦ λαοῦ.
>
> The Lord your God will raise up for you from your brothers a
> prophet like me. Listen to him in whatever he tells you. And it will
> be that everyone who does not listen to that prophet will be utterly
> rooted out of the people.

> *Deut 18:15*: προφήτην ἐκ τῶν ἀδελφῶν σου ὡς ἐμὲ ἀναστήσει σοι κύριος ὁ
> θεός σου, αὐτοῦ ἀκούσεσθε

> *Deut 18:16*: κατὰ πάντα, ὅσα ᾐτήσω παρὰ κυρίου τοῦ θεοῦ σου

> *Deut 18:19*: καὶ ὁ ἄνθρωπος, ὃς ἐὰν μὴ ἀκούσῃ ὅσα ἐὰν λαλήσῃ ὁ προφήτης
> ἐπὶ τῷ ὀνόματί μου, ἐγὼ ἐκδικήσω ἐξ αὐτοῦ.

> *Lev 23:29*: πᾶσα ψυχή, ἥτις μὴ ταπεινωθήσεται ἐν αὐτῇ τῇ ἡμέρᾳ ταύτῃ,
> ἐξολεθρευθήσεται ἐκ τοῦ λαοῦ αὐτῆς.

Deuteronomy 18:15 has been reworked; the possessive personal pronouns are changed from singular to plural, and clauses are rearranged.
Phrases from Deut 18:16, 19 round out the first sentence. The second sentence is composed of elements from Deut 18:19 and Lev
23:29.[121] The warning of Leviticus is taken from a section on Day
of Atonement regulations (Lev 23:26–32). Again the analysis of the
quotation reveals a quite sophisticated scribal composition.

There are strong indications that this quotation derives not from
Luke but from an earlier *testimonia* collection. (1) Conflated passages,
which occur regularly in TCs, are not characteristic of Luke.[122] The

---

[121] Jan de Waard denies any influence from Lev 23:29 here, arguing instead that
the wording can be traced back to a translation of the targum reading of Deut
18:19 (*A Comparative Study of the Old Testament Text in the Dead Sea Scrolls and in the
New Testament* [STDJ 4; Leiden: Brill, 1965] 21–24). The parallel between Luke's
quotation and Lev 23:29, however, is too close to overlook.

[122] See Bock (*Proclamation from Prophecy*, 192): "this mixed form is more characteristic of a traditional source than of Lucan style." Litke argues for Lukan redaction, but his proposal (citing E. Richard) that Acts 3:21 and the quotation in 3:22

same combination of Deut 18:15–19 and Lev 23:29 also appears in Ps.-Clement *Hom.* 3.55.3, though this may simply be due to dependence on Acts.[123] (2) Deuteronomy 18:15–19 was widely used in both Jewish and Christian circles as a messianic passage. 4QTestimonia 5–7 and the Samaritan Pentateuch conflated Deut 18:18–19 with Deut 5:28–29.[124] Luke quotes the same LXX-deviant text of Deut 18:15 in Acts 7:37 (Stephen's speech), and important allusions to this passage are found in accounts of Jesus' transfiguration (Mark 9:7 par.) and in John 6:14.[125] (3) The passage diverges somewhat from Luke's normal style: although Luke is careful elsewhere to distinguish Moses from the prophets (Luke 24:27, 44; Acts 26:22), here Moses is included as one of the prophets (3:21–22, 24).[126] This is again an indication that Luke is working with a source that does not exactly correspond to his own outlook.

After an editorial comment emphasizing that "these days" were predicted by the prophets (v 24), Luke adds a final quotation: "You are the descendants of the prophets and of the covenant that God gave to your ancestors, saying to Abraham":

Acts 3:25b: Καὶ ἐν τῷ σπέρματί σου [ἐν]ευλογηθήσονται πᾶσαι αἱ πατριαὶ τῆς γῆς.
And in your descendants all the families of the earth shall be blessed.
Gen 22:18: καὶ ἐνευλογηθήσονται ἐν τῷ σπέρματί σου πάντα τὰ ἔθνη τῆς γῆς[127]

The English translation is misleading here: "your descendants" actually translates a singular "your seed" (τῷ σπέρματί σου) which in at

---

are structurally parallel is not persuasive ("Luke's Knowledge," 255–56). C.K. Barrett sees the conflation as a possible indication of Luke's use of "a collection of *testimonia*" (*A Critical and Exegetical Commentary on the Acts of the Apostles* [ICC; 2 vols.; Edinburgh: T & T Clark, 1994] 1. 210).

[123] Bruce (*Acts*, 145) leaves open the possibility that both Luke and the Ps.-Clementine passage draw on a "testimony collection."

[124] For further discussion of the eschatological prophet-like-Moses at Qumran (esp. 1QS 9.11), see Collins, *Scepter*, 113–14.

[125] Dodd, *Scriptures*, 53–57; Lindars, *Apologetic*, 204–10. Lindars holds that Luke has taken over his quotation from the "apologetic of response" (p. 210).

[126] So Holtz, *Zitate bei Lukas*, 77–79. It should be noted, however, that the passages are not strictly comparable—in these other instances Luke uses "Moses" to refer to a section of scriptures, here the reference is more to the person of Moses.

[127] Barrett (*Acts*, 212) refers to this as a conflation of Gen 12:3; 18:18; and 22:18. However, it is easier to see this as a slight adaptation of Gen 22:18; in any case the inclusion of ἐν τῷ σπέρματί makes it clear that Gen 22:18 is the primary text in view.

least some early Christian contexts was understood as a reference
to Christ (see Gal 3:16). The passage is taken from the story of Abraham's near sacrifice of Isaac, where God's promises are a reward
for Abraham's obedience.

What originally drew Deut 18:15–19, Lev 23:29, and Gen 22:18
together? Deut 18:15–19 and Gen 22:18, as noted above, were interpreted messianically in some early Christian circles. The connection
between Gen 22:18 and Lev 23:29 is more involved. The context
in Leviticus speaks of the Day of Atonement, when sacrifices are
offered for the sin of the people. A first-century Jewish interpretive
tradition saw in Genesis 22 Isaac's voluntary offering of himself as
a sacrifice, an understanding that formed the roots of the later rabbinic concept of the *Akedah* and its developed theology of atoning
sacrifice.[128] Christians early on made the connection between the
binding of Isaac and their understanding of the atoning sacrifice of
Jesus.[129]

This proposal, admittedly less than compelling at first glance, gains
persuasive power when one considers *Barnabas* 7, a reading of the
Day of Atonement ritual as a type of Christ's crucifixion. *Barnabas*
7.3c reads:

> But moreover when he was crucified "he was given to drink vinegar
> and gall." Listen how the priests of the Temple foretold this. The com-
> mandment was written: "Whosoever does not keep the fast shall die
> the death," and the Lord commanded this because he himself was
> going to offer the vessel of the spirit as a sacrifice for our sins, in
> order that the type established in Isaac, who was offered upon the
> altar, might be fulfilled.

---

[128] On this tradition, see Geza Vermes, *Scripture and Tradition in Judaism: Haggadic
Studies* (SPB 4; Leiden: Brill, 1961) 193–227. On Isaac's voluntary sacrifice, see
Josephus *Ant.* 1.232; 4 Macc 13:12; *Ps.-Philo* 32.3. The full-blown atonement theology is clear in *Lev. Rab.* 29.9: "So when the children of Israel commit sin, and
do evil, remember on their behalf the Binding of Isaac." This text is explicitly connected with the seventh month, i.e., the month in which the Day of Atonement is
celebrated (see Vermes, *Scripture and Tradition*, 213).

[129] See ibid., 218–27; Vermes understands Acts 3:25 as a clear reference to the
Genesis story (p. 221). Paul's remark in Rom 8:23, "He who did not withhold his
own Son, but gave him up for all of us," is often seen as an echo of Gen 22:16,
although not necessarily a reflection on atonement; see Dunn, *Romans* 1. 501. On
the possible influence of the binding of Isaac on the narratives of Jesus' baptism,
see Stegner, *Narrative Theology*, 13–31. The bound Isaac as a type of Christ is found
in early Christian TCs; see sect. 3.4.4 (on Melito) above and the further references
there.

The author of *Barnabas*, reflecting on the crucifixion, quotes Lev 23:29 (in a form deviating from the LXX, MT, and Acts!) and immediately comments that the sacrifice of Isaac is a type of Christ's sacrifice. *Barnabas*'s interpretation is explicit: Christ's death is a sacrifice for our sins. *Barnabas* here is likely drawing on a *testimonia* source that combined anti-cultic polemic with positive cultic typologies (e.g. paschal lamb, scapegoat, high priest) of Christ.[130]

I conclude, then, that Luke's source in Acts 3:22–25 was a *testimonia* source that included Deut 18:15–19, Lev 23:29, and Gen 22:18. This collection begins by portraying Jesus as the awaited prophet-like-Moses (Deuteronomy 18), but interprets this messianic image with a text from Lev 23:29, and thus evokes the background of the Day of Atonement and its atoning sacrifices. Genesis 22:18 added the image of Isaac as a further type of Christ's atoning sacrifice.[131] It appears that Luke made little direct use of this original exegetical background: he refers the quotations not to Jesus' death but rather to his second advent (vv 20–21); the passage on the seed is not used christologically or in reference to atonement, but rather to link the contemporary generation with their ancestors the prophets (vv 25–26).[132] This tension between the apparently original purposes of these quotations and Luke's own purposes in his composition is a further indication that Luke here is taking over a source.

(b) *Acts 13:16b–41: A Review of Scriptural History*
In Acts 13:16b–41 Paul's speech in the synagogue of Antioch of Pisidia is presented. The speech can be summarized in the following way:

13:16b–22: A quick review of Israel's history: exodus from Egypt, time in the wilderness, conquest of Canaan, times of the judges, Samuel, Saul, and David. The review, emphasizing God's purpose behind all these events, culminates in God's selection of David as king (v 22).[133]

---

[130] For a discussion of Skarsaune's view that both *Barnabas* and Justin draw on this *testimonia* source, see sect. 3.9.2 above.

[131] Bock makes the tentative suggestion that these quotations are drawn from a tradition "centered upon OT parallels to Jesus' suffering that compared it to atonement and substitution concepts which, in turn, were drawn from themes current in the Jewish exegesis of Genesis 22" (*Prophecy and Pattern*, 196).

[132] Luke does maintain the focus on forgiveness of sin, however (3:19).

[133] For a similar analysis, see Holtz, *Zitate bei Lukas*, 131.

13:23–31: Jesus is linked to David as David's "seed" promised by God. After references to John the Baptist, Jesus' death and resurrection are proclaimed as being in accordance with God's will in scripture. The "residents of Jerusalem and their rulers" unconsciously fulfilled the prophets by condemning Jesus.[134]

13:32–41: Ps 2:7 is presented as a *testimonium* to the resurrection. Isaiah 55:3 and Ps 16 (15):10 are quoted as *testimonia* that Jesus did not experience corruption, in contrast to David (cf. Acts 2:24–31). Forgiveness of sins through Jesus is proclaimed, and the speech ends with a warning quoted from Hab 1:5.

The historical summary in 13:16b–22 is of most interest here. This summary is an example of a genre well known in Jewish writing, the historical overview emphasizing God's guidance of the events.[135] While of course based on scripture, the narrative shows an interest in precise dates that goes beyond explicit scriptural information.[136] The culmination of this survey (v 22) reads: "And when he [God] had removed him [Saul], he made David their king. In his testimony about him he said, 'I have found David, son of Jesse, to be a man after my heart, who will carry out all my wishes." This "witness" (μαρτυρήσας) by God is not found in any one text, but is rather a conflation, as the following synopsis shows:

> *Acts 13:22*: εὗρον Δαυὶδ τὸν τοῦ Ἰεσσαί, ἄνδρα κατὰ τὴν καρδίαν μου, ὃς ποιήσει πάντα τὰ θελήματά μου.
> I have found David, son of Jesse, to be a man after my heart, who will carry out all my wishes.
>
> *1 Kingdoms 13:14* (1 Sam 13:14): καὶ νῦν ἡ βασιλεία σου οὐ στήσεται, καὶ ζητήσει κύριος ἑαυτῷ ἄνθρωπον κατὰ τὴν καρδίαν αὐτοῦ, καὶ ἐντελεῖται κύριος αὐτῷ εἰς ἄρχοντα ἐπὶ τὸν λαὸν αὐτοῦ.
>
> *Ps 88:21*: εὗρον Δαυιδ τὸν δοῦλόν μου, ἐν ἐλαίῳ ἁγίῳ μου ἔχρισα αὐτόν.
>
> *Isa 44:28*: ὁ λέγων Κύρῳ φρονεῖν, καὶ Πάντα τὰ θελήματά μου ποιήσει·

---

[134] Jesus' cross is described as the "tree" (v 29); this language goes back to the earliest stages of Christian reflection on the crucifixion (see sect. 3.10 above).

[135] Historical summaries emphasizing God's guidance appear already in the Hebrew scriptures: Deut 26:5–10; Psalms 78, 105, 136. The "re-written Bible" genre (sect. 2.5.1 above), and, on a smaller scale, the scriptural *exempla* collections (see sects. 2.6.3, 3.5.4, and 4.2.1b above) are closely related.

[136] E.g., "he gave them their land as an inheritance for about four hundred and fifty years" (vv 19–20); Saul reigned for forty years (v 21). The precise referent of the four hundred and fifty years is obscure (Barrett, *Acts*, 634); the date for Saul's reign is known by Josephus *Ant.* 6.378 (although cf. *Ant.* 10.143, where a figure of ten years is given).

1 Clem. 18.1: Τί δὲ εἴπωμεν ἐπὶ τῷ μεμαρτυρημένῳ Δαυίδ πρὸς ὃν εἶπεν ὁ θεός· Εὗρον ἄνδρα κατὰ τὴν καρδίαν μου, Δαυὶδ τὸν τοῦ Ἰεσσαί, ἐν ἐλέει αἰωνίῳ ἔχρισα αὐτόν.[137]

The base text is 1 Sam 13:14; the originally third person narrative has been reworked so that it is now a first person speech by God. The opening phrase is adapted from Ps 88:21, with "son of Jesse" replacing "my servant." The last phrase derives from Isa 44:28 (where it is applied to Cyrus).[138]

It is difficult to suppose that the historical summary and its concluding quotation are Luke's creations.[139] The details of the summary (e.g., specific references to Saul) have no connection with Luke's overall interests; most tellingly, there is no conceivable reason for Luke to produce so complex a quotation as that found in Acts 13:22. The evidence points to previous extensive exegetical activity which Luke found in a source.

1 Clement 18.1 is closely related to Acts 13:22 and provides a clue to the quotation's background. Both texts (1) conflate Ps 88:21 and 1 Sam 13:14; (2) read τὸν τοῦ Ἰεσσαί in place of τὸν δοῦλόν μου; (3) present God speaking in the first person; (4) introduce their quotations with a form of μαρτυρέω; and (5) place their quotations in a wider context of a historical overview/*exempla* list.[140] Does *1 Clement* simply take over the quotation from Acts here? Two observations suggest otherwise: (1) *1 Clement* lacks any reference to Acts final phrase: ὃς ποιήσει πάντα τὰ θελήματά μου; (2) *1 Clement* extends the quotation of Ps 88:21 past what appears in Acts, though in an LXX-deviant form! We can propose that *1 Clem.* 18.1 and Acts 13:22 are

---

[137] Greek text in Karl Bihlmeyer, ed., *Die apostolischen Väter: Neuarbeitung der Funkschen Ausgabe*, vol. 1 (3d ed.; Tübingen: Mohr-Siebeck, 1970) 35–81.

[138] So Holtz, *Zitate bei Lukas*, 134. Max Wilcox rejects this last proposal in favor of a Semitic background. The Targum to 1 Sam 13:14 reads: נבר עביד ועותיה: "a man doing his will," and lacks any reference to "a man after God's heart." Wilcox argues that the author of the conflation in Acts used phrases from both the Hebrew original ("a man after his own heart") and the Aramaic tradition (*The Semitisms of Acts* [Oxford: Oxford University Press, 1965] 21–24). Wilcox's proposed use of both targumic and Hebrew translation of the same verse, however, is less likely than positing the influence of Isa 44:28 (see Litke, "Luke's Knowledge," 134).

[139] Even Litke, who attributes nearly all quotations to Lukan composition, finds Acts 13:22 only "probably" attributable to Luke (ibid., 135).

[140] *1 Clement* 17–18 presents a deliberative *exempla* collection on the humility of famous scriptural figures, culminating in David.

independent witnesses to a tradition which combined 1 Sam 13:14
and Ps 88:21.[141]

Can this common source be more narrowly defined? The context
of *1 Clement* 17–18 and Acts 13:16b–21 suggests that the quotation
was originally part of a scriptural historical review or *exempla* collection. 1 Samuel 13:14 and Ps 88:21 are obviously connected by
Davidic references; the presence of a text referring to Cyrus (Isa
44:28) in Acts makes it probable that a more general messianic thread
drew these texts together.[142] This messianic emphasis is also apparent in the use of the LXX-deviant τὸν τοῦ Ἰεσσαί, which some have
seen as an allusion to (the messianically understood) Isa 11:1, 10.[143]
I suggest, then, that the source was a Jewish scriptural-historical
review, emphasizing God's divine guidance, that culminated in God's
selection of David, the ideal, "messianic" king.

The question remains, however, regarding the relationship of this
historical overview source with the rest of Paul's speech. Important
studies, remarking on the speech's overall coherence, have analyzed
the entire passage as an example of a typical Jewish sermon form.[144]
Luke certainly presents the speech in this way: Paul speaks in the
synagogue after "the reading of the law and the prophets" (v 15).
The most probable reconstruction, then, is that the author of the
whole (13:16b–41) has matched reflections on Jesus' death and resurrection with an originally Jewish survey that culminated with David.
The purpose is to demonstrate the superiority of Jesus over David,
presenting Jesus as the true fulfillment of Israel's royal messianic
hopes. Whether the author of the whole is Luke or Luke's source
is open to question.[145]

---

[141] On the independence of *1 Clement*, see Bock, *Prophecy and Pattern*, 243; Holtz,
Zitate bei Lukas, 135, with further references. Holtz adds the general consideration
that *1 Clement* does not seem to know Acts.

[142] Cyrus, of course, is explicitly referred to as מָשִׁיחַ (χριστός) in Isa 45:1, the
only non-Israelite to receive this designation in the Hebrew scriptures.

[143] Holtz, *Zitate bei Lukas*, 134. Holtz finds that the conflations, in particular the
reference to Jesse, give the whole passage a "messianic ring" (p. 135).

[144] See Bowker, "Speeches in Acts," 101–4 (proem homily); Wills, "Form of the
Sermon," 278–80 ("word of exhortation" form). See above, sect. 1.16.2, for discussion on these studies.

[145] Another often suggested candidate for a *testimonium* reading in the speeches in
Acts is the quotation of Amos 9:11–12 with Isa 45:21 in Acts 15:16–18 (see Hodgson,
"Testimony," 368–69; Hans Conzelmann, *Acts of the Apostles* [Hermeneia; Philadelphia:
Fortress, 1987] 117). This case is ambiguous, however, as the non-standard read-
ings may be attributable to textual traditions witnessed at Qumran (see de Waard,
Comparative Study, 24–27).

4.4.3 *Common Early Christian* Testimonia *in Acts*

In addition to the above evidence for use of written *testimonia* sources, I now present a brief overview of the general use of well-known Christian *testimonia* in Acts:

Scripture in Acts Speeches	Function	Parallels
1:20: Ps 69:26	Ps 69 is the Psalm of the righteous sufferer; here the curses of the righteous one's enemies are applied to Judas.	Ps 69: Eph 4:8; John 12:17; Rom 15:3; Passion Narrative allusions to Ps 69:22[146]
2:34: Ps 110:1	Jesus' exaltation	Gospels, Paul, Hebrews[147]
4:11: Ps 118:22 (A)	Jesus is the rejected stone, now the cornerstone	Stone *testimonia*[148]
4:25: Ps 2:1–2	Herod and Plate united against Jesus	Ps 2:1–2 in passion TCs;[149] Ps 2:7 in Gospel baptism and transfiguration accounts (also Acts 13:33)
8:32: Isa 53:7–8	Jesus as sheep led to slaughter	Passion narrative; Passion TCs

Luke is clearly in touch with a wide-ranging early Christian *testimonia* tradition. Luke presupposes that these texts have a self-evident meaning that his readers will recognize, and thus can apply them directly for proof of his arguments. In contrast, when Luke quotes Ps 16 (15):8–11 in Acts 2:25–28 and Ps 16 (15):10 in Acts 13:35, these texts must be followed by exegetical arguments that demonstrate

---

[146] On Psalm 69, see Lindars, *Apologetic*, 99–110.
[147] See sect. 5.3 below.
[148] See sect. 5.6 below.
[149] See Crossan, *Cross*, 60–75.

their applicability to Jesus. Indeed, part of the argument in both cases is the quotation of self-evident *testimonia* (Ps 110 [109]:1 in Acts 2:34–35; Ps 2:7 in Acts 13:33) to support the exegetical point. While the possibility exists that these *testimonia* came to Luke in the form of a written TC,[150] it is just as possible that Luke's choice was influenced by more general oral traditions.

4.4.4 *Rhetorical Functions of Luke's* Testimonia

Luke is quite explicit about his understanding of scripture as forensic proof. Paul's activity in the synagogues is summarized as a forensic effort to prove to Jews that the messiah is Jesus: Paul "argued with them from the scriptures, explaining and proving (διανοίγων καὶ παρατιθέμενος) that it was necessary for the Messiah to suffer and to rise from the dead, and saying, 'This is the Messiah, Jesus whom I am proclaiming to you'" (17:2–3); "Paul was occupied with proclaiming the word, testifying (διαμαρτυρόμενος) to the Jews that the Messiah was Jesus" (18:5; cf. 9:22; 28:23). Similar terminology describes the efforts of Apollos: "for he powerfully refuted the Jews in public, showing (ἐπιδεικνύς) by the scriptures that the Messiah is Jesus" (18:28). This forensic characteristic seems to be based on the conviction that it is a scriptural necessity that the messiah suffer, die, and rise (3:18; 13:27–29; 17:2–3).[151]

Kurz has well observed that scripture, even though it has divine authority, is not employed as a *direct* proof in Luke-Acts.[152] That is, for Luke, and indeed for Justin, proof-texts are not applied directly to Jesus' life: further arguments must first establish that "messianic" scriptures apply to Jesus and not to someone else. Proof from prophecy, then, is employed in two stages, taking the form of the following rhetorical enthymeme:[153]

---

[150] Bruce makes this suggestion for the use of Psalm 69 in Acts 1:20 (*Acts*, 110).

[151] The scriptural necessity of the suffering and death had already been foreshadowed in Luke 18:31–34; 22:37; and of course the programmatic statement in 24:44–47.

[152] Kurz, "Christological Proof," 111–12. Cf. Quintilian's view that even *divina testimonia* cannot be applied without further argument when they are not clearly related to a case (*Inst.* 5.7.35).

[153] The enthymeme is the rhetorical counterpart to the logical syllogism (*Rhet.* 1.2.8).

Major premise: According to scripture, the Christ must die and rise.
Minor premise: Jesus did die and rise, as shown by witnesses.
Conclusion: Jesus is the Christ.[154]

Kurz identifies two forms of this proof from prophecy: a schematic enthymeme in which the second term is often simply assumed (e.g., Acts 17:2b–3) and a more complex form in which argument is based explicitly on scriptural quotations (e.g., Acts 2:22–36).[155]

Kurz is correct to emphasize both the rhetorical background and the indirect nature of scriptural proof. Nevertheless, it should be emphasized that Kurz's schematic provides Christian assumptions which would not be shared by Jewish opponents. Luke assumes that Paul and others will also have to argue the major premise, that the Christ will have to suffer (e.g., Acts 17:3: διανοίγων καὶ παρατιθέμενος ὅτι τὸν χριστὸν ἔδει παθεῖν καὶ ἀναστῆναι ἐκ νεκρῶν). With Lindars, we can assume that this passion apologetic was a major motivating force in early Christian use of scripture.

4.4.5 *Conclusions*

Like Matthew, Luke uses his *testimonia* as forensic proof—he is explicit in claiming that scriptural passages can be used to prove Christian (especially messianic) claims. Luke makes use of widespread early Christian *testimonia*: Ps 110:1; the stone *testimonia*, the use of Isaiah 53; these are perhaps known to him from oral tradition. At the same time, Luke has taken over more detailed *testimonia* compositions as sources for his speeches: a typological reflection on Christ's atoning death (Acts 3:22–25) and a scriptural history review which showed that Israel's history culminates not in David but in Jesus Christ.

4.5 *Christ's Superiority to the Angels: A* Testimonia *Collection in Heb 1:5–2:8*

4.5.1 *Overview of the Catena in Heb 1:5–2:8*

The author of the letter to the Hebrews concludes his or her majestic christological reflection in Heb 1:3–4 thus: "When he had made purification for sins, he sat down at the right hand of the Majesty

---

[154] Kurz, "Christological Proof," 119–20.
[155] Ibid., 114–34.

on high, having become as much superior to angels as the name he has inherited is more excellent than theirs." As a proof of the superiority of the Son over the angels, Hebrews presents a string of *testimonia*:

Hebrews	Parallels
1:5: Ps 2:7	Gospel baptismal and Transfiguration texts;[156] Acts 13:33
1:5: 2 Sam 7:14 (=1 Chr 17:13)	4QEschatMidr;[157] 2 Cor 6:18;[158] Rev 21:7
1:6: Deut 32:43[159]	Other NT uses of Song of Moses (sect. 4.2.1d)
1:7: Ps 104:4	
1:8–9: Ps 45:7–8	Justin *Dial.* 38.4; 56.14; Irenaeus *Proof* 47; *A.H.* 3.6.1
1:10–12: Ps 102:25–28	
1:13: Ps 110:1	See sect. 5.3 below
2:6: Ps 8:4–6	See sect. 5.3.2 below

This collection shows many of the classic characteristics of a TC: vague citation formulas,[160] brief quotations connected with καὶ πάλιν and καί; use of texts well represented in other TCs; a parallel in a literarily independent text (see below on *1 Clement*). After the TC proper in Heb 1:5–13 (with a concluding comment in 1:14), and a

---

[156] See the discussion above (sect. 4.3.2c) on Matt 12:18a.

[157] 4QEschatological Midrash also references Ps 2:1–2; see 2.7.7a above.

[158] See sect. 4.2.1f above.

[159] The exact source of this quotation is disputed. Some commentators see an adapted reference to LXX Ps 97 (96):7, while others point to Deut 32:43 (from the "Song of Moses"). The closest parallel to the wording in Hebrews, however, occurs in the version of the Song of Moses included in the Greek Psalter (witnessed in Codex Alexandrinus): καὶ προσκυνησάτωσαν αὐτῷ πάντες οἱ ἄγγελοι θεοῦ. See the discussion in Harry W. Attridge, *The Epistle to the Hebrews* (Hermeneia; Philadelphia: Fortress, 1989) 57. On the Song of Moses as a popular *testimonia* source, see above on Rom 12:19 (sect. 4.2.1d).

[160] Hebrews 2:6: "But someone has testified somewhere" (διεμαρτύρατο δέ πού τις λέγων); cf. 4:4. The indefinite phrase, however, may well reflect a "common homiletical practice," and not necessarily indicate ignorance of the precise scriptural context; see Attridge, *Hebrews*, 70–71.

parenetic section (Heb 2:1–4), the author returns to the theme of the Son's superiority to the angels, quoting a final text: Ps 8:4–6 (Heb 2:6b–8a). In the exegesis of the text (vv 8b–9), the author understands "you made him for a little while lower than the angels," to refer to Christ's earthly ministry: the glory comes after his death.[161]

4.5.2 *Evidence for Hebrews's Use of a Previous* Testimonia *Collection: Parallel with* 1 Clem. *36:2–6*

1 Clement 36:2–6 is a close parallel to the Hebrews catena. Although *1 Clem.* 36:2–6 presents an abbreviated version, it is clear that it and Hebrews share some kind of literary connection: they both use ἀπαύγασμα; they share an LXX-deviant quotation;[162] they share a τοσούτῳ . . . ὅσῳ structure by which Christ's greatness over the angels is compared to the greatness of his name over theirs; and they both support their claim of Christ's superiority with a TC. The TC in *1 Clement* includes three of the seven proof-texts given in Hebrews: Ps 104 (103):4; Ps 2:7–8; and Ps 110:1. A comparison between the introductions to the respective TCs follows:

Hebrews 1:3–4	*1 Clem.* 36.2b
³<u>ὃς ὢν ἀπαύγασμα τῆς δόξης</u> καὶ χαρακτὴρ τῆς ὑποστάσεως αὐτοῦ, φέρων τε τὰ πάντα τῷ ῥήματι τῆς δυνάμεως αὐτοῦ, καθαρισμὸν τῶν ἁμαρτιῶν ποιησάμενος ἐκάθισεν ἐν δεξιᾷ τῆς μεγαλωσύνης ἐν ὑψηλοῖς, ⁴<u>τοσούτῳ κρείττων</u> γενόμενος τῶν <u>ἀγγέλων ὅσῳ διαφορώτερον</u> παρ' αὐτοὺς <u>κεκληρονόμηκεν ὄνομα.</u>	<u>ὃς ὢν ἀπαύγασμα τῆς</u> μεγαλωσύνης αὐτοῦ, <u>τοσούτῳ μείζων</u> ἐστὶν ἀγγέλων , <u>ὅσῳ διαφορώτερον ὄνομα κεκληρονόμηκεν.</u>

It is not surprising, in light of these points of connection, that many scholars conclude that *1 Clement* depends literarily on Hebrews.[163]

Two major considerations, however, challenge this conclusion.

---

[161] This understanding is similar to the classic two advents pattern of the *testimonia* literature. The author's understanding of a future consummation in which everything would be in subjection to Christ echoes Paul's explication in 1 Cor 15:24–28.

[162] LXX Ps 103:4 reads πῦρ φλέγον; Hebrews and *1 Clement* read πυρὸς φλόγα.

[163] See Gareth Lee Cockerill, "Heb 1:1–14, *1 Clem.* 36:1–6 and the High Priest

(1) Although *1 Clement* 36 explicitly refers to Jesus as "high priest" (ἀρχιερεύς) this does not necessarily prove dependence on Hebrews. *Clement* in fact has a different conception of Christ's high priesthood than that of Hebrews: most noticeably, *Clement* does not explicitly link the office with Christ's death. In any case, early Christian typologies picturing Jesus as high priest are hardly limited to Hebrews: Ernst Käsemann and Gerd Theissen have traced both Hebrews's and *1 Clement*'s high priest christology to a common liturgical source,[164] and both Justin's and *Barnabas*'s *testimonia* sources know a high priest typology.[165] (2) If one assumes *1 Clement*'s dependence on Hebrews, no clear rationale or pattern for *1 Clement*'s abbreviations and adaptations *vis à vis* Hebrews is evident.[166] The possibility that both Hebrews and *1 Clement* draw on the same *testimonia* tradition must be considered an open one.[167]

4.5.3   *Original Form and Function of the* Testimonia *Collection in Heb 1:5–2:8*

What can we say about the original form and function of this proposed TC? The quotations themselves are an odd mixture of popular Christian and Jewish *testimonia* (Psalms 2 and 110 [109]) and more idiosyncratic texts (Ps 104 [103]:4; Ps 102 [101]:25–28). Three exegetical activities are discernible within the catena:

(1) Texts collected around the catch-word "son" (Ps 2:7; 2 Sam 7:14)—these are established royal messianic *testimonia* in both Jewish and Christian circles.

Title," *JBL* 97 (1978) 437–40; Paul Ellingworth, "Hebrews and *1 Clement*: Literary Dependence or Common Tradition?" *BZ* 23 (1979) 264–65; Attridge, *Hebrews*, 6–7. Attridge is particularly persuaded by the identity of the transitional link introducing the catena (the comparison of names) in Hebrews and *1 Clement*.

[164] Käsemann, *The Wandering People of God: An Investigation of the Letter to the Hebrews* (Minneapolis: Augsburg, 1984; orig. pub. 2d ed.; Göttingen: Vandenhoeck & Ruprecht, 1957) 170; Theissen, *Untersuchungen zum Hebräerbrief* (SNT 2; Gütersloh: Mohn, 1969) 34–37.

[165] E.g., *Dial.* 42.1; 115–16; *Barn.* 7.9; see Skarsaune, *Prophecy*, 309–13. Crossan holds that the details of the crowning and robing of Jesus in the original passion narrative derive from a high priest typology (of Joshua) (*Cross*, 128, 132–33, 157–58).

[166] Cockerill, "High Priest," 438, offers a few *ad hoc* suggestions, but nothing close to a coherent pattern of intentional adaptation.

[167] Even Attridge (*Hebrews*, 7), who judges that *1 Clement* depends on Hebrews for this passage, nevertheless concludes, "Much of this catena was probably a traditional collection celebrating the exaltation of Christ."

(2) Texts collected around the catch-word "angels" (Deut 32:43; Ps 104 [103]:4)

(3) "Two powers" texts collected and applied to the "son" (Ps 45 [44]:7–8; Ps 102 [101]:25–28; Ps 110 [109]:1)

Steps one and two are fairly straightforward: the quotations are selected in order to establish the unique status of the "son" as God's chosen one, and "angel" passages are collected to demonstrate the subordinate status of angels. Step three is a further effort to establish the status of the "son" by applying "two powers" texts to him.

The "two powers in heaven" tradition, condemned by the early rabbis, has been well charted by Alan F. Segal.[168] Segal has traced this movement, with its interest in intermediary powers between God and the world, in Philo, rabbinic literature, various Jewish intertestamental texts, and early Christian literature. Characteristic of this movement was speculation on scriptural texts which contain references to two Gods or Lords (often occurring in OT theophanies where God appears to humans in angelic form).

Justin and Irenaeus provide ample proof that "two powers" speculation formed part of early Christian TCs. Within his longer discussion of OT theophanies, which he interprets as appearances of Christ (*Dialogue* 56–60), Justin draws on a TC made up of passages that speak of two Lords or two Gods: Gen 19:23; Ps 110 (109):1; and Ps 45 (44):6–7.[169] In *Proof* 47–48, Irenaeus, probably in dependence on Justin, also combines Ps 45 (44):7–8 and Psalm 110 (as proof that "the Father is Lord and the Son is Lord, and the Father is God and the Son is God"),[170] but also adds, independently of Justin, a tendentious form of Isa 45:1 in *Proof* 49.[171] In section 5.3.5 below, I provide further examples of "two powers" speculation (involving Ps 110 [109]:1, Ps 45 [44]:6–7), and Isa 45:1) in *Barnabas*, Tertullian, and Novatian.

---

[168] Segal, *Two Powers in Heaven: Early Rabbinic Reports about Christianity and Gnosticism* (SJLA 25; Leiden: Brill, 1977).

[169] See Skarsaune, *Prophecy*, 126, 209; see also Per Beskow, *Rex Gloriae: The Kingship of Christ in the Early Church* (Stockholm/Göteborg/Uppsala: Almqvist & Wiksell, 1962) 84–86. *Dialogue of Timothy and Aquila* fol. 81 combines Ps 110 (109):1 with Gen 19:24 to prove that Christ is the "counselor" of God.

[170] *Proof* 44–46 echoes the theophanies presented in *Dial.* 56–60; see also *A.H.* 3.6.1.

[171] See sect. 5.3.6 below for discussion of the "Christianized" reading of Isa 45:1.

Two of the texts, then, are clearly part of Christian "two powers" speculation: (1) *Ps 45:7 (44:6)*: "Your throne, O God, is for ever
and ever." Addressing the king directly as "God," this psalm picks
up the royal ideology of Ps 2:7 and 2 Sam 7:14, in which the Israelite
king was closely identified with God. (2) *Ps 110 (109):1*: "The Lord
said to my Lord." The attraction of this "two powers" phrase was
one factor that made Ps 110:1 the most frequently quoted passage
in the NT.

The applicability of the third text, Ps 102 (101):25–28 ("In the
beginning, Lord, you founded the earth. . . ."), is not obvious at first
glance. T.F. Glasson, however, rightly notes the significance of the
immediate context of these verses. Psalm 102 (101):19–21 reads "The
Lord looked upon the earth from heaven . . . to proclaim the name
of the Lord in Zion." The two "Lords" of this passage would have
provided exegetical license to identify one of them with the "son,"
and to apply the quoted verses to him.[172]

The original TC, then, was composed to establish the divine or
"Lordly" status of the son of God over against the status of angels.
David Hay remarks that "the questions about angels sound more
rhetorical than serious,"[173] but this is to underestimate significantly
the role of angelic speculation in the theological thought world of
Second Temple Judaism and early Christianity. The work of Segal,
and more recently of Jarl Fossum, has clearly shown the central part
that interest in angels played in the wider reflection on intermediary powers between God and the world.[174] This reflection took a
variety of forms: messianic angelology (e.g., Michael in the book of
Daniel); the possibly angelic figure of Melchizedek (11QMelchizedek);
and Philo's understanding of the Logos (sometimes described as an
angel).[175] Christian conceptions of Christ as an angel are evident in

---

[172] Glasson, "'Plurality of Divine Persons' and the Quotations in Hebrews I.6FF.,"
NTS 12 (1965–66) 271. Glasson also argues that Deut 32:43, quoted above in the
TC, also drew attention as a "two powers" quotation. His contention that in the
reading καὶ προσκυνησάτωσαν αὐτῷ πάντες ἄγγελοι θεοῦ, the αὐτῷ and the θεοῦ
would have been taken as two references to God is perhaps pressing the text too far.

[173] Hay, *Right Hand*, 39.

[174] Fossum (*The Name of God and the Angel of the Lord: Samaritan Concepts of Intermediation
and the Origin of Gnosticism* [WUNT 36; Tübingen: Mohr-Siebeck, 1985]) emphasizes
Samaritan traditions on the hypostasized divine Name and of the Angel of the Lord
as forerunners of the gnostic concept of the demiurge (see p. iii).

[175] See Attridge, *Hebrews*, 51–52.

the *Gospel of Thomas*;[176] Justin;[177] *Shepherd of Hermas*;[178] and *Apostolic Constitutions*.[179] This angel christology is found in TCs as late as Cyprian.[180] The TC in Hebrews is representative of the efforts in other Christian circles to *distinguish* Christ from the angels, emphasizing his superiority over them. This same effort is apparent in other Christian uses of the Ps 8:7/Ps 110:1 *testimonia*, where the angels are likely one of the "powers" which are subjected to Christ.[181]

4.5.4 *Conclusions*

The catena in Hebrews 1–2 is most likely not the work of the author of Hebrews; rather it is a reflection of the intense scriptural activity centered on Jesus Christ. The collection witnesses to an early controversy on Jesus' status over against angels; the collector seeks to establish Jesus' superiority. To this end, he gathered royal messianic texts (Psalm 2 and 2 Samuel 7) to demonstrate Jesus' unique status as God's son; he further gathered "two powers" passages to prove that Jesus is the "second" Lord or God spoken of in scripture. The messianic texts, Ps 110:1, and Psalm 8 in all likelihood already had an established christological meaning by the time they are incorporated into the catena.

---

[176] *Gos. Thom.* 13: "Simon said to him, 'You are like a righteous angel.'" Coptic text and ET in A. Guillaumont, et al., eds., *The Gospel according to Thomas: Coptic Text Established and Translated* (Leiden: Brill; New York: Harper, 1959).

[177] Justin frequently argues that Christ is called an angel on the basis of his appearance in OT angelic theophanies (e.g., Abraham's visitors at Mamre; the burning bush) and his role as God's messenger. Thus *Dial.* 56.4 claims, in the context of discussing the theophany at Mamre, "there is another God and Lord subject to the Maker of all things; who is also called an angel, because he announces to men whatsoever the Maker of all things—above whom there is no other God—wishes to announce to them." See also *1 Apol.* 63.5; *Dial.* 56.10; 58.3; 59.1; 60.1–4; 128.4. As with the title "stone," the title "angel" is so well established that Justin can simply include it casually in his lists of christological titles: *Dial.* 34.2; 61.1; 86.3; 100.4; 126.1.

[178] In *Herm. Vis.* 5.2; *Sim.* 7.5; 9.1.1–3 Christ is called an angel. However, in *Sim.* 8.3.3 Michael is called "the great and glorious angel" and in *Sim.* 9.12.7–8 the "Son of God" is distinct from "the glorious angels." Bakker points out that the christology of *Shepherd of Hermas* does not clearly distinguish between the angel Michael and Christ ("Christ an Angel?" 257).

[179] *Ap. Const.* 8.12.

[180] Cyprian *Quir.* 2.5: "That Christ is as once Angel and God."

[181] 1 Corinthians 15:24–27; Eph 1:20–23; 1 Pet 3:22 (explicit reference to angels). See below, sect. 5.3.2 for further discussion of these texts. Cf. also Paul's association of angels and powers in Rom 8:38.

CHAPTER FIVE

FIVE *TESTIMONIA* TRADITIONS IN
THE NEW TESTAMENT

5.1   *Overview of the Chapter*

In this chapter, I will trace *testimonia* traditions which extend across
a spectrum of NT writings. I consider the use of a messianic text
cluster (Gen 49:10–11; Num 24:17; and Isa 11:1, 10); the interpretation of Ps 110:1; the "hardening" tradition (based on Isa 6:9–10);
the interpretation of Zech 12:10 as a "second advent" text; and the
"stone" tradition. As above, I will consider the function of these *testimonia* in each work; evidence that the NT quotations are drawn
from previous *testimonia* sources (Jewish or Christian); and reflect on
the original form of these *testimonia* sources.

5.2   *New Testament Use of Jewish Messianic* Testimonia

5.2.1   *Second Temple Interpretations of Gen 49:10; Num 24:17;
and Isa 11:1, 10*

There is ample evidence that three of the texts that Justin presents
in *1 Apology* 32—Gen 49:10–11; Num 24:17; and Isa 11:1, 10—were
all well established messianic proof-texts in pre-Christian Jewish circles. These texts were read messianically both individually and as a
part of larger collections. These texts thus demonstrate continuity between Jewish and Christian scriptural traditions, and show that there
was indeed a core group of texts, interpreted messianically by both
Jews and Christians, which could serve as common ground for Jewish-
Christian debate. In what manner, or even whether, such debates
actually took place, however, is a further question.

Three targumic traditions—Targum Onqelos, Targum Ps.-Jonathan,
and the Fragmentary Targum—interpret Gen 49:10–11 with explicit
references to the messiah.[1] Ps.-Jonathan and the Fragmentary Targum

---

[1] See Levey, *Messiah*, 7–11.

emphasize the warlike characteristics of the messiah, whose garments will be saturated with his enemies' blood.

While the dating of the targums is notoriously uncertain, evidence from Qumran provides decisive proof for pre-Christian messianic understanding of these texts. 4QGenesis Pesher[a] 5, for example, gives the following interpretation of Gen 49:10:

> A sovereign shall [not] be removed from the tribe of Judah. While Israel has the dominion, there will [not] lack someone who sits on the throne of David. For the staff is the covenant of royalty, the thousands of Israel are the feet. Until the messiah of justice comes, the branch of David. For to him and to his descendants has been given the covenant of royalty over his people for all everlasting generations, which he has observed.[2]

The "Branch of David" (צמח) (see Jer 23:5; 33:15) is closely associated with the "Prince of the Congregation" in several texts. 1QRule of the Blessings (1QSb) contains a blessing of the messianic "Prince of the Congregation," who is described in language based on Isa 11:1–5, but also with elements from Gen 49:9 and Num 24:17.[3] The "Branch" and the "Prince" depict an eschatological, warlike Davidic figure.[4] In the Pesher on Isaiah (4QpIsa[a]), this messianic Branch is identified with the shoot from the stump of Jesse (Isa 11:1).[5]

Outside of Qumran, the *Psalms of Solomon* 17 records the hope for a Davidic messiah with language dependent on Isa 11:1–4.[6] The language of Isa 11:1–5 also influenced descriptions of later eschatological figures: the "man from the sea" destroys his enemies with a stream of fire flowing from his mouth (4 Ezra 13:10; cf. Isa 11:4); the depiction of the "Elect One" from the Similitudes of *Enoch* echoes Isa 11:2 (*1 Enoch* 49:3–4).[7]

Num 24:17 ("a star shall come out of Jacob, and a scepter shall rise out of Israel") was interpreted messianically in many strands of Second Temple Judaism.[8] Already in the LXX tradition, ἄνθρωπος

---

[2] Hebrew in B.Z. Wacholder and M.G. Abegg, *A Preliminary Edition of the Unpublished Dead Sea Scrolls*, Facsicle Two (Washington, D.C.: Biblical Archaeological Society, 1991–92) 212–15; ET in *Scrolls*, 215.

[3] Prigent, "Testimonia messianiques," 419–20; Collins, *Scepter*, 60–61.

[4] See Collins, *Scepter*, 56–63. In this section, Collins discusses the Pesher on Isaiah, 4Q285 (a probable fragment of the War Scroll), and 4QGenesis Pesher[a].

[5] Ibid., 58.

[6] Ibid., 53–56.

[7] Ibid., 65.

[8] See Geza Vermes, *Scripture and Tradition*, 59–60, 165.

was read for the Hebrew "scepter." Smit Sibinga argues that a variant reading ἡγούμενος for ἄνθρωπος may well have arisen due to the
influence of the messianically interpreted Gen 49:10, as messianic
proof-texts influenced one another in the *testimonia* tradition.[9] Targums
Onqelos and Ps.-Jonathan provide explicitly messianic translations.[10]
Even Philo, who normally shows little interest in messianic figures,
understands ἄνθρωπος as an eschatological warrior who will subdue
the world.[11] The attribution of this prophecy to the revolutionary
leader Kosiba (better known as Bar Kochba: Son of the Star) is well
known.[12] The passage figures in several of the most important Qumran
sectarian documents: the Damascus Document (CD 7.18–21), the
War Scroll (1QM 11:5–7) and 4QEschatological Midrash.

Certain texts examined above (1QRule of the Blessings; LXX variant of Num 24:17) suggest that these messianic texts were read as
collections. The description of a priestly eschatological figure in
Testament of Levi 18 provides a further example of combined images.[13]
Verse 3 clearly alludes to Num 24:17:

> And his star shall rise in heaven like a king; kindling the light of knowl-
> edge as day is illumined by the sun. And he shall be extolled by the
> whole inhabited world.

The chapter has further allusions to our messianic cluster: Gen 49:10
(18.1: common use of ἐκλείψει) and Isa 11:2 (18.7: πνεῦμα συνέσεως)
and Isa 11:9 (18.5: imagery of the knowledge of the Lord poured
out on the earth like the waters of the sea).[14] The *Testament of Judah*
24 combines Num 24:17 with the messianic phrases "branch of God
Most High" and "from your root a stem shall arise" (Isa 11:1, 10).
As with *Testament of Levi* 18, Jewish messianic traditions can be detected
beneath the Christian redaction in this chapter.[15]

The above survey demonstrates that we can speak of a "messianic" tradition that was fairly consistent among various groups in

---

[9] Smit Sibinga, *Old Testament Text*, 139.

[10] See Levey, *Messiah*, 21–23.

[11] See Peder Borgen, "There Shall Come Forth a Man: Reflections on the
Messianic Ideas in Philo," in Charlesworth, ed., *The Messiah*, 341–61.

[12] For the tradition of Rabbi Akiba's attribution of Num 24:17 to Kosiba, see
y. Taʾan 68d.

[13] Greek text in H.W. Hollander, H.J. de Jonge, and Th. Korteweg, eds., *The
Testaments of the Twelve Patriarchs: A Critical Edition of the Greek Text* (PVTG 1.2; Leiden:
Brill, 1978); ET in *OTP* 1. 788–95. Though admitting a Christian influence on this
text, Collins (*Scepter*, 92) argues for a Jewish messianic core.

[14] See Prigent, "Testimonia messianiques," 422–23.

[15] So Collins, *Scepter*, 92.

Second Temple Judaism.[16] A consistent portrait of a warrior messiah who would destroy Israel's enemies, restore the Davidic kingship, and institute an era of unending peace can be traced.[17] The three texts studied above, Num 24:17, Gen 49:10–11, and Isa 11:1–10, were at the heart of this messianic expectation, and were often conflated in quotations and allusions. Although Collins warns that we cannot know how widespread or significant messianic expectation was among various Jewish groups in the first century CE, we can conclude that "when interest in messianic expectation arose, however, there was at hand a body of tradition that could be used to articulate it."[18] This "body of tradition" may well have included written collections of messianic proof-texts.

5.2.2 *New Testament Interpretation of Gen 49:10–11; Num 24:17; and Isa 11:1, 10*

This constellation of messianic texts is used widely, if subtly, in the NT.

In Revelation, the *testimonia* passages have attained such authority that they can be applied without argument as titles of Jesus:

Rev 5:5: ἰδοὺ ἐνίκησεν ὁ λέων ὁ ἐκ τῆς φυλῆς Ἰούδα, ἡ ῥίζα Δαυίδ
See, the Lion of the tribe of Judah, the Root of David, has conquered
The titles are drawn from Gen 49:9 and Isa 11:1, 10 respectively.
Rev 22:16: ἐγώ εἰμι ἡ ῥίζα καὶ τὸ γένος Δαυίδ, ὁ ἀστὴρ ὁ λαμπρὸς ὁ πρωϊνός
I am the root and the descendant of David, the bright morning star.

Here Isa 11:1, 10 is used again, this time in combination with a "star" reference, perhaps an allusion to Num 24:17.[19] Skarsaune comments that the influence of Isa 11:1, 10 and Num 24:17 on these christological titles in Revelation represents a "later stage" in which Christians added traditional Jewish *testimonia* to their proof-text collections.[20] But this appeal to a later stage is hardly necessary: the familiar use of these titles in Revelation, together with an already

---

[16] Referring to the interpretation of Num 24:17, together with other examples, Vermes can conclude: "In inter-testamental Judaism there existed a fundamental unity of exegetical tradition" (*Post-Biblical Jewish Studies* [SJLA 8; Leiden: Brill, 1975] 49).
[17] See Collins, *Scepter*, 68.
[18] Ibid., 67.
[19] So Skarsaune, *Prophecy*, 261.
[20] Ibid.

traditional use of Isa 11:10 in Rom 15:12 (sect. 4.2.1c above), suggests that Jewish messianic *testimonia* were applied to Jesus from the beginning stages of scriptural reflection on him.[21]

In the context of arguing that Jesus was from the tribe of Judah and not from the Levi (the tribe of the Aaronic priesthood), the author of Hebrews asserts:

> *Heb 7:14*: πρόδηλον γὰρ ὅτι ἐξ Ἰούδα ἀνατέταλκεν ὁ κύριος ἡμῶν
> For it is evident that our Lord was descended from Judah

Though the NRSV translates "descended," the basic meaning of the verb ἀνατέλλω actually is "(to cause) to rise or spring up."[22] Connected with the phrase ἐξ Ἰούδα, however, this passage is manifestly an allusion to the constellation of messianic references (Gen 49:10; Num 24:17; Isa 11:1, 10), together with the closely related messianic images of the branch and star:

> *Gen 49:10*: οὐκ ἐκλείψει ἄρχων ἐξ Ἰούδα
> A leader shall not be lacking from Judah
> *Num 24:17*: ἀνατελεῖ ἄστρον ἐξ Ἰακώβ
> A star shall arise from Jacob
> *Jer 23:5*: καὶ ἀναστήσω τῷ Δαυὶδ ἀνατολὴν δικαίαν
> And I will raise up for David a righteous branch (lit. "arising")[23]
> *Zech 6:12b*: Ἰδοὺ ἀνήρ, Ἀνατολὴ ὄνομα αὐτῷ, καὶ ὑποκάτωθεν αὐτοῦ ἀνατελεῖ, καὶ οἰκοδομήσει τὸν οἶκον Κυρίου
> Behold a man, whose name is Branch, and he shall spring up from beneath it, and he shall build the house of the Lord.[24]

In claiming that Jesus' descent from Judah is "evident," Hebrews draws on a messianic *testimonia* tradition that combined various scriptural

---

[21] Philipp Vielhauer ("Paulus und das alte Testament," in L. Abramowski and J.F.G. Goeters, eds., *Studien zur Geschichte und Theologie der Reformation: Festschrift für E. Bizer* [Neukirchen-Vluyn: Neukirchener, 1969] 41; repr. in Philipp Vielhauer, *Oikodome: Aufsätze zum Neuen Testament*, vol. 2 [TBü 65; Munich: Kaiser, 1979] 204 n. 31) also reckons with a pre-Pauline messianic application of Isa 11:10 to Jesus.

[22] In addition to variations of this standard meaning, *LSJ* offers the definition "of persons, originate," (s.v. II 2b) but the only example provided is Heb 7:14!

[23] Ἀνατολή is the LXX translation of the Hebrew צֶמַח = branch, sprout. On messianic interpretation of "branch" (and the related "shoot" of Isa 11:1, 10) see Collins, *Scepter*, 58–62.

[24] Philo gives an important interpretation of this passage in *Confusion of Tongues* 63–64: "that incorporeal being who in no respect differs from the divine image ... the Father of the universe has caused him to spring up as the eldest son ... the firstborn ... imitating the ways of his father, has formed such and such species, looking to his archetypal patterns." Greek text and ET in F.H. Colson and G.H. Whitaker, *Philo*, vol. 4 (LCL; Cambridge, MA; London: Heinemann, 1949).

images in order to prove that the messiah came from Judah. The author hardly constructed this complex by him or herself: the point in the context of Hebrews is that Jesus is a *high priest* from Judah, and therefore reflection on Jesus as Davidic messiah is not in view.[25] Rather, Hebrews has simply taken over a traditional messianic reflection with little concern for its original purpose.

The messianic use of ἀνατολή is also evident in Luke 1:78, where Zechariah prophesies that "the dawn from on high (ἀνατολὴ ἐξ ὕψους) will break upon us."[26] Justin also knows a messianic *testimonia* source linked by the catch-words ἀνατέλλω/ἀνατολή (*Dialogue* 32 and 120–21). Both passages combine ἀνατέλλω/ἀνατολή texts, an LXX-deviant form of Gen 49:10, other messianic passages (Num 24:18, Isa 11:1, 10 in 1 *Apology* 32; Zech 6:12 in *Dialogue* 120–21), and the theme of the gentiles putting their hope in the messiah.[27]

The *testimonia* tradition behind Heb 7:14 should also be compared with other early Christian *testimonia* that "prove" that the messiah must come from Judah: Matt 2:6 (Mic 5:1/2 Sam 5:2)[28] and John 7:41–42 (general reference to scripture). Closely related are passages that presuppose that Jesus is the son of David: Matt 1:1; 9:27; 15:22; Mark 10:47 par.; Luke 1:32; 2:4; Rom 1:3; 2 Tim 2:8; Rev 5:5; 22:16. As we have seen, traditions in Rom 1:3, Rev 5:5, and 22:16 are based directly on *testimonia* exegetical activity.[29]

We must also reckon with the compositional use of these messianic passages: Num 24:17 likely lies behind Matthew's account of the Magi;[30] Gen 49:11 influences the Synoptic accounts of Jesus' messianic entry into Jerusalem;[31] and Isa 11:1, 10 is the most probable source behind Matt 2:23.[32]

---

[25] See also Attridge, *Hebrews*, 201: "In referring to the fact that Christ has 'sprung' (ἀνατέταλκεν) from Judah, he [the author] does use metaphorical language evocative of the messianic prophecies of the branch and the star that will arise as Yahweh's agent, but these prophecies, too, remain very much in the background."

[26] For a messianic interpretation of this passage, see Joseph A. Fitzmyer, *The Gospel According to Luke I–IX* (AB 28; New York/London: Doubleday, 1981) 387. Fitzmyer also cites the use of ἀνατέλλω in *T. Naph.* 8.2 and *T. Gad* 8.1, which refer to salvation arising in Israel.

[27] See Skarsaune, *Prophecy*, 84–85.

[28] See sect. 4.3.2a above.

[29] On Rom 1:3, see 4.2.1c above.

[30] See esp. Matt 2:1–3 (Brown, *Birth of the Messiah*, 195–96).

[31] Mark 11:1–11 par.; see J. Blenkinsopp, "The Oracle of Judah and the Messianic Entry," *JBL* 80 (1961) 55–64.

[32] See sect. 4.3.2b above.

This brief survey indicates that the common view that Second Temple Jewish messianic texts were not applied to Jesus in earliest Christianity should be modified.[33] Christian writers across a broad spectrum in fact simply *presuppose* that Jesus is the Davidic messiah, and expend their exegetical energy establishing other points.

5.2.3   *Patristic Interpretation of Gen 49:10–11; Num 24:17; and Isa 11:1, 10*

Justin presents these three texts in *1 Apology* 32, the beginning of Skarsaune's proposed kerygma source, as *testimonia* to the first advent of the messiah. Genesis 49:10 has been altered to express a further messianic meaning,[34] and a non-LXX Gen 49:11 is interpreted as an allegory of Christ's blood (the blood of the grape) and the church (the robe). Justin then presents a conflation of Num 24:17b, Isa 11:1b, and Isa 51:5b; he attributes the whole to Isaiah.[35]

Justin's non-LXX text of Gen 49:10 was a popular *testimonium* among later Christian authors. It is used by Ps.-Gregory, Irenaeus, the Ps.-Clementine *Homilies*, and Novatian.[36] Syriac Christian traditions also echo this variant in their quotations.[37] LXX readings can be found in TCs of Ps.-Epiphanius *Test.* 5.1; Athanasius *On the Incarnation* 40.3; and Eusebius *Proof* (approximately forty times). Genesis 49:10 is often cited together with Isa 11:1 or 11:10: Hippolytus *Antichrist* 7–9, Cyprian *Quir.* 1.21; and Eusebius *Proof* 7.3.55.

Genesis 49:11 serves a dual purpose in patristic *testimonia* literature. Verse 11a (tying his colt to a vine) was associated with Zech

---

[33] Variants of this view include the following: (1) The earliest Christians were more interested in a scriptural passion apologetic than a messianic apologetic *per se* (e.g., Skarsaune, *Prophecy*, 261); and (2) Jesus (and his followers) rejected the militaristic, nationalistic messianism of Second Temple Judaism and instead redefined the meaning of "messiah."

[34] Justin reads: οὐκ ἐκλείψει ἄρχων ἐξ Ἰουωδα οὐδὲ ἡγούμενος ἐκ τῶν μηρῶν αὐτοῦ ἕως ἂν ἔλθῃ ᾧ ἀπόκειται ("A ruler will not fail from Judah, nor a leader from his loins, until *he come for whom it is reserved*"); the LXX reads: ἕως ἂν ἔλθῃ τὰ ἀποκείμενα αὐτῷ ("until the things which are reserved have come for him"). See Skarsaune, *Prophecy*, 25–29, for detailed analysis.

[35] See ibid., 50–52.

[36] Ps.-Gregory *Testimonies* 2; Irenaeus *Proof* 57; Ps.-Clementine *Hom* 3.49.1; and Novatian *Trin.* 9. See Hatch, "Early Quotations," 168–69, for discussion and further references.

[37] *Acts of Thomas*; Isaac of Antioch; Aphrahat; and Ephrem; see Murray, *Church and Kingdom*, 282–84.

9:9 as a prophecy for Jesus' entry into Jerusalem.[38] Verse 11b was understood, with Justin, as an allegory of Christ's blood washing believers.[39] Cyprian (*Quir.* 1.21) goes his own way: he cites Gen 49:8–12 under the heading, "That the Gentiles should rather believe in Christ," focusing apparently on 49:10d: "he is the hope of the nations."

Num 24:17, the prophecy on a star coming out of Jacob, is often found in the same combination of texts which we find in Justin. Ps.-Gregory *Testimonies* 2 adds Num 24:17 and Isa 10:33–34; 11:1–5, 10 to Gen 49:10. Irenaeus *Proof* 57–59, most likely in dependence on Justin, discusses Gen 49:10 (non-LXX), Num 24:17, and Isa 11:1–10 in that order.[40] While Justin reads ἡγούμενος in his Num 24:17 quotation, other writers read the LXX ἄνθρωπος, giving it a christological interpretation. Thus Cyprian, Athanasius, and Lactantius understand, "A star shall arise out of Jacob, and a man shall rise up from Israel" as a proof of the human and divine nature of Christ.[41]

The connection of Num 24:17 with the narrative of the star at Christ's birth in Bethlehem, implicit in Matthew, is made explicit in later writings. Justin links the Numbers passage and the birth narrative recorded in "the memoirs of his apostles" (*Dial.* 106.4),[42] as does Irenaeus (*Proof* 58; *A.H.* 3.9.2).[43]

5.2.4   *Conclusions on the Messianic* Testimonia

We have good evidence from pre-Christian Judaism, the NT, and patristic writings that Gen 49:10, Num 24:17, and Isa 11:1, 10 were understood as prophecies of the royal messiah. These texts thus show a marked continuity in messianic belief between certain forms of Judaism and early Christianity, and potentially served as a common ground for debate over their applicability to Jesus. Evidence from

---

[38] Clement of Alexandria *Teacher* 1.15.3; Ps.-Epiphanius *Test.* 37.2.

[39] Irenaeus *Proof* 57; Tertullian *Marc.* 4.40.6.

[40] Irenaeus gives the same exegesis as Justin for most of these passages. Smit Sibinga, however, argues that Justin and Irenaeus are independent, with Irenaeus preserving the earlier form of their common tradition (*Old Testament Text*, 49).

[41] Cyprian *Quir.* 2.10; Athanasius *Incarn.* 33.4; Lactantius *D.I.* 4.13. Lactantius also cites Isa 11:1–2 and 11:10 in the same context as a proof for Christ's humanity.

[42] In *Dial.* 126.1, Justin can simply refer to "star" (ἄστρον) as one of the titles of Christ.

[43] For discussion of these texts as well as further traditions of the star and the birth of Jesus, see Daniélou, *Theology*, 216–24.

all three bodies of literature indicates that these texts (together with other, related scriptures) were read as part of larger collections and often conflated. It is therefore likely that the texts were circulated in written collections analogous to 4QTestimonia and 4QEschatological Midrash. In the NT they are used compositionally (e.g., in the birth narrative and in the titles found in Revelation): their applicability is taken for granted.

5.3   *Psalm 110:1 as an Early Christian* Testimonium

To begin my study of the use of Ps 110 (109):1, I present the MT and LXX texts:

> *MT Ps 110:1*: נאם יהוה לאדני שב לימיני עד־אשית איביך הדם לרגליך
> The Lord says to my lord, "Sit at my right hand until I make your enemies your footstool."
>
> *LXX Ps 109:1*: Εἶπεν ὁ κύριος τῷ κυρίῳ μου Κάθου ἐκ δεξιῶν μου, ἕως ἂν θῶ τοὺς ἐχθρούς σου ὑποπόδιον τῶν ποδῶν σου.
> The Lord said to my lord, "Sit at my right hand, until I place your enemies as a footstool of your feet."

As is well known, Ps 110 (109):1 is the scriptural passage with the greatest number of citations or definite allusions in the NT.[44] This passage is a fundamental *testimonium* to the exaltation of Jesus after his death; it is found in a broad range of NT writings and is already a firmly established *testimonium* in Paul's time. Many studies have addressed the early Christian use of Psalm 110; the most comprehensive is David M. Hay's *Glory at the Right Hand*.[45] As another comprehensive survey of early Christian use of this Psalm would have little to add to Hay's study, I will instead focus on a narrower goal. Limiting the study to Ps 110:1, I will investigate the process by which this passage came to be identified as a *testimonium* to Christ's exaltation. Although no definitive conclusions can be drawn, I will offer five models which may help to shed some light on how Ps 110:1 came to have this function in early Christian writings.

---

[44] The index of UBSGNT lists eight citations and ten allusions. Even this number is too small, as indicated in the table below. For the sake of convenience in this section, I will refer only to the numbering of the MT (i.e., Ps 110:1) rather than to the strictly more accurate designation, Ps 110 (109):1.

[45] For a brief summary of Hay's work, see sect. 1.13 above.

5.3.1   *Overview of Early Christian Use of Ps 110:1*

Psalm 110:1 has three basic parts:

(a) *Introduction*: "The Lord said to my Lord"
(b) *The exaltation/enthronement*: "Sit at my right hand"
(c) *The subjection of the Lord's enemies*: "until I make your enemies your footstool."

Following is a table laying out references to Ps 110:1 in Christian literature before Justin. This overview is an adaptation of Hay's tabular summary.[46]

Text	Reference	Function
(1) Mark 12:36 (see par. below).	Q 1a–c	proves that the Christ should be called "Lord" and not "son of David" (spoken by Jesus)
(2) Matt 22:44	Q 1a–c	same
(3) Luke 20:42	Q 1a–c	same
(4) Mark 14:62 (see par. below)	A 1b	describes Jesus' (= Son of Man's) future vindication (at Jesus' trial)
(5) Matt 26:64	A 1b	same
(6) Luke 22:69	A 1b	same
(7) Mark 16:19	A 1b	describes Jesus' ascension
(8) Acts 2:33–36	Q 1a–c	proves that Jesus, not David, was exalted as Lord and Christ; from here Christ pours out the Pentecost gifts of the Spirit
(9) Acts 5:31	A 1b	describes how God exalted Jesus as leader and savior
(10) Acts 7:55–56	A 1b	describes Jesus as the exalted Son of Man[47] (Stephen's vision)
(11) Rom 8:34	A 1b	describes how the exalted Christ Jesus intercedes for the faithful

---

[46] Hay, *Right Hand*, 45–46.

[47] Cf. Hegesippus's account of the martyrdom of James, where Jesus is described as the Son of Man sitting at the right hand of the great power and about to come on the clouds (*apud* Eusebius *H.E.* 2.23.13). The account of Stephen's vision itself is strongly reminiscent of the Synoptic accounts of Christ's prediction at his trial.

(table cont.)

Text	Reference	Function
(12) 1 Cor 15:25	A 1c	proves that Christ must reign until his enemies are subjected
(13) Eph 1:20–22	A 1bc	describes God's exaltation of Jesus over other powers as head of the church
(14) Eph 2:6[48]	A 1b	describes believers' raising and exaltation with Christ
(15) Col 3:1	A 1b	describes Christ's exaltation, in which believers share
(16) Heb 1:3	A 1b	describes the exaltation of Jesus after he made purification for sins
(17) Heb 1:13	Q 1bc	proves the superiority of Christ over the angels
(18) Heb 8:1	A 1b	describes Jesus as high priest in glory
(19) Heb 10:12–13	A 1bc	describes the exaltation of the high priest Jesus after his sacrifice; his waiting for the subjection of his enemies
(20) Heb 12:2	A 1b	describes Jesus' vindication and exaltation after suffering
(21) 1 Pet 3:22	A 1bc	describes exaltation of Christ and subjection of powers in context of believers' salvation through baptism
(22) Rev 3:21[49]	A 1b	describes exaltation to the heavenly throne of believers who "conquer," just as Christ was exalted to God's throne
(23) *1 Clem.* 36.5–6	Q 1bc	proves the superiority of Christ over the angels

[48] This passage lacks the characteristic "right hand" terminology, but the verb "seated" and the association with Eph 1:20–22 ensure that an allusion to Ps 110:1 is intended.

[49] Again the "right hand" terminology is lacking, but the reference to "sitting" on the throne with Christ and God in exaltation is a strong indication that Ps 110:1 is intended.

(table cont.)

Text	Reference	Function
(24) Polycarp *Phil.* 2.1	A 1bc	describes Christ's exaltation and subjection of powers in context of exhorting believers— they too will be raised
(25) *Barn.* 12.10–11	Q 1a–c	proves that the Christ is Son of God and not David's Son
(26) *Sib. Or.* 2.241–45	A 1b	describes Christ as judge; conflation with Dan 7:13
(27) *Apoc. Peter* 6	A 1b	describes Christ as judge; conflation with Dan 7:13
(28) *Asc. Isaiah* 10.14; 11.32	A 1bc A 1b	describes glorious ascension of Christ after judgment
(29) *Apocr. Jas.* 14.30–31	A 1b	describes Jesus' imminent ascension to glory
(30) *Excerpt of Theodotus* 62.1–2.	Q 1b	describes the "psychic" (ψυχικός) Christ sitting at the right hand of the Demiurge until the consummation

All texts use Ps 110:1 in reference to an exaltation or vindication of Jesus after his death. This exaltation is associated in various ways with Jesus' resurrection, ascension, second advent, and subjection of powers to him. Some quotations have a clear forensic purpose (proving the appropriateness of the title "Lord": 1–3; 8; 25), while the allusions are often used compositionally to describe events. Christ's activity at the right hand is variously portrayed: interceding for believers (11, 18); waiting (19); pouring out the Spirit (8); giving repentance and forgiveness of sins (9); reigning universally (12, 14); and judging (26–27). The exaltation of Christ is often identified with a parallel exaltation of the believer (14, 15, 22, 24). Use of Ps 110:1 cuts across many independent streams of early Christian literature, from the Gospels to Revelation, from Polycarp to the gnostic *Apocryphon of James*.

When these Christian writers quote Ps 110:1, the LXX reading ἐκ δεξιῶν is always used. The majority of the allusions, however, use constructions with δεξιά: ἐν δεξιᾷ (Rom 8:34; Col 3:1; Eph 1:20; 1 Pet 3:22; Heb 1:3; 8:1; 10:12; 12:2); τῇ δεξιᾷ (Acts 2:33; 5:31); ἐπὶ δεξιᾷ (*Sib. Or.* 2.243).[50] Especially striking is the use in Hebrews: the four allusions read ἐν δεξιᾷ, while the quotation in Heb 1:13 uses the LXX ἐκ δεξιῶν. Romans 8:34; 1 Pet 3:22; and the Acts quotations lack reference to the "sitting"; they simply speak of the right hand of God. We can conclude that these allusions are drawn from an authoritative source other than the LXX.[51]

Hay provides a valuable discussion of possible "indirect sources" for Ps 110:1.[52] *Barnabas* 12.10–11; Heb 1:13; and *1 Clem.* 36.5–6 appear to draw on "collections of scriptural testimonies."[53] Several of the allusions derive from "primitive church confessions or hymns."[54] He draws two implications from this evidence: (1) a given author's allusions to Ps 110:1 do not necessarily show direct acquaintance with scripture: the author may simply know the intermediary source; (2) intermediary sources not only provided early Christian writers their phrasing, but also with theological interpretation.[55]

Hay's conclusions on the widespread use of intermediary sources for this central scriptural passage are important for this study. They confirm that the earliest Christian writers did not always make direct use of scripture, but depended on mediating sources that provided both adapted scriptural passages and their *authoritative interpretation*. Hay's further distinction between *testimonia* sources and confessional/hymnic sources is also valuable. This confirms the observation made several times in this study that intermediary sources were

---

[50] These allusions are clearly to Ps 110:1, as shown by verbal parallels (esp. "sitting" or "right hand") or other clues in the context (e.g., earlier references to Psalm 110). Other scriptural references to the right hand of God (e.g., Ps 80:17; *Test. Job* 33) are most likely not in view (see Hay, *Right Hand*, 17 n. 9).

[51] It is theoretically possible that the allusions are based on another Greek translation or on direct access to the Hebrew (ἐν δεχιᾷ is in fact a natural translation of the MT). Nevertheless, we have no scriptural manuscript evidence for such a reading.

[52] Hay, *Right Hand*, 38–43. See sect. 1.14 above on non-scriptural sources.

[53] On *Barn.* 12.10–11, see below; on the Hebrews 1/*1 Clement* 36 parallel, see 4.5.2 above.

[54] Hay (*Right Hand*, 39–40) offers the following criteria to identify use of these sources: (1) The close, non-LXX parallels between certain allusions (Rom 8:34; 1 Pet 3:22; Col 3:1) suggest a common source. (2) The "sheer superfluity" of some of the allusions (Col 3:1 and Polycarp *Phil.* 2.1) indicate that earlier material is taken over into a new setting. Hay's argument is that the Ps 110:1 allusions add little or nothing to the sense of the passages in which they occur, and are therefore likely to be stock phrases. (3) Many allusions appear "in settings indicative of creed-like origins." In addition to the above references, Hay refers to Eph 1:20–23; 2:4–10; Heb 1:2b–3; Mark 14:62; 16:19 (pp. 40–43). All references are given with a wealth of secondary citations.

[55] Ibid., 43–45. This accords well with the evidence presented in this study that exegetical comments usually accompany the proof-texts in *testimonia* sources.

not limited to *testimonia* collections strictly defined, but took the form of historical surveys, passages with commentary, and dialogues.

Nevertheless, Hay does make one implicit contrast between TCs and confessional/hymnic sources with which I take issue. He holds that

> no single scriptural passage is regularly cited by early Christians along-side Ps 110.1.... [T]he passage most often linked with it, Ps 8.7, might have been connected with it independently by various Christians simply because of the similarity of the two psalm texts.[56]

This comment undervalues evidence for common traditions (involv-ing the combination of Ps 110:1 with texts like Ps 8:6) which under-lie independent NT writings. In my analysis below, I hope to show that even the earliest confessional or hymnic uses of Ps 110:1 pre-suppose prior exegetical activity in which the christological meaning of the psalm was established in connection with other texts, most notably Dan 7:13 and Ps 8:6.

5.3.2 *Second Temple Jewish Use of Ps 110:1*

In contrast to the messianic *testimonia* (Gen 49:10; Num 24:17; and Isa 11:1, 10), Ps 110:1 seems not to have been an established Jewish messianic *testimonium* which Christians could simply have taken over and applied to Jesus. The psalm itself refers to the enthronement of a historical Davidic king.[57] Hay's survey of the pre-Christian evi-dence produces scant results: an allusion in *Test. Job* 33.3; possible references in the Enoch literature; use by the Hasmoneans (1 Macc 14:41; *As. Mos.* 6.1); and later rabbinic references.[58] He concludes from this that pre-Christian Jews held a variety of interpretations, including messianic applications. Yet his evidence for messianic inter-pretation is rabbinic, and should be considered doubtful for Second Temple Judaism.[59] More accurate is John J. Collins's simple conclusion:

---

[56] Ibid., 44–45.

[57] The precise date and original intention of Psalm 110 is much debated; pro-posals on the date have ranged from pre-exilic times to the Maccabean era. A *crux* is the function of v 4, which the Maccabees certainly applied to themselves (see 1 Macc 14:41), but which may also have been applied to earlier combinations of priestly and royal office (see Allen, *Psalms*, 83–86).

[58] Hay, *Right Hand*, 19–33, esp. 33.

[59] See the critical remarks in Joseph A. Fitzmyer, Review of Hay, *Glory at the Right Hand*, *CBQ* 36 (1974) 595. Fitzmyer concludes that "we still do not have any clear evidence" for a pre-Christian Jewish messianic interpretation of Ps 110:1.

"The psalm does not figure prominently in pre-Christian Jewish literature."[60]

If Ps 110:1 did not have a clearly messianic meaning in pre-Christian Jewish circles, it stands to reason that early Christians established this meaning through their own exegetical activity. In order to study more closely this interpretive activity, I turn now to consideration of individual quotations and allusions, beginning with our earliest Christian examples in Paul's letters.

5.3.3 *Christian Interpretation of Ps 110:1 with Ps 8:6*

(a) *Paul's Use of Ps 110:1; 1 Cor 15:25–27 and Rom 8:34*

> *1 Cor 15:25–27:* [25]δεῖ γὰρ αὐτὸν βασιλεύειν ἄχρι οὗ θῇ πάντας τοὺς ἐχθροὺς ὑπὸ τοὺς πόδας αὐτοῦ. [26]ἔσχατος ἐχθρὸς καταργεῖται ὁ θάνατος· [27]πάντα γὰρ ὑπέταξεν ὑπὸ τοὺς πόδας αὐτοῦ. ὅταν δὲ εἴπῃ ὅτι πάντα ὑποτέτακται, δῆλον ὅτι ἐκτὸς τοῦ ὑποτάξαντος αὐτῷ τὰ πάντα.
>
> [25]For he must reign until he has put all his enemies under his feet. [26]The last enemy to be destroyed is death. [27]For "God has put all things in subjection under his feet." But when it says, "All things are put in subjection," it is plain that does not include the one who put all things in subjection under him.
>
> *Ps 8:7:* καὶ κατέστησας αὐτὸν ἐπὶ τὰ ἔργα τῶν χειρῶν σου, πάντα ὑπέταξας ὑποκάτω τῶν ποδῶν αὐτοῦ,
>
> You have appointed him over the works of your hands; you have subjected all things under his feet

Verses 25–27 of 1 Corinthians 15 occur in the context of Paul's arguments for the reality of resurrection, introduced in 1 Cor 15:12–19. Two principles are evident in Paul's reasoning: (1) Christ is raised first, then at his coming (παρουσία) those who belong to Christ (vv 20, 24), and (2) Christ's role is understood in parallel with Adam: just as all die in Adam, so all shall be raised in Christ (vv 22–23). Paul then describes the events of the end, when Christ will hand over the kingdom to God after he has destroyed every ruler and every authority and power (v 24).

The next verses (25–27), based on Ps 110:1 and Ps 8:7, explicate these events of the end. These scriptures are not cited directly, but are rather used compositionally, woven into the narrative. At the same time, as evidenced by the use of δεῖ in v 25, this scripturally

---

[60] Collins, *Scepter*, 142.

based narration also functions as a kind of proof: these events must occur, for they are in scripture.[61]

"For he must reign until he has put all his enemies under his feet" (v 25) is a clear allusion to Ps 110:1. Several changes from the LXX are evident: (1) a third person narrative replaces God's first person speech; (2) the phrasing πάντας and ὑπὸ τοὺς πόδας αὐτοῦ is likely due to the influence of Ps 8:7;[62] (3) Christ instead of God is the subject of the action; (4) the replacement of ἕως ἄν by ἄχρι οὗ emphasizes the temporal end of the kingship.[63]

After the comment, "The last enemy to be destroyed is death" (v 26), Ps 8:6 is quoted. Again the scriptural passage is substantially modified: (1) second person discourse is changed to third person narrative; (2) ὑπὸ τοὺς πόδας replaces ὑποκάτω τῶν ποδῶν; (3) the subject is changed from God to Christ.[64] Paul completes his description by declaring that the Son, too, will finally be subjected to the Father, "so that God may be all in all" (v 28).

The whole of 1 Cor 15:25–27, then, is a carefully adapted Christian reflection on the end times based on Ps 110:1 and Ps 8:7. Through textual conflations and the attribution to Christ of God's actions recorded in scripture, an eschatological narrative is produced in which Christ is portrayed as the Lord of all creation, triumphant even over death itself. Did Paul himself compose this prophetic vision?

The first consideration is that Paul is not the only Christian author who has combined Ps 110:1 and Ps 8:6 (8:7 LXX). There are a range of literarily independent combinations (which I present below): Mark 12:36 (par. Matt 22:44); Eph 1:20–22; Heb 1:13–2:8; 1 Pet 3:22; and Polycarp *Phil.* 2.1. The whole context of Ps 8:5–7 drew the special attention of these Christian writers:[65]

---

[61] See also Conzelmann, *1 Corinthians*, 272, for a scriptural understanding of the δεῖ in this passage. This concept of the scriptural necessity of events is of course a hallmark of the scriptural TCs studied in chapter three above (e.g., *Barn.* 5.13; Melito *Homily* 57; Irenaeus *Proof* 75; Tertullian *A.J.* 10.4) which argue for the scriptural necessity of Christ's suffering.

[62] So Jan Lambrecht, "Paul's Christological Use of Scripture in 1 Cor. 15:20–28," *NTS* 28 (1982) 505 n. 16; repr. in idem, *Pauline Studies* (BETL 115; Leuven: Leuven University Press, 1994) 132; Hay, *Right Hand*, 36.

[63] See Lambrecht, "Use of Scripture," 132.

[64] Whether the subject of the verbs in this section is Christ or God is a matter of dispute; the issue is thoroughly discussed in Lambrecht, "Use of Scripture," 506–12.

[65] My translation from the LXX. I translate in a non-inclusive manner to preserve the force of "son of man."

> *Ps 8:5–7:* ⁵What is man, that you are mindful of him? or the son of
> man, that you are concerned about him? ⁶You have made him a
> little less than angels; you have crowned him with glory and honor;
> ⁷and you have set him over the works of your hands: you have put
> all things (πάντα) under his feet.

These verses, originally understood as referring to humans in gen-
eral, are applied by Christians to Christ. Combined with the exalted
"Lord" title of Ps 110:1, the powerful composite image of Jesus as
Lord over all creation (so evident in 1 Cor 15:24–27) emerges.

Consideration of Paul's other use of Ps 110:1, in Rom 8:34,
confirms the importance of Psalm 8, although the Psalm itself is not
used directly:

> *Rom 8:34:* Χριστὸς Ἰησοῦς⁶⁶ ὁ ἀποθανών, μᾶλλον δὲ ἐγερθείς, ὃς καὶ ἐστιν
> ἐν δεξιᾷ τοῦ θεοῦ, ὃς καὶ ἐντυγχάνει ὑπὲρ ἡμῶν.
> Christ Jesus, who died, yes, who was raised, who is at the right
> hand of God, who indeed intercedes for us.

The passage occurs in the context of Paul's reflections on the love
of God in Christ for believers (8:31–39). Verse 32 is central:

> *Rom 8:32:* ὅς γε τοῦ ἰδίου υἱοῦ οὐκ ἐφείσατο ἀλλὰ ὑπὲρ ἡμῶν πάντων
> παρέδωκεν αὐτόν, πῶς οὐχὶ καὶ σὺν αὐτῷ τὰ πάντα ἡμῖν χαρίσεται;
> He who did not withhold his own Son, but gave him up for all of
> us, will he not with him also give us everything else?

Dunn rightly sees in the τὰ πάντα a reference to all of creation, echoing the τὰ πάντα of 1 Cor 15:27, itself derived from Psalm 8.⁶⁷ Not
only does τὰ πάντα most often carry this meaning in Paul,⁶⁸ but it
fits the context of Paul's discussion in Rom 8:18–30 regarding the
"creation subjected to futility" and the future glory of creation and
believers, set out in terms of an Adam-Christ typology (cf. 1 Cor
15:21–22).⁶⁹ Romans 8:38–39, then, with its insistence that the believer
will overcome death, angels, rulers, and "anything else in creation"

---

⁶⁶ Ἰησοῦς is lacking in B and D.
⁶⁷ Dunn, *Romans 1.* 502; see also Ulrich Wilckens, *Der Brief an die Römer (Röm
6–11)* (EKKNT 6/2; Zürich/Einsiedeln/Cologne: Benziger; Neukirchen-Vluyn:
Neukirchener, 1980) 173–74.
⁶⁸ Dunn refers to Rom 11:36; 1 Cor 8:6; 11:12; Phil 3:21; Col 1:16–17; Eph
1:10–11, 23; 3:9; 4:10.
⁶⁹ See also James D.G. Dunn, *Christology in the Making: A New Testament Inquiry into
the Origins of the Doctrine of the Incarnation* (Philadelphia: Westminster, 1980) 107–12
for the details of the Adam (identified with the sinful humanity and decaying creation) and Christ (identified with restored humanity and creation) typology.

echoes the imagery of 1 Cor 15:24–27. Dunn sums up well: "Christ again [is] understood as the one who fulfills God's mandate for man (Ps 8:6), but precisely as the head of a new humanity who share his sonship and his devolved authority."[70] Paul's reference to Christ's glorification at the right hand (Rom 8:34) presupposes a line of thought in which Psalm 8 plays a vital role.[71]

In Romans as in 1 Corinthians, Paul knowingly employs Ps 110:1 and Ps 8:6 as established *testimonia*: he assumes that his audience accepts the applicability of these passages to the Christ events. He has no need to quote the passages directly; they are already deeply embedded in Christian teaching and liturgy.[72] A quick review of other NT combinations of Ps 110:1 and Ps 8:6 provides further confirmation that Paul was not the first to make this link: it is well established in the Christian tradition when he writes.

(b) *Polycarp* Phil. *2.1b*

> *Polycarp Phil. 2.1b*: πιστεύσαντες εἰς τὸν ἐγείραντα τὸν κύριον ἡμῶν Ἰησοῦν Χριστὸν ἐκ νεκρῶν καὶ δόντα αὐτῷ δόξαν καὶ θρόνον ἐκ δεξιῶν αὐτοῦ· ᾧ ὑπετάγη τὰ πάντα ἐπουράνια καὶ ἐπίγεια, ᾧ πᾶσα πνοὴ λατρεύει
> believing on him who raised up our Lord Jesus Christ from the dead and gave him glory, and a throne on his right hand, to whom are subject all things in heaven and on earth, whom all breath serves[73]

The context is parenetic, with Polycarp exhorting his readers to "serve God in fear and truth." The lengthy adjectival phrases describing Christ and God's work in Christ are not directly relevant to the context and indicate that Polycarp is quoting a fixed formula.[74]

---

[70] Dunn, *Romans* 2. 502. See also Gordon D. Fee, *The First Letter to the Corinthians* (NICNT; Grand Rapids: Eerdmans, 1987) 757 n. 55: "Christ as *man* is thus the representative 'Man' to whom all things are subjected."

[71] Philippians 3:20–21 is a further parallel; here Christ's role in renewing the believer is described with terms from Ps 8:6 but not Ps 110:1.

[72] On Rom 8:34 as a pre-Pauline confession, see Hay, *Right Hand*, 40 (with bibliography); on the wider pre-Pauline background to both the Romans and 1 Corinthians passages, see Martin Hengel, "Psalm 110 und die Erhöhung des Auferstandenen zur Rechten Gottes," in Cilliers Breytenbach and Henning Paulsen, eds., *Anfänge der Christologie: Festschrift für Ferdinand Hahn zum 65. Geburtstag* (Göttingen: Vandenhoeck & Ruprecht, 1991) 45–56; and idem, "Hymnus und Christologie," in Wilfrid Haubeck und Michael Bachmann, eds., *Wort in der Zeit: Neutestamentliche Studien. Festgabe für Karl Heinrich Rengstorf zum 75. Geburtstag* (Leiden: Brill, 1980) 9–13 (ET = "Hymns and Christology," in idem, *Between Jesus and Paul: Studies in the Earliest History of Christianity* [Philadelphia: Fortress, 1983] 85–88).

[73] Greek text in Bihlmeyer, *Apostolischen Väter*, 114–20; ET based on Lake, *Apostolic Fathers*, 282–301.

[74] On this point, see Hay, *Right Hand*, 40. Henning Paulsen speaks in this context

(c) *1 Pet 3:22*

> *1 Pet 3:22*: ὅς ἐστιν ἐν δεξιᾷ [τοῦ] θεοῦ πορευθεὶς εἰς οὐρανὸν ὑποταγέντων
> αὐτῷ ἀγγέλων καὶ ἐξουσιῶν καὶ δυνάμεων.[75]
> who [Jesus Christ] has gone into heaven and is at the right hand
> of God with angels, authorities, and powers made subject to him.

The opening phrase of this verse, ὅς ἐστιν ἐν δεξιᾷ τοῦ θεοῦ, an exact
parallel to the opening phrase of Rom 8:34,[76] appears in an explicitly baptismal context (v 21). Achtemeier's comments, representative
of current scholarship, may be summarized: the passage reflects "early
creedal material" which the author reworks creatively; the passage
shares traditions with other NT passages but is not dependent literarily on them; with his use of ἐν δεξιᾷ, the author indicates "his
dependence on tradition rather than on the psalm directly."[77]

(d) *Heb 1:13–2:8*
I argued above (sect. 4.5) that both Ps 110:1 (Heb 1:13) and Ps
8:5–6 (Heb 2:6–8a) formed part of a scriptural TC taken over by
the author of Hebrews. Although the four allusions (Heb 1:3; 8:1;
10:12–13; 12:2) are formally independent of Psalm 8, the interpretation given of Ps 8:4–6 in Heb 2:6–10 (Jesus was for a time made
a little lower than the angels, but is now crowned with glory and
honor) is the framework within which Ps 110:1 is understood in the
epistle.[78]

(e) *Eph 1:20–23*

> *Eph 1:20–23*: [20]ἣν ἐνήργησεν ἐν τῷ Χριστῷ ἐγείρας αὐτὸν ἐκ νεκρῶν καὶ
> καθίσας ἐν δεξιᾷ αὐτοῦ ἐν τοῖς ἐπουρανίοις
> [21]ὑπεράνω πάσης ἀρχῆς καὶ ἐξουσίας καὶ δυνάμεως καὶ κυριότητος
> καὶ παντὸς ὀνόματος ὀνομαζομένου, οὐ μόνον ἐν τῷ αἰῶνι τούτῳ ἀλλὰ καὶ
> ἐν τῷ μέλλοντι·

of Polycarp's use of "traditional christological statements" (Walter Bauer and Henning
Paulsen, *Die Briefe des Ignatius von Antiochia und der Polykarpbrief* [HNT 18; Die
Apostolischen Väter II; 2d ed.; Tübingen: Mohr-Siebeck, 1985] 115).

[75] The τοῦ is lacking in ℵ* B Ψ 33.

[76] See Hengel, "Psalm 110," 46, on a possible hymnic common background to
these two expressions.

[77] Achtemeier, *First Peter*, 273. F.L. Cross, no doubt seeking more precision than
is possible, identified 1 Pet 3:18–22 as a paschal baptismal creed (*I. Peter: A Paschal
Liturgy* [London: Mowbray, 1954] 31–32).

[78] See the comments of Dunn (*Christology*, 108–11) on the importance of this interpretation of Psalm 8.

²²καὶ πάντα ὑπέταξεν ὑπὸ τοὺς πόδας αὐτοῦ

καὶ αὐτὸν ἔδωκεν κεφαλὴν ὑπὲρ πάντα τῇ ἐκκλησίᾳ

²³ἥτις ἐστὶν τὸ σῶμα αὐτοῦ, τὸ πλήρωμα τοῦ τὰ πάντα ἐν πᾶσιν πληρουμένου

²⁰God put this power to work in Christ when he raised him from the dead and seated him at his right hand in the heavenly places, ²¹far above all rule and authority and power and dominion, and above every name that is named, not only in this age but the age to come. ²²And he has put all things under his feet and has made him the head over all things for the church, ²³which is his body, the fullness of him who fills all in all.

This passage shows the continued use of the Ps 110:1/Ps 8:6 tradition in Pauline circles. Ephesians re-interprets these traditional theological images: the subjection is present, not future; the church and the headship of Christ are emphasized in the explication of πάντα.⁷⁹

(f) *Mark 12:36 (par. Matt 22:44)*

Mark 12:36: αὐτὸς Δαυὶδ εἶπεν ἐν τῷ πνεύματι τῷ ἁγίῳ, Εἶπεν κύριος τῷ κυρίῳ μου· Κάθου ἐκ δεξιῶν μου, ἕως ἂν θῶ τοὺς ἐχθρούς σου ὑποκάτω τῶν ποδῶν σου.

David himself, by the Holy Spirit, declared, "The Lord said to my Lord, Sit at my right hand, until I put your enemies under your feet.'"

Mark's ὑποκάτω τῶν ποδῶν (also in Matt 22:44) shows the influence of Ps 8:6.⁸⁰ The pericope relates Jesus' contention that the title "Lord" is more appropriate for the messiah than "son of David." The whole force of Jesus' point presupposes that Psalm 110 is understood as a messianic *testimonium*: simply quoting the psalm proves that the messiah should be called "Lord."⁸¹ If, as shown above, Psalm 110 did not have a clearly messianic meaning in pre-Christian Jewish circles, then

---

⁷⁹ Joachim Gnilka lists some potential sources for this passage: a christological hymn; liturgical material; a meditation on a confession of faith; a creed expressed in a form that was not yet fixed. He plausibly suggests that this material was developed in a pedagogical life-setting and quickly adopted into the worship service of a Christian community (*Der Epheserbrief* [HTKNT 10/2; Freiburg/Basel/Vienna: Herder, 1971] 93–94).

⁸⁰ See Hay, *Right Hand*, 35–36; Hengel, "Psalm 110," 54–55; Ulrich Luz, *Das Geschichtsverständnis des Paulus* (BEVT 49; Munich: Kaiser, 1968) 344–45. Many witnesses of Mark conform the reading to the LXX ὑποπόδιον (e.g., ℵ A L Δ Θ); but the parallel in Matthew supports the non-LXX reading as original (see *TCGNT*, 111). Luke 20:42–43 reads the LXX (except in D it, where ὑποκάτω is read, probably under the influence of the parallels).

⁸¹ This presupposition is also evident in the quotation of Ps 110:1 in Acts 2:34–35: David is not messiah/Lord (he did not ascend to heaven), rather the ascended Christ is messiah/Lord.

the Synoptic accounts presuppose a Christian exegetical activity that *established* this meaning.

To sum up: behind each of the above examples where Ps 110:1 is quoted as a self-evident messianic *testimonium*, we must presuppose a stage of reflection in which Ps 110:1 attained this status with the help of Ps 8:4–6. Psalm 110:1 supplied the imagery of glorification/vindication, as well as a rather clear reference to royal status (sitting at the right hand of God implying enthronement). Psalm 8:4–6 provided an Adam-Christ typology: Ps 8:4–5a (especially "you made him a little lower than the angels") understood as humanity in its weakness and proneness to sin, was identified with Adam; Ps 8:5b–6, understood as humanity restored to its original vocation of glorious rule over creation, was applied to Christ. This view of Christ as representative of renewed humanity makes understandable the frequent application of Christ's glory to believers (Eph 2:6; Col 3:1; Rev 3:21; Polycarp *Phil.* 2.1).

The Adam-Christ interpretation of Psalm 8 is reflected in the later two-advent schema which underlies much of the patristic *testimonia* literature. Tertullian includes "you have made him a little lower than angels" in his first advent TC (*Marc.* 3.7.2), but "will crown him with glory and honor, and put all things under his feet" in his second advent TC (*Marc.* 3.7.5).[82]

5.3.4 *Christian Interpretation of Ps 110:1 with Dan 7:13*

We must distinguish the connection of Ps 110:1 with the "son of man" of Psalm 8 from other NT "Son of Man" traditions, in which Ps 110:1 is combined with Dan 7:13 ("one like a son of man coming with the clouds of heaven").[83] Although I cannot enter into the notoriously complex discussion over the precise meaning(s) of "Son of Man" in the NT, I argue that we can distinguish between two exegetical traditions:

(1) *Christ as the Heavenly Son of Man*: derived from reflections on Daniel 7, mediated through conceptions of angelic intermediary powers, and found in the *Similitudes of Enoch*, *4 Ezra*, and in the Gospels.[84]

---

[82] See sect. 3.5.4 above for a summary of this two advents chapter in Tertullian.

[83] In the following, I use "Son of Man" as an eschatological title and "son of man" as a generic reference to humanity, though of course the distinction in individual cases is not always clear.

[84] See Collins, *Scepter*, 173–94, for a description of the Jewish texts.

(2) *Christ as Representative Human*: the tradition presented above, derived from Psalm 8 and involving an Adam-Christ typology in which Christ is the representative of a renewed humanity.[85]

Martin Hengel does not seem to distinguish clearly enough between these two traditions when he suggests that 1 Cor 15:45, 47 provides evidence for Paul's knowledge of the Son of Man tradition (presumably the heavenly Son of Man as found in the Synoptics); and that Stephen's vision (Acts 7:55–56) combines elements from Psalm 8 and Ps 110:1.[86] More accurate are the observations of Hay and Dunn, who doubt that Paul had contact with the Danielic Son of Man tradition.[87]

The linking of Ps 110:1 with eschatological Danielic Son of Man traditions is most obvious in the Synoptic passion accounts. Jesus' answer to the high priest at his trial conflates Ps 110:1b with Dan 7:13:

> *Mark 14:62*: καὶ ὄψεσθε τὸν υἱὸν τοῦ ἀνθρώπου ἐκ δεξιῶν καθήμενον τῆς δυνάμεως καὶ ἐρχόμενον μετὰ τῶν νεφελῶν τοῦ οὐρανοῦ.
> and you will see the Son of Man seated at the right hand of the Power, and coming with the clouds of heaven.
> *Matt 26:64*: ἀπ' ἄρτι ὄψεσθε τὸν υἱὸν τοῦ ἀνθρώπου καθήμενον ἐκ δεξιῶν τῆς δυνάμεως καὶ ἐρχόμενον ἐπὶ τῶν νεφελῶν τοῦ οὐρανοῦ.
> *Luke 22:69*: ἀπὸ τοῦ νῦν δὲ ἔσται ὁ υἱὸς τοῦ ἀνθρώπου καθήμενος ἐκ δεξιῶν τῆς δυνάμεως τοῦ θεοῦ.
> *Dan 7:13* (Theodotion): καὶ ἰδοὺ μετὰ τῶν νεφελῶν τοῦ οὐρανοῦ ὡς υἱὸς ἀνθρώπου ἐρχόμενος ἦν καὶ ἕως τοῦ παλαιοῦ τῶν ἡμερῶν ἔφθασεν καὶ ἐνώπιον αὐτοῦ προσηνέχθη.

---

[85] But see Francis J. Moloney ("The Reinterpretation of Psalm VIII and the Son of Man Debate," *NTS* 27 [1981] 656–72) who argues on the basis of targumic evidence that the son of man in Psalm 8 was understood as a messianic figure in the 1st cent. CE. Given the uncertain dating of the targum, however, the argument is less than convincing. No doubt other sources also influenced "representative human" speculation and Adam-Christ typology, including the many Adam traditions known from Philo and other intertestamental texts (see Segal, *Two Powers*, 189; Dunn, *Christology*, 101–7). Anthony J. Chvala-Smith ("The Boundaries of Christology: 1 Corinthians 15:20–28 and its Exegetical Substructure" [Ph.D. diss., Marquette University, 1993] 114–23) rightly points to the influence of Gen 1:26–28 in the development of this tradition.

[86] Hengel, "Psalm 110," 54. I hold that Stephen's vision owes more to the traditions deriving from Dan 7:13.

[87] Hay considers it only a possibility that Paul had the titular "Son of Man" in mind in 1 Cor 15:25 (*Right Hand*, 109); for Dunn, both Paul and Hebrews have no contact with the eschatological Son of Man concept (associated with Dan 7:13) in the Gospels (*Christology*, 91).

Dan 7:13 (LXX): καὶ ἰδοὺ ἐπὶ τῶν νεφελῶν τοῦ οὐρανοῦ ὡς υἱὸς ἀνθρώπου ἤρχετο, καὶ ὡς παλαιὸς ἡμερῶν παρῆν, καὶ οἱ παρεστηκότες παρῆσαν αὐτῷ.[88]

All the Synoptics read the LXX of Ps 110:1b (δύναμις is used as a circumlocution for God). All three replace the "lord" of Ps 110:1 with the "Son of Man" from Dan 7:13; Matthew and Mark make the reference explicit by quoting ἐρχόμενος μετὰ τῶν νεφελῶν τοῦ οὐρανοῦ from Daniel. The Danielic image of the one like a Son of Man coming on the clouds is understood eschatologically: all three Gospels have similar images in their accounts of Jesus' eschatological discourse (see Mark 13:26; Matt 24:30; Luke 21:27). This identification of the "lord" (Ps 110:1) with the eschatological Son of Man is also made in Acts 7:55–56 (Jesus = Son of Man = one standing at God's right hand). In Matt 19:28 (Son of Man, thrones, twelve judges) and Matt 25:31 (Son of Man as the eschatological King), the Son of Man is identified as the royal messianic ruler.[89]

We have in Jesus' confession to the high priest a compositional use of Ps 110:1 and Dan 7:13. The conflation of texts is hardly due to an *ad hoc* inspiration of the evangelists; rather it points to an earlier stage of exegetical activity in which the image of Jesus' exaltation (Ps 110:1) is combined with the image of the eschatological Son of Man from Daniel. Psalm 110:1 can be used as an implicit *testimonium*, showing that the "Son of Man" will be exalted, because its meaning has been established by this earlier exegetical activity. Other Christian conflations of Ps 110:1/Dan 7:13 (*Sib. Or.* 2.241–45 and *Apoc. Peter* 6) follow Matt 19:28 and 25:31 in casting Jesus in the role of eschatological judge.[90] I shall consider further the Synoptic allusions, and their possible use of Zech 12:10, in my section on the second advent (sect. 5.5 below).

---

[88] Although the Jewish translator Theodotion of Ephesus was active in the mid-2d. cent. CE, quotations from the Theodotion recension (an attempt to bring the Old Greek translations closer to the proto-MT) show that this translation effort began in the 1st cent. BCE. Some scholars thus refer to a "Ur-Theodotion," but I will simply use "Theodotion" with the understanding that it refers to a translation earlier than the "historical Theodotion." Theodotion's edition of Daniel replaced the Old Greek version in the LXX at an early date. See Leonard J. Greenspoon, "Theodotion, Theodotion's Version," *ABD* 6. 447–48. Mark's μετά reflects Theodotion, while Matthew's ἐπί is drawn from the LXX.

[89] These Matthean passages are very likely influenced by the *Similitudes* of *1 Enoch* (Dunn, *Christology*, 78; Collins, *Scepter*, 177).

[90] It should be noticed that the Son of Man in Dan 7:13 arrives on the scene *after* the judgment; the portrayal of the Son of Man as a judge seems dependent on exegetical traditions evident in the *Similitudes* of *1 Enoch* (see, e.g., 69.27).

Anthony J. Chvala-Smith has argued that the "exegetical substructure" to 1 Cor 15:20–28 involves reflection on Ps 110:1, Psalm 8, and Daniel 7—i.e., a conflation of the two traditions which I have outlined. Chvala-Smith also finds that Paul has taken over the combination of Psalm 110 and Psalm 8 from previous Christian tradition;[91] Paul's achievement is to further combine it with Daniel 7.[92] Chvala-Smith plausibly holds that the language of "kingdom," "power," "authority," derive ultimately from Daniel 7, although his suggestion that Paul has reinterpreted the Son of Man from Daniel 7 in a messianic sense is less convincing. Chvala Smith's work is especially important in identifying the literary form in which Paul combined these texts and traditions: the apocalypse. We can easily imagine that other early Christians transmitted scriptural *testimonia* reflections in the form of short apocalyptic narratives such as we find in 1 Cor 15:20–28.

5.3.5 *Psalm 110:1 and the High Priest Typology*

Although I will not study in any detail the Christian use of Ps 110:4, "The Lord has sworn and will not change his mind, 'You are a priest forever according to the order of Melchizedek'," some observations are necessary. Hebrews of course makes extensive use of this verse in developing its image of Jesus as high priest. This image's influence on Hebrews's interpretation of Ps 110:1 is patent:

> *1:3*: *When he had made purification for sins*, he sat down at the right hand of the Majesty on high,
> *8:1*: We have such a *high priest*, one who is seated at the right hand of the throne of the Majesty in the heavens,
> *10:12*: But when Christ had offered for all time *a single sacrifice for sins*, he sat down at the right hand of God.

Although Hebrews is apparently the only Christian text before Justin to make use of Ps 110:4,[93] the interpretation of Christ as high priest is not so maverick as first appears. The *testimonia* sources of both Justin *Dialogue* 42 and *Barnabas* 7 know a Jesus as high priest typology;[94] I have already argued (sect. 4.4.2a above) that a TC on Jesus' death as an atoning sacrifice underlies Acts 3:22–25. It would not

---

[91] Chvala-Smith, "Boundaries of Christology," 124.
[92] See ibid., 127–73 on the role of Daniel 7.
[93] So Hay, *Right Hand*, 50.
[94] See Skarsaune, *Prophecy*, 307–13.

be surprising, then, if the traditional formula used by Paul in Rom 8:34, "Christ Jesus who died, who was raised, who is at the right hand of God, who indeed intercedes for us," involves a combination of imagery from Ps 110:1 and a high priest typology.[95] This typology was worked out not only on the basis of Ps 110:4, but also on the basis of reflection on such passages as Zechariah 3 (Joshua the high priest) and passages on the Day of Atonement (e.g., Lev 23:29).

5.3.6   *Psalm 110:1 and "Two Powers" Testimonia*

I showed above (sect. 4.5.3) that Ps 110:1 was a part of "two powers" *testimonia* collections in Justin and Irenaeus, and that the "two powers" tradition was one of the sources behind the catena in Hebrews. I will briefly add further evidence of this tradition here. In *Barn.* 12:10–11, the author contends that Jesus is not "son of man" but "son of God"; and that Jesus is not "David's son" but rather the Lord. As proof, *Barnabas* quotes Ps 110:1 and Isa 45:1 in its popular "Christianized" form. This latter text, instead of reading the LXX "The Lord God said to my anointed Cyrus" (τῷ χριστῷ μου Κύρῳ), reads "The Lord said to my anointed Lord" (τῷ χριστῷ μου κυρίῳ) (i.e., "Christ my Lord").[96] *Barnabas*'s major interest here (establishing that Jesus is "son of God") fits awkwardly with the point of the adapted quotation (Jesus is "Lord").[97] For *Barnabas*, then, "son of God" and "Lord" are interchangeable. Though showing some connection with the Synoptic accounts of Jesus' debate with Jewish authorities (Mark 12:35–37 par.), the complete rejection of the terms "David's son" and "son of man" for Jesus point to *Barnabas*'s use of an tradition independent from the Synoptics.[98]

The combination of the tendentious Isa 45:1 with Ps 110:1 remained a staple in the *testimonia* literature. Tertullian and Novatian show an ironic development in the function of the adapted Isa 45:1/Ps 110:1: against Christians who hold to the identity of Father and Son, they use the texts to prove that Christ and God *are distinct!*[99] Ps.-Gregory

---

[95] So Hengel, "Psalm 110," 50.

[96] The reading κυρίῳ may easily have come into a textual tradition through scribal error, although we have no extant LXX evidence. I agree with Kraft ("Isaiah," 342 n. 36) that the change was most likely an intentional Christian alteration, although no sure conclusion can be made.

[97] See Hay, *Right Hand*, 38; Carleton Paget, *Barnabas*, 161.

[98] So Carleton Paget, *Barnabas*, 161; Köhler, *Matthäusevangeliums*, 119.

[99] Tertullian *Prax.* 11.7–8; he also reads the adapted Isa 45:1 in *Prax.* 28 and

(*Test.* 16) has the combination in his chapter "On the unbelief of the Jews and the church of the gentiles"; Lactantius (*Inst.* 4.12.17–18) includes it as proof of Christ's ascension. The Christianized Isa 45:1 also appears in TCs without Ps 110:1.[100]

The above citations provide solid evidence for the enduring presence of Ps 110:1 in collections of "two powers" texts.[101] In some authors, most clearly in Irenaeus's *Proof* and in Novatian's *On the Trinity*, these texts are part of catechetical material.[102] Although the evidence goes well beyond NT times, the fact that a non-standard text such as Isa 45:1 was still quoted as authoritative scripture in the second through the fourth centuries indicates that the roots of its authority run deep. The "two powers" interpretation of Ps 110:1 may represent the beginnings of this authoritative tradition.

5.3.7   *Psalm 110:1 and the Two Advents Pattern*

In the two advents pattern of much of Christian *testimonia* literature, Ps 110:1 is of course included as a proof-text of Christ's glorious advent. Irenaeus *A.H.* 4.33.11 provides a good example:

> For some of them, beholding Him in glory, saw His glorious life at the Father's right hand; others beheld him coming on the clouds of glory as the Son of Man; and those who declared regarding Him, "They shall look on Him whom they have pierced," indicating his [second] advent, concerning which He Himself says, "Do you think that when the Son of man comes, he shall find faith on earth?"[103]

This passage should be compared with the two advents schema in Tertullian *Marc.* 3.7 (sect. 3.5.4d above). Although Tertullian does not include Ps 110:1 among his glorious advent texts, it is noteworthy that he includes Dan 7:13; Ps 8:6, and Zech 12:10, i.e., all texts that "traveled with" Ps 110:1 in early Christian reflections. We must

---

A.J. 7.2 (here it proves Christ's universal rule). Novatian *Trin.* 26.6–7 distinguishes between Christ and God (Ps 2:7–8 and Gen 19:24 are also included in this chapter); in *Trin.* 9.8, Ps 110:1 appears in a traditional TC as a proof of the resurrection. On Tertullian, see sect. 3.5.4 above; on Novatian, sect. 3.5.9.

[100] See Cyprian *Quir.* 1.21, "That the Gentiles should rather believe in Christ." For further discussion of the widespread use of Isa 45:1, see Kraft, "Christian Transmission," 214, 216 n. 3; idem, "Isaiah," 342.

[101] Segal also holds that Ps 110:1 may have been interpreted as a "two powers" text (*Two Powers*, 207); see also Beskow, *Rex Gloriae*, 84.

[102] On catechetical TCs in these authors, see sect. 3.4.6c (Irenaeus *Proof*) and 3.5.9 (Novatian).

[103] The allusions are to Ps 110:1; Dan 7:13; Zech 12:10; and to Luke 18:8.

reckon with the possibility that Irenaeus and Tertullian reproduce here a very early Christian exegetical tradition in which texts were collected under the more general humiliation/glorification schema. This more general classification is one possible explanation for the wide range of applications: Jesus' resurrection, ascension, second advent, activity as ruler/judge would all be subsumed under the general heading of glorification. The oldest collections may have simply applied the texts to Christ's glorification/vindication after death; later interpretations would then have made more specific applications.[104]

5.3.8 *Ps 110:1 and the Substructure of New Testament Theology*

To what extent did Ps 110:1 influence NT theology? Specifically, is it the major inspiration behind Christian application of the title "Lord" to Jesus? C. H. Dodd, while admitting that "various Hellenistic usages affected the development of the idea of *Kyrios* in early Christian theology," nevertheless held that the fundamental influence was Psalm 110.[105] Dodd is certainly correct to emphasize a Jewish scriptural background rather than a background of the hellenistic mystery religions for the immediate source of the κύριος title.[106]

Yet the bald contention that interpretation of Ps 110:1 was fundamental to the development of the κύριος title is open to serious qualification on two grounds. First, the initial attraction of Ps 110:1 may have been only part of what was a larger pattern of scriptural reflection on two heavenly powers in early Christianity and contemporary Judaism. This reflection was of course not inspired completely by a desire to explicate difficult scriptural passages; philosophical

---

[104] The alternative, of course, is that two advents collections are later combinations of disparate traditions. The hypothesis of the earlier, more general collections should not be dismissed too quickly, however; I will take up this question again in the discussion on the second advent (sect. 5.4 below).

[105] "But since the title 'Lord' is given to Christ in a *testimonium* which is as clearly primitive as anything we have, it seems unnecessary to go farther for the origin of the usage, however it may have been extended and enriched in meaning from other sources" (Dodd, *Scriptures*, 121).

[106] Dodd's position is also held by Martin Hengel (*The Son of God: The Origin of Christology and the History of Jewish-Hellenistic Religion* [Philadelphia: Fortress, 1976] 77–83). Hengel argues that κύριος was not a typical title for the mystery religions, indeed "we have no evidence for mysteries in Syria in the first century" (pp. 77–78). On the other hand, he cites evidence from Qumran (11Q Melchizedek) in which the angelic mediator Melchizedek is characterized with attributes of God (pp. 80–83).

reflection on the role of powers intermediate between humanity and divinity was also a motivating factor.[107] Secondly, it is clear that early christological reflection on Jesus as Lord could be formulated without reference to Ps 110:1; the famous christological hymn in Phil 2:6–11 is an obvious example.[108] Even when Ps 110:1 is used directly, the above study has shown that its meaning as a *testimonium* is dependent not on its intrinsic value, but rather on its combination with other texts (Ps 8:6; Dan 7:13, other "glorious advent" texts) and theological images (high priest typology). In short, it is difficult to single out the precise influence of Ps 110:1 as distinct from a host of other influences on the title "Lord" and related christological beliefs.

This is not to deny, however, the far-reaching influence of Ps 110:1. Once established as a *testimonium*, the imagery of the "session at the right hand" became a part of Christian worship (hymns, liturgy), confessions, and eventually part of formal creeds.[109] While the passage did not give rise to Christian beliefs in Jesus' exaltation, heavenly enthronement, and universal rule, it did provide striking language with which to express these beliefs. Hay well points out that the "session" was a way of expressing the supreme exaltation of Christ without diminishing the sovereignty of God the Father, and of describing the uniquely close relationship of Christ and God while still maintaining a clear distinction.[110] The twin applications of this *testimonium* are clear in Tertullian and Novatian: they quote Ps 110:1 in one context to support Christ's glorious exaltation and universal rule, and in another to prove Christ's distinctiveness from God.

---

[107] Philo's scriptural exegesis is the most obvious example of this philosophical motivation, but he was hardly an isolated case. See Thomas H. Tobin (*The Creation of Man: Philo and the History of Interpretation* [CBQMS 14; Washington, D.C.: Catholic Biblical Association of America, 1983]) on exegetical traditions that Philo has taken over from Jewish predecessors.

[108] The Philippians hymn does include a scriptural allusion, but to Isa 45:23 (Phil 2:10–11); other scholars see in the δοῦλος of v 7 an allusion to Isa 53:3, 11. For discussion of other NT christological exaltation texts that do not refer to Ps 110:1, see Philipp Vielhauer, "Ein Weg zur neutestamentlichen Christologie? Prüfung der Thesen Ferdinand Hahns," *EvT* 25 (1965) 24–72; repr. in idem, *Aufsätze zum Neuen Testament* (TBü 31; Munich: Kaiser, 1965) 171.

[109] See Kelly, *Creeds*, 151. Kelly, commenting on the phrases "ascended into the heavens" and "sits at the right hand of the father" of the ancient creed of the Roman church, concludes that "ultimately the ideas contained in these clauses go back to *Ps.* 110,1."

[110] Hay, *Right Hand*, 159.

5.3.9   *Conclusions on Ps 110:1 as a* Testimonium

The study of Ps 110:1 has given us some valuable insights into early
Christian use of scripture. A central conclusion is that Paul, our earliest NT author, is already alluding to Ps 110:1 as a firmly established christological *testimonium*. I have argued that the messianic
significance of this passage could not be assumed in pre-Christian
Jewish circles, and it follows that Christian scriptural interpreters
established this meaning before Paul. We have seen some hints of
the forms which this interpretive process took: Ps 110:1 was the
object of a search of the scriptures for "two powers" terminology; it
was used in composing early christological confessions and hymns;
it was combined with Ps 8:6 and Dan 7:13; it formed part of extensive two advent collections and of specific TCs aimed at demonstrating Christ's superiority to the angels. Scholarship has yet to grapple
with the full implications of this intense oral and written scriptural
activity in its historical reconstruction of earliest Christianity.[111]

Christian use of Ps 110:1 does not correspond to Dodd's model
of the use of textual blocks. Outside of the much used first verse,
only v 4 received Christian attention (and that only in Hebrews)
before the time of Justin. The interpretation of the passage reflects
both a remarkable unity across many different NT writings—it is
always referred to the exaltation of Christ after his death—and a noteworthy diversity—being applied to Christ's resurrection, ascension,
second advent, role as judge, and analogously applied to believers.
The passage is used forensically (most obviously in the Hebrews TC),
but even more importantly it is used compositionally, providing important terminology and imagery for expressing the relationship of the
glorified Christ with God. Its theological influence is subtle: although
it was hardly constitutive of early Christian beliefs, its use was so
widespread that we can suppose that it influenced later theological
thought, e.g., in offering language which allowed the expression of
both the near identity yet also the clear distinction between God
and Christ.

---

[111] I am assuming that an oral worship tradition is an adequate explanation for
the combination of Ps 110:1 and Ps 8:6, often expressed in hymnic and confessional formulas. The TC in Hebrews, the quotation of conflated texts in Mark
12:36 (Matt 22:44) and Mark 14:62 (par.), and the presence of Ps 110:1 in "two
powers" collections likely derive from written sources.

5.4 *Isaiah 6:9–10 and the Hardening Tradition*

Craig A. Evans has written a comprehensive survey on the use of Isa 6:9–10 in Second Temple Jewish and early Christian literature.[112] I shall use Evans's work in sketching the main outlines of these interpretive traditions, while considering some implications for *testimonia* research.

5.4.1 *Isaiah 6:9–10 in the MT, Qumran, and Greek Translations*

I first present Isa 6:9–10 in its original setting in the Hebrew scriptures, and then explore a range of interpretive traditions in which later readers struggled to understand this passage in which God commands Isaiah to make the heart of the people dull and to stop up their ears. The setting of this passage in Isaiah 6 is the heavenly throne room, where Yahweh gives Isaiah his commission as a prophet:

⁹ויאמר לך ואמרת לעם הזה
שמעו שמוע ואל־תבינו
וראו ראו ואל־תדעו
¹⁰השמן לב־העם הזה
ואזניו הכבד ועיניו השע
פן־יראה בעיניו ובאזניו ישמע
ולבבו יבין ושב ורפא לו

⁹Go and say to this people:
"Keep listening but do not comprehend;
keep looking, but do not understand."
¹⁰Make the mind of this people dull,
and stop their ears, and shut their eyes,
so that they may not look with their eyes, and listen with their ears,
and comprehend with their minds, and turn and be healed

With its use of Hiphil (causative) imperatives, the passage is uncompromising in its insistence that the prophet harden the people.

A quick survey of the versions indicates that this image of God deliberately hardening people may have been theologically unacceptable in some circles, and hence was softened in different ways. In 1QIsaiah[a] for example, the following version is read:[113]

---

[112] Evans, *To See and Not Perceive: Isaiah 6.9–10 in Early Jewish and Christian Interpretation* (JSOTSup 64; Sheffield: JSOT, 1989).

[113] Col. 6, ll. 2–5. Hebrew text in Millar Burrows with J.C. Trever and W.H. Brownlee, eds., *The Dead Sea Scrolls of St. Mark's Monastery* (New Haven, CT: The American Schools of Oriental Research, 1950).

⁹וִיואמר לך ואמרתה לעם הזה
שמעו שמוע ו<u>על</u> תבינו
ראו ראו ו<u>על</u> תדעו
¹⁰<u>השמ</u> לב העם הזה
ואוניו הכבד ועיניו השע
פן יראה בעיניו ובאוניו ישמעו
<u>בלבבו</u> יבין ושב ורפא לו

1QIsaᵃ essentially follows the MT, but several minor divergences (underlined above) may well be significant.

Each divergence, taken by itself, may be attributed simply to scribal error or textual variation. William Hugh Brownlee, however, followed by Evans, makes a plausible case that in fact these changes reveal a pattern of deliberate alterations designed to soften the sense of the passage.[114]

(1) The MT אל ("not") is replaced by על. This change may simply be an example of orthographic variance.[115] Brownlee, however, argues for an intentional change: "Keep listening but do not comprehend" is changed to "Keep on listening, *because* you may understand."[116] Brownlee is probably correct in seeing this change as intentional rather than due to scribal error, since the same change is made in 9c.[117]

(2) In v 10a, the final ן of השמן ("make dull" from the root שמן) is omitted, resulting in the reading השמ ("make appalled or desolate" from the root שמם).[118] Brownlee offers a passage from the Qumran hymns to illustrate how this verb was used in other contexts:

---

[114] The following discussion is based on Brownlee, *The Meaning of the Qumrân Scrolls for the Bible, with Special Attention to the Book of Isaiah* (New York: Oxford University Press, 1964) 186–88; Evans, *To See*, 54–56.

[115] This is one explanation suggested by Eduard Y. Kutscher (*The Language and Linguistic Background of the Isaiah Scroll [1QIsaᵃ]* [STDJ 6; Leiden: Brill, 1974] 410, 506). Under the category of "weakening of laryngeals and pharyngeals, Kutscher notes that the Isaiah scroll replaces the MT א with ע, and gives this passage as an example.

[116] Apparently Brownlee has in mind the meanings given in *BDB* s.v. על II. f. (b): "on account of; on the basis of," or III.c: "because." Evans takes the על as an abbreviation for על אשר (*To See*, 55; cf. BDB s.v. על III. a.).

[117] Kutscher also suggests, "The scribe erroneously supposed the word to be the preposition אל and changed both instances to על" (Kutscher, *Isaiah Scroll*, 410). Yet this amounts to the same conclusion reached by Brownlee: whether "erroneously" or not, the scribe has avoided the implications of the negative אל.

[118] Kutscher also suggests that "the scribe found it difficult to understand the verb שמן in conjunction with לב, whereas שמם, which is found over a 100 times was more intelligible to him; cf. ישתומם לבי Ps. cxliii 4" (ibid., 292). F. J. Morrow ("The Text of Isaiah at Qumran," [Ph.D. diss., Catholic University of America, 1973] 27) also reckons with an intentional change (cited in Evans, *To See*, 54).

my eyes are blind from having seen evil,
my ears, through hearing the shedding of blood,
my heart is horrified (הׁשמ) at wicked schemes (1QH 15.2–3)[119]

Brownlee holds that this passage is essentially a reinterpretation of the images in Isa 6:9–10. God does not harden the speaker, rather the speaker is hardened on account of the wickedness around him or her. This reinterpretation, Brownlee further suggests, echoes one already made in MT Isa 33:15:

[Those who walk righteously and speak uprightly]
who stop their ears from hearing of bloodshed
and shut their eyes from looking on evil

Thus the translation of the Isaiah scroll can be seen as participating in a wider tradition (witnessed in Isa 33:15 and in the Hodayoth) which reinterpreted Isa 6:9–10.

(3) In v 9d ולבבו יבין is replaced by בלבבו יבין, changing the meaning from the negative "(lest) it the understand" to a positive admonition to understand.[120]

It is perhaps coincidental that these textual variations may all be understood as altering the passage's meaning, but the overall pattern of the changes indicates that they are intentional. Brownlee plausibly concludes that through minor alterations in the text, the Qumran scribe(s) have completely reinterpreted the sense of the passage: the people are hardened *against* evil and bloodshed; God's intention (through the prophet) is still to lead the people to healing. This interpretive use of textual variants is a well established scribal practice at Qumran, one that Stendahl rightly emphasized in positing his "school" model.

The LXX also gives a translation of Isa 6:9–10 which reinterprets its original sense:

---

[119] Hebrew text of 1QHᵃ (1QHodayothᵃ) in E.L. Sukenik, *The Dead Sea Scrolls of the Hebrew University* (Jerusalem, 1954–55); ET in *Scrolls*, 317–61.

[120] Brownlee, *Qumrân Scrolls*, 186; Evans, *To See*, 55. If one wishes to deny that this latter change is intentional, alternative explanations are difficult to find. Thus Joseph R. Rosenbloom concludes that it is "another variation without sensible explanation. That the scribe may have been copying from dictation does not help.... This particular section indicates the difficulty of narrowing down the method of copying the MS and a consistent pattern for its deviations from the MT" (*The Dead Sea Isaiah Scroll: A Literary Analysis. A Comparison with the Masoretic Text and the Biblia Hebraica* [Grand Rapids: Eerdmans, 1970] 14).

⁹ Ἀκοῇ ἀκούσετε καὶ οὐ μὴ συνῆτε
καὶ βλέποντες βλέψετε καὶ οὐ μὴ ἴδητε·
¹⁰ἐπαχύνθη γὰρ ἡ καρδία τοῦ λαοῦ τούτου,
καὶ τοῖς ὠσὶν αὐτῶν βαρέως ἤκουσαν
καὶ τοὺς ὀφθαλμοὺς αὐτῶν ἐκάμμυσαν,
μήποτε ἴδωσιν τοῖς ὀφθαλμοῖς καὶ τοῖς ὠσὶν ἀκούσωσιν
καὶ τῇ καρδίᾳ συνῶσιν
καὶ ἐπιστρέψωσιν καὶ ἰάσομαι αὐτούς.

⁹Keep listening, but you will never understand
Keep looking, but you will never see
¹⁰For the mind of this people is dulled
and their ears hear with difficulty
and they have shut their eyes
lest they see with their eyes and hear with their ears
and understand with their heart
and turn—and I will heal them.

The use of future verb tenses in verse nine is a standard LXX rendering of the Hebrew imperatives.[121] In verse ten, however, it is apparent that the translator wishes to avoid the implication that God (through Isaiah) has deliberately hardened the people. The causative command of the MT: "Make the mind of this people dull" has become a statement of fact: "the mind of this people is dulled." The Hebrew imperative "shut their eyes" has become "they have shut their eyes." The people are obdurate, but the LXX avoids saying that God has deliberately caused this state.[122]

The Greek recensions of the LXX, although their normal tendency is to translate more closely to the Hebrew, follow the LXX in avoiding the causative sense of the MT verbs.[123]

---

[121] E.g., futures are used to translate the commandments in the decalogue. While Evans acknowledges this possibility, he nevertheless maintains (in light of the changes in v 10, on which see below) that the force of these futures is predictive (*To See*, 62, esp. n. 12). This is in fact how the NRSV takes the sense, when it renders Matt 13:14b (= LXX Isa 6:9): "You will indeed listen, but never understand, and you will indeed look, but never perceive." Given the Hebrew imperative, however, it is most natural to understand the Greek in the same way.

[122] See Evans, *To See*, 62–63. Isac Leo Seeligmann's study of LXX translation techniques found three ways of rendering the causative Hebrew verbs: (1) using the verb as an object of ποιέω; (2) finding a Greek equivalent for the causative notion; and (3) using "transitive or even passive forms of verbs, thereby completely altering the construction and even the meaning" (*The Septuagint Version of Isaiah: A Discussion of its Problems* [Leiden: Brill, 1948] 55). This third technique is obviously employed in this passage.

[123] See Evans, *To See*, 64–65. Symmachus, for example, renders, ὁ λαός οὗτος τὰ ὦτα ἐβάρυνε, καὶ τοὺς ὀφθαλμοὺς αὐτοῦ ἔμυσε for v 10a. See also Evans's analysis of the Aramaic and Syriac versions (pp. 69–80).

5.4.2   *Hardening Traditions in the Hebrew Scriptures*

Isaiah 6:9–10 is not the only scriptural text which holds that God hardens people, even his own chosen people:

> *Exod 9:12*: But the Lord hardened the heart of Pharaoh, and he would not listen to them, just as the Lord had spoken to Moses.[124]
> *Deut 29:4*: But to this day the Lord has not given you a mind to understand, or eyes to see, or ears to hear.
> *Isa 29:10*: For the Lord has poured out upon you a spirit of deep sleep; he has closed your eyes, you prophets, and covered your heads, you seers.
> *Isa 63:17*: Why, O Lord, do you make us stray from your ways and harden our heart, so that we do not fear you?

Other texts retain the images of seeing and not understanding, of hearing, and not comprehending, but they attribute responsibility to the people:

> Hear this, O foolish and senseless people,
> who have eyes, but do not see,
> who have ears, but do not hear. (Jer 5:21)

> Mortal, you are living in the midst of a rebellious house,
> who have eyes to see but do not see,
> who have ears to hear but do not hear. (Ezek 12:2–3a)

This (re)interpretation of the seeing/hearing imagery occurs also in Second Isaiah: "Hear, you deaf; and look, you blind, that you may see!" (Isa 42:18). The state of blindness and deafness is not seen as permanent: hope is held out for a reversal of fortune.[125]

In sum, the hardening tradition in the Hebrew scriptures includes "hard" versions, in which God is the subject of the hardening, together with "softer" versions, which give more credit to human action. The metaphor of blindness and deafness can be seen both as a permanent

---

[124] "Harden" is expressed by חזק D stem. Already in the Exodus narrative itself, the struggle to express the relationship between human and divine agency is evident, resulting in a variety of explanations: "he [Pharaoh] hardened his heart (8:15 = MT 8:11) (כבד H stem); "But Pharaoh's heart was hardened (8:19 = MT 8:15) (חזק G stem).

[125] Some scholars understand Isa 6:12–13 as a hopeful interpretive addition to the originally completely negative account of the prophet's commission. Thus Otto Kaiser (*Isaiah 1–12: A Commentary* [OTL 16; Philadelphia: Westminster, 1972] 84): "But the conclusion of v. 13 is also secondary, because it gives a positive sense to the comparison between the survivors and the growth that springs up after the felling of the tree . . . while its original sense was negative."

state ordained by God, or a temporary state that may be overcome
(Second Isaiah, Deut 29:4). This same ambiguity is carried over into
early Christian reflections.

5.4.3 *The Hardening Tradition in Paul*

Paul does not quote Isa 6:9–10 directly, but I hope to show that he
is certainly familiar with scriptural hardening traditions related to
this passage. In 2 Cor 3:14, he says of the Israelites at the time of
Moses, "But their minds were hardened (ἐπωρώθη)." A few lines later,
Paul maintains (perhaps of unbelievers in general): "In their case the
god of this world has blinded (ἐτύφλωσεν) the minds of the unbelievers, to keep them from seeing the light of the gospel of the glory
of Christ, who is the image of God" (2 Cor 4:4). Paul knows both
"hard" and "soft" versions of the hardening tradition.

We have evidence, however, that Paul was not the first Christian
to make use of this tradition. The term πωρόω gives us our first hint.
This verb, together with its cognate noun πώρωσις, occurs a striking number of times in a variety of NT texts, always in the sense
of a hardening of the heart or mind:[126]

> *Mark 6:52*: οὐ γὰρ συνῆκαν ἐπὶ τοῖς ἄρτοις, ἀλλ᾽ ἦν αὐτῶν ἡ καρδία
> πεπωρωμένη.
> for they [the disciples] did not understand about the loaves, but
> their hearts were hardened.
> *Mark 8:17*: οὔπω νοεῖτε οὐδὲ συνίετε; πεπωρωμένην ἔχετε τὴν καρδίαν
> ὑμῶν;
> Do you still not perceive or understand? Are your hearts hardened?
> *John 12:40*: τετύφλωκεν αὐτῶν τοὺς ὀφθαλμοὺς καὶ ἐπώρωσεν αὐτῶν τὴν
> καρδίαν,
> He has blinded their eyes and hardened their heart.
> *Rom 11:7*: ἡ δὲ ἐκλογὴ ἐπέτυχεν· οἱ δὲ λοιποὶ ἐπωρώθησαν,
> The elect obtained it, but the rest were hardened.
> *Mark 3:5*: συλλυπούμενος ἐπὶ τῇ πωρώσει τῆς καρδίας αὐτῶν
> he was grieved at their hardness of heart.
> *Rom 11:25*: πώρωσις ἀπὸ μέρους τῷ Ἰσραὴλ γέγονεν
> a hardening has come over part of Israel.
> *Eph 4:18*: ἀπηλλοτριωμένοι τῆς ζωῆς τοῦ θεοῦ διὰ τὴν ἄγνοιαν τὴν οὖσαν
> ἐν αὐτοῖς, διὰ τὴν πώρωσιν τῆς καρδίας αὐτῶν
> [They are] alienated from the life of God because of ignorance and
> hardness of heart.

---

[126] See also the use of πωρόω in *Herm. Man.* 4.2.1; 12.4.4; and πώρωσις in
Theophilus *Autolycus* 2.35, in the sense of hardness of heart.

This widespread NT use of πωρόω/πώρωσις is the more remarkable since the verb πωρόω is found only twice in the LXX (Job 17:7; Prov 10:20 A) (neither time in the sense of hardening of heart or mind); πώρωσις does not occur at all. This usage, then, may be taken as a signal to a common early Christian source.

Romans 9–11 provides insight into Paul's understanding of the hardening tradition in general, and of the term πωρόω in particular. These chapters are dominated by Paul's reflection on various forms of the hardening tradition as he struggles to discern Israel's fate in God's plan. In Rom 9:11–18, Paul provides scriptural examples (Jacob/Esau; Pharaoh) to demonstrate that God has mercy on, or hardens, whomever he chooses; Rom 9:19–29 reflects further on his theme, with *testimonia* demonstrating God's sovereign will in choosing a remnant from both Jews and gentiles. Paul's quotation of a "stone" *testimonium* (Isa 28:16/Isa 8:14) in Rom 9:33 reflects a hard form of the hardening tradition: God himself has laid a stumbling stone in Zion.[127] Among his wide-ranging scriptural reflections in Romans 10, Paul includes two *testimonia* that are well established in Christian TCs designed to "prove" God's rejection of Israel: Isa 53:1 (10:16) and Isa 65:2 (10:21).[128]

In Rom 11:7–10, Paul returns specifically to the theme of hardening: "What then? Israel failed to obtain what it was seeking. The elect obtained it, but the rest were hardened (ἐπωρώθησαν)." With the introduction, "as it is written," Paul explicates his understanding of πωρόω by presenting two *testimonia*, the composite Deut 29:3/Isa 29:10, and Ps 69 (68):23–24:

> *Rom 11:8*: Ἔδωκεν αὐτοῖς ὁ θεὸς πνεῦμα κατανύξεως, ὀφθαλμοὺς τοῦ μὴ βλέπειν καὶ ὦτα τοῦ μὴ ἀκούειν, ἕως τῆς σήμερον ἡμέρας.
> God gave them a sluggish spirit, eyes that would not see and ears that would not hear, down to this very day.
>
> *Deut 29:3*: καὶ οὐκ ἔδωκεν κύριος ὁ θεὸς ὑμῖν καρδίαν εἰδέναι καὶ ὀφθαλμοὺς βλέπειν καὶ ὦτα ἀκούειν ἕως τῆς ἡμέρας ταύτης.
> And the Lord God did not give you a heart to know and eyes to see and ears to hear until this day.
>
> *Isa 29:10*: ὅτι πεπότικεν ὑμᾶς κύριος πνεύματι κατανύξεως καὶ καμμύσει τοὺς ὀφθαλμοὺς αὐτῶν καὶ τῶν προφητῶν αὐτῶν καὶ τῶν ἀρχόντων αὐτῶν

---

[127] On this passage see below, sect. 5.6.
[128] Isa 53:1 is used in John 12:38; *1 Clem.* 16.3; Justin 1 *Apol.* 50; *Dial.* 13.3; 42.2; 114.2; 118.4; Isa 65:2 is used in *Barn.* 12.4; Justin 1 *Apol.* 35, 38; *Dial.* 97.2.

because the Lord has made you drink a spirit of deep sleep, and he will close their eyes and [the eyes] of their prophets and of their rulers.

Rom 11:9–10: καὶ Δαυὶδ λέγει· Γενηθήτω ἡ τράπεζα αὐτῶν εἰς παγίδα καὶ εἰς θήραν καὶ εἰς σκάνδαλον καὶ εἰς ἀνταπόδομα αὐτοῖς, σκοτισθήτωσαν οἱ ὀφθαλμοὶ αὐτῶν τοῦ μὴ βλέπειν καὶ τὸν νῶτον αὐτῶν διὰ παντὸς σύγκαμψον.

And David says, "Let their table become a snare and a trap, a stumbling block and a retribution for them; let their eyes be darkened so that they cannot see, and keep their backs forever bent."

Ps 68:23–24: γενηθήτω ἡ τράπεζα αὐτῶν ἐνώπιον αὐτῶν εἰς παγίδα καὶ εἰς ἀνταπόδοσιν καὶ εἰς σκάνδαλον· σκοτισθήτωσαν οἱ ὀφθαλμοὶ αὐτῶν τοῦ μὴ βλέπειν, καὶ τὸν νῶτον αὐτῶν διὰ παντὸς σύγκαμψον.

Let their table before them become a snare and a retribution and a stumbling block; let their eyes be darkened so that they cannot see, and keep their backs forever bent.

The quotation from Deuteronomy is slightly adapted to sharpen the hardening sense: the Lord has not merely withheld the faculties of comprehension (as in Deuteronomy) but has *actively* given the people a spirit of stupor (πνεῦμα κατανύξεως—a phrase taken from Isa 29:10). The quotation of Ps 69 (68):23–24 follows the LXX, except for some minor deviations which do not affect the sense: omission of ἐνώπιον, replacement of ἀνταπόδοσις with ἀνταπόδομα, and the addition of καὶ εἰς θήραν.

Several considerations point towards a non-Pauline origin of Rom 11:7–10:

(1) the *testimonia* are introduced by πωρόω, a word widespread in the NT; (2) there are no obvious reasons for attributing the LXX deviations in the Psalm 69 quotation to Paul;[129] (3) the passages used (especially Psalm 69 and Isaiah 29) are present in diverse early Christian texts;[130] and (4) the text conflations and LXX-deviant readings are general characteristics of TCs.[131]

---

[129] Καὶ εἰς θήραν is probably introduced into the psalm under the influence of the similar Ps 35 (34):8. On the pre-Pauline character of this adapted version of Ps 68:22–23, see Luz, *Geschichtsverständnis*, 98. Koch (*Schrift als Zeuge*, 138) also considers it possible that a pre-Pauline form is witnessed here, though he denies that this points to the use of a TC.

[130] On Psalm 69, see Lindars, *Apologetic*, 99–108; Isa 29:13 is an important *testimonium* quoted in Mark 7:6–7/Matt 15:8–9. On this point, see Lindars, "Second Thoughts," 175.

[131] Other supporters of the position that Paul is drawing on a "florilegium" in Rom 11:7–10 include Ernst Käsemann, *An die Römer* (HNT 8a; 3d ed.; Tübingen: Mohr-Siebeck, 1974) 292; and Wilckens, *Römer*, 238.

After acknowledging that God has hardened Israel, Paul creatively interprets the tradition: this hardening was God's way of providing an opening for the gentiles into God's plan of salvation:

> *Rom 11:25–6*: So that you may not claim to be wiser than you are, brothers and sisters, I want you to understand this mystery (μυστήριον): a hardening (πώρωσις) has come upon part of Israel, until the full number of the Gentiles has come in. And so all Israel will be saved . . .

Paul presupposes that his Roman readers know the "hardening" tradition; his own contribution is to teach them that this hardening is partial, that it has opened the way to the gentiles, and that eventually all Israel will be saved.[132] Not surprisingly, Paul supports his teaching with a scriptural *testimonium*: a conflation of Isa 59:20–21/ Isa 27:9. Again there are good reasons to think that this quotation is not Paul's own composition, but rather a previous scriptural reflection which he has taken over and applied to the new situation.[133]

5.4.4 *The Hardening Tradition and the Gospel of John*

Next for consideration is John's quotation of an adapted version of Isa 6:9–10 at John 12:40 that actually makes use of πωρόω:

τετύφλωκεν αὐτῶν τοὺς ὀφθαλμοὺς
καὶ ἐπώρωσεν αὐτῶν τὴν καρδίαν,
ἵνα μὴ ἴδωσιν τοῖς ὀφθαλμοῖς
καὶ νοήσωσιν τῇ καρδίᾳ καὶ στραφῶσιν,
καὶ ἰάσομαι αὐτούς.

He has blinded their eyes
and hardened their heart,
lest they should see with their eyes,
and perceive with their heart and turn
for me to heal them. (John 12:40)

John places his quotation of Isa 6:9–10 in a climactic section in the Gospel: the summary at the end of Jesus' public ministry (John 12:36b–50). Although Jesus had performed so many signs, the people did not believe. As *testimonia* to this unbelief, John presents Isa

---

[132] Dunn rightly concludes that "Paul understood it [i.e., the 'mystery'] as a revelation given particularly to himself to make known" (*Romans* 2. 678).

[133] See sect. 4.2.1c above for discussion on this *testimonium* as a pre-Pauline composition.

53:1: "Lord, who has believed our message, and to whom has the arm of the Lord been revealed?" and the adapted version of Isa 6:9–10. John adds the comment: "Isaiah said this because he saw his glory and spoke about him" (John 12:41).

Comparison of this passage with the hardening traditions known to Paul shows that the Gospel is in touch with widespread Christian *testimonia* tradition. John's combination of Isa 53:1 and Isa 6:9–10 as hardening *testimonia* echoes Paul's use of them in Romans 9–11 (Isa 53:1 in Rom 10:16; allusions to Isa 6:9–10 in 11:7, 25); John's τυφλόω parallels 2 Cor 4:4; and his use of πωρόω shares in the πωρόω tradition examined above.[134]

The hardening tradition, as expressed in John 12, parallels many Johannine themes. Consonant with the Gospel's emphasis on Jesus' signs, John specifies that the unbelief brought about by this hardening is a lack of belief in Jesus' signs (12:38). In line with John's emphasis on seeing/belief imagery, John's quotation of Isa 6:9–10 lacks any reference to the hearing/ears of the original version.[135] John's interest in the pre-incarnate Christ is likely alluded to in the comment that Isaiah saw his glory (12:41).[136] Finally, John's tendency towards a dualistic or deterministic outlook (however one may define these terms) is reflected in the comment that the people *could not* believe (οὐκ ἠδύνατο πιστεύειν) because he (i.e., God) had blinded them (John 12:39–40a).[137] To what extent these theological ideas were already present in the tradition taken over by John, and how much they are due to his creative adaptation, is difficult to assess.

---

[134] The variant reading ἐπήρωσεν in John 12:40 has strong support (p[66,75] ℵ), and is in fact accepted by some scholars as original (see M.J.J. Menken, "Die Form des Zitates aus Jes 6,10 in Joh 12,40: Ein Beitrag zum Schriftgebrauch des vierten Evangelisten," *BZ* 32 [1988] 192–94). Nevertheless, the judgment of *TCGNT* (p. 238) that the variant arose "in an attempt to supply a somewhat more suitable verb" is to be preferred.

[135] See Menken, "Jes 6,10," 195–96.

[136] 12:41 is usually understood as John's reference to a targumic tradition in which Isaiah sees not the Lord directly, but the "glory" of the Lord (see Raymond E. Brown, *The Gospel according to John I–XII* [AB 29; Garden City, NY: Doubleday, 1966] 486–87).

[137] It is possible that John actually intends Jesus to be the subject of the blinding: cf. John 9:39: "Jesus said, 'For judgment I came into the world, that those who do not see may see, and those who see may become blind'"; 12:36b: "After Jesus had said this, he departed and hid from them."

5.4.5   Carol Stockhausen: The "Exegetical Substructure" to Paul and John

An important study by Carol Kern Stockhausen sheds more light on the common exegetical background linking these hardening texts.[138] In her analysis of 2 Cor 3:1–4:6, Stockhausen uses the guiding image of a "text pool" in which texts related to one another are linked together on the basis of vocabulary or content similarities. Her text pool behind 2 Cor 3:7–18 includes Isa 6:1–11; Isa 29:10–12; and Deut 29:1–4.[139] All these texts belong to the hardening tradition examined above. The particular value of Stockhausen's work is her ability to show the influence of these background ("substructure") texts on the specific details of Paul's account in Corinthians. In Paul's reworking of the narrative of Moses' veil (Exod 34:29–36), specific details in Paul's account that are not found in the Exodus passage can be traced back to these underlying *testimonia*:

2 Cor 3:13–16	Hardening Texts (Substructure)
v 13: Moses actively prevents the people from seeing	Isa 6:9–10
v 14a: their minds were hardened (ἐπωρώθη)	Isa 6:9–10/Hardening Tradition
v 14: the Israelite's understanding of scripture is veiled "to this very day" (ἄχρι γὰρ τῆς σήμερον ἡμέρας) (also v 15 ἕως σήμερον)	Deut 29:3: The Lord has not given faculties of understanding (heart, eyes, ears) "until this day" (ἕως τῆς ἡμέρας ταύτης)
vv 14–15: People cannot read (ἀναγινώσκω) scripture properly, because of the veil over their minds	Isa 29:10: "and he [the Lord] shall close their eyes, and the eyes of their prophets and their rulers." Vv 11–12 refer to a sealed book that neither the learned nor the unlearned can read; also influence of Isa 6:9–10.
v 16: but when one turns (ἐπιστρέψῃ) to the Lord	Isa 6:10d: and they turn (ἐπιστρέψωσιν) and I heal them

---

[138] Stockhausen, *Moses' Veil and the Glory of the New Covenant: The Exegetical Substructure of 2 Cor 3:1–4:6* (AnBib 116; Rome: Pontifical Biblical Institute, 1989).

[139] Ibid., 140–46.

In her summary, Stockhausen displays the complex intertextual links between these "hardening" texts (Isa 6:9–10; Deut 29:3; Isa 29:10) and the texts which undergird Paul's exegesis in 1 Cor 3:1–6 (Exodus 34 and 36 narratives read in light of texts from Jeremiah 38–39 and Ezekiel 11 and 36).[140]

Behind the texts of Paul and John we find a common hardening tradition which included Isa 6:9–10 (apparently read in a non–LXX version with πωρόω and τυφλόω), Isa 53:1; Isa 29:10; and Deut 29:3.[141] What Stockhausen refers to as a "textual pool" likely took the form of a TC on the hardening/rejection of Israel by God—a collection which would fit well into the broader anti-Jewish *testimonia* tradition which was traced in chapter three above.

5.4.6 *Later Pauline Traditions*

Luke places Isa 6:9–10 at the climax of his entire work in the context of Paul's preaching in Rome. Paul meets with the Roman Jewish leaders, "testifying (διαμαρτυρόμενος) to the kingdom of God and trying to convince them about Jesus both from the law of Moses and from the prophets" (Acts 28:23).[142] Some are convinced, and others "refused to believe." Paul quotes LXX Isa 6:9–10 as a *testimonium* to this Jewish unbelief, and announces that he will go to the gentiles since "they will listen." The account in Acts represents a classic expression of the early Christian hardening *testimonia* tradition: it explicitly links the "hardening" to an inability to interpret scripture rightly (cf. 2 Cor 3:14–15); it uses a form of Isa 6:9–10 as a proof-text; and it expresses a definitive rejection of the Jews in favor of gentile Christians (cf. the TCs examined in chapter three above).[143]

While there is no reason to doubt that the use of Isa 6:9-10 in Acts 28 relies on "a tradition where it was remembered that the apostle had used the text to explain Jewish unbelief,"[144] it is equally clear that the Acts account misses the individual creativity that Paul brought to the hardening tradition (e.g., the "partial" hardening and the eventual salvation of "all Israel" worked out in Romans). Luke

---

[140] See her summary figure, *Moses' Veil*, 148.

[141] On the modified textual form of Isa 6:9–10, see ibid., 142 n. 102.

[142] Cf. the use of μαρτυρέω and cognates in the *testimonia* tradition (e.g., in Justin's *testimonia* sources: sect. 3.4.1a above).

[143] Luke lacks the characteristic πωρόω/πώρωσις vocabulary, as he quotes a strictly LXX text.

[144] Evans, *To See*, 81.

appears to rely more on general Christian tradition than on specifically Pauline sources for his reconstruction of Paul's discourse at this point.

This uncompromising reading of the hardening tradition is also evident in Eph 4:17–24, but here it is applied to the gentiles. Readers are admonished not to live as the gentiles, who lack understanding and are alienated from God because of their ignorance and hardness (πώρωσις) of heart. Ephesians is unique in its application of the tradition specifically to gentiles.

5.4.7 *The Hardening Tradition in Mark*

Mark applies the hardening tradition of Isa 6:9–10 specifically to the reception of Jesus' parables. After publicly delivering the parable of the sower, Jesus explains privately to his disciples: "To you has been given the secret (τὸ μυστήριον) of the kingdom of God, but for those outside everything is in parables (ἐν παραβολαῖς),"

> *Mark 4:11–12*: ἵνα βλέποντες βλέπωσιν καὶ μὴ ἴδωσιν, καὶ ἀκούοντες ἀκούωσιν καὶ μὴ συνιῶσιν, μήποτε ἐπιστρέψωσιν καὶ ἀφεθῇ αὐτοῖς.
> so that they may indeed see but not perceive, and may indeed hear but not understand; lest they should turn again, and be forgiven.

The passage differs markedly from the LXX and the MT: (1) the Markan version is much abridged; (2) Mark's verbs are 3rd person rather than the LXX 2nd person; (3) the "seeing" and "hearing" clauses are reversed; (4) Mark's last phrase, καὶ ἀφεθῇ αὐτοῖς, replaces the LXX καὶ ἰάσομαι αὐτούς. This final change corresponds to the targumic reading.[145]

Mark draws a clear distinction between those "who have been given the secret of the kingdom of God" and "those outside" for whom everything is in parables. Mark therefore follows the "hard" line of the tradition: the ἵνα . . . μήποτε construction makes it clear that Jesus' intention in speaking in parables is that "those outside" not perceive, understand, or turn to be forgiven.[146] In this sense Mark is close to

---

[145] Ibid., 92. The targum reads ושתביק להון: "and it be forgiven them."

[146] Evans records various scholarly attempts to avoid the conclusion that the construction should be understood in the sense of purpose (*To See*, 92–99), but correctly concludes that the phrase should be taken as "telic" or purposive. Matthew 13:13 considerably softens the hardening tradition which the evangelist found in Mark: he changes the purposive ἵνα to the neutral ὅτι and avoids πώρωσις/πωρόω terms (Matthew goes on to quote the LXX Isa 6:9–10 in vv 14b–15). Luke similarly softens the tradition: he lacks πώρωσις and πωρόω, and although he retains

the theology of the Johannine and Pauline (2 Cor 4:4) versions, which themselves hearken back to the original Hebrew reading.

In Lindars's evaluation, Mark 4 belongs to the second stage of the apologetical application of the hardening tradition. For Lindars, the tradition was first applied to explain the unbelief of Jews when confronted with the church's *kerygma*, then was "read back" at a secondary stage into Jesus' ministry, where it was used to explain why only certain people recognized the messianic character of his ministry.[147] Lindars's contention that the application to the Jews is primary, however, should be challenged.[148] Our earliest witness, Paul, already knows an application both to Jews (2 Cor 3:14) and to nonbelievers in general (2 Cor 4:4). The application of the tradition to Jews, moreover, presupposes a clear distinction between Christians and Jews, a distinction that would have taken some time to emerge in earliest Christianity.

I propose instead that the earliest version of the hardening tradition may go back to Jesus' earliest followers, or indeed to Jesus himself. Jesus' teaching was certainly rejected or misunderstood by some within his own lifetime, and it is *a priori* probable that, as reflected in the Gospels, Jesus made a distinction between teachings given to his closest followers and teachings given to the crowds. Mark 4:10–12, then, may derive from this early stage. This is not to insist that the account goes back to Jesus exactly as it stands, but rather that it may well faithfully represent very early scriptural reflection, and need not be considered secondary.

Mark shows contact with the πωρόω/πώρωσις tradition in three other texts which describe those with hardened hearts: Mark 3:5 (applied to the Pharisees) and Mark 6:52 and 8:17–18 (applied to the disciples). Without addressing the implications of Mark's application of the hardening tradition to the disciples, I simply note the flexibility of the tradition and reiterate that this need not be seen as a derivative of an original hardening tradition applied only to Jews.

---

the purposive ἵνα in his rendering of Mark's adapted version, he does omit Mark's μήποτε clause (Luke 8:10b) (see Evans, *To See*, 115–27).

[147] Lindars, *Apologetic*, 159–67. Lindars holds that a parallel secondary development applied the tradition to an apologetic for preaching to the gentiles.

[148] See sect. 1.13 above for my more general criticism that Lindars's model of stages is overly schematic.

5.4.8   *Patristic Use of the Hardening Tradition*

I briefly note a few examples of the early Christian hardening tradition outside the NT.[149] Justin makes two clear allusions to the adapted version of Isa 6:9–10:

> *Dial. 12.2*: ἔτι γὰρ τὰ ὦτα ὑμῶν πέφρακται, οἱ ὀφθαλμοὶ ὑμῶν πεπήρωνται, καὶ πεπάχυται ἡ καρδία.
> For your ears are closed, your eyes are blinded, and your heart is hardened.
> *Dial. 33.1*: τὰ δὲ ὦτα ὑμῶν πέφρακται, καὶ αἱ καρδίαι πεπώρωνται.[150]
> But your ears are shut up, and your hearts are made dull.

The reference in *Dialogue* 12 is in the middle of an anti-cultic TC; here Justin falsely attributes the reference to Jeremiah. Justin knows the πωρόω tradition as it is reflected in the NT, using the verb itself in *Dial.* 33.1 and the closely related πηρόω in *Dial.* 12.2. The use of this vocabulary, the false attribution, and Justin's probable literary independence from John all argue that Justin is not directly dependent on the NT here, but is another witness to common written *testimonia* sources.[151]

Explicit use of Isa 6:9–10 in TCs on Israel's rejection of Christ are found in Tertullian *Marc.* 3.6.5 and Cyprian *Quir.* 1.3. A related tradition, common in anti-cultic TCs and likely dependent on Matt 19:7–8, is that the Mosaic law was given to Israel because of its hardness of heart: *Barn.* 9.5; Irenaeus *A.H.* 4.15.2.[152]

5.4.9   *Conclusions on the Hardening Tradition: Form and Function*

The hardening tradition is applied in a variety of ways in the NT: both to Jews and to gentiles, both in a "hard" manner (God hardens people) and in a "softer" version (people allow themselves to be hardened). Isaiah 6:9–10 is a key text in the NT hardening tradition; some Christians used an authoritative non-standard version of it which employed πωρόω and perhaps τυφλόω. This modified text was certainly not read in a scriptural manuscript, but was part of a

---

[149] On this subject, see Evans, *To See*, 147–62.

[150] πεπήρωνται is read in the corrected A manuscript.

[151] Skarsaune concludes that *Dial.* 12.1 and 33.1 are allusions to the adapted Isa 6:10 as witnessed in John 12:40, but probably depend on an intermediary source (*Prophecy*, 106).

[152] The phrase found in these passages is not from the πωρόω group but rather σκληροκαρδία.

testimonia source. Justin shows the continuity of this *testimonia* tradition into the mid-second century. As is typical of the *testimonia* tradition, Isa 6:9–10 was often combined with related texts such as Isa 29:10 and Deut 29:3.

I have suggested that the earliest application of the tradition was likely made to unbelievers in general, rather than to Jews specifically. By the time of Paul's letter to the Romans, however, a "hard" anti-Jewish version had been firmly established (see Rom 11:7–10) and Paul had to labor mightily to modify this understanding. We can conclude that the life-setting of much of the tradition was a Semitic milieu: the "hard" reading of Isa 6:9–10 presupposes the Hebrew text, and the versions in Mark 4 and John 12 show contact with targumic traditions.

While we can speak broadly of a common NT tradition, it is also apparent that the tradition was open to individual modification (especially evident in John and Paul). Stockhausen's work is valuable in showing the dialectical relationship between Paul's individual scriptural reflection (on Exodus 34) and the Christian scriptural traditions which had already been established before he wrote.[153]

Scriptural *testimonia* function as forensic proofs from prophecy: these things (especially the fate of the Jews) are written in scripture, thus their occurrence is predetermined and must take place. This sense is especially clear in John. Paul, however, appears to think more in terms of a *scriptural pattern*: the current situation of unbelief and hardening fits into a scriptural pattern of the unbelief, hardening, and the response of the remnant. It is significant that Paul unfolds his interpretation of the hardening tradition in the context of a historical overview in Romans; the current situation is simply a (final?) chapter in the story of God's relationship with his people. While John employs Isa 6:9–10 as a forensic proof within his deterministic scheme in 12:36b–40;[154] for Paul, the hardening tradition takes

---

[153] Regarding shared scriptural traditions used by John and Paul, Stockhausen concludes: "I suggest that it is not a relationship between Paul and John, but a common background drawn originally from a catena of scripture texts which formed a matrix and pattern for early Christian thought and early Christian texts. I consider my own work on II Cor. 3 as a contribution to the discovery of such a network of concrete background texts and the analysis of its probable structure" (*Moses' Veil*, 139 n. 98). It is precisely this sort of *testimonia* background that I would claim to have uncovered in this analysis of the early Christian hardening tradition.

[154] This section is certainly deterministic (v 39: "and so they *could not* believe"), but this does not imply that the thought-world of the entire Gospel is deterministic.

the form of *exempla* in a historical pattern—but a pattern that is still to be fully worked out.

5.5 *Zechariah 12:10 and The Two Advents* Testimonia

Zechariah 12:10 is a common text in the patristic two advents TCs studied in chapter three.[155] The phrase "and they shall look at the one whom they have pierced" (MT) is present in three literarily independent passages in the NT: Matt 24:30, Rev 1:7, and John 19:37. The textual form in all three passages deviates from both the MT and LXX. Before examining these texts, however, I must briefly discuss the Hebrew and Greek versions of Zech 12:10 which may have been available to these writers.

5.5.1 *MT Zechariah 12:10 and the Versions*

The MT of Zech 12:10 reads as follows:

> And I will pour out a spirit of compassion and supplication in the house of David and the inhabitants of Jerusalem, so that, when they look on the one whom they have pierced (והביטו אלי את אשר־דקרו), they shall mourn for him, as one mourns for an only child, and weep bitterly over him, as one weeps over a firstborn.

The relevant phrase has some ambiguities. אלי may be vocalized אֵלַי (they shall look "upon me," whom they have pierced, as in the MT) or אֱלֵי (a poetic form of the preposition אֶל: they shall look "upon" the one whom they have pierced). The particle את can be read either as a marker of the object or as the preposition "with." Since the Lord is the speaker in Zech 12:10, if the MT pointing is followed and את is understood as an accusative marker, then the sense is that the Lord is the object of the piercing.[156] Obviously such a reading would have been attractive to early Christians as a prophecy of the crucified Lord.

The LXX, apparently in an attempt to avoid this strongly anthropomorphic reading, renders the phrase καὶ ἐπιβλέψονται πρός με ἀνθ᾽

---

[155] See esp. the analysis of Tertullian *Marc.* 3.7. in sect. 3.5.4d.

[156] In this analysis I follow Maarten J.J. Menken's discussion, "The Textual Form and the Meaning of the Quotation from Zechariah 12:10 in John 19:37," *CBQ* 55 [1993] 498–99).

ὧν κατωρχήσαντο: "and they shall look upon me because they have mocked me (lit. 'they have danced')."[157]

> *Zech 12:10*: καὶ ἐκχεῶ ἐπὶ τὸν οἶκον Δαυιδ
> καὶ ἐπὶ τοὺς κατοικοῦντας Ιερουσαλημ
> πνεῦμα χάριτος καὶ οἰκτιρμοῦ,
> <u>καὶ ἐπιβλέψονται πρός με ἀνθ᾽ ὧν κατωρχήσαντο</u>
> καὶ κόψονται ἐπ᾽ αὐτὸν κοπετὸν ὡς ἐπ᾽ ἀγαπητὸν
> καὶ ὀδυνηθήσονται ὀδύνην ὡς ἐπὶ πρωτοτόκῳ.
> And I will pour upon the house of David,
> and upon the inhabitants of Jerusalem,
> a spirit of grace and compassion:
> and they shall look upon me, because they have mocked me,
> and they shall make lamentation for him, as for a beloved friend,
> and they shall grieve intensely, as for a firstborn son.

This Greek translation was achieved by reading the MT דקרו as רקדו, most likely an intentional transposition of the ד and ר that would have been seen as a legitimate exegetical procedure.[158] The other versions offer a variety of translations: Aquila understands the את as "with" ("*with* the one whom they have pierced"); Theodotion follows the MT closely: καὶ ἐπιβλέψονται πρός με ὃν ἐξεκέντησαν ("and they shall look on me whom they have pierced"); and the targum renders a quite periphrastic ויבעון מן קדמי על דאטלטלו ("and they shall pray before me for those who were exiled").[159]

5.5.2 *A Christian Adaptation of Zech 12:10 in Matt 24:30; Rev 1:7; and John 19:37*

Turning to the use of Zech 12:10 in the NT, we see that Matthew has conflated his adapted version of Zech 12:10 with Dan 7:13:

> *Matt 24:30*: καὶ τότε φανήσεται τὸ σημεῖον τοῦ υἱοῦ τοῦ ἀνθρώπου ἐν οὐρανῷ,
> καὶ τότε κόψονται πᾶσαι αἱ φυλαὶ τῆς γῆς
> <u>καὶ ὄψονται τὸν υἱὸν τοῦ ἀνθρώπου</u>
> <u>ἐρχόμενον ἐπὶ τῶν νεφελῶν τοῦ οὐρανοῦ</u> μετὰ δυνάμεως καὶ δόξης πολλῆς·
> Then will appear the sign of the Son of man in heaven,
> and then all the tribes of the earth will mourn,

---

[157] The sense seems to be that of dancing insultingly; Menken, "Zechariah," 499.

[158] See ibid., 499–500, for discussion and further examples.

[159] For these and other versions, see ibid., 501; text of Greek versions in Frederick Field, ed., *Origenis Hexaplorum quae supersunt* (2 vols.; Oxford: Clarendon, 1867, 1875; repr. Hildesheim: Olms, 1964); Aramaic text of the targum in Alexander Sperber, ed., *The Bible in Aramaic*, vol. 3: *The Latter Prophets according to Targum Jonathan* (2d impression; Leiden/New York/Cologne: Brill, 1992).

and they will see the Son of man
coming on the clouds of heaven with power and great glory.
Dan 7:13 (LXX): καὶ ἰδοὺ ἐπὶ τῶν νεφελῶν τοῦ οὐρανοῦ ὡς υἱὸς ἀνθρώπου
ἤρχετο,
And behold he comes as a son of man upon the clouds of heaven

Matthew's κόψονται πᾶσαι αἱ φυλαὶ τῆς γῆς echoes elements of LXX
Zech 12:12–14: Καὶ κόψεται ἡ γῆ . . . Πᾶσαι αἱ ὑπολελειμμέναι φυλαί.
Ὄψονται corresponds to no extant scriptural version. The setting in
Matthew is Jesus' eschatological discourse; the "sign of the Son of
Man" is one of the heavenly signs of the end times when the Son
of Man "will gather his elect from the four winds" (Matt 24:29–31).
Matthew's phrase corresponds to Mark 13:26: καὶ τότε ὄψονται τὸν
υἱὸν τοῦ ἀνθρώπου ἐρχόμενον ἐν νεφέλαις μετὰ δυνάμεως πολλῆς καὶ
δόξης, and Luke 21:27: καὶ τότε ὄψονται τὸν υἱὸν τοῦ ἀνθρώπου ἐρχόμενον
ἐν νεφέλῃ μετὰ δυνάμεως καὶ δόξης πολλῆς.

In an unattributed saying at the beginning of Revelation, the same
combination of Zech 12:10 with Dan 7:13 is evident:

> *Rev 1:7*: Ἰδοὺ ἔρχεται μετὰ τῶν νεφελῶν, καὶ ὄψεται αὐτὸν πᾶς ὀφθαλμὸς
> καὶ οἵτινες αὐτὸν ἐξεκέντησαν, καὶ κόψονται ἐπ᾽ αὐτὸν πᾶσαι αἱ φυλαὶ
> τῆς γῆς.
> Behold, he is coming with the clouds, and every eye will see him,
> every one who pierced him; and all tribes of the earth will wail on
> account of him.

In addition to the common conflation of Zechariah and Daniel, both
Matthew and Revelation read the non-scriptural κόψονται πᾶσαι αἱ
φυλαὶ τῆς γῆς, and both use ὄψομαι in their versions of Zech 12:10,
although this verb does not appear in any Greek manuscript of the
text. Revelation differs, however, in making πᾶς ὀφθαλμός the subject of ὄψομαι, and employing ἐκκεντέω (in agreement with the Greek
recensions)[160] to express the "piercing" of Zech 12:10.

John presents his version as a *testimonium* to the soldier's piercing
(νύσσω) Jesus' side after Jesus' death on the cross.

> *John 19:37*: Ὄψονται εἰς ὃν ἐξεκέντησαν.
> They shall look on him whom they have pierced.

While John lacks any reference to Dan 7:13 in this passage, his
ἐκκεντέω reflects the same usage in Revelation, and his ὄψομαι parallels the use in Revelation and Matthew.

---

[160] Aquila, Theodotion, Symmachus.

What is the relationship between these three texts? Given the differences between the versions, together with lack of evidence for dependence on other grounds, literary dependence among these texts can be ruled out.[161] Rather, the passages reveal a common use of a modified version of Zech 12:10. Lindars reconstructs this common source as follows:[162]

καὶ ὄψονται εἰς ὃν ἐξεκέντησαν
καὶ κόψονται ἐπ᾽ αὐτὸν πᾶσαι αἱ φυλαὶ τῆς γῆς

Perrin agrees with Lindars's reconstruction, holding only that ἐπιβλέψεται was read originally in this tradition in place of ὄψονται.[163] Menken's more cautious analysis is perhaps to be preferred. He agrees that ὄψονται εἰς ὃν ἐξεκέντησαν was part of the "standard early Christian version of Zech 12:10ab"; the second part of this passage was less constant, although κόψονται and φυλή always "figure in it."[164]

It is clear from the above survey that this early Christian version of Zech 12:10 was never part of a scriptural manuscript tradition; it is drawn from a *testimonia* source. Was this original *testimonium* oral or written? While Lindars (originally) and Menken argue for oral tradition,[165] it is difficult to maintain that such precise verbal agreements as exist between Matthew and Revelation are due merely to oral tradition, particularly when standard written scriptural versions would likely have been known and influential. Indeed Lindars himself later reconsidered his opinion, and offered this adapted form of Zech 12:10 as an example of a text deriving from a written "little gospel," as postulated by Prigent.[166]

What of the common use of ὄψομαι, a reading not witnessed in any manuscript? Perrin makes the attractive suggestion that the reading ὄψονται arose within a Christian pesher process as a play on words with κόψονται.[167] Menken further points out that ὄψομαι is often used with second advent texts.[168] Against Lindars and Perrin, who posit that Zech 12:10 was originally used as an apologetical

---

[161] So Menken, "Zechariah," 497.
[162] Lindars, *Apologetic*, 124.
[163] Perrin, "Christian Pesher," 153.
[164] Menken, "Zechariah," 497.
[165] Lindars, *Apologetic*, 127; Menken, "Zechariah," 498 n. 10.
[166] Lindars, "Second Thoughts," 174.
[167] Perrin, "Christian Pesher," 153.
[168] Menken, "Zechariah," 502: Mark 9:1 par.; 13:26 par.; Matt 5:8; Luke 3:6; 13:28; 17:22; Heb 9:28; 12:14; 1 John 3:2; Rev 22:4.

text applied to Jesus' crucifixion, one can easily argue that the rendering ὄψονται εἰς ὃν ἐξεκέντησαν was worked out from the start to apply to Christ's future coming in glory.[169] The seeming exception to this, John's application of Zech 12:10 to the piercing at the crucifixion, is explained by this Gospel's particular understanding of the crucifixion itself as a "lifting up" (3:14–15; 8:28; 12:32) and a glorification (12:23), as well as by the Gospel's identification of "seeing" with faith and salvation. John has taken a traditional "second advent" text and fit it into his "realized eschatology" by applying it to the crucifixion itself.[170]

We can perhaps go further. As we saw above, the Synoptic parallels (Mark 13:26/Luke 21:27) to Matt 24:30 also employ the word ὄψονται in their accounts of the coming Son of Man. Perrin sees in these texts (together with the ὄψεσθε of Mark 14:62) allusions to the adapted form of Zech 12:10.[171]

> *Matt 24:30*: καὶ τότε κόψονται πᾶσαι αἱ φυλαὶ τῆς γῆς
> <u>καὶ ὄψονται τὸν υἱὸν τοῦ ἀνθρώπου ἐρχόμενον</u> ἐπὶ τῶν νεφελῶν τοῦ οὐρανοῦ
> μετὰ δυνάμεως καὶ δόξης πολλῆς·
> *Mark 13:26*: <u>καὶ τότε ὄψονται τὸν υἱὸν τοῦ ἀνθρώπου ἐρχόμενον</u> ἐν νεφέλαις
> μετὰ δυνάμεως πολλῆς καὶ δόξης.
> *Luke 21:27*: <u>καὶ τότε ὄψονται τὸν υἱὸν τοῦ ἀνθρώπου ἐρχόμενον</u> ἐν νεφέλῃ
> μετὰ δυνάμεως καὶ δόξης πολλῆς.

Matthew's version can be seen as the most original of the three. The accounts of Mark and Luke make perfect sense without a reference to "seeing" the Son of Man; indeed, the subject of this "seeing" is ambiguous in them. This ambiguity is explained if we posit that Mark and Luke have edited a version such as that found in Matthew. Together with the clear evidence for a widespread Christian reading of Zech 12:10 with ὄψομαι (Matt 24:30, John 19:37, and Rev 1:7), these considerations make it possible to see ὄψονται as an

---

[169] See Lindars, *Apologetic*, 125; Perrin, "Christian Pesher," 153. David Wenham is open to the possibility of an original function as a second advent text: "It is quite as likely that the testimonium with its reference to remorse after the piercing was understood from the beginning to refer to a post-crucifixion event, i.e., as a prophecy of the parousia" (*Eschatological Discourse*, 318).

[170] So Menken, "Zechariah," 511. On the general subject of John's use and reinterpretation of traditional *testimonia*, see D. Moody Smith, "The Setting and Shape of a Johannine Narrative Source," *JBL* 95 (1976) 237; C.K. Barrett, "The Old Testament in the Fourth Gospel," *JTS* n.s. 48 (1947) 165–68; see also John's use of the "hardening" tradition in 5.3.5 above.

[171] Perrin, "Christian Pesher," 153–55.

allusion to a Christianized Zech 12:10.[172] I suggest, therefore, that
a reading similar to that of Matthew existed in a pre-Synoptic source
(perhaps the independent eschatological discourse posited by Wenham)
and has been edited by Mark and then, following Mark, by Luke.

The independent conflation of Zech 12:10 and Dan 7:13 again is
significant. We have seen that both texts were applied to the second advent of Christ in early Christian collections. If, as argued
above, ὄψομαι is a reference to the Christianized form of Zech 12:10,
then we can also see in Mark 14:62 (καὶ ὄψεσθε τὸν υἱὸν τοῦ ἀνθρώπου
ἐκ δεξιῶν καθήμενον τῆς δυνάμεως) a conflation of Zech 12:10, Dan
7:13, and Ps 110 (109):1.[173] These early conflations do not establish
conclusively the existence of written TCs in which these texts were
gathered: we may perhaps attribute the parallel conflations to common oral *testimonia* or to common midrashic techniques. Yet when
we consider the weight of the evidence—widespread independent
use of a Christianized reading of Zech 12:10 and parallel conflations
in independent authors—it is difficult not to posit some kind of common written source. Whether we should think of this written source
as a two advents TC or as an eschatological discourse which makes
heavy compositional use of scripture is not clear; nor is it necessary
to decide the case in this present discussion.

5.5.3 *Zechariah 12:10 in* Didache *and Justin*

Within the description of the "last days" in *Didache* 16.8 there occurs
a parallel to these passages: τότε ὄψεται ὁ κόσμος τὸν κύριον ἐρχόμενον
ἐπάνω τῶν νεφελῶν τοῦ οὐρανοῦ. This short passage shows points of
contact with several different formulations: ὄψεται is connected with
the Zech 12:10 tradition underlying Matt 24:30; John 19:37; and
particularly Rev 1:7 (ὄψεται πᾶς ὀφθαλμός); the ἐρχόμενον ἐπάνω τῶν
νεφελῶν τοῦ οὐρανοῦ of course reflects Dan 7:13. *Didache* shows independence from these traditions, however, in its use of the preposition ἐπάνω and, more significantly, in its having κύριος in place of
υἱὸς τοῦ ἀνθρώπου.[174]

Justin references Zech 12:10 as one of the *testimonia* for Christ's

---

[172] So Wenham, *Eschatological Discourse*, 316.
[173] As proposed in Perrin, "Christian Pesher," 155.
[174] Köster concludes that *Did.* 16.6–8 is independent of the Synoptics: he posits
a Jewish apocalypse as a common source for *Did.* 16.8 and Mark 13:25 (par.)
(*Synoptische Überlieferung*, 184–90, esp. 188–89).

second advent. The form of his text reflects the NT tradition which we have been studying:

> *1 Apol. 52.12*: κόψονται φυλὴ πρὸς φυλήν, καὶ τότε ὄψονται εἰς ὅν ἐξε-κέντησαν (in context of discussion on Christ's two advents).
> *Dial. 14.8*: καὶ ὄψεται ὁ λαὸς ὑμῶν καὶ γνωριεῖ εἰς ὅν ἐξεκέντησαν (two advents context; with allusion to Dan 7:13 and falsely attributed to Hosea).[175]
> *Dial. 32.2*: Here Justin shows that Zech 12:10 functions as a bridge between the two advents: "one in which he was pierced by you (ἐξεκεντήθη ὑφ᾽ ὑμῶν); a second, when you shall know him whom you have pierced (ἐπιγνώσεσθε εἰς ὅν ἐξεκέντησατε)."[176]

Justin thus reads the same Christianized text form of Zech 12:10 which was isolated in the NT passages above, although there is no reason to suppose that he depends directly on the NT for this quotation.[177]

5.5.4   Barnabas *7: Two Advents and Two Goats on the Day of Atonement*

The basic adapted Christian form of Zech 12:10 is also visible in *Barn.* 7.9. In *Barnabas* 7 the author presents a reflection on the Day of Atonement ritual of the two goats as a type of the atoning suffering and death of Jesus. Verse nine reads as follows:

> What does this mean? Listen: "the first goat is for the altar, but the other is accursed," and note that the one who is accursed is crowned, because then, "they will see him" (ὄψονται) on that day with the long scarlet robe on his body, and they will say, "Is not this he whom we once crucified and rejected and pierced (κατακεντήσαντες) and spat upon? Of a truth it was he who then said that he saw the Son of God."

The passage presupposes the Christianized version of Zech 12:10: ὄψονται is read with κατακεντέω (cognate to ἐκκεντέω).[178]

Barnabas 7, then, combines the two advents schema, the Christian version of Zech 12:10, and the two goats of the Day of Atonement ritual. Leviticus 16 describes this ritual: Aaron is to select two goats:

---

[175] Menken observes that although Justin has inserted καὶ γνωριεῖ into the basic text form, he retains the preposition εἰς, resulting in the clumsy γνωριεῖ εἰς ("Zechariah," 496). This shows that Justin, far from relying on a vague "oral tradition," is refer-ring to a non-scriptural written *Vorlage* which he regards as authoritative.

[176] On Justin's clumsy reading ἐπιγνώσεσθε εἰς, see the preceding note.

[177] See also Justin *Dial.* 64.7 and 118.1 for further references to Zech 12:10.

[178] See Menken, "Zechariah," 496.

one is to be sacrificed as a sin-offering; upon the head of the other, Aaron is ritually to place the sins of the people, and drive the animal out into the wilderness. *Barnabas* describes several details of this practice (including ritual abuse of the second goat) known from Mishnaic tractates.[179] In the process of showing that ritual practices are types of Christ's passion, *Barnabas* also shows knowledge of details which parallel details from the Synoptic passion narratives:

Ritual Type	Fulfillment	Parallels
7.3: "Whosoever does not keep the fast [i.e., on the Day of Atonement], shall die the death" (Lev 23:29)	The Lord to offer "the vessel of the spirit" as a sacrifice for sins	Acts 3:22–25
7.3: Isaac	Christ's offering	Acts 3:22–25[180]
7.4: Priests eat the entrails of the goat unwashed with vinegar (ὄξος)	7.3: "when he was crucified he was given to drink vinegar (ὄξος) and gall (χολή)"	Gospel Passion accounts[181]
7.7: The other [goat] is accursed (ἐπικατάρατος)	7.7: "Notice how the type (ὁ τύπος) of Jesus is manifested."	*Gal 3:10–13*: Paul applies Deut 21:23 "Cursed (ἐπικατάρατος) is everyone who hangs on a tree" to Jesus
7:8–9: Abuse of the scape-goat: ἐμπτύω; κατακεντέω; σταυρόω; ἐξουθενέω	Abuse of Jesus	Gospel accounts of abuse; κατακεντέω from adapted Zech 12:10/two advents tradition; ἐξουθενέω in Luke 23:11; Acts 4:11[182]

---

[179] See the analysis in Carleton Paget, *Barnabas*, 134–40.

[180] See my analysis of a TC behind Acts 3:22–25 which also reflects on the Day of Atonement and Jesus (sect. 4.4.2a).

[181] See the detailed discussion in Lindars, *Apologetic*, 100–102; Crossan, *Cross*, 208–18.

[182] See Lindars, *Apologetic*, 81–82; Crossan, *Cross*, 127, for use of ἐχουθενέω in the NT passion tradition and Isa 53:3.

(table cont.)

Ritual Type	Fulfillment	Parallels
7.8: "bind the scarlet wool (τὸ ἔριον τὸ κόκκινον) about its head"	7.9: "the one that is accursed is crowned, because then 'they will see him' on that day with the long scarlet robe (ποδήρης κόκκινος)"[183]	Crowning with thorns in Gospels; Soldiers put scarlet robe (χλαμὺς κόκκινη) on Jesus (Matt 27:28); Moses uses ἔριον κοκκίνον to sprinkle blood (Heb 9:19); Vision of Son of Man in ποδήρης (Rev 1:13); Intermediary reference to Zech 3:1–5, a scene in which the high priest Joshua (= Jesus [Ιησοῦς]), removes filthy garments, is clothed with a ποδήρης, and is crowned.

I will not attempt here to trace out the possible lines of literary relationships or the use of common tradition implicit in the above parallels. I simply wish to show in some detail that the Day of Atonement/two advents reflection which *Barnabas* knows is intimately tied to a passion narrative.[184]

5.5.5 *The Two Goats/Two Advents Tradition in Justin and Tertullian*

The identification of a two advents schema with the two goats of the Day of Atonement ritual also appears in Justin *Dial.* 40.4–5 and Tertullian *Marc.* 3.7.7 (= *A.J.* 14.9–10). Justin's account occurs within a longer section presenting various cultic typologies: Jesus as the Passover Lamb (*Dial.* 40.1–4), the offering of fine flour as a type of the Eucharist; circumcision as a type of the true circumcision (*Dialogue*

---

[183] See Crossan, *Cross*, 128, on the allusion to Zech 3:1–5; Skarsaune, *Prophecy*, 309, on the Zechariah 3 allusion and a further connection with Rev 1:13. Crossan rightly refers to Tertullian *Marc.* 3.7.7 which connects Zechariah 3 with the two goats ritual.

[184] On the complex relationships here, see Crossan, *Cross*, 124–29; Carleton Paget, *Barnabas*, 134–40; Köster, *Synoptische Überlieferung*, 152–56; Skarsaune, *Prophecy*, 309.

41).[185] The recognition theme from Zech 12:10 is implicit in Justin's account, yet unlike *Barnabas*, Justin holds that the reason for recognition is not the similarity of the two goats but rather that the events occur in Jerusalem. This difference, together with Justin's lack of reference to any of the extra-biblical rituals described in *Barnabas*, shows that the accounts are independent.[186]

Tertullian's account occurs within his long two advents TC. Within this collection, he refers explicitly to Zech 12:10 and to the high priest Joshua (Zechariah 3) as a type of Christ. Tertullian's narrative is close to that of *Barnabas*: both refer to non-scriptural details of the scarlet wool, the abuse of the scapegoat, and the eating of the sacrificed goat by the priests. Yet Tertullian differs in understanding the second advent as occurring already in the eucharist:

> While the other [i.e., the second goat], by being offered up for sins, and given to the priests of the temple for meat, afforded proofs of his second appearance, when (after all sins have been expiated) the priests of the spiritual temple, that is, the church, are to enjoy the flesh, as it were, of the Lord's own grace, whilst the residue go away from salvation without tasting it. (*Marc.* 3.7.8)[187]

Although Tertullian may know *Barnabas*'s and even Justin's discourse, the differences between them have led some scholars to understand his account as an independent witness.[188]

5.5.6 *Conclusions on Zech 12:10 and the Two Advents Tradition: Form and Function*

The Hebrew of Zech 12:10–14, with its potential application to the Lord being pierced and "all tribes" mourning, must have attracted Christian attention from the earliest times. Although it may have been applied as a *testimonium* to the crucifixion, all our extant evidence indicates that it was applied to the second, glorious advent of Christ from the beginning.[189] The investigation of NT and early Christian

---

[185] Skarsaune, *Prophecy*, 295–307. The source used by Justin here, Skarsaune argues, combined anti-cultic polemic with cultic typologies.

[186] See Crossan, *Cross*, 129; Carleton Paget, *Barnabas*, 138.

[187] This eucharistic application is possibly already in view in *Barnabas* in the reflection on the priestly meal and on Christ as "offering my flesh for my new people" (*Bam.* 7.3–5, esp. v 5).

[188] See the discussion in Carleton Paget (*Barnabas*, 138–39) and Crossan (*Cross*, 131).

[189] Whether this "second advent" referred to Christ's resurrection or to his eventual return as judge is a separate question which I do not address here.

forms of Zech 12:10 indicates that it was transmitted, independently of scriptural manuscripts, in the form ὄψονται εἰς ὅν ἐξεκέντησαν. It is likely that it was transmitted in collections with similar second advent texts, such as Dan 7:13, in the form of a TC, a text and commentary collection, or perhaps already as part of an eschatological discourse.

Barnabas 7 and its parallels in Justin and Tertullian show the combination of the two advents *testimonia* tradition with reflection on the two goats of the Day of Atonement ritual. The two goats represent not only the advent in lowliness and the advent in glory, but also the advent as the crucified one and the advent in the eucharist.[190] This pattern fits in well with the *testimonia* sources analyzed by Skarsaune, in which anti-cultic *testimonia* were combined with cultic typologies which in turn were connected with Christian sacraments.[191]

Barnabas 7 presents not only the combination of a two advents pattern and two goats typology, but also details of Christ's passion (see table above). In this sense, *Barnabas* 7 is strictly parallel to John 19:31–37, which itself combines a passion narrative, a cultic typological interpretation of Christ's death, and a two advents *testimonium*:

> *John 19:31–34: Passion Narrative* (set on the day of Preparation): the breaking of the crucified men's legs and the soldier's spear thrust
> *John 19:36: Cultic Type*: Jesus as the Paschal Lamb: "None of his bones shall be broken" (Ps 34 [33]:21 with influence from Exod 12:10, 46 and Num 9:12)[192]
> *John 19:37: Two Advents Testimonium*: "They shall look on the one whom they have pierced."

These elements, I suggest, were already combined in the earliest reflections on the death of Jesus: (1) a narrative based on historical memories; (2) interpretation of Jesus as the fulfillment of a cultic type; (3) interpretation of Jesus within a two advents schema, i.e., as a suffering righteous one who is eventually glorified in resurrection (and second advent in judgment?).

---

[190] See Carleton Paget, *Barnabas*, 140; Prigent, *Testimonia*, 108.

[191] See sect. 3.9.2 above.

[192] For an analysis of this *testimonium*, see Maarten J.J. Menken, "The Old Testament Quotation in John 19, 36: Sources, Redaction, Background," in Frans van Segbroeck, et al., eds., *The Four Gospels 1992: Festschrift Frans Neirynck* (3 vols.; BETL 100; Leuven: Leuven University Press/Peeters, 1992) 3. 2101–18.

5.5.7   *Excursus on Crossan's Interpretation of* Barnabas *7*

Crossan identifies *Barnabas* 7 as an intermediary stage in the development of the passion narrative. As Crossan has it, the first activity of Christian scribes after the crucifixion was to gather scriptural *testimonia* which showed "a dialectic of persecution and vindication." In this particular case the Day of Atonement ritual in Leviticus 16 was chosen because of its dialectic of the two goats.[193] The connections drawn between the ritual and Jesus in *Barnabas* 7 is what Crossan refers to as "passion prophecy" or "exegetical discourse."[194] Only then were various passion prophecies such as this written up into a passion narrative; thus the passion prophecy of *Barnabas* 7 "knows nothing at all about passion stories."[195] For Crossan, it is the exegetical work exemplified in *Barnabas* 7 that provided the details of the ritual abuse in the eventual passion narrative.

Crossan is correct to emphasize that the collection of passion/vindication lists (*testimonia*), and even the development of small-scale "prophetic-fulfillment units" was a process that was independent of and/or interactive with gospel narrative traditions well into the third century.[196] Crossan is most likely incorrect, however, to claim that units such as *Barnabas* 7 have no knowledge of a passion narrative.

For Crossan's claim to be substantiated, we should find in *Barnabas* 7 only general references to the dialectic of suffering and vindication. But as we have seen, the suffering/vindication (two advents) schema is only one axis of *Barnabas* 7—in fact the author's main concern is the Day of Atonement ritual. Indeed, if suffering/vindication patterns were the sole focus of the "search of scripture," then the "two goats" of Leviticus 16 would never have been chosen. On the contrary, the Day of Atonement text was likely chosen because of prior conviction that Jesus' death is atoning (*Barn.* 7.2).

From Crossan's analysis, we should similarly have expected to find generic references to scriptural abuse and mockery. What we find instead are obscure references to non-scriptural rituals involving abuse and mockery! It is far more likely that the author of *Barnabas* 7, familiar with such passion narrative details as the scarlet robe, sought types of these narrative details in scripture and other authoritative

---

[193] Crossan, *Who Killed Jesus?* 120.
[194] Ibid., 121; see also idem, "Lists," 243.
[195] Crossan, *Who Killed Jesus?* 123.
[196] Crossan, "Lists," 241.

traditions than that he scoured scriptural and non-scriptural traditions looking for general symbols of suffering and vindication.

Finally, if *Barn.* 7.3–5 is indeed a reference to eucharistic practice, then it is plausible that the author found a type of this practice in Jewish ritual, but much more difficult to imagine that a bare reference to washing with vinegar can have struck him as a useful suffering/vindication *testimonium*.

While it is not necessary to suppose that *Barnabas* 7 knew the canonical passion narratives as we have them,[197] it is clear that *Barnabas* is familiar with both *testimonia* traditions and some form of the passion narrative. We can conclude that he was a member of a Christian community in which he was taught a theological understanding of Jesus' death as atoning, that he was familiar with eucharistic traditions, and hence that he cannot be characterized as a lone "searcher of the scriptures" looking for suffering/vindication patterns.

5.6   *Stone* Testimonia *in the New Testament*

By the time of Justin, the title "stone" for Jesus is so well established that Justin can simply make the identification without further argument.[198] In the following, I shall explore the scriptural background to this stone tradition. After surveying the Jewish background to the stone traditions, I discuss five NT stone traditions: (1) interpretations of Jesus as the rejected cornerstone (Ps 118 [117]:22); (2) the imagery of the stumbling stone set in Zion (Rom 9:33; 1 Pet 2:6–8); (3) *testimonia* and stone metaphors for the Christian community and the temple; (4) gospel portraits of Jesus and the stone *testimonia*; and (5) the designation of Peter as the "rock" and foundation stone (Matt 16:18). Finally, I will provide some examples of the continuity of the stone *testimonia* tradition into the patristic era. Four passages are central to the stone *testimonia* tradition: Isa 8:14; Isa 28:16; Ps 118 (117):22; and Dan 2:34, 44–45.

---

[197] Carleton Paget (*Barnabas*, 139) and Köster (*Synoptische Überlieferung*, 152–56) argue for the independence of *Barnabas* from the canonical narratives.
[198] See *Dial.* 34.2; 86.2–3; 100.4; 126.1.

5.6.1 *Second Temple Jewish Background to the Stone* Testimonia

Pre-Christian Jewish interpretations of Isa 28:16 and Dan 2:34, 44–45 are of particular importance for the Christian stone tradition. The Daniel 2 passages were part of the eschatological imagery in at least some first-century Jewish circles:

> And when these things come to pass and the signs occur which I showed you before, then my Son will be revealed, whom you saw as a man coming up out of the sea. Then, when all the nations hear his voice, all the nations shall leave their own lands and the warfare that they have against one another; and an innumerable multitude shall be gathered together, as you saw, desiring to come and conquer him. But he shall stand on the top of Mount Zion. And Zion shall come and be made manifest to all people, prepared and built, as you saw *the mountain carved out without hands.* (4 Ezra 13:32–36, NRSV)

This important passage identifies an eschatological Mount Zion, the mount of the temple, with the mountain of Daniel 2. The "man of the sea," associated with interpretations of the Danielic "Son of Man," also figures prominently in the vision.[199]

Josephus, in the course of his exposition of the book of Daniel, provides a further tantalizing hint that some Jews gave the Danielic stone a potentially dangerous eschatological interpretation:

> And Daniel also revealed to the king the meaning of the stone, but I have not thought it proper to relate this, since I am expected to write of what is past and done and not of what is to be ... (*Ant.* 10.210)[200]

Many scholars read here an understandable reluctance on the part of Josephus to divulge a Jewish eschatological or messianic interpretation threatening to his Roman patrons.[201]

An important interpretive background may likewise be traced for Isa 28:16 in the varieties of Second Temple Judaism, beginning already with the LXX rendition:

> *MT Isa 28:16*: See I am laying in Zion a foundation stone, a tested stone, a precious cornerstone, a sure foundation: "One who trusts will not panic."

---

[199] On 4 Ezra 13, see Collins, *Scepter*, 183–87.
[200] Greek text and ET in Ralph Marcus, trans., *Josephus*, vol. 6: *Jewish Antiquities, Books IX–XI* (LCL; Cambridge, MA; London: Heinemann; 1937).
[201] See Lloyd Gaston, *No Stone on Another: Studies in the Significance of the Fall of Jerusalem in the Synoptic Gospels* (NovTSup 23; Leiden: Brill, 1970) 219 n. 3.

LXX Isa 28:16: Ἰδοὺ ἐγὼ ἐμβαλῶ εἰς τὰ θεμέλια Σιων λίθον πολυτελῆ ἐκλεκτὸν ἀκρογωνιαῖον ἔντιμον εἰς τὰ θεμέλια αὐτῆς, καὶ ὁ πιστεύων <u>ἐπ᾽ αὐτῷ</u> οὐ μὴ καταισχυνθῇ.

Behold, I will lay for a foundation in Zion a stone, a costly, chosen, precious cornerstone for its foundation, and the one trusting in it [him?] will not be put to shame.

The addition ἐπ᾽ αὐτῷ is of most interest: Joachim Jeremias holds that the reading ἐπ᾽ αὐτῷ is "the oldest example of Messianic interpretation of an OT stone statement."[202] This conclusion is open to serious question, however, as the referent of αὐτῷ is ambiguous, the addition is lacking in the LXX B text, and, even granted that the LXX A text has a messianic meaning, this may be due to Christian influence.[203]

The targum to Isa 28:16 has transformed the stone into a king:

Behold I will appoint in Zion a king, a strong king, powerful and terrible. I will make him strong and powerful, says the prophet, but the righteous who have believed in these things shall not be dismayed when distress comes.

Again, of course, the uncertain dating of this targumic tradition makes its use for recovering first-century understandings difficult.

All in all, the evidence for a pre-Christian messianic interpretation of Isa 28:16 must be considered weak.[204]

A more promising witness to a first-century Jewish reading of Isa 28:16 is found in the Dead Sea Scrolls. Isaiah 28:16 played an important part in expressing the self-understanding of the Qumran community as the renewed temple—a place holy and set apart.[205] In the Rule of the Community, the following passage refers to the Community council, a body consisting of twelve men and three priests:

[5]the Community council shall be founded on truth, like an everlasting plantation, a holy house for Israel and the foundation of the holy of [6]holies for Aaron, true witnesses for the judgment and chosen by the will (of God) to atone for the earth and to render [7]the wicked their retribution. It[206] will be the tested rampart, the precious cornerstone

---

[202] Jeremias, "λίθος," *TDNT* 4. 268–80; esp. 272. Jeremias proceeds to provide a wealth of rabbinic citations for messianic readings of stone passages (pp. 272–73).

[203] So Gaston, *No Stone*, 219.

[204] *Pace* Dunn (*Romans* 2. 583–84) who considers a pre-Christian messianic interpretation of Isa 28:16 likely.

[205] See the impressive case presented in Gaston, *No Stone*, 163–76.

[206] The subject here is ambiguous: it may refer to the council in particular or

that does not ⁸whose foundations do not shake or tremble in their place. It will be the most holy dwelling ⁹for Aaron with total knowledge of the covenant of justice and in order to offer a pleasant aroma; and it will be a house of perfection and truth in Israel. (1QS 8.5–9)²⁰⁷

Lloyd Gaston comments correctly that here we see the Community taking over the temple's role not only as the dwelling place of God, but also providing the means of atonement which had previously been effected by the sacrifices of the Jerusalem temple.²⁰⁸

Gaston offers two further texts from the hymns of the Community in which Isa 28:16 is used compositionally:

> The deep thunders at my sigh, [my soul nears] the gates of death
> I am like someone entering a fortified city,
> and looking for shelter in the rampart until salvation.
> My God, I lean on your truth,
> for you place the foundation upon rock,
> and the beams to the correct size, and the plumb line [. . .]
> tested stone for a strong building which will not shake.
> All those who enter there will not stagger,
> for a foreigner will not penetrate it;
> its gates are armoured gates which do not permit entry. (1QH 14.24b–28a)

> You placed me like a sturdy tower, like a high wall,
> you founded my building upon rock
> and everlasting foundations as my base,
> all my walls are like a tested wall which will not shake. (1QH 15.8–9)

The targum's rendering of the last phrase of Isa 28:16 as "the righteous who believed in these things shall not be dismayed when distress

---

to the community as a whole. García Martínez supplies "the Community" in his translation, and Gaston too prefers this rendering (*No Stone*, 168). The context, however, supports a specific reference to the council here (so Achtemeier, *1 Peter*, 155 n. 74). The point is not essential, as 4QIsaiah Pesherᵈ shows that both the council and the wider community could be described as stones: "and your foundations are sapphires [Isa 54:11] [its interpretation]: they will found the council of the Community, the priests and the people; the assembly of their elect, like a sapphire stone in the midst of stones."

²⁰⁷ Hebrew text of 1QS (1QRule of the Community) in Millar Burrows, ed., *The Dead Sea Scrolls of St. Mark's Monastery*, vol. 2; fasc. 2: *The Manual of Discipline* (New Haven, CT: American Schools of Oriental Research, 1951); ET in *Scrolls*, 3–19.

²⁰⁸ Gaston, *No Stone*, 169. See also 1QS 9.3–4 on the holy Community's role in establishing "the spirit of holiness in truth eternal, in order to atone for the fault of the transgression and for the guilt of sin and for approval for the earth, without the flesh of burnt offerings and without the fats of sacrifice."

come" shows that these Qumran readings also parallel a targumic tradition.[209]

Finally, the epithet "rock" (צור) given to Yahweh in the Jewish scriptures may have contributed to the later messianic or eschatological interpretations of the stone passages.[210] This image of God as a rock, intriguingly, is expressly avoided in the LXX: of the forty references in the Hebrew scriptures, only once is the image carried over into the LXX (2 Kgs 22:2). The metaphor is most often replaced by a simple reference to God.[211]

5.6.2 *New Testament Uses of Stone* Testimonia

(a) *Jesus as the Rejected (but Ultimately Vindicated) Cornerstone*

As a conclusion to Jesus' parable on the vineyard and the tenants (Mark 12:1–11), Ps 118 (117):22–23 is quoted in a straightforward LXX text:

> *Mark 12:10–11*: λίθον, ὃν ἀπεδοκίμασαν οἱ οἰκοδομοῦντες, οὗτος ἐγενήθη εἰς κεφαλὴν γωνίας· παρὰ Κυρίου ἐγένετο αὕτη, καὶ ἔστιν θαυμαστὴ ἐν ὀφθαλμοῖς ἡμῶν.
> The stone that the builders rejected has become the cornerstone, this was the Lord's doing, and it is amazing in our eyes.

The parable is certainly intended as an allegory (see Mark 12:12): Jesus is identified as the son, and further symbolized as the rejected stone that will become the cornerstone. The connection between the parable and the quotation was likely facilitated by the play on words: בֵּן (son) and אֶבֶן (stone).[212] This connection, together with the witness of the *Gospel of Thomas* 65–66 (which also follows its version of the parable with a clear allusion to Ps 118:22), indicates that the quotation was the original, scriptural key to the allegory.

---

[209] See ibid., 172. The verb for staggering/shaking in the Qumran hymns is the Hiphil. of זוע; the targum uses the cognate יודעזעון.

[210] Jeremias, "λίθος," 273; see Deut 32:4; 2 Sam 23:3; Isa 26:4; 30:39; Ps 62:3, 7.

[211] See Ken Derry, "One Stone on Another: Towards an Understanding of Symbolism in *The Epistle of Barnabas*," *Journal of Early Christian Studies* 4 (1996) 526 n. 35. Thus in Deut 32:4, "The Rock (הצור), his work is perfect," becomes simply θεός, ἀληθινὰ τὰ ἔργα αὐτοῦ. On this see the thorough study of Staffan Olofsson, *God is My Rock: A Study of Translation Technique and Theological Exegesis in the Septuagint* (ConB OT Ser. 31; Stockholm: Almqvist & Wiksell, 1990).

[212] Gundry, *Matthew: A Commentary on his Handbook for a Mixed Church under Persecution* (2d ed.; Grand Rapids: Eerdmans, 1994) 429; Klyne Snodgrass, *The Parable of the Wicked Tenants* (WUNT 27; Tübingen: Mohr-Siebeck, 1983), esp. 113–18.

Matthew 21:33–46 and Luke 20:9–19 follow Mark here, quoting the LXX Psalm 118 (117) passage as a conclusion to the allegorical parable. Matthew gives the allegory an explicitly anti-Jewish interpretation: "the kingdom of God will be taken away from you and given to a people that produces the fruits of the kingdom" (21:43). Luke quotes only Ps 118 (117):22, and immediately adds:

> *Luke 20:18*: πᾶς ὁ πεσὼν ἐπ᾿ ἐκεῖνον τὸν λίθον συνθλασθήσεται·
> ἐφ᾿ ὅν δ᾿ ἂν πέσῃ, λικμήσει αὐτόν.
> Everyone who falls on that stone will be broken to pieces;
> and it will crush anyone on whom it falls.

This allusion itself is a composite one: the first part echoes the stone of stumbling as found in Isa 8:14–15:

> *Isa 8:14–15a*: καὶ ἐὰν ἐπ᾿ αὐτῷ πεποιθὼς ᾖς, ἔσται σοι εἰς ἁγίασμα,
> καὶ οὐχ ὡς λίθου προσκόμματι συναντήσεσθε αὐτῷ
> οὐδὲ ὡς πέτρας πτώματι . . .
> διὰ τοῦτο ἀδυνατήσουσιν ἐν αὐτοῖς πολλοὶ καὶ πεσοῦνται καὶ συντριβή-
> σονται,
> And if you trust in him, he shall be a sanctuary for you,
> and you shall not come against him as against a stumbling stone,
> neither as against a rock of falling. . . .
> Therefore many among them shall be weak, and fall, and be crushed.

The second part of Luke's image derives from the stone in Dan 2:34, the stone cut from a mountain without hands (ἐτμήθη λίθος ἐξ ὄρους ἄνευ χειρῶν) and (in vv 44–45) identified as a kingdom that will last forever and crush and grind to powder all other kingdoms.[213]

In the speech reported in Acts 4:11, Peter makes a clear allusion to Ps 118 (117):22:

> *Acts 4:11*: οὗτός ἐστιν ὁ λίθος, ὁ ἐξουθενηθεὶς ὑφ᾿ ὑμῶν τῶν οἰκοδόμων, ὁ
> γενόμενος εἰς κεφαλὴν γωνίας.
> This one is the stone that was rejected by you, the builders; it has
> become the cornerstone.

Here Luke has replaced the LXX word for rejection (ἀποδοκιμάζω) (which he uses in Luke 20:17) with ἐξουθενέω. It is hardly a casual

---

[213] See Lindars, *Apologetic*, 184, on the tracing of these allusions. Matthew 21:44 has essentially the same addition, though its omission in 44 D 33 and other witnesses makes the reading textually suspect. Whether original or an accretion, however, Matt 21:44 witnesses to the strong tendency for scriptural stone texts to attract other scriptural stone passages.

change: ἐξουθενέω is a key word in Christian reflection on Christ's passion, as can be seen below:

Mark 9:12: καὶ πῶς γέγραπται ἐπὶ τὸν υἱὸν τοῦ ἀνθρώπου ἵνα πολλὰ πάθῃ καὶ ἐξουδενηθῇ.
Luke 23:11: ἐξουθενήσας δὲ αὐτὸν [καὶ] ὁ᾽ Ἡρῴδης σὺν τοῖς στρατεύμασιν
Barn. 7.9: Οὐχ οὗτός ἐστιν, ὅν ποτε ἡμεῖς ἐσταυρώσαμεν ἐξουθενήσαντες καὶ κατακεντήσαντες καὶ ἐμπτύσαντες;

Lindars plausibly suggests that this use of ἐξουθενέω is derived from Isa 53:3 (in the Aquila, Symmachus, and Theodotion recensions).[214] With Lindars and Crossan, therefore, we can speak of two "rejection" themes in the NT, one based on Ps 118 (117):22 and using ἀποδοκιμάζω, the other likely derived from Isa 53:3 with ἐξουθενέω.[215] Acts 4:11 represents a confluence of these two streams.[216]

With his combination of Ps 118 (117):22; Isa 8:14; and Dan 2:34, 44–45, Luke therefore shows contact with exegetical reflection that applied a complex network of stone images to Jesus. Each text serves a distinct function:

Ps 118 (117):22: Shows that Jesus has been rejected (by unbelievers in general/Jews in particular) but is ultimately vindicated (by his resurrection/ascension/second advent)
Isa 8:14–15: Demonstrates the ambiguity of trust in Christ: for those who trust he is a sanctuary (ἁγίασμα), for those who do not, he is a stumbling stone or rock of falling
Daniel 2: Intensifies the negative effects of those who oppose Christ: they will be crushed

(b) *The Stumbling Stone Set in Zion (Rom 9:33; 1 Pet 2:6–8)*

In the context of his scriptural meditation on God's plan for Israel in Romans 9–11, Paul cites a conflation of Isa 28:16 and Isa 8:14. This text belongs to the "hard" hardening tradition known to Paul (see sect. 5.4.3): God is portrayed as intentionally placing a stumbling stone in Zion.

---

[214] Ibid., 81–82. The LXX reads ἠτιμάσθη.

[215] Lindars, *Apologetic*, 81–92; Crossan, *Cross*, 126–27. In the passion predictions, Mark 8:31 uses ἀποδοκιμάζω; Mark 9:12 has ἐξουθενέω.

[216] A further link between "stone" traditions and the Isaian servant is to be found already in one of the "servant songs": "The Lord God helps me; therefore I have not been disgraced; therefore I have set my face like flint"—a text which was to become part of *Barnabas*'s "stone" collection (6.3b).

Rom 9:33: Ἰδοὺ τίθημι ἐν Σιὼν λίθον προσκόμματος καὶ πέτραν σκανδάλου,
καὶ ὁ πιστεύων ἐπ᾽ αὐτῷ οὐ καταισχυνθήσεται.

See, I am laying in Zion a stone that will make people stumble, a
rock that will make them fall, and whoever believes in him will not
be put to shame.

LXX Isa 28:16: Ἰδοὺ ἐγώ ἐμβαλῶ εἰς τὰ θεμέλια Σιων λίθον πολυτελῆ
ἐκλεκτὸν ἀκρογωνιαῖον ἔντιμον εἰς τὰ θεμέλια αὐτῆς, καὶ ὁ πιστεύων ἐπ᾽
αὐτῷ οὐ μὴ καταισχυνθῇ.

MT Isa 28:16: הנני יסד בציון אבן אבן   בחן
פנת יקרת מוסד מוסד   המאמין לא יחיש

See, I am laying in Zion a foundation stone, a tested stone, a precious cornerstone, a sure foundation: "One who trusts will not panic."

LXX Isa 8:14: καὶ ἐὰν ἐπ᾽ αὐτῷ πεποιθὼς ᾖς, ἔσται σοι εἰς ἁγίασμα, καὶ οὐχ
ὡς λίθου προσκόμματι συναντήσεσθε αὐτῷ οὐδὲ ὡς πέτρας πτώματι.

MT Isa 8:14: והיה למקדש ולאבן נגף   ולצור מכשול

He will become a sanctuary, a stone one strikes against, a rock one
stumbles over.

The base text of the quotation is Isa 28:16, with interpretive elements brought in from Isa 8:14. The quotation of Isa 8:14 is closer
to the sense of the Hebrew, indicating either a recourse to the original or (most likely) the use of one of the Greek recensions preserved
in Aquila, Symmachus, and Theodotion.[217] The quotation of Isa 28:16
shows contact with both the Hebrew (omission of "foundation" of
Zion) and the Greek (retention of ἐπ᾽ αὐτῷ);[218] in its omission of τὰ
θεμέλια it differs from the readings preserved in the LXX recensions. This non-standard reading of Isa 28:16 has a remarkable parallel in 1 Pet 2:6:

Rom 9:33: Ἰδοὺ τίθημι ἐν Σιὼν λίθον προσκόμματος καὶ πέτραν σκανδάλου,
καὶ ὁ πιστεύων ἐπ᾽ αὐτῷ οὐ καταισχυνθήσεται.

1 Pet 2:6: Ἰδοὺ τίθημι ἐν Σιὼν λίθον ἀκρογωνιαῖον ἐκλεκτὸν ἔντιμον καὶ ὁ
πιστεύων ἐπ᾽ αὐτῷ οὐ μὴ καταισχυνθῇ.

Both Romans and 1 Peter read the non-standard Ἰδοὺ τίθημι ἐν Σιὼν
λίθον and retain the ἐπ᾽ αὐτῷ reading of LXX A. 1 Peter does not
insert the material from Isa 8:14 at this point, but rather continues
with quotations from LXX Ps 117:22 (1 Pet 2:7) and then adds Isa
8:14 (1 Pet 2:8), the latter in a non-LXX version exactly parallel to
that in Romans.

There are three options to explain the common non-standard

---

[217] See Stanley, *Language of Scripture*, 123–24; Koch, *Schrift als Zeuge*, 58–60.
[218] Koch, *Schrift als Zeuge*, 69–71.

reading Ἰδοὺ τίθημι ἐν Σιὼν λίθον: (1) that Romans depends on 1 Peter; (2) that 1 Peter depends on Romans; or (3) that both texts draw on a common source for their adapted version of Isa 28:16. There is nearly unanimous scholarly agreement that there is no direct literary relationship between Romans and 1 Peter. It is difficult to imagine the author of 1 Peter disentangling Paul's composite quotation and quoting Isa 28:16 and Isa 8:14 (with a slight adjustment to Isa 28:16) with Ps 118 (117):22 between them. On the other hand, dependence of Romans on 1 Peter is *prima facie* unlikely: why would Paul select only two of three texts and conflate them?[219] Recent commentaries by Achtemeier and J. Ramsey Michaels represent the consensus that 1 Peter and Romans are in fact drawing on a common source.[220]

Stanley and Koch present the following arguments for their view that the form of Isa 28:16 witnessed in 1 Peter and Romans goes back to a common Christian tradition: (1) it deviates strikingly from the LXX, MT, and any other extant version; (2) there is no reason to think that the changes from the LXX or MT are attributable to Paul or 1 Peter, since they fit the context of neither work closely; (3) this common form can easily be given a christological interpretation: God has laid Christ as a cornerstone in Zion; those who believe in him will not be put to shame. While Koch attributes this common "source" to oral tradition, his notion of a christological oral tradition is quite vague, and he gives no convincing reason to prefer this explanation over a common written source.[221]

Koch further argues that Isa 28:16 and Isa 8:14 were first conflated by Paul, and that the use of both texts in 1 Pet 2:6–8, though not directly dependent on Romans, nevertheless depends on a more general "tradition deriving from Paul."[222] Stanley, however, rightly rejects this proposal: the fact that both Paul and 1 Peter use the same non-LXX text of Isa 8:14 in close conjunction with a "christianized" version

---

[219] See Kraft, "Isaiah," 344–45; Koch, *Schrift als Zeuge*, 69; Stanley, *Language of Scripture*, 120 n. 109.

[220] "While the similarities point to a common source, the differences indicate an independent use of it" (Achtemeier, *1 Peter*, 159); "Peter is therefore probably not dependent on Paul for his quotations but on an early collection of messianic proof texts" (Michaels, *1 Peter* [WBC 49; Waco, TX: Word, 1988] 94).

[221] Koch, *Schrift als Zeuge*, 69–71; idem, "Christologischen Schriftgebrauch," 178–84. Stanley (*Language of Scripture*, 121–22) remains noncommittal on the question of the use of oral or written sources.

[222] See Koch, "Schriftgebrauch," 182.

of Isa 28:16 could hardly have occurred independently.[223] This independent but exactly parallel use of two non-standard texts makes the conclusion that both 1 Peter and Paul drew on a written "stone" text collection almost inevitable.[224]

It remains to consider the function of the stone texts in each author. In the specific context of Rom 9:30–33, Paul declares that Israel did not fulfill the law because it did not pursue it ἐκ πίστεως but rather ὡς ἐξ ἔργων. This striving ὡς ἐξ ἔργων is the stumbling block over which Israel has stumbled. Lindars is perhaps correct to conclude that Paul does not have a directly christological interpretation in view here: the stone is not Christ *per se*, but rather the role of Christ in God's plan for Israel.[225] Nevertheless, it is likely that Paul is simply extending the meaning of an original directly christological interpretation of Jesus as the stumbling stone.

1 Peter 2 reveals a range of functions for the stone imagery. In 1 Pet 2:4, the image is attributed directly to Christ: "Come to him, a living stone (λίθος ζῶν), though rejected (ἀποδεδοκιμασμένον) by mortals yet chosen and precious (ἐκλεκτὸς ἔντιμος) in God's sight" (allusions to Ps 118 [117]:22 and Isa 28:16). The image then slips almost imperceptibly to an application to followers of Christ: "like living stones (ὡς λίθοι ζῶντες) let yourselves be built into a spiritual house (οἰκοδομεῖσθε οἶκος πνευματικός), to be a holy priesthood, to offer spiritual sacrifices acceptable to God through Jesus Christ" (1 Pet 2:5). Finally, the catena of proof-texts (1 Pet 2:6–8), together with interpretive comments, echoes the point of Rom 9:33 precisely: "To you who believe, he is precious; but for those who do not believe he is a stumbling stone."

The common TC that has been posited for 1 Peter and Romans was almost certainly part of a *testimonia* tradition on God's rejection

---

[223] Stanley, *Language of Scripture*, 120–21 n. 109.

[224] Koch challenges the TC hypothesis on the grounds that the same "stone" texts are not cited by independent authors: Paul does not use Ps 118 (117):22; the Synoptics do not employ Isa 28:16 or 8:14 (though I dispute this last claim above); *Barn.* 6:2–4 lacks Isa 8:14 and cites Isa 28:16 in a textual form different from Paul ("Christologischen Schriftgebrauch," 184). Koch's objections, however, rest on a rigid, Harris-type model of a single fixed written TC: the evidence presented in this study suggests rather a more fluid model of a flexible school life-setting in which TCs were produced and transmitted.

[225] "The stone is not a symbol of Christ, but a vivid poetic image. The consequence of belief in Christ, or of unbelief, is *like* a precious stone in your way. If you see it and take hold of it, you have got something of real value. If you are blind, it trips you up" (Lindars, *Apologetic*, 178).

of Israel and election of the gentiles as the new chosen people.[226] As so often in the *testimonia* literature, these events are understood as pre-ordained because they are written in scripture: "They stumble because they disobey the word, as they were destined to do (εἰς ὃ καὶ ἐτέθησαν) (1 Pet 2:8b).[227]

(c) *Stone* Testimonia, *the Community, and the Temple*

The imagery of believers as the living stones of a new temple, οἶκος πνευματικός (1 Pet 2:5), is paralleled in many other NT passages.[228] We have seen that this image of the community as the new temple is "proved" by a TC in 2 Cor 6:14–7:1: "We are the temple of the living God" (2 Cor 6:16b) (see sect. 4.2.1f above). In Eph 2:20–22, the new community brought together by Christ is described with a series of building images that climax in a temple metaphor: the believers are "built upon the foundations of the apostles and the prophets, with Christ Jesus himself as the cornerstone" (ἐποικοδομηθέντες ἐπὶ τῷ θεμελίῳ τῶν ἀποστόλων καὶ προφητῶν, ὄντος ἀκρογωνιαίου αὐτοῦ Χριστοῦ Ἰησοῦ), they are "a holy temple (ναὸς ἅγιος) in the Lord" in whom they are built together (συνοικοδομέω) into a dwelling place (κατοικητήριον) of God in the spirit.[229]

The imagery continues into the apostolic period. Ignatius (*Eph.* 9.1) refers to his readers as "stones of the temple of the Father, made ready for the building of God the Father" (ὡς ὄντες λίθοι ναοῦ πατρός, ἡτοιμασμένοι εἰς οἰκοδομὴν θεοῦ πατρός).[230] In *Barnabas* 16, an extended attack on the Jewish Temple (TC in 16.3–5, with commentary) is followed by a passage on believers being led into an "incorruptible temple" (*Barn.* 16.9). Although *Barnabas*'s meaning is not clear, he apparently identifies the new temple with Christians: "God truly dwells in us, in the habitation which we are" (v 8). Influence of a stone *testimonium* is perhaps visible in *Barn.* 16.7, with

---

[226] See 1 Pet 2:9: "you are a chosen race, a royal priesthood, a holy nation, God's own people"; and the quotation of Hos 2:23 in 1 Pet 2:10 (quoted also in Rom 9:25).

[227] The connection between the use of τίθημι here and in the quotation of Isa 28:16 (1 Pet 2:6) is noteworthy.

[228] E.G. Selwyn correctly interprets οἶκος πνευματικός as "God's true temple" (*St. Peter* 160, 286–91). That 1 Peter has the temple in mind is ensured by the following references in the verse to priesthood and sacrifice.

[229] Cf. the parallel sequence of thought in Eph 4:15–16, where Christ is depicted as the head of the body of believers.

[230] Greek text and ET in Lake, *Apostolic Fathers* 1. 172–277.

the reference to the Jewish temple as "like a temple really built with hands (ὡς ἀληθῶς οἰκοδομητὸς ναὸς διὰ χειρός)" (cf. the Danielic ἄνευ χειρῶν).[231] Finally, the *Shepherd of Hermas* Vision 3 and Similitude 9 develop the metaphor whereby believers are the stones (λίθοι) that make up the tower (πύργος) which is the church.

Paul's identification of the individual's body with the temple of God in 1 Cor 3:16–17; 6:19 is perhaps best understood as an extension of the metaphor of the community as temple.[232] The concept of the community as temple is also a constitutive element in the NT parenetic tradition centered on building metaphors (οἰκοδομή, οἰκοδομέω).[233] Nor should the temple allusions be limited to "stone" words and the οἰκοδομέω word group; Gaston rightly recognizes that λίθος, πέτρα, and ἀκρογωνιαῖος should be studied together with θεμέλιος and even στῦλος (Gal 2:9; Rev 3:12) as part of an overall image.[234] Indeed apostles are portrayed as the foundation of the community in Matt 16:18; Eph 2:20; 2 Tim 2:19; and Rev 21:9. 2 Timothy 2:19 is of special interest, in that it forms an exact parallel to Isa 28:16 in picturing a firm foundation with an inscription on a stone.[235]

(d) *Jesus, the Temple, and Stone* Testimonia

With this widespread network of stone *testimonia* and temple imagery evident in the NT, it is not surprising that these traditions are also found in the Gospel portraits of Jesus. Statements that Jesus would destroy the temple and rebuild it are witnessed in a variety of independent traditions:

---

[231] Cf. also Acts 7:48, where Stephen, after noting that Solomon built the temple, argues that God has no need of a human-made habitation: ἀλλ' οὐχ ὁ ὕψιστος ἐν χειροποιήτοις κατοικεῖ. Both *Barnabas* and Acts use Isa 66:1 as an anti-temple *testimonium*.

[232] See Gaston, *No Stone*, 180.

[233] See Acts 20:32; Rom 14:19; 1 Cor 8:1; 10:23; 14:12; 2 Cor 10:8; 12:19; 13:10; 1 Thess 5:11; Jude 20. On the general OT background of Paul's use of the "building" tradition, see Philipp Vielhauer, "Oikodome: Das Bild vom Bau in der christlichen Literatur vom Neuen Testament bis Clemens Alexandrinus," in idem, *Oikodome*, 113–15; on the particular relationship to temple imagery, see Otto Michel, "οἶκος," *TDNT* 5. 139. My point here is only that the scriptural background, including the temple imagery, is an important element of the οἰκοδομέω parenetic tradition; this does not rule out other important influences from Jewish and hellenistic sources.

[234] Gaston, *No Stone*, 195, 214.

[235] Ibid., 197–98.

Mark 14:58: "I will destroy this temple that is made with hands, and in three days I will build another, not made with hands." (par. Matt 26:61; omitting "not made with human hands")

Mark 15:29: "Aha! You who would destroy the temple and build it in three days, save yourself, and come down from the cross." (par. Matt 27:40)

John 2:19–21: "Destroy this temple, and in three days I will raise it up . . . But he was speaking of the temple of his body."

Acts 6:14: "for we have heard him say that this Jesus of Nazareth will destroy this place and will change the customs that Moses handed on to us."

Gospel of Thomas 71: Jesus said: "I shall destroy [this] house, and no one will be able to [re]build it."

Also to be noted is Jesus' answer to his disciple's question about the temple: "Do you see these great buildings? Not one stone will be left here upon another; all will be thrown down" (Mark 13:2).

This temple tradition is again connected with specific stone *testimonia*. Lindars rightly sees in the χειροποίητος/ἀχειροποίητος of Mark 14:58 an allusion to Dan 2:34, 44–45 (ἄνευ χειρῶν).[236] The exchange in Mark 13:1–2 explicitly connects λίθοι with the temple. Latin textual traditions add to Mark 13:2 "and in three days another will be raised without hands," thereby showing the influence of a *testimonia* reflection which combined images of the destruction of the temple, the accusations against Jesus, (perhaps) a reference to Jesus' resurrection, and Dan 2:34, 44–45.[237]

A recent trend in historical Jesus research has centered on the importance of Jesus' challenge to the temple. For E.P. Sanders, Jesus' symbolic action in the temple (Mark 11:15–19) is key for reconstructing Jesus' intentions. Sanders argues that Jesus' action was meant not as a "cleansing" but as a symbolic destruction of the temple as a prelude to the inauguration of the kingdom of God and the construction of the eschatological temple.[238] N.T. Wright agrees with the centrality of the temple action in reconstructing Jesus' intentions: in predicting the destruction of the temple, Jesus implicitly claimed to be the royal messiah with authority to destroy and rebuild the

---

[236] Lindars, *Apologetic*, 68–69.

[237] See ibid.; Bakker, "Old-Latin Gospels," 1–8. The addition is witnessed in D W it Cyprian.

[238] Sanders, *Jesus and Judaism* (Philadelphia: Fortress, 1985) 61–76; idem, *The Historical Figure of Jesus* (London: Penguin, 1993) 253–62.

temple.[239] Crossan too finds in Jesus' action a symbolic destruction, although he sees no messianic intent.[240] Space precludes even a cursory discussion of these complex historical Jesus issues, but I suggest that pursuing connections between the NT stone traditions (so often connected with temple imagery) and Jesus' own intentions in regard to the temple is a fruitful avenue for future research.[241]

(e) *Peter and the Stone* Testimonia *(Matt 16:18)*

We saw above that in addition to Christ and the church, stone traditions were also applied to Peter.[242] The application is already present in the NT: Jesus names the disciple Simon "Cephas" ("rock") in all four Gospels.[243] In Peter's confession of Jesus as the messiah as recorded in Matt 16:13–23, the stone imagery is further developed. Jesus responds to Peter's confession:

> [17]Blessed are you, Simon son of Jonah! For flesh and blood has not revealed this to you , but my Father in heaven. [18]And I tell you, you are Peter, and on this rock I will build my church, and the gates of Hades will not prevail against it. [19]I will give you the keys of the kingdom of heaven, and whatever you bind on earth will be bound in heaven, and whatever you loose on earth will be loosed in heaven. (Matt 16:17–19)

Otto Betz has shown well the important parallels between the imagery here and the Qumran community's self-understanding as the new temple (using Isa 28:16 as the guiding metaphor).[244] Both the Qumran texts and Matthew 16 picture a community built on a solid rock,

---

[239] Wright, *Christian Origins and the Question of God*, vol. 2: *Jesus and the Victory of God* (Minneapolis: Fortress, 1996) 490–93. Wright explicitly links this interpretation of the temple action with the interpretation of the parable of the wicked tenants (pp. 497–501).

[240] Crossan, *The Historical Jesus: The Life of a Mediterranean Jewish Peasant* (San Francisco: HarperSanFrancisco, 1991) 357–59.

[241] On this connection, see Seyoon Kim, "Jesus—The Son of God, the Stone, the Son of Man, and the Servant: The Role of Zechariah in the Self-Identification of Jesus," in Gerald F. Hawthorne and Otto Betz, eds., *Tradition and Interpretation in the New Testament: Essays in Honor of E. Earle Ellis for his 60th Birthday* (Grand Rapids: Eerdmans; Tübingen: Mohr-Siebeck, 1987) 134–48. Kim draws some interesting connections, but is often highly speculative.

[242] The Peter stone tradition is most developed in Syriac literature (see Murray, *Church and Kingdom*, 205–38, 295–97, 353).

[243] Matt 16:18; Mark 3:16; Luke 6:14; John 1:42.

[244] Betz, "Felsenmann und Felsengemeinde (Eine Parallele zu Mt 16:17–19 in den Qumranpsalmen)," *ZNW* 48 (1957) 49–77. See sect. 5.6.1 above on the interpretation of Isa 28:16 at Qumran.

strong enough to withstand the elemental forces of chaos and evil.[245] Although a majority of scholars dismiss this passage as unhistorical, Ben F. Meyer's case that it represents Jesus' aim of building an eschatological temple in the form of his community of disciples is worthy of consideration in light of the above discussions.[246]

5.6.3   *The Patristic Stone* Testimonia

In the following I provide an overview of stone collections outside of the NT in the first three centuries of the common era. I begin with *Barn.* 6.2b–4a, perhaps the earliest collection outside the NT. The author of *Barnabas* presupposes that his readers know a tradition in which Christ is called the stone. He is concerned that his readers have a correct understanding of this symbol: "Is then our hope on a stone? God forbid. But he means that the Lord placed his flesh in strength" (6.3).[247] For *Barnabas*, then, this image applies to Christ's self-control in the suffering of the passion.

Barnabas introduces the collection, "And again the Prophet says that he was placed as a strong stone (λίθος) for crushing" (6:2b). The reference to being placed (ἐτέθη) may allude either to Isa 50:7[248] or to an adapted text of Isa 8:14 (see Rom 9:33 and 1 Pet 2:6).[249] The phrase λίθος . . . εἰς συντριβήν alludes to Isa 8:15[250] or Dan 2:34, 45.[251] The very difficulty of pinpointing precise scriptural

---

[245] Cf. the imagery of Matt 16:18 with Isa 28:18: "Then your covenant with death will be annulled, and your agreement with Sheol will not stand." Cf. further the compositional use of Isa 28:16–18 in the Hodayoth (sect. 5.6.1 above).

[246] Meyer, *The Aims of Jesus* (London: SCM, 1979) 185–97. The Qumran and the NT evidence provide numerous parallels to the imagery of the community as eschatological temple; Sanders and others have argued forcefully for the historicity of Jesus' intention to destroy the current temple and replace it with the eschatological community of his followers.

[247] The implied objection is actually made in the *Dialogue of Athanasius and Zacchaeus* 111–12: "Do you mean that the Wisdom of God became a stone?" (quoted in Barnard, "Testimonies," 122). Derry rightly points out that some of the stone imagery in *Barnabas* is negative: tables of stone broken by Moses (4.7–8); hearts of stone (6:14); see Derry, "One Stone," 519–20.

[248] So Prigent, *Testimonia*, 171.

[249] So Harris, *Testimonies* 1. 31.

[250] So Prigent, *Testimonia*, 171. After speaking of the λίθος and πέτρα in the previous verse, Isa 8:15 declares that "many among them" shall be weak, and fall, and be crushed (συντριβήσονται).

[251] Barnard offers this as a possibility ("Testimonies," 121). These passages speak of the stone which will destroy the four kingdoms of Daniel's vision. The lack of συντρίβω in Daniel tells against an allusion.

references argues that Barnabas is employing the imagery of what is already a well-known combination of texts. The following references can be identified with more precision.

Barnabas	LXX
6:2b: Ἰδού, ἐμβαλῶ εἰς τὰ θεμέλια Σιὼν λίθον πολυτελῆ, ἐκλεκτόν, ἀκρογωνιαῖον, ἔντιμον.	Isa 28:16a Ἰδοὺ ἐγὼ ἐμβαλῶ εἰς τὰ θεμέλια Σιων λίθον πολυτελῆ, ἐκλεκτὸν, ἀκρογωνιαῖον, ἔντιμον.
6:3a: Καὶ ὃς ὁ πιστεύων εἰς αὐτὸν ζήσεται εἰς τὸν αἰῶνα.	Isa 28:16b: καὶ ὁ πιστεύων ἐπ' αὐτῷ οὐ μὴ καταισχυνθῇ.
6:3b: Καὶ ἔθηκέ με ὡς στερεὰν πέτραν.	Isa 50:7: ἀλλὰ ἔθηκα τὸ πρόσωπόν μου ὡς στερεὰν πέτραν.
6:4a: λίθον ὃν ἀπεδοκίμασαν οἱ οἰκοδομοῦντες, οὗτος ἐγενήθη εἰς κεφαλὴν γωνίας.	Ps 118:22: λίθον ὃν ἀπεδοκίμασαν οἱ οἰκοδομοῦντες, οὗτος ἐγενήθη εἰς κεφαλὴν γωνίας.
6:4b: Αὕτη ἐστὶν ἡ ἡμέρα ἡ μεγάλη καὶ θαυμαστή, ἣν ἐποίησεν ὁ κύριος.	Ps 118:24: Αὕτη ἡ ἡμέρα ἣν ἐποίησεν ὁ κύριος.

The passages witness to an odd combination of precise LXX quotation and free paraphrase. *Barnabas* closely follows Isa 28:16 LXX (i.e., not the non-LXX form witnessed in Romans and 1 Peter), yet then gives a very free paraphrase of Isa 28:16–17a. *Barnabas* continues with an adapted form of Isa 50:7, although the author knows the LXX version (5:14). Psalm 118 (117):22 is quoted accurately; the author, however, then skips over v 23 and gives what appears to be a free rendering of Ps 118 (117):24.

Isaiah 28:16 and Ps 118 (117):22 are well-established *testimonia* in the NT, yet *Barnabas* shows no direct dependence on NT text forms or exegesis. Nevertheless, the author knows an authoritative tradition, incorporating both LXX and non-LXX texts, in which stone passages are applied to Christ. Given his use of extensive non-LXX TCs, it is most likely that this stone tradition too was passed down to him as a written collection. As a Christian teacher, he provided his readers with a certain exegesis of this collection: he applies it to Christ's steadfastness during his passion. It is possible that the author added other texts (e.g., Isa 50:7) to a collection that had been handed down to him.[252]

To demonstrate the widespread popularity and range of functions which the stone *testimonia* served, I present the following summary table. The summary draws on citations collected by Harris (*Testimonies* 2. 60–61), Barnard ("Testimonies," 117), Kraft ("Isaiah," 344–45) and my own research.

Author/Work	Stone Texts	Function
Justin *Dial.* 70.1	Dan 2:34	Polemic against super-natural birth of Mithras;
Dial. 76.1	Dan 2:34 (w. Dan 7:13)	Christ's supernatural birth;
Dial. 86.2–3	Gen 28:18 (A)	Christ called a stone in many passages;
Dial. 90.4	Exod 17:9–12 (A)	Stone a symbol of Christ;
Dial. 113.6–7	Josh 5:2 (A)	Stone knives = Jesus' and apostles' words; second circumcision
Dial. 114.2–5[253]	Various allusions	Second circumcision; titles of Christ
Sib. Or. 1.345–46	Isa 28:16, 8:14 (A)	Beautiful stone from Egypt against which Hebrews will stumble;
Sib. Or. 8.254		Title of Christ
Irenaeus *A.H.* 3.21.7 *A.H.* 4.20.11	Dan 2:34/Isa 28:16 Dan 2.34	Christ's supernatural birth; One of the symbols of Christ
Hippolytus *Antichrist* 26 *Ref.* 5.2.35	Dan 2:34 (A) (w. Dan 7:13) Ps 118:22; Isa 28:16; Dan 2:34 (A) (w. Homeric citations)	Christ's future universal reign Naasenes attribute passages to Adam
Dial. Tim. and Aq. Fol. 99	Exod 17:12 (A)	Moses' stone a type of the true stone

---

[252] See Barnard, "Testimonies," 122.

[253] In several passages, "stone" is one of a series of Christ's titles: *Dial.* 34.2; 100.4; 126.1. In *Dial.* 36.1, even Trypho admits that the prophets had said that Christ was to be called a stone.

(table cont.)

Author/Work	Stone Texts	Function
Tertullian *Marc.* 3.7.3; *A.J.* 14.2–3	Isa 8:14; Ps 118:22; Dan 2:34 (w. Dan. 7:13)	Isa 8:14 refers to Christ's humble advent; others to his glorious advent
Marc. 5.5.9	Isa 28:16; 8:14	Christ a stone; stumbling stone for Marcion
A.J. 9:22 (cf. *Marc.* 3.16.4)	Josh 5:2 (A)	stone knife = Christ's precepts
Marc 4.13.6	Isa 8:14 (A)	Christ names Simon "Peter" since "stone" titles are particularly fit for Christ himself
Marc. 5.17.16	Eph 2:20 and Ps 118:22	Paul learns Christ is corner-stone from OT "figure"
Dial. Ath. and Zac. 111–12.	Isa 28:16; 8:14 (form = Rom 9:33)	Zaccheus asks if the Wisdom of God became a stone
Dream of Nero 10.1–2	Gen 28:18, 22; Ps 126:1; Isa 28:16	Only the stone of Christ can build house of God
Cyprian *Quir.* 2.16	Isa 28:16; Ps 118:21–26; Zech 3:8–9; Deut 27:8; Josh 24:26–27; Acts 4:8–12; Gen 28:11–22 (A); Exod 17:12; 1 Sam 6:15; 1 Sam 17:49; 1 Sam 7:12	Christ also is called a stone
Quir. 2.17–18	Dan 2:31–35 and Isa 2:2–4; Ps 24:3–6	Stone (Christ) shall become a mountain, and the gentiles will come to the mountain
Firmicus Maternus *Error* 20:1–6	Isa 28:16; Ps 118:22–23; Zech 3:8–9; Deut 27:8; Josh 24:26–27; Dan 2:31–34.	Polemic against followers of Mithras: Christ is the true stone.

(table cont.)

Author/Work	Stone Texts	Function
Origen *In Joh.* 1.23.41	Ps 118:22–23; Matt 21:42, 44; Acts 4:11	One of Christ's titles
Acts of Peter 24	Dan 2:34; Ps 118:22; Isa 28:16 (w. Dan 7:13)	Christ's supernatural origin
Eusebius *Proof* 1.7	Isa 28:16; Ps 118:22	Christ the cornerstone between Jews and Christians (cf. Eph 2:20)
Proph. Select. 3.42		
Methodius *Sermon on Sim.* 6	Ps 118:22 (A)	One of Christ's titles
Ps.-Epiphanius *Test.* 13	Dan 2:34 Isa 8:14; 28:16 (form = Rom 9:33); Zech 3:9; 4:10	Supernatural birth; That he is a stone
Ps.-Gregory *Test.* 8	Isa 28:16; Ps 118:22 (A)	Christ's resurrection and building of the church.
Cyril of Jer. *Catech.* 10.3; 15:28	Dan 2:34; Ps 118:2; Isa 28:16 (A)	One of Christ's titles
Aphrahat *Dem.* 1.16.1–21.9	Ps 118:22; Isa 28:16; Luke 20:18; Dan 2:34–44; Zech 4:7; Zech 3:9	Prophets called Christ the "rock."
Acts of the Eastern Martyrs (intro.)	Dan 2:34; Matt 16:18; Isa 28:16; Ps 118:22; Rom 9:33; Matt 7:24–25 (A)	Church is built from stones of the martyrs
Ephrem *EC.* 21.21 (Diatessaron comm.)	Ps 118:22; Dan 2:34; Gen 28:11 (A)	Christ = Stone[254]

5.6.4 *Conclusions on the Stone* Testimonia: *Form and Function*

Again our study has found ample evidence that stone texts were interpreted as a collection already in NT times: Paul and 1 Peter

---

[254] See Murray for further examples of Ephrem's numerous stone allusions (*Church and Kingdom*, 208–12).

know a written TC which was apparently drawn together as a scriptural proof against unbelievers (Jews?) who did not accept Christian beliefs; the quotation of Ps 118 (117):22 in Luke 20:18 already shows the influence of stone texts in Daniel 2 and Isa 8:14–15. This broad collection supplies both positive (precious cornerstone) and negative (stone of stumbling) images. Early Christian stone imagery is profoundly ambivalent.

Lindars understood the application of Ps 118 (117):22 in Acts 4:11 as the "first" stage of the apologetic: Jesus' resurrection/vindication was interpreted as a literal fulfillment of this scriptural vindication of the rejected cornerstone.[255] Gaston, however, offers an important alternative: the image of Christ as cornerstone is secondary to the fundamental image of the community as the temple. The above analysis has shown how pervasive this metaphor is in the NT: not only do many texts explicitly link the community and the temple, but the widespread NT parenetic traditions involving οἰκοδομέω often presuppose the image of the community as the temple. In this sense, the elusive effort to find a pre-Christian messianic background for the christological interpretation of stone texts is misplaced: the most important background is the use of Isa 28:16 at Qumran to support the community's claim to be the solid rock of refuge and indeed even the new Temple.

In the second century, *Barnabas* and Justin can simply allude to "stone" as a meaningful title for Jesus Christ.[256] Stone collections contain both explicit quotations (Dan 2:34; Ps 118:22; Isa 8:14, 28:16 are central) and allusions to narratives (Moses' stone; Joshua's stone knives). The stone texts carry a bewildering variety of christological symbolism:

(1) Christ's supernatural birth
(2) Christ as a stone of stumbling (e.g., to Jews and Marcion)
(3) Christ's humility *and* his glory
(4) Christ's universal reign
(5) Christ's endurance of suffering
(6) Christ's teachings
(7) Christ as the cornerstone between Jews and gentiles

---

[255] Lindars, *Apologetic*, 170.
[256] See Kurz ("Christological Proof," 210): "Justin's failure to comment on this title *Stone* would seem to indicate that it was too familiar to need justification."

The stone symbolism is also applied to followers of Christ; Peter and the apostles are at times singled out for special emphasis. Some of the symbolism seems to have been mediated through NT interpretations, e.g., Christ as the cornerstone between Jew and gentile (Eph 2:20); believers as the stones of the church (1 Pet 2:5); and Peter as the foundation stone (Matt 16:18).

The stone texts quoted are characterized by great diversity in text forms (both LXX and LXX-deviant), text combinations, and functions.[257] This diversity should not be allowed to obscure the striking continuity: stone imagery is widely understood as a meaningful description of Christ and/or Christians; and a common fund of *testimonia* are used to articulate this meaning. The complex dynamics of the patristic tradition are to be explained by multiple factors: direct use of scripture, borrowing from previous authors, oral traditions (liturgical or homiletical), individual creativity, and "school" traditions (written TCs and commentaries).

---

[257] See esp. Kraft, "Isaiah," 344–45 for the textual variety.

CONCLUSIONS

Rather than again provide a summary of my results, which I have
done at the end of major sections, I will offer what I see as some
implications of this study's conclusions for the scholarly reconstruction of early Christianity.

Conclusion 1: Authoritative written *testimonia* existed in New Testament
times. This is probable by analogy with excerpt collections from contemporary Greco-Roman literature, Qumran documents, and later
patristic collections; it is made virtually certain by the presence of authoritative non-standard quotations found in various strands of the
NT itself. The close verbal parallels, shared by independent witnesses, to Christian versions of Zech 12:10, Isa 6:9–10, and Isa 28:16
are especially persuasive. These written *testimonia* no doubt originally
circulated in many forms: in proof-text collections (seen in Rom 9:33
and 1 Peter 2; the Hebrews 1–2 catena); in dialogues (at least as early
as *Jason and Papiscus*, a source used by Justin); in eschatological discourses (employed in the Synoptics with an adapted version of Zech
12:10); in historical (scriptural *exempla*) reviews (Acts 13); and in narratives about Jesus (Matthew's formula citations). Some forms of these
written *testimonia* are already known to Paul.

    Implications: If authoritative written *testimonia* date back to the ear-
    liest stages of Christian tradition, then a paradigm which attrib-
    utes the earliest Jesus traditions to oral transmission and assigns
    written traditions to a later stage is inadequate. While the model
    of early = oral and later = written may fit the transmission of
    Jesus' sayings, in the case of scriptural reflection on the Christ
    events it is probable that both oral and written traditions were
    transmitted from the earliest stages after the death of Jesus. This
    evidence virtually requires that some of the earliest followers of
    Jesus were trained interpreters of scripture.

    Once the existence of these written works is admitted, the pic-
ture of early Christian literary relationships becomes correspond-
ingly more complex. Thus, for example, in comparing the synoptic
versions of the eschatological coming of the Son of Man, it is

Matthew (24:30), not Mark (13:26) who appears to preserve the version closest to the original (see sect. 5.5.2).

In recent work on the passion narrative, scholars such as John Dominic Crossan have recognized the significance of intense early scribal activity. Crossan rightly speaks of *testimonia* lists and exegetical discourses which precede the canonical writings. At the same time, however, his model of scribes searching the scriptures for persecution/vindication passages is too limited. Followers of Jesus were also looking for other scriptural patterns (e.g., Christ as the fulfillment of sacrificial types) and passages which corresponded to known details of Jesus' life.

Continued research into the relationship between narratives of Jesus' life and scriptural reflection on that life will no doubt shed further light on both of these early Christian literary efforts.

Conclusion 2: The basic criteria for detecting use of written *testimonia* collections, refined by a century of scholarly discussion in NT, Second Temple, and patristic studies, remain valid today (see chapter one conclusions, point seven, for a summary). The burden of proof now lies with those who would deny that Christians used written scriptural collections beginning in NT times.

Implications: This study has demonstrated that the insights of older scholars (J. Rendel Harris, George Milligan, Vincent Henry Stanton) are still worth recovering for the debate today. In particular, the genuine insights of Harris have been too lightly dismissed on the basis of his more idiosyncratic views (e.g., that early Christians used a single Testimony Book). Similarly, insights from patristic and Qumran research must continue to be a part of NT study; indeed the boundaries between these fields are, from a scholarly point of view, artificial.

Conclusion 3: *Testimonia* traditions show a high degree of sophistication, implying access to a variety of variant readings (in Greek, Hebrew, and Aramaic traditions), an intimate knowledge of scripture, and training in scribal techniques such as text conflation and adaptation.

Implications: Given this degree of sophistication, the attribution of many of these quotations to the final authors and redactors of the NT is unrealistic. In the case of Paul, many of his quotations are far too complex to have been composed during the course of dictation: we must suppose that he himself composed them at an earlier stage or that he has taken over another's work. In the case of the gospel writers, it is hard to suppose that Matthew, for example, would have composed the intricate adapted version of Isa 42:1–4 as a "fulfillment quotation" to his narrative (Matt 12:18–21).

Conclusion 4: Some early Christians knew only excerpt collections, not the entire corpus of scripture or even whole books. This situation was certainly the case with gentile converts to Christianity who had little exposure to Judaism: their first access to scripture would have been in the form of extracts used in catechesis. We see an example of this in Onesimus's request to Melito to provide a list of OT books together with christologically relevant extracts.

   Implications: C.H. Dodd's suggestion that a quotation evoked the wider scriptural context must be accepted with caution: in some cases this wider context simply may not have been known. Although Traugott Holtz's position that Luke did not directly know the Pentateuch or the historical books remains unproven, he rightly questions the uncritical assumption of many scholars that NT writers had a thorough knowledge of, let alone access to, the entire body of Jewish scriptures.

Conclusion 5: *Testimonia* were used as direct quotations, allusions, and as models for composition in early Christian literature. It is difficult to assess whether direct quotations and TCs proper are earlier than compositional use of scripture. Messianic passages, for example, are used allusively and compositionally in Hebrews and Revelation, but it is possible that this use presupposes an earlier explicit collection of, and reflection on, these passages from Genesis, Numbers, and Isaiah (cf. the analogy of 4QTestimonia). This study has shown repeatedly how the *testimonia* seem to have gained their authoritative status as part of larger collections, whether messianic, "two powers," "two advent," or "stone" collections.

   Implications: Recent trends in scholarship emphasizing an intertextual approach to the NT (e.g., Richard B. Hays's *Echoes of Scripture in the Letters of Paul*) are a promising development, allowing scholars to identify scriptural allusions more accurately. At the same time, further research into the *process* of how certain scriptures came to attain authoritative status (and the role of scriptural collections in that process) is necessary.

Conclusion 6: *Testimonia* traditions are not limited to NT times, but continued to be passed down well into the patristic era and beyond. This continuity does not necessarily imply direct dependence on the NT: a major conclusion of this study is that *testimonia* collections were transmitted *independently* of the NT and other authoritative early Christian literature.

Implications: A corollary to this conclusion is that later patristic evidence may shed a clearer light on NT traditions. Crossan rightly makes this one of his principles in his work on the passion narratives. In this study, for example, we have seen that the combination of references to Isaac and the Day of Atonement in *Barnabas* 7 clarifies the scriptural traditions in Acts 3:22–25. Patristic witnesses to Zech 12:10 establish that this text was understood as a "second advent" passage: this illuminates John's particular theological understanding that Jesus' death already inaugurated eschatological, "second advent" events.

Conclusion 7: The *testimonia* and the exegetical comments which accompanied them were considered authoritative by a wide variety of independent NT witnesses. The applicability of Ps 110:1, for example, to Jesus' vindication was accepted without question in the Synoptics, Paul, and Hebrews. Already in NT times, "Christianized" versions of Zech 12:10 and Isa 28:16 are quoted as scriptural, although they never formed part of scriptural manuscripts.

Implications: Further research into the source of the authority of the *testimonia* is necessary. This study has suggested that the *testimonia* were part of the earliest authoritative catechesis and general Christian teaching, yet the life-setting of these Christian "schools" remains vague. Older suggestions that the *testimonia* were collected under the authority of the disciples or Jesus himself must of course be treated with extreme caution, but should not be dismissed out of hand.

In the continuing debate concerning unity and diversity in early Christianity, the *testimonia* traditions are a witness in the case for unity. Nevertheless, the precise manner in which these authoritative traditions were passed down (in catechesis, authoritative discourses, and/or liturgical traditions—especially hymns) is still quite unclear.

Conclusion 8: The *testimonia* show a range in their rhetorical or persuasive force. They are employed as proofs from prophecy to supply a kind of forensic proof for Christian claims (the principle that all things written in scripture *must* take place is important here), but they are also employed to illustrate a larger scriptural pattern in which the Christ events may be understood.

> *Implications*: There is a continued need for studies such as that of Reinhold Liebers, who has isolated a group of scriptural quotations in the NT that refer not to specific texts, but to general scriptural patterns that were applied to Jesus and John the Baptist. While there is no need to argue, with Liebers, that such general references are earlier than explicit proof-text collections, his study nevertheless is a reminder that early Christian use of scripture spanned a range of rhetorical force.

In investigating the varied issues raised by the *testimonia* hypothesis, this study has uncovered the world of the earliest Christian scribes. They were an anonymous group, but their activity of selecting, editing, conflating, and applying the scriptures of Israel to the Christ events decisively shaped subsequent Christian life and thought. They were a group with two commitments: one to understanding and obeying God's will in sacred scriptures, and the other to understanding and obeying God's will as expressed in Jesus Christ. Their great achievement was to combine these two tasks, tasks that others saw as mutually exclusive. Although scholars of early Christianity today no longer share all of the methods or even the presuppositions with which these scribes worked, we still have much to learn from their often brilliant, creative, and committed interpretation of the scriptures.

BIBLIOGRAPHY

1 PRIMARY SOURCES

1.1 Hebrew Bible

Elliger, K., and W. Rudolph, eds., *Biblia Hebraica Stuttgartensia* (Stuttgart: Deutsche Bibelgesellschaft, 1984).

1.2 New Testament

Aland, Barbara, et al., eds., *The Greek New Testament* (4th ed.; Stuttgart: Deutsche Bibelgesellschaft, 1994).
Novum Testamentum Graece (26th ed.; Stuttgart: Deutsche Bibelgesellschaft, 1979).
Aland, Kurt, ed., *Synopsis Quattuor Evangeliorum* (13th ed.; Stuttgart: Deutsche Bibelgesellschaft, 1985).

1.3 Septuagint and Targum

Academia Litterarum Gottingensis, *Septuaginta: Vetus Testamentum Graecum* (Göttingen: Vandenhoeck & Ruprecht, 1931–).
    Vol. 1: Wevers, John William, ed., *Genesis* (1974).
    Vol. 2/2: Wevers, John William, ed., *Leviticus* (1986).
    Vol. 3/1: Wevers, John William, ed., *Numeri* (1982).
    Vol. 3/2: Wevers, John William, ed., *Deuteronomium* (1977).
    Vol. 10: Rahlfs, Alfred, ed., *Psalmi cum Odis* (2d ed.; 1967).
    Vol. 13: Ziegler, Joseph, ed., *Duodecim Prophetae* (3d ed.; 1984).
    Vol. 14: Ziegler, Joseph, ed., *Isaias* (3d ed.; 1983).
    Vol. 16/2: Ziegler, Joseph, ed., *Susanna, Daniel, Bel et Draco* (1954).
Field, Frederick, ed., *Origenis Hexaplorum quae supersunt* (2 vols.; Oxford: Clarendon, 1867, 1875; repr. Hildesheim: Olms, 1964).
Klein, Michael L., *The Fragment-Targums of the Pentateuch According to their Extant Sources* (2 vols.; AnBib 76; Rome: Biblical Institute, 1980).
Rahlfs, Alfred, *Septuaginta* (Stuttgart: Deutsche Bibelgesellschaft, 1935).
Sperber, Alexander, *The Bible in Aramaic: Based on Old Manuscripts and Printed Texts* (2d impression; 5 vols.; Leiden/New York/Cologne: Brill, 1992).
Stenning, J.F., *The Targum of Isaiah* (Oxford: Clarendon, 1949).

1.4 Second Temple Jewish Authors

Burrows, Millar, J.C. Trever and W.H. Brownlee, eds., *The Dead Sea Scrolls of St. Mark's Monastery* (New Haven, CT: The American Schools of Oriental Research, 1950).
Burrows, Millar, ed., *The Dead Sea Scrolls of St. Mark's Monastery*, vol. 2; fasc. 2: *The Manual of Discipline* (New Haven, CT: American Schools of Oriental Research, 1951).
Colson, F.H., and G.H. Whitaker, *Philo*, vol. 4 (LCL; Cambridge, MA; London: Heinemann, 1949).
Charlesworth, James, *The Old Testament Pseudepigrapha* (2 vols.; London/New York: Doubleday, 1983–85).
Discoveries in the Judean Desert (Oxford: Clarendon, 1955–).
    Vol. 4: Sanders, James A., ed., *The Psalms Scroll of Qumrân Cave 11 (11QPs^a)* (1965).

Vol. 5: Allegro, John M., ed., *Qumrân Cave 4 I (4Q158–4Q186)* (1968).

Vol. 6: de Vaux, Roland, and J.T. Milik, eds., *Qumrân Grotte 4 II (4Q128–4Q157): Archéologie, Teffillin, Mezuzot et Targums* (1977).

Vol. 14: Ulrich, Eugene, et al. eds., *Qumran Cave 4 IX: Deuteronomy, Joshua, Judges, Kings* (1995).

García Martínez, Florentino, *The Dead Sea Scrolls Translated: The Qumran Texts in English* (2d ed.; Leiden/New York/Cologne: Brill; Grand Rapids: Eerdmans, 1996).

Horst, P.W. van der, ed., *The Sentences of Pseudo-Phocylides* (SVTP 4; Leiden: Brill, 1978).

Lohse, Eduard, ed., *Die Texte aus Qumran: Hebräisch und Deutsch* (Darmstadt: Wissenschaftliche Buchgesellschaft, 1971).

Marcus, Ralph, trans., *Josephus*, vol. 6: *Jewish Antiquities, Books IX–XI* (LCL; Cambridge, MA; London: Heinemann; 1937).

Sukenik, E.L., ed., *The Dead Sea Scrolls of the Hebrew University* (Jerusalem, 1954–55).

Wacholder, Ben Zion and Martin G. Abegg, eds., *A Preliminary Edition of the Unpublished Dea Sea Scrolls: The Hebrew and Aramaic Texts from Cave Four* (4 vols.; Washington, D.C.: Biblical Archaeological Society, 1991).

Woude, A.S. van der, "Melchisedek als himmlische Erlösergestalt in den neugefundenen eschatologischen midraschim aus Qumran-Höhle XI.," *OTS* 14 (1965) 354–73.

Yadin, Yigdal, ed., *Megillat ham-migdash (The Temple Scroll)* (3 vols. and supp.; Jerusalem: Israel Exploration Society, 1977).

Young, D., ed., *Theognis, Ps-Pythagoras, Ps.-Phocylides, Chares, Anonymi Aulodia, Fragmentarum Teleiambicum* (Biblioteca Script. Graec. et Rom. Teubneriania; 2d ed.; Leipzig: BSB Teubner, 1971).

1.5   *Greco-Roman Authors*

Babbit, Frank Cole, ed., *Plutarch's Moralia*, vol. 1 (LCL; London: Heinemann; New York: Putnam, 1927).

Bury, R.G., ed., *Plato: Laws*, vol. 2 (LCL; Cambridge, MA: Harvard University Press; London: Heinemann, 1926).

Butler, H.E., ed., *The Institutio Oratoria of Quintilian*, vol. 2 (LCL; Cambridge, MA: Harvard University Press; London: Heinemann, 1939).

Caplan, Harry, ed., *Rhetorica ad Herennium* (LCL; Cambridge, MA: Harvard University Press, 1954).

Diels, Hermann, ed., *Doxographi Graeci* (4th ed.; Berlin: de Gruyter, 1965).

Dillon, John, ed., *Alcinous: The Handbook of Platonism* (Clarendon Later Ancient Philosophers; Oxford: Clarendon, 1993).

Freese, John Henry, ed., *Aristotle: The "Art" of Rhetoric* (LCL; London: Heinemann; New York: Putnam, 1926).

Grenfell, Bernard P., and Arthur S. Hunt, eds., *The Hibeh Papyri* (Egypt Exploration Society, Graeco-Roman Memoirs 7, 32; 2 vols.; London: Egypt Exploration Fund, 1906, 1955).

Guéraud, O. and P. Jouget, eds., *Un Livre d'écolier du III* siècle avant J.-C* (Publications de la Société royale égyptienne de Papyrologia, textes et documents; 2 vols.; Cairo: Institut française d'archéologie orientale, 1938).

Gummere, Richard M., ed., *Seneca Ad Lucilium Epistulae Morales*, vol. 1–2 (LCL; Cambridge, MA: Harvard University; London: Heinemann, 1917).

Helmbold, W.C., ed., *Plutarch's Moralia*, vol. 6 (LCL; London: Heinemann; Cambridge, MA: Harvard University Press, 1939).

Hense, Otto, and C. Wachsmuth, eds., *Ioannis Stobaei Anthologium* (5 vols.; Berlin: Weidmann, 1884–1912; repr. 1968).

Hicks, R.D., ed., *Diogenes Laertius: Lives of Eminent Philosophers*, vol. 2 (LCL; London: Heinemann; New York: Putnam, 1925).

Hubbell, H.M., ed., *Cicero De Inventione, De Optimo Genere Oratorum, Topica* (LCL; London: Heinemann; Cambridge, MA: Harvard University Press, 1949).

———, ed., *Cicero: Topica* (LCL; Cambridge, MA: Harvard University Press, 1949).

Marchant, E.C., ed., *Xenephon: Memorabilia and Oeconomicus* (LCL; London: Heinemann; New York: Putnam, 1923).

Melmoth, W., and W.M.L. Hutchinson, eds., *Pliny: Letters*, vol. 1 (LCL; London: Heinemann; New York: Macmillan, 1915).

Norlin, George, ed., *Isocrates* vol. 1 (LCL; Cambridge, MA: Harvard University Press, 1928).

Pack, Roger Ambrose, ed., *The Greek and Latin Literary Texts from Greco-Roman Egypt* (2d ed.; Ann Arbor: University of Michigan Press, 1965).

Schubart, W. and U. von Wilamowitz-Moellendorff, eds., *Griechische Dichterfragmente* (Berliner Klassikertexte 5/2; Berlin, 1907).

Smith, Robin, trans., *Aristotle: Topics: Books I and VIII* (Clarendon Aristotle Series; Oxford: Clarendon, 1996).

1.6 Early Christian Authors

Bensly, R.L., ed., *The Fourth Book of Ezra, the Latin Version Edited from the MSS* (Texts S 3.2; Cambridge: Cambridge University Press, 1895).

Karl Bihlmeyer, ed., *Die apostolischen Väter: Neuarbeitung der Funkschen Ausgabe*, vol. 1 (3d ed.; Tübingen: Mohr-Siebeck, 1970).

Bratke, Edward, ed., *Evagrii Altercatio Legis inter Simonem Iudaeum et Theophilum Christianum* (CSEL 45; Scriptores Eclesiastici Minores Saec IV V VI; Vindobona: Tempsky; Lipsia: Freytag, 1904).

Braun, René, ed., *Tertullian: Contre Marcion, Livre III* (SC 399; Paris: Cerf, 1994).

Chadwick, Henry, ed., *Origen: Contra Celsum* (Cambridge: Cambridge University Press, 1953).

Conybeare, F.C., ed., *Anecdota Oxoniensia: The Dialogues of Athanasius and Zacchaeus and of Timothy and Aquila* (Classical Series Pt. 8; Oxford: Clarendon, 1898).

Damme, Dirk van, ed., *Pseudo-Cyprian Adversus Judaeos. Gegen die Judenchristen: Die älteste lateinische Predigt* (Paradosis 22; Freiburg, Switzerland: Universitätsverlag, 1969).

Diercks, Gerard Frederick, ed., *Novatiani Opera* (CChr Series Latina 4; Turnhout: Brepols, 1972).

Dobschütz, Ernst von, *Das Kerygma Petri kritisch untersucht* (TU 11/1; Leipzig: Hinrichs, 1893).

———, "A Collection of Old Latin Bible Quotations: *Somnium Neronis*," *JTS* 16 (1914–15) 1–27.

Ferrar, W.J., ed., *The Proof of the Gospel* (2 vols.; Translations of Christian Literature Series 1; New York: Macmillan; London: SPCK, 1920; repr. Grand Rapids: Baker, 1981).

Gaisford, Thomas, ed., *Eusebius: Eclogae Propheticae* (Oxford: Academic, 1842).

Goodspeed, Edgar, ed., *Die ältesten Apologeten: Texte mit kurzen Einleitungen* (Göttingen: Vandenhoeck & Ruprecht, 1914; repr. 1984).

Guillaumont, A., et al., eds., *The Gospel according to Thomas: Coptic Text Established and Translated* (Leiden: Brill; New York: Harper, 1959).

Hall, Stuart George, ed., *Melito of Sardis: On Pascha and Fragments* (Oxford Early Christian Texts; Oxford: Clarendon, 1979).

Heikel, Ivar A., ed., *Eusebius Werke 6: De Demonstratio Evangelica* (GCS 23; Berlin: Hinrichs, 1913).

Hennecke, Edgar and Wilhelm Schneemelcher, eds., *New Testament Apocrypha*, vol. 2: *Writings Relating to the Apostles, Apocalypses and Related Subjects* (Cambridge: James Clarke; Louisville, KY: Westminster/John Knox, 1991).

Hort F.J.A., and Joseph B. Mayor, eds., *Clement of Alexandria: Miscellanies Book VII* (London: Macmillan, 1902; repr. Greek and Roman Philosophy; New York/London: Garland, 1987).

Hotchkiss, Robert V., ed., *A Pseudo-Epiphanius Testimony Book* (SBLTT 4; Early Christian Literature Series 1; Missoula, MT: Scholars Press/SBL, 1974).

Kannengieser, Charles, ed., *Sur l'Incarnation du Verbe* (SC 199; Paris: Cerf, 1973).

Lake, Kirsopp, ed., *The Apostolic Fathers* (LCL; 2 vols.; London: Heinemann; New York: Macmillan, 1912).

Marcovich, Miroslav, ed., *Hippolytus Refutatio Omnium Haeresium* (Patristische Texte und Studien 25; Berlin/New York: de Gruyter, 1986).

———, *Iustini Martyris Apologiae pro Christianis* (Patristische Texte und Studien 38; Berlin/New York: de Gruyter, 1994).

———, *Iustini Martyris Dialogus cum Tryphone* (Patristische Texte und Studien 47; Berlin/New York: de Gruyter, 1994).

Martin, Joseph, ed., *Commodiani Carmina, Claudii Marii Victorii Alethia* (CChr Series Latina 118; Turnhout: Brepols, 1960).

Migne, J., ed., *Ps.-Gregory of Nyssa: Delecta Testimonia Adversus Judaeos* (PG 46.194–234).

Monat, Pierre, ed., *Lactance: Institutions Divines, Livre IV* (SC 377; Paris: Cerf, 1992).

Mondésert, C., C. Matray, and H.-I. Marrou, eds., *Clement: Le Pédagogue*, vol. 3 (SC 158; Paris: Cerf, 1970).

Pierre, Marie-Joseph, ed., *Aphraate le Sage Persan: Les Exposés* (2 vols.; SC 349, 359; Paris: Cerf, 1988).

Prigent, Pierre and Robert A. Kraft, eds., *Epître de Barnabé* (SC 172; Paris: Cerf, 1971).

Roberts, Alexander, and James Donaldson, eds., *The Ante-Nicene Fathers: Translations of the Writings of the Fathers down to A.D. 325* (10 vols.; Buffalo: The Christian Literature Publishing Company, 1885–96; American repr. of Edinburgh ed).

Roberts, C.H., "Two Biblical Papyri in the John Rylands Library, Manchester," *BJRL* 20 (1936) 241–44.

Robertson, Robert Gerald, "The Dialogue of Timothy and Aquila: A Critical Text, Introduction to the Manuscript Evidence, and an Inquiry into the Sources and Literary Relationships" (Ph.D. diss., Harvard University, 1989).

Robinson, James M., ed., *The Nag Hammadi Library* (3d ed.; San Francisco: HarperSanFrancisco, 1990).

Rousseau, Adelin, ed., *Démonstration de la Prédication Apostolique* (SC 406; Paris: Cerf, 1995).

Sevrin, Jean-Marie, ed., *L'Exégèse de l'Âme (NH II, 6)* (Bibliothèque Copte de Nag Hammadi, Section "Textes" 9; Québec: Presses de l'Université Laval, 1983).

Smith, Joseph P., ed., *Irenaeus: Proof of the Apostolic Preaching* (ACW 16; Westminster, MD: Newman; London: Longmans, Green, 1952).

Stählin, Otto, ed., *Clemens Alexandrinus* (GCS 17; Berlin: Akademie, 1960–80).

Tränkle, Hermann, ed., *Q.S.F. Tertulliani Adversus Iudaeos: Mit Einleitung und kritischem Kommentar* (Wiesbaden: Steiner, 1964).

Unger, Dominic J. and John J. Dillon, eds., *St. Irenaeus of Lyons: Against the Heresies*, vol. 1 (ACW 55; New York/Mahwah, NJ: Paulist, 1992).

Vouaux, Léon, *Les Actes de Pierre: Introduction, Textes, Traduction et Commentaire* (Paris: Letouzey et Ané, 1922).

2 SECONDARY LITERATURE

Achtemeier, Paul J., "Towards the Isolation of Pre-Markan Miracle Catanae," *JBL* 89 (1970) 265–91.

———, "The Origin and Function of the Pre-Marcan Miracle Catanae," *JBL* 91 (1972) 198–221.

———, *A Commentary on First Peter* (Hermeneia; Minneapolis: Fortress, 1996).

Albright, W.F., "A Biblical Fragment from the Maccabean Age: The Nash Papyrus," *JBL* 56 (1937) 145–76.

Allegro, J.M., "Further Messianc References in Qumran Literature," *JBL* 75 (1956) 174–87.

Allen, Leslie C., *Psalms 101–150* (WBC 21; Dallas: Word, 1983).

Attridge, Harry W., *The Epistle to the Hebrews* (Hermeneia; Philadelphia: Fortress, 1989).

Audet, Jean Paul, "L'hypothèse des Testimonia: remarques autour d'un livre récent," *RB* 70 (1963) 381–405.

Aune, David E., "Oral Tradition and the Aphorisms of Jesus," in H. Wansbrough, ed., *Oral Gospel*, 59–106.

Bailey, James L. and Lyle D. Vander Broek, *Literary Forms in the New Testament: A Handbook* (Louisville, KY: Westminster/John Knox, 1992).

Bakker, Adolphine, "Testimony Influence in the Old Latin Gospels," in H.G. Wood, *Amicitiae*, 1–14.

———, "Christ an Angel? A Study of Early Christian Docetism," *ZNW* 32 (1933) 255–65.

Bardy, Gustave, "Introduction," to idem, ed., *Théophile d'Antioche: Trois Livres à Autolycus* (SC 20; Paris: Cerf, 1948) 7–56.

Barnard, L.W., "The Use of Testimonies in the Early Church and in the Epistle of Barnabas," in idem, *Studies in the Apostolic Fathers and their Background* (New York: Schocken, 1966) 109–35.

Barnes, Timothy D., *Constantine and Eusebius* (Cambridge, MA/London: Harvard University Press, 1981).

———, *Tertullian: A Historical and Literary Study* (Oxford: Clarendon, 1985).

Barns, John, "A New Gnomologium: With Some Remarks on Gnomic Anthologies," *Classical Quarterly* 44 (1950) 126–37; 45 (1951) 1–19.

Barrett, C.K., "The Old Testament in the Fourth Gospel," *JTS* n.s. 48 (1947) 155–69.

———, *A Critical and Exegetical Commentary on the Acts of the Apostles* (ICC; 2 vols.; Edinburgh: T & T Clark, 1994).

Barthélemy, Dominique, "Redécouverte d'un chaînon manquant de l'histoire de la Septante," *RB* 60 (1953) 18–29; repr. in Cross and Talmon, *Qumran and Biblical Text*, 127–39.

———, *Les Devanciers d'Aquila: Première publication intégrale du texte des fragments du Dodécaprophéton* (VTSup 10; Leiden: Brill, 1963).

Bauer, Walter and Henning Paulsen, *Die Briefe des Ignatius von Antiochia und der Polykarpbrief* (HNT 18; Die Apostolischen Väter II; 2d ed.; Tübingen: Mohr-Siebeck, 1985).

Benoît, André, "Irénée *Adversus haereses* IV 17, 1–5 et les Testimonia," in F.L. Cross, ed., *Studia Patristica*, vol. 4/2 (TU 79; Berlin: Akademie, 1961) 20–27.

Benoît, André, M. Philenko, and C. Vogel, eds., *Paganisme, Judaïsme, Christianisme: Influences et affrontements dans le monde antique: Mélanges offerts à Marcel Simon* (Paris: Boccard, 1978).

Benoît, André, and Pierre Prigent, eds., *La Bible et les pères: Colloque de Strasbourg October 1–3* (Paris: Presses Universites de France, 1971).

Berger, Klaus, "Hellenistische Gattungen im Neuen Testament," *ANRW* 2.25.2. 1031–1432.

Beskow, Per, *Rex Gloriae: The Kingship of Christ in the Early Church* (Stockholm/Göteborg/Uppsala: Almqvist & Wiksell, 1962).

Betz, Hans Dieter, "2 Cor 6:14–7:1: An Anti-Pauline Fragment?" *JBL* 92 (1973) 88–108; repr. in idem, *Paulinische Studien: Gesammelte Aufsätze III* (Tübingen: Mohr-Siebeck, 1994) 20–45.

———, "The Sermon on the Mount: Its Literary Genre and Function," *JR* 59 (1979) 285–97; repr. in idem, *Essays on the Sermon on the Mount* (Philadelphia: Fortress, 1985) 1–16.

Bindley, T. Herbert, "Papias and the Matthean Oracles," *CQR* 84 (1917) 31–43.

———, Review of J. Rendel Harris, *Testimonies*, *JTS* 22 (1920–21) 279–82.

Black, Matthew, "The Christological Use of the Old Testament in the New Testament," *NTS* 18 (1971/72) 1–14.

———, Πᾶσαι ἐξουσία αὐτῷ ὑποταγήσονται (Ps 110:1; Dan 7:13; 1 Cor 15:24–27; Eph 1:20–21; 1 Pet 3:22) in Morna D. Hooker and S.G. Wilson, eds., *Paul and Paulinism: Essays in Honour of C.K. Barrett* (London: SPCK, 1982) 74–82.

Blenkinsopp, J., "The Oracle of Judah and the Messianic Entry," *JBL* 80 (1961) 55–64.

Bloch, Renée, "Midrash," *DBSup* 5/29: 1263–80; repr. in William Scott Green, ed., *Approaches to Early Judaism: Theory and Practice* (BJS 1; Missoula, MT: Scholars Press, 1978) 29–50.

Bock, Darrell L., *Proclamation from Prophecy and Pattern: Lucan Old Testament Christology* (JSNTSup 12; Sheffield: JSOT, 1986).

Bonsirven, Joseph, *Exégèse Rabbinique et Exégèse Paulinienne* (Bibliothèque de Théologie Historique; Paris: Beauchesne, 1938).

Borgen, Peder, *Bread from Heaven: An Exegetical Study of the Concept of Manna in the Gospel of John and the Writings of Philo* (NovTSup 10; Leiden: Brill, 1965).

———, "There Shall Come Forth a Man: Reflections on the Messianic Ideas in Philo," in J.H. Charlesworth, ed., *Messiah*, 341–61.

Bousset, Wilhelm, *Jüdischchristlicher Schulbetrieb in Alexandria und Rom: Literarische Untersuchungen zu Philo und Clemens von Alexandria, Justin und Irenäus* (FRLANT n.F. 6/23; Göttingen: Vandenhoeck & Ruprecht, 1915).

Bowker, J.W., "Speeches in Acts: A Study in Proem and Yelammedenu Form," *NTS* 14 (1967–68) 96–111.

Box, G.H., "The Value and Significance of the Old Testament in Relation to the New," in Arthur S. Peake, *The People and the Book: Essays on the Old Testament* (Oxford: Clarendon, 1925) 433–67.

Braun, Michael A., "James' Use of Amos at the Jerusalem Council: Steps toward a Possible Solution of the Textual and Theological Problems (Acts 15)," *JETS* 20 (1977) 113–21.

Braun, Roddy, *1 Chronicles* (WBC 14; Dallas: Word, 1986).

Brooke, George J., *Exegesis at Qumran: 4QFlorilegium in its Jewish Context* (JSOTSup 29; Sheffield: JSOT, 1985).

Brown, Raymond E., *The Gospel According to John* (AB 29; 2 vols.; Garden City, N.Y.: Doubleday, 1966, 1970).

———, *The Death of the Messiah: From Gethsemane to the Grave. A Commentary on the Passion Narratives in the Four Gospels* (2 vols.; AB Reference Library; New York/London: Doubleday, 1993).

———, *The Birth of the Messiah: A Commentary on the Infancy Narratives in the Gospels of Matthew and Luke* (AB Reference Library; updated ed.; New York/London: Doubleday, 1993).

Brownlee, W.H., *The Meaning of the Qumrân Scrolls for the Bible, with Special Attention to the Book of Isaiah* (New York: Oxford University Press, 1964).

Bruce, F.F., *The Acts of the Apostles: The Greek Text with Introduction and Commentary* (3d ed.; Grand Rapids: Eerdmans; Leicester: Apollos, 1990).

———, *The Epistle to the Hebrews* (NICNT; rev. ed.; Grand Rapids: Eerdmans, 1990).

Büchsel, Friedrich, "παραδίδωμι," *TDNT* 2. 169–73.

Bultmann, Rudolf, Review of Otto Michel, *Paulus und seine Bibel*, *TLZ* 58 (1933) col. 157.

Burkitt, F. Crawford, *The Gospel History and its Transmission* (2d ed.; Edinburgh: T & T Clark, 1907).

Burney, Charles Fox, *The Aramaic Origin of the Fourth Gospel* (Oxford: Clarendon, 1922).

Cameron, Alan, *The Greek Anthology from Meleager to Planudes* (Oxford: Clarendon, 1993).

Carleton Paget, James, *The Epistle of Barnabas: Outlook and Background* (WUNT 2/64; Tübingen: Mohr-Siebeck, 1994).

Carrington, Phillip, *The Primitive Christian Catechism* (Cambridge: Cambridge University Press, 1940).

Cerfaux, Lucien, "Vestiges d'un florilège dans 1 Cor 1.18–3.24," *RHE* 27 (1931) 521–34; repr. in idem, *Recueil Cerfaux* 2. 319–32.

———, "Un chapitre du Livre des 'Testimonia' (P. Ryl. Gk. 460)," *ETL* 14 (1937) 69–74; repr. in idem, *Recueil Cerfaux* 2. 219–26.

———, "Citations scripturaires et tradition textuelle dans le Livre des Actes," in *Aux sources de la tradition chretienne: Mélanges M. Goguel* (Bibliothèque theologique; Neuchâtel: Delachaux & Niestle, 1950) 43–51; repr. in idem, *Recueil Cerfaux* 2. 93–103.

———, *Recueil Cerfaux: Etudes d'Exégèse et d'Histoire Religieuse de Monseigneur Cerfaux* (2 vols.; BETL 6–7; Gembloux: Duculot, 1954).

Chadwick, Henry, "Florilegium," *RAC* 7 (1969) cols. 1131–59.

Charlesworth, James H., ed., *The Messiah: Developments in Earliest Judaism and Christianity: The First Princeton Symposium on Judaism and Christian Origins* (Minneapolis: Fortress, 1992).

Chvala-Smith, Anthony J., "The Boundaries of Christology: 1 Corinthians 15:20–28 and its Exegetical Substructure" (Ph.D. diss., Marquette University, 1993).

Cockerill, Gareth Lee, "Heb 1:1–14, *1 Clem.* 36:1–6 and the High Priest Title," *JBL* 97 (1978) 437–40.

Collins, John J., Review of Annette Steudel, *Der Midrasch zur Eschatologie*, *JBL* 114 (1995) 314–16.

———, *The Scepter and the Star: The Messiahs of the Dead Sea Scrolls and Other Ancient Literature* (AB Reference Library; New York/London: Doubleday, 1995).

Conzelmann, Hans, *First Corinthians* (Hermeneia; Philadelphia: Fortress, 1975).

———, *Acts of the Apostles* (Hermeneia; Philadelphia: Fortress, 1987).

Cosby, Michael R., *The Rhetorical Composition and Function of Hebrews 11 in Light of Example Lists in Antiquity* (Macon, GA: Mercer University Press, 1988).

Credner, Karl August, *Beiträge zur Einleitung in die biblischen Schriften*, vol. 2: *Das alttestamentliche Urevangelium* (Halle: Waisenhaus, 1838).

Cross, F.L., *I. Peter: A Paschal Liturgy* (London: Mowbray, 1954).

Cross, Frank Moore, "The History of the Biblical Text in the Light of Discoveries in the Judean Desert," *HTR* 57 (1964) 281–99; repr. in idem and Shemaryahu Talmon, eds., *Biblical Text*, 177–95.

Cross, Frank Moore, and Shemaryahu Talmon, eds., *Qumran and the History of the Biblical Text* (Cambridge, MA/London: Harvard University Press, 1975).

Crossan, John Dominic, *The Cross That Spoke: The Origins of the Passion Narrative* (San Francisco: Harper & Row, 1988).

———, "Lists in Early Christianity: A Response to *Early Christianity, Q and Jesus*," *Semeia* 55 (1991) 235–43.

———, *The Historical Jesus: The Life of a Mediterranean Jewish Peasant* (San Francisco: HarperSan Francisco, 1991).

Culpepper, R. Alan, *The Johannine School* (SBLDS 26; Missoula, MT: Scholars Press, 1975).

Dahl, Nils, "The Crucified Messiah," in idem, *The Crucified Messiah and other Essays* (Minneapolis: Augsburg, 1974) 10–36; repr. in D.H. Juel, ed., *Jesus the Christ*, 27–47.

Daniélou, Jean, *The Theology of Jewish Christianity* (The Development of Christian Doctrine before the Council of Nicaea 1; London: Darton, Longman & Todd, 1964).

————, *Etudes d'exégèse judéo-chrétienne (Les Testimonia)* (Théologie Historique 5; Paris: Beauschesne, 1966).

————, *Gospel Message and Hellenistic Culture* (A History of Early Christian Doctrine before the Council of Nicaea 2; London: Darton, Longman & Todd; Philadelphia: Westminster, 1973).

————, "Les testimonia de Commodien," in Antonio Maddalena, et al., eds., *Forma Futuri: Studi in Onore de Cardinale Michele Pellegrino* (Turin: Bottega d'Erasmo, 1975) 59–69.

————, *The Origins of Latin Christianity* (A History of Early Christian Doctrine before the Council of Nicaea 3; London: Darton, Longman & Todd; Philadelphia: Westminster, 1977).

Davies, W.D., *Paul and Rabbinic Judaism: Some Rabbinic Elements in Pauline Theology* (2d ed.; London: SPCK, 1955).

Delling, Gerhard, "παραλαμβάνω," *TDNT* 4. 11–14.

Derry, Ken, "One Stone on Another: Towards an Understanding of Symbolism in *The Epistle of Barnabas*," *Journal of Early Christian Studies* 4 (1996) 515–28.

Dibelius, Martin, "Zur Formgeschichte des Neuen Testaments (auserhalb der Evangelien)," *TR* 3 (1931) 207–42.

Dillistone, F.W., *C.H. Dodd: Interpreter of the New Testament* (Grand Rapids: Eerdmans, 1977).

Dimant, Devorah, "Use and Interpretation of Mikra in the Apocrypha and Pseudepigrapha," in M.J. Mulder, ed., *Mikra*, 379–420.

Dodd, C.H., *The Apostolic Preaching and its Developments* (London: Hodder & Stoughton, 1936).

————, *The Johannine Epistles* (MNTC; London: Hodder & Stoughton, 1946).

————, *Scriptures of the Old Testament in the New* (London: Athlone, 1952).

————, *According to the Scriptures: The Sub-structure of New Testament Theology* (London: Nisbet, 1952).

Doeve, Jan Willem, *Jewish Hermeneutics in the Synoptic Gospels and Acts* (Assen: Van Gorcum, 1954).

Döpke, Johann Christian Karl, *Hermeneutik der neutestamentlichen Schriftsteller* (Leipzig: Vogel, 1829).

Driver, G.R., *The Judean Scrolls: The Problem and a Solution* (New York: Schocken, 1965).

Drummond, James, *An Inquiry into the Character and Authorship of the Fourth Gospel* (London: Williams & Norgate, 1903).

Duncan, Julie A., "Considerations of 4QDt^j in Light of the 'All Souls Deuteronomy' and Cave 4 Phylactery Texts," in Julio Trebolle Barrera and Luis Vegas Montaner, eds., *The Madrid Qumran Congress: Proceedings of the International Congress on the Dead Sea Scrolls* (STDJ 11; 2 vols.; Leiden/New York/Cologne: Brill; Madrid: Editorial Complutense, 1992) 1. 199–215.

Dunn, James D.G., *Christology in the Making: A New Testament Inquiry into the Origins of the Doctrine of the Incarnation* (Philadelphia: Westminster, 1980).

————, *Romans* (WBC 38; 2 vols.; Dallas, TX: Word, 1988).

Ellingworth, Paul, "Hebrews and *1 Clement*: Literary Dependence or Common Tradition?" *BZ* 23 (1979) 262–69.

Ellis, E. Earle, *Paul's Use of the Old Testament* (Edinburgh: Oliver & Boyd, 1957; repr. Grand Rapids: Baker, 1981).

————, "Midrash, Targum and New Testament Quotations," in idem and Max Wilcox, eds., *Neotestamentica et Semitica: Studies in Honour of Matthew Black* (Edinburgh: T & T Clark, 1969) 61–68.

————, "Midrashic Features in the Speeches of Acts," in Albert Descamps and Andre de Halleux, eds., *Mélanges bibliques en hommage au R.P. Béda Rigaux* (Gembloux: Duculot, 1970) 303–12.

———, *Prophecy and Hermeneutic in Early Christianity* (Grand Rapids: Baker, 1993; orig. pub. WUNT 18; Tübingen: Mohr-Siebeck, 1978).

Eshel, Esther, "4QDeut^n—A Text That Has Undergone Harmonistic Editing," *HUCA* 62 (1991) 148–52.

Evans, Craig A., *To See and Not Perceive: Isaiah 6.9–10 in Early Jewish and Christian Interpretation* (JSOTSup 64; Sheffield: JSOT, 1989).

Evans, Craig A. and James A. Sanders, eds., *Paul and the Scriptures of Israel* (JSNT 83; Studies in Scripture in Early Judaism and Christianity 1; Sheffield: JSOT, 1993).

Fee, Gordon D., *The First Letter to the Corinthians* (NICNT; Grand Rapids: Eerdmans, 1987).

Findlay, J.A., "The First Gospel and the Book of Testimonies," in H.G. Wood, *Amicitiae*, 57–71.

Fishbane, Michael, *Biblical Interpretation in Ancient Israel* (Oxford: Clarendon, 1985).

———, "Use, Authority and Interpretation of Mikra at Qumran," in M.J. Mulder, ed., *Mikra*, 339–78.

Fitzmyer, Joseph A., "'4QTestimonia' and the New Testament," *TS* 18 (1957) 513–37; repr. in idem, *Semitic Background*, 59–89.

———, "The Use of Explicit Old Testament Quotations in Qumran Literature and in the New Testament," *NTS* 7 (1960–61) 297–333; repr. in idem, *Semitic Essays* 3–58.

———, "Qumran and the Interpolated Paragraph in 2 Cor 6:14–7:1," *CBQ* 23 (1961) 271–80.

———, "Further Light on Melchizedek from Qumran Cave 11," *JBL* 86 (1967) 25–41; repr. in idem, *Semitic Background*, 245–67.

———, *Essays on the Semitic Background of the New Testament* (SBLSBS 5; Missoula, MT: Scholars Press, 1974).

———, Review of David M. Hay, *Glory at the Right Hand*, *CBQ* 36 (1974) 594–95.

———, *The Gospel According to Luke I–IX* (AB 28; New York/London: Doubleday, 1981).

———, *Romans: A New Translation with Introduction* (AB 33; New York/London: Doubleday, 1993).

Fontaine, Jacques and Charles Pietri, eds., *Le monde latin antique et la Bible* (Paris: Beauchesne, 1985).

Fortna, Robert T., *The Fourth Gospel and its Predecessor* (Philadelphia: Fortress, 1988).

Fossum, Jarl, *The Name of God and the Angel of the Lord: Samaritan and Jewish Concepts of Intermediation and the Origin of Gnosticism* (WUNT 36; Tübingen: Mohr-Siebeck, 1985).

Frankfurter, David T.M., "The Origin of the Miracle-List Tradition and its Medium of Circulation," in D.J. Lull, ed., *SBLSP 1990*, 344–74.

Frend, W.H.C., "Jews and Christians in Third Century Carthage," in A. Benoît, et al., eds., *Paganisme*, 185–94.

Froidevaux, Léon-Marie, "Sur trois textes cites par Saint Irenee," *RSR* 44 (1956) 408–21.

Furnish, Victor Paul, *II Corinthians* (AB 32A; Garden City, NY: Doubleday, 1984).

Gamble, Harry Y., *Books and Readers in the Early Church: A History of Early Christian Texts* (New Haven/London: Yale University Press, 1995).

Gaston, Lloyd, *No Stone on Another: Studies in the Significance of the Fall of Jerusalem in the Synoptic Gospels* (NovTSup 23; Leiden: Brill, 1970).

Gerhardsson, Birger, *Memory and Manuscript: Oral Tradition and Written Transmission in Rabbinic Judaism and Early Christianity* (Lund: Gleerup, 1961).

———, *The Origins of the Gospel Traditions* (Philadelphia: Fortress, 1979).

———, *The Gospel Tradition* (Mälmo: Gleerup, 1986).

Glasson, T.F., "'Plurality of Divine Persons' and the Quotations in Hebrews I.6FF.," *NTS* 12 (1965–66) 270–72.

————, "Old Testament Testimonies and their Transmission: A Letter from C.H. Dodd to Dr. T.F. Glasson," *ExpTim* 87 (1975/76) 21–22.

Gnilka, Joachim, *Der Epheserbrief* (HTKNT 10/2; Freiburg/Basel/Vienna: Herder, 1971).

Goshen-Gottstein, M.H., "The Psalms Scroll (11PsQ^a): A Problem of Canon and Text," *Textus* 5 (1966) 22–33.

Gough, Robert, *The New Testament Quotations Collated with the Scriptures of the Old Testament* (London: Walton and Maberly, 1855).

Grant, Robert M., "Irenaeus and Hellenistic Culture," *HTR* 42 (1949) 41–51.

————, "Introduction," to idem, ed., *Theophilus of Antioch: Ad Autolycum* (Oxford Early Christian Texts; Oxford: Clarendon, 1970) ix–xxv.

Grant, Robert M., Review of Oskar Skarsaune, *Proof from Prophecy*, *CH* 57 (1988) 216.

Grech, Prosper, "Testimonia and Modern Hermeneutics," *NTS* 19 (1973) 318–24.

Greenspoon, Leonard J., "Theodotion, Theodotion's Version," *ABD* 6. 447–48.

Gregory, John Burslem, *The Oracles Ascribed to Matthew by Papias of Hierapolis: A Contribution to the Criticism of the New Testament* (London/New York: Longmans, Green, 1894). Originally published anonymously.

Guignebert, Charles, Review of J. Rendel Harris, *Testimonies*, *RHR* 81 (1920) 58–69.

Gundry, Robert H., *The Use of the Old Testament in St. Matthew's Gospel* (NovTSup 18; Leiden: Brill, 1967).

————, *Matthew: A Commentary on his Handbook for a Mixed Church under Persecution* (2d ed.; Grand Rapids: Eerdmans, 1994).

Harnack, Adolf von, Review of Edwin Hatch, *Essays in Biblical Greek*, *TLZ* 15 (1890) 297–301.

————, *History of Dogma*, vol. 1 (New York: Russell & Russell, 1958) (trans. of 3d German ed. [1894]).

Harris, J. Rendel, *Testimonies* (2 vols.; Cambridge: Cambridge University Press, 1916–20).

Reviews

Guignebert, Charles, *RHR* 81 (1920) 58–69.

Bindley, T. Herbert, *JTS* 22 (1920–1) 279–82.

Lagrange, M.-J., *RevB* 30 (1921) 612–14.

————, *Nicodemus* (Evergreen Essays 4; Cambridge: Heffer, 1932).

Harris, William V., *Ancient Literacy* (Cambridge, MA/London: Harvard University Press, 1989).

Hatch, Edwin, *The Organization of the Early Christian Churches: Eight Lectures Delivered before the University of Oxford in the year 1880* (London: Rivington, 1881; repr. New York: Burt Franklin, 1972).

————, *Essays in Biblical Greek* (Oxford: Clarendon, 1889).

————, *The Influence of Greek Ideas and Usages upon the Christian Church* (London: Williams and Norgate, 1890; repr. as *The Influence of Greek Ideas on Christianity* [New York: Harper, 1957]).

Hay, David M., *Glory at the Right Hand: Psalm 110 in Early Christianity* (SBLMS 18; Nashville/New York: Abingdon, 1973).

Review

Fitzmyer, Joseph A., *CBQ* 36 (1974) 594–95.

Hays, Richard B., *Echoes of Scripture in the Letters of Paul* (New Haven/London: Yale University Press, 1989).

Hemmerdinger, B., "Remarques sur l'ecdotique de Saint Irénée," in F.C. Cross, ed., *Studia Patristica*, vol. 3 (TU 78; Berlin: Akademie, 1961) 68–71.

Hengel, Martin, *The Son of God: The Origin of Christology and the History of Jewish-Hellenistic Religion* (Philadelphia: Fortress, 1976).

————, *The Atonement: The Origin of the Doctrine in the New Testament* (Philadelphia: Fortress; London: SCM, 1981).

———, "Hymnus und Christologie," in Wilfrid Haubeck and Michael Bachmann, eds., *Wort in der Zeit: Neutestamentliche Studien. Festgabe für Karl Heinrich Rengstorf zum 75. Geburtstag* (Leiden: Brill, 1980) 1–23 (ET = "Hymns and Christology," in idem, *Between Jesus and Paul: Studies in the Earliest History of Christianity* [Philadelphia: Fortress, 1983] 78–96).

———, "The Old Testament in the Fourth Gospel," *HBT* 12 (1990) 19–41.

———, "Psalm 110 und die Erhöhung des Auferstandenen zur Rechten Gottes," in Cilliers Breytenbach and Henning Paulsen, eds., *Anfänge der Christologie: Festschrift für Ferdinand Hahn zum 65. Geburtstag* (Göttingen: Vandenhoeck & Ruprecht, 1991) 43–73.

Hense, F., "Johannes Stobaios," *PW* 19/2 (1938) 2549–86.

Hilgenfeld, A., "Die alttestamentlichen Citate Justin's in ihrer Bedeutung für die Untersuchung über seine Evangelien," *Theologische Jahrbücher* 9 (1850).

Hills, Julian V., *Tradition and Composition in the Epistula Apostolorum* (HDR 24; Minneapolis: Fortress, 1990).

———, "Tradition, Redaction, and Intertextuality: Miracle Lists in Apocryphal Acts as a Test Case," in David J. Lull, ed., *SBLSP 1990*, 375–90.

———, "The Three 'Matthean' Aphorisms in the *Dialogue of the Savior* 53," *HTR* 84 (1991) 43–58.

Hirsch, Emanuel, *Geschichte der Neuern Evangelischen Theologie im Zusammenhang mit den allgemeinen Bewegungen des europäischen Denkens* (5 vols.; 3d ed.; Münster: Stenderhoff, 1984).

Hock, Ronald F., and Edward N. O'Neil, *The Chreia in Ancient Rhetoric. I. The Progymnasmata* (SBLTT 27; Graeco-Roman Religion Series 9; Atlanta: Scholars Press, 1986).

Hodgson, Robert, "The Testimony Hypothesis," *JBL* 98 (1979) 361–78.

———, "1 Thessolonians 4:1–12 and the Holiness Tradition," in Kent H. Richards, ed., *SBL 1982 Seminar Papers* (SBLSP 21; Chico, CA: Scholars Press, 1982) 199–215.

———, "Paul the Apostle and First Century Tribulation Lists," *ZNW* 74 (1983) 59–80.

———, "On the *Gattung* of Q: A Dialogue with James M. Robinson," *Bib* 66 (1985) 73–95.

———, "Valerius Maximus and Gospel Criticism," *CBQ* 51 (1988) 502–10.

———, "Valerius Maximus and the Social World of the New Testament," *CBQ* 51 (1989) 683–93.

Holtz, Traugott, *Untersuchungen über die alttestamentlichen Zitate bei Lukas* (TU 104; Berlin: Akademie, 1968).

Hommes, N.J., *Het Testamoniaboek: Studiën over OT Citaten in het NT en bij de Patres. Met Critische Beschouwingen over de Theorieën van J. Rendel Harris en D. Plooy* (Amsterdam: Noord-Hollandsche Uitgevers-Maatschappij, 1935).
Review
Kraemer, August, *Philologische Wochenschrift* 58 (1938) cols. 73–83.

Hooker, Morna Dorothy, *Jesus and the Servant: The Influence of the Servant Concept of Deutero-Isaiah in the New Testament* (London: SPCK, 1959).

Horsley, Richard A., "'Like One of the Prophets of Old': Two Types of Popular Prophets at the Time of Jesus," *CBQ* 47 (1985) 435–63.

———, "'Messianic' Figures and Movements in First-Century Palestine," in J.H. Charlesworth, ed., *Messiah*, 276–95.

Horst, P. W. van der, "Pseudo-Phocylides and the New Testament," *ZNW* 69 (1978) 187–202.

———, "Pseudo-Phocylides Revisited," *JSP* 3 (1988) 3–30.

———, "Pseudo-Phocylides," *ABD* 5. 348

Hunter, Archibald M., *Paul and his Predecessors* (rev. ed.; Philadelphia: Westminster, 1961).

Hvalvik, Reidar, *The Struggle for Scripture and Covenant: The Purpose of the Epistle of Barnabas and Jewish-Christian Competition in the Second Century* (WUNT 2/82; Tübingen: Mohr-Siebeck, 1996).

Jaeger, Werner, *Paideia: The Ideals of Greek Culture* (3 vols.; 2d ed.; New York: Oxford University Press, 1945).

Jeremias, Joachim, "λίθος," *TDNT* 4. 268–80.

Juel, Donald, *Messianic Exegesis: Christological Interpretation of the Old Testament in Early Christianity* (Philadelphia: Fortress, 1988).

———, ed., *Jesus the Christ: Historical Origins of Christological Doctrine* (Minneapolis: Fortress, 1991).

Kaiser, Otto, *Isaiah 1–12: A Commentary* (OTL 16; Philadelphia: Westminster, 1972).

Kaiser, Walter C. "The Promise to David in Psalm 16 and its Application in Acts 2:25–33 and 13:32–37," *JETS* 22 (1980) 219–229.

Kannengieser, Charles, "Le témoignage des *lettres festales* de Saint Athanase sur la date de l'Apologie *Contre les païens—Sur l'incarnation du Verbe*," *RSR* 52 (1964) 91–100; repr. in idem, *Arius and Athanasius: Two Alexandrian Theologians* (Hampshire: Variorum, 1991).

———, "Les citations bibliques du traité athanasien 'Sur l'incarnation du Verbe' et les testimonia," in A. Benoît and P. Prigent, *Bible*, 135–60.

Käsemann, Ernst, *The Wandering People of God: An Investigation of the Letter to the Hebrews* (Minneapolis: Augsburg, 1984; orig. pub., 2d ed.; Göttingen: Vandenhoeck & Ruprecht, 1957).

———, *An die Römer* (3d ed.; HNT 8a; Tübingen: Mohr-Siebeck, 1974).

Keck, Leander, "The Function of Romans 3:10–18: Observations and Suggestions," in Jacob Jervell and Wayne A. Meeks, eds., *God's Christ and his People: Studies in Honor of N.A. Dahl* (Oslo: Universitetsforlaget, 1977) 141–57.

Kelly, J.N.D., *Early Christian Creeds* (3d ed.; New York: Longman, 1972).

Kennedy, George A., *A New History of Classical Rhetoric* (Princeton, NJ: Princeton University Press, 1994).

Kim, Seyoon, "Jesus—The Son of God, the Stone, the Son of Man, and the Servant: The Role of Zechariah in the Self-Identification of Jesus," in Gerald F. Hawthorne and Otto Betz, eds., *Tradition and Interpretation in the New Testament: Essays in Honor of E. Earle Ellis for his 60th Birthday* (Grand Rapids: Eerdmans; Tübingen: Mohr-Siebeck, 1987) 134–48.

Kistemaker, Simon, *The Psalm Citations in the Epistle to the Hebrews* (Amsterdam: van Soest, 1961).

Kloppenborg, John S., *The Formation of Q: Trajectories in Ancient Wisdom Collections* (Studies in Antiquity and Christianity; Philadelphia: Fortress, 1987).

Koch, Dietrich-Alex, "Beobachtungen zum christologischen Schriftgebrauch in den vorpaulinischen Gemeinden," *ZNW* 71 (1980) 174–91.

———, *Die Schrift als Zeuge des Evangeliums: Untersuchungen zur Verwendung und zum Verständnis der Schrift bei Paulus* (BHT 69; Tübingen: Mohr-Siebeck, 1986).

Köhler, Wolf-Dietrich, *Die Rezeption des Matthäusevangeliums in der Zeit vor Irenäus* (WUNT 2/24; Tübingen: Mohr-Siebeck, 1987).

Köster, Helmut, *Synoptische Überlieferung bei den Apostolischen Vätern* (TU 65; Berlin: Akademie, 1957).

Kraemer, August, Review of N.T. Hommes, *Het Testimoniaboek*, *Philologische* 58 (1938) cols. 73–84.

Kraft, Robert A., "Barnabas' Isaiah Text and the 'Testimony Book' Hypothesis," *JBL* 79 (1960) 336–50.

———, "The Epistle of Barnabas: Its Quotations and their Sources" (Ph.D. diss., Harvard University, 1961).

———, "Barnabas' Isaiah Text and Melito's Paschal Homily," *JBL* 80 (1961) 371–73.

———, "A Note on the Oracle of Rebecca (Gen xxv.23)," *JTS* n.s. 13 (1962) 318–20.

————, Review of Pierre Prigent, *Les Testimonia dans le christianisme primitif*, *JBL* 81 (1962) 316–17.

————, "Christian Transmission of Greek Jewish Scriptures: A Methodological Probe," in A. Benoît, et al., *Paganisme*, 207–26.

————, "Towards Assessing the Latin Text of '5 Ezra': The 'Christian' Connection," *HTR* 79 (1986) 158–69.

Kretzmann, Paul Edward, *The Liturgical Element in the Earliest Forms of the Medieval Drama, with Special Reference to the English and German Plays* (Studies in Language and Literature, University of Minnesota 4; Minneapolis: Bulletin of the University of Minnesota, 1916).

Küchler, Max, *Frühjüdische Weisheitstraditionen: Zum Fortgang weisheitlichen Denkens im Bereich des frühjüdischen Jahweglaubens* (OBO 26; Freiburg: Universitätsverlag; Göttingen: Vandenhoeck & Ruprecht, 1979).

Kurz, William Stephen, "The Function of Christological Proof from Prophecy for Luke and Justin" (Ph.D. diss., Yale University, 1976).

Kutscher, E.Y., *The Language and Linguistic Background of the Isaiah Scroll (I Q Isa^a)* (STDJ 6; Leiden: Brill, 1974).

Lagrange, M.-J., Review of J. Rendel Harris, *Testimonies*, *RevB* 30 (1921) 612–14.

Lambrecht, Jan, "Paul's Christological Use of Scripture in 1 Cor. 15,20–28," *NTS* 28 (1982) 502–27; repr. in idem, *Pauline Studies* (BETL 115; Leuven: Leuven University Press, 1994) 125–49.

Lane, William R., "A New Commentary Structure in 4Q Florilegium," *JBL* 78 (1959) 343–46.

Levey, Samson H., *The Messiah: An Aramaic Interpretation. The Messianic Exegesis of the Targum* (HUCM 2; Cincinnati/New York: Hebrew Union College/Jewish Institute of Religion, 1974).

Liebers, Reinhold, *Wie Geschrieben Steht: Studien zu einer besonderen Art frühchristlichen Schriftbezuges* (Berlin/New York: de Gruyter, 1993).

Lietzmann, Hans, *An die Galater* (HNT 10; 4th ed.; Tübingen: Mohr-Siebeck, 1923).

Lindars, Barnabas, *New Testament Apologetic: The Doctrinal Significance of the Old Testament Quotations* (Philadelphia: Westminster, 1961).
 Review
 Sparks, H.F.D., *JTS* 13 (1962) 399–401.

————, "Second Thoughts IV: Books of Testimonies," *ExpTim* 75 (1963/64) 173–75.

————, "The Place of the OT in the Formation of New Testament Theology," *NTS* 23 (1976/77) 59–66.

Litke, Wayne Douglas, "Luke's Knowledge of the Septuagint: A Study of the Citations in Luke-Acts" (Ph.D. diss., McMaster University, 1993).

Llewelyn, S.R., ed., *New Documents Illustrating Early Christianity*, vol. 7 (The Ancient History Documentary Research Centre, North Ryde, New South Wales, Australia: Macquarie University, 1994).

Long, A.A., *Hellenistic Philosophy: Stoics, Epicureans, Sceptics* (New York: Scribner, 1974).

Longenecker, Richard, *Biblical Exegesis in the Apostolic Period* (Grand Rapids: Eerdmans, 1975).

Lübbe, John, "A Reinterpretation of 4Q Testimonia," *RevQ* 12 (1986) 187–97.

Lull, David J., ed. *SBL 1990 Seminar Papers* (SBLSP 29; Atlanta: Scholars Press, 1990).

Lupieri, Edmondo, *Il cielo è il mio trono. Is. 40,12 e 66,1 nella tradizione testimoniara* (Temi e testi 28; Rome: Edizioni di storia e letteraura, 1980).

————, "Novatien et les *Testimonia* d'Isaïe," in Elizabeth A. Livingstone, ed., *Studia Patristica*, vol. 17/2 (Oxford/New York: Pergamon, 1982) 803–7.

Luz, Ulrich, *Das Geschichtsverständnis des Paulus* (BEVT 49; Munich: Kaiser, 1968).

Mann, Jacob, *The Bible as Read and Preached in the Old Synagogue: A Study in the Cycles of the Readings from the Torah and the Prophets, and in the Structure of the Midrashic*

Homilies (2 vols.; Cincinnati, 1940; New York, 1966; repr. Library of Biblical Studies; New York: KTAV, 1971).

Manson, T.W., "The Argument from Prophecy," *JTS* n.s. 46 (1949) 129–36.

Marcovich, Miroslav, "Hippolytus and Heraclitus," in F.L. Cross, ed., *Studia Patristica*, vol. 7 (TU 92; Berlin: Akademie, 1966) 255–64.

Marcus, Joel, *The Way of the Lord: Christological Exegesis of the Old Testament in the Gospel of Mark* (Louisville, KY: Westminster/John Knox, 1992).

Marrou, Henri I., *A History of Education in Antiquity* (Wisconsin Studies in Classics; Madison: University of Wisconsin Press, 1982).

Massaux, Edouard, *The Influence of the Gospel of Matthew on Christian Literature before St. Irenaeus* (ed. Arthur J. Bellenzoni; 3 vols.; Macon, GA: Mercer University Press, 1990; orig. pub., Universitas Catholica Lovaniensis Dissertationes; Louvain: Universitaires de Louvain, 1950).

McCready, Wayne O., "A Second Torah at Qumran?" *SR* 14 (1985) 5–15.

McGuckin, Paul, "The Non-Cyprianic Scripture Texts in Lactantius' *Divine Institutes*," *VC* 36 (1982) 145–63.

McKane, William, *Proverbs: A New Approach* (Philadelphia: Westminster, 1970).

Mehat, André, Review of Pierre Prigent, *Les Testimonia dans le christianisme primitif*, *RHE* 58 (1963) 149–51.

———, "L'hypothèse des Testimonia à l'épreuve des stromates: remarques sur les citations de l'Ancien Testament chez Clément d'Alexandrie," in A. Benoît and P. Prigent, *Bible*, 229–42.

Menken, M.J.J., "Die Form des Zitates aus Jes 6:10 in Joh 12:40: Ein Beitrag zum Schriftgebrauch des vierten Evangelisten," *BZ* 32 (1988) 189–209.

———, "The Old Testament Quotation in John 19,36: Sources, Redaction, Background," in Frans van Segbroeck, ed., *The Four Gospels 1992: Festschrift Frans Neirynck* (3 vols.; BETL 100; Leuven: Leuven University Press/Peeters, 1992) 3. 2101–18.

———, "The Textual Form and the Meaning of the Quotation from Zech 12:10 in John 19:37," *CBQ* 55 (1993) 494–511.

Metzger, Bruce, "The Formulas Introducing Quotations of Scripture in the New Testament and the Mishna," *JBL* 70 (1951) 297–307.

Meyer, Ben F., *The Aims of Jesus* (London: SCM, 1979).

———, "The Pre-Pauline Formula in Rom 3:25–26a," *NTS* 29 (1983) 198–208.

Michaels, J. Ramsey, *1 Peter* (WBC 49; Waco, TX: Word, 1988).

Michel, Otto, *Paulus und seine Bibel* (BFCT 2/18; Gütersloh: Bertelsmann, 1929; repr. Darmstadt: Wissenschaftliche Buchgesellschaft, 1972).
Review
Bultmann, Rudolf, *TLZ* 58 (1933) col. 157.

———, "οἶκος," *TDNT* 5. 119–59.

Miller, Merrill P., "The Function of Isa 61:1–2 in 11Q Melchizedek," *JBL* 88 (1969) 467–69.

———, "Targum, Midrash, and the Use of the Old Testament in the New," *JSJ* 2 (1971) 29–82.

Milligan, George, *The New Testament Documents: Their Origin and Early History* (London: Macmillan, 1913).

Minde, Hans-Jurgen van der, *Schrift und Tradition bei Paulus: Ihr Bedeutung und Funktion im Römerbrief* (Paderborner Theologische Studien 3; Munich/Paderborn/Vienna: Schöning, 1976).

Moffatt, James, *An Introduction to the Literature of the New Testament* (International Theological Library; New York: Scribner, 1911).

Moloney, Francis J., "The Reinterpretation of Psalm VIII and the Son of Man Debate," *NTS* 27 (1981) 656–72.

Monat, Pierre, "Les *testimonia* bibliques de Cyprien à Lactance," in J. Fontaine and
C. Pietri, *Monde latin*, 499–507.

———, *Lactance et la Bible: Une propédeutique latine à la lecture de la Bible dans l'Occident constantinien* (2 vols.; Paris: Etudes Augustiniennes, 1982).

Morrow, F.J., "The Text of Isaiah at Qumran," (Ph.D. diss., Catholic University of America, 1973) [n.v.].

Moule, C.F.D., *The Birth of the New Testament* (3d ed.; San Francisco: Harper & Row, 1982).

Mueller, James R., *The Five Fragments of the Apocryphon of Ezekiel: A Critical Study* (JSPSup 5; Sheffield: Sheffield Academic Press, 1994).

Mulder, Martin Jan, *Mikra: Text, Translation, Reading and Interpretation of the Hebrew Bible in Ancient Judaism and Early Christianity* (CRINT 2/1; Assen/Maastricht: Van Gorcum; Philadelphia: Fortress, 1988).

Murray, Robert, *Symbols of Church and Kingdom: A Study in Early Syriac Tradition* (Cambridge: Cambridge University Press, 1975).

———, "Some Rhetorical Patterns in Early Syriac Literature," in Robert H. Fischer, ed., *A Tribute to Arthur Vööbus: Studies in Early Christian Literature and Its Environment, Primarily in the Syrian East* (Chicago: Lutheran School of Theology at Chicago, 1977) 109–31.

Nautin, Pierre, "C.r. de la conférence annuelle," in *Annuaire de l'EPHE*, Vᵉ sect., Sc. Rel. 1967/68 (Paris) 162–67 [n.v.].

Neill, Stephen, and Tom Wright, *The Interpretation of the New Testament: 1861–1986* (2d ed.; Oxford/New York: Oxford University Press, 1988).

Neusner, Jacob, *Aphrahat and Judaism: The Christian-Jewish Argument in Fourth-Century Iran* (SPB 19; Leiden: Brill, 1971).

———, *Midrash in Context: Exegesis in Formative Judaism* (The Foundations of Judaism: Method, Teleology, Doctrine, Part One: Method; Philadelphia: Fortress, 1983).

Neusner, Jacob, William Scott Green, and Ernest S. Frerichs, eds., *Judaisms and Their Messiahs* (Cambridge: Cambridge University Press, 1987).

Neyrey, Jerome H., "The Thematic Use of Isaiah 42, 1–4 in Matthew 12," *Bib* 63 (1982) 457–73.

Nickelsburg, George W.E., *Resurrection, Immortality, and Eternal Life in Intertestamental Judaism* (HTS 26; Cambridge, MA: Harvard University Press, 1972).

———, "The Bible Rewritten and Expanded," in Michael E. Stone, ed., *Jewish Writings of the Second Temple Period: Apocrypha, Pseudepigrapha, Qumran Sectarian Writings, Philo, Josephus* (CRINT 2/2; Assen: Van Gorcum; Philadelphia: Fortress, 1984) 89–156.

Niebuhr, Karl-Wilhelm, *Gesetz und Paränese: Katechismusartige Weisungsreihen in der frühjüdischen Literatur* (WUNT 2/28; Tübingen: Mohr-Siebeck, 1987).

Nilson, Jon, "To Whom is Justin's *Dialogue with Trypho* Addressed?" *TS* 38 (1977) 538–46.

Nock, Arthur Darby, "The Apocryphal Gospels," *JTS* n.s. 11 (1960) 63–70.

O'Neill, J.C., "The Lost Written Records of Jesus' Words and Deeds Behind Our Records," *JTS* n.s. 42 (1991) 483–504.

Olofsson, Staffan, *God is My Rock: A Study of Translation Technique and Theological Exegesis in the Septuagint* (ConB OT Ser. 31; Stockholm: Almqvist & Wiksell, 1990).

Osborn, Eric Francis, *Justin Martyr* (BHT 47; Tübingen: Mohr-Siebeck, 1973).

Perrin, Norman. "Mark xiv 62: The End Product of a Christian Pesher Tradition?" *NTS* 13 (1965–66) 150–55.

———, *Rediscovering the Teachings of Jesus* (New York/Evanston: Harper & Row; London: SCM, 1967).

Perrot, Charles, "The Reading of the Bible in the Ancient Synagogue," in M.J. Mulder, ed., *Mikra*, 137–59.

Peters, Melvin K.H., "Septuagint," *ABD* 5. 1093–1104.

Plooij [Plooy], Daniel, *Studies in the Testimony Book* (Verhandelingen der Koninklijke Akademie van Wetenschappen te Amsterdam, Literature Sect. 32/2; Amsterdam: Noord-Hollandsche Uitgevers-Maatschappij, 1932).

Porton, Gary G., "Midrash: Palestinian Jews and the Hebrew Bible in the Greco-Roman Period," *ANRW* 2.19.2. 103–38.

Prigent, Pierre, "Quelques testimonia messianiques: leur histoire littéraire de Qoumrân aux Pères de l'église," *TZ* 15 (1959) 419–30.

——, *Les Testimonia dans le christianisme primitif: L'Epître de Barnabé 1–16 et ses sources* (EBib, Paris: Gabalda, 1961).

Reviews

Kraft, Robert A., *JBL* 81 (1962) 316–17.

Stegemann, H., *ZKG* 73 (1962) 142–53.

Méhat, André, *RHE* 58 (1963) 149–51.

——, "Les récits évangeléliques de la Passion et l'utilisation des 'Testimonia,'" *RHR* 161 (1962) 130–32.

——, *Justin et l'Ancien Testament: L'Argumentation scriptuaire du traité de Justin contre toutes les hérésies comme source principale du dialogue avec Tryphon et de la première apologie* (Paris: Gabalda, 1964).

Quasten, Johannes, *Patrology* (3 vols.; Westminster, MD: Newman; Utrecht/Antwerp: Spectrum, 1950–60).

Reijners, G.Q., *The Terminology of the Holy Cross in Early Christian Literature as Based upon Old Testament Typology* (Graecitas Christianorum Primaeva Fascicle 2; Nijmegen: Dekker & Van de Vegt, 1965).

Rese, Martin, *Alttestamentliche Motive in der Christologie des Lukas* (SNT 1, Gütersloh: Mohn, 1969).

Roberts, Colin H., "Books in the Graeco-Roman World and in the Old Testament," in P.R. Ackroyd and C.F. Evans, eds., *The Cambridge History of the Bible*, vol. 1: *From the Beginnings to Jerome* (Cambridge/New York: Cambridge University Press, 1970).

Robinson, James M., "LOGOI SOPHON: On the Gattung of Q" in idem and Helmut Koester, eds., *Trajectories through Early Christianity* (Philadelphia: Fortress, 1971) 71–113.

Rosenbloom, Joseph R., *The Dead Sea Isaiah Scroll: A Literary Analysis. A Comparison with the Masoretic Text and the Biblia Hebraica* (Grand Rapids: Eerdmans, 1970).

Rothfuchs, Wilhelm, *Die Erfüllungszitate des Matthäus-Evangeliums* (BWANT 8; Stuttgart: Kohlhammer, 1969).

Ruether, Rosemary Radford, "The *Adversus Judaeos* Tradition in the Church Fathers: The Exegesis of Christian Anti-Judaism," in Paul E. Szarmcah, ed., *Aspects of Jewish Culture in the Middle Ages* (Albany: State University of New York Press, 1979) 27–50; repr. in Jeremy Cohen, ed., *Essential Papers on Judaism and Christianity in Conflict: From Late Antiquity to the Reformation* (New York/London: New York University Press, 1990) 174–89.

Sanday, William, *The Gospels in the Second Century: An Examination of the Critical Part of a Work Entitled "Supernatural Religion"* (London: Macmillan, 1876).

Sanday, William, and Arthur C. Headlam, *A Critical and Exegetical Commentary on the Epistle to the Romans* (ICC; Edinburgh: T & T Clark, 1895).

Sanders, E.P., *Jesus and Judaism* (Philadelphia: Fortress, 1985).

——, *The Historical Figure of Jesus* (London: Penguin, 1993).

Sanders, James A., "Cave 11 Surprises and the Question of Canon," in D.N. Freedman and J.C. Greenfield, eds., *New Directions in Biblical Archaeology* (Garden City, NY: Doubleday, 1969) 101–16.

——, "The Qumran Psalms Scroll (11QPs^a) Reviewed," in M. Black and W. Smalley, eds., *On Language, Culture, and Religion: In Honor of Eugene A. Nida* (Approaches to Semiotics 56; The Hague/Paris: Mouton, 1974) 79–99.

Sanders, Jack T., *Ben Sira and Demotic Wisdom* (SBLMS 28; Chico, CA: Scholars, 1983).

Saxer, Victor, "La Bible chez les Pères latins du IIIe siècle," in J. Fontaine and C. Pietri, *Monde latin*, 339–69.

Schelke, K.H., "Cento," *RAC* 2 (19) cols. 972–73.

Schuchard, Bruce G., *Scripture within Scripture: The Interrelationship of Form and Function in the Explicit Old Testament Citations in the Gospel of John* (SBLDS 133, Atlanta: Scholars, 1992).

Schürer, Emil; rev. eds.: Geza Vermes, Fergus Millar, Matthew Black, Martin Goodman, *The History of the Jewish People in the Age of Jesus Christ (175 B.C.–A.D. 135)* (3 vols.; Edinburgh: T & T Clark, 1973).

Scopello, Maddalena, "Les testimonia dans le traite de l'exégèse de l'âme (Nag Hammadi, II, 6)," *RHR* 191 (1977) 159–71.

Seeligmann, Isac Leo, *The Septuagint Version of Isaiah: A Discussion of its Problems* (Leiden: Brill, 1948).

Segal, Alan F., *Two Powers in Heaven: Early Rabbinic Reports about Christianity and Gnosticism* (SJLA 25; Leiden: Brill, 1977).

Sellew, Philip, "Oral and Written Sources in Mark 4.1–34," *NTS* 36 (1990) 234–67.

Selwyn, Edward Carus, *The Oracles of the New Testament* (London/New York: Hodder & Stoughton, 1912).

Selwyn, Edward Gordon, *The First Epistle of St. Peter: The Greek Text with Introduction, Notes and Essays* (2d ed.; London: Macmillan, 1947).

Sibinga, Joost Smit, *The Old Testament Text of Justin Martyr I: The Pentateuch* (Leiden: Brill, 1963).

Simon, Marcel, *Verus Israel: A Study of the Relations between Christians and Jews in the Roman Empire (135–425)* (Littman Library of Jewish Civilization; Oxford: Oxford University Press, 1986; orig. pub. Bibliotheque des Ecoles francaises d'Athenes et de Rome; Paris: Boccard, 1948).

Skarsaune, Oskar, *The Proof from Prophecy. A Study in Justin Martyr's Proof-Text Tradition: Text-Type, Provenance, Theological Profile* (NovTSup 56; Leiden: Brill, 1987).
Review
Grant, Robert M., *CH* 57 (1988) 216.

Skehan, Patrick W., "The Period of the Biblical Texts from Khirbet Qumran," *CBQ* 19 (1957) 435–40.

———, "Qumran and Old Testament Criticism," in M. Delcor, ed., *Qumrân: sa piété, sa théologie et son milieu* (BETL 46; Louvain: Duculot, 1978) 163–82.

Smith, D. Moody, "The Use of the Old Testament in the New," in James M. Efird, ed., *The Use of the Old Testament in the New and Other Essays in Honor of William Franklin Stinespring* (Durham, NC: Duke University Press, 1972) 3–65.

———, "The Setting and Shape of a Johannine Narrative Source," *JBL* 95 (1976) 231–41.

Snodgrass, Klyne, *The Parable of the Wicked Tenants* (WUNT 27; Tübingen: Mohr-Siebeck, 1983).

Sparks, H.F.D., Review of Barnabas Lindars, *New Testament Apologetic*, *JTS* n.s. 13 (1962) 399–401.

Stanley, Christopher D., *Paul and the Language of Scripture: Citation Technique in the Pauline Epistles and Contemporary Literature* (SNTSMS 69; Cambridge: Cambridge University Press, 1990).

———, "The Importance of 4QTanhumim (4Q176)," *RevQ* 15 (1992) 569–82.

———, "The Redeemer Will Come ἐκ Σιων: Rom 11.26–7 Revisited," in C.A. Evans and J.A. Sanders, eds., *Paul and the Scriptures*, 118–42.

Stanton, Graham N., "5 Ezra and Matthean Christianity in the Second Century," *JTS* n.s. 28 (1977) 67–83.

Stanton, Vincent Henry, *The Gospels as Historical Documents* (3 vols.; Cambridge: Cambridge University Press, 1906–20).

Starratt, Alfred Byron, "The Use of the Septuagint in the Five Books against Heresies by Irenaeus of Lyons" (Ph.D. diss., Harvard University, 1952).

Stather Hunt, B.P.W., *Primitive Gospel Sources* (New York: Philosophical Library, 1951).

Stegemann, H., Review of Pierre Prigent, *Les Testimonia dans le christianisme primitif*, *ZKG* 73 (1962) 142–53.

Stegner, William Richard, *Narrative Theology in Early Jewish Christianity* (Louisville, KY: Westminster/John Knox, 1989).

Stemmer, Peter, ed., *Hermann Samuel Reimarus, Vindicatio dictorum Veteris Testamenti in Novo allegatorum 1731: Text der Pars I und Conspectus der Pars II* (Göttingen: Vandenhoeck & Ruprecht, 1983).

Stendahl, Krister, *The School of St. Matthew and its Use of the Old Testament* (2d ed., Philadelphia: Fortress, 1968).

Steudel, Annette, *Der Midrasch zur Eschatologie aus der Qumrangemeinde (4QMidrEschat^{a,b}): Materielle Rekonstruktion, Textbestand, Gattung und traditionsgeschichtliche Einordnung des durch 4Q174 ("Florilegium") und 4Q177 ("Catena A") repräsentierten Werkes aus den Qumranfunden* (STDJ 13; Leiden/New York/Cologne: Brill, 1994).
Review
Collins, John J., *JBL* 114 (1995) 314–16.

Stockhausen, Carol Kern, *Moses' Veil and the Glory of the New Covenant: The Exegetical Substructure of 2 Cor 3:1–4:6* (AnBib 116; Rome: Pontifical Biblical Institute, 1989).

Strecker, Georg, *Der Weg der Gerechtigkeit: Untersuchung zur Theologie des Matthäus* (FRLANT 82; 3d ed.; Göttingen: Vandenhoeck und Ruprecht, 1971).

Sundberg, Albert C., "On Testimonies," *NovT* 3 (1959) 268–81.

Swete, Henry Barclay, *The Apocalypse of St. John: The Greek Text with Introduction, Notes, and Indices* (3d ed., London: Macmillan, 1911; repr. Grand Rapids: Eerdmans, 1951).

———, *An Introduction to the Old Testament in Greek* (2d ed.; rev. Richard R. Ottley; New York: Cambridge: Cambridge University Press, 1914); repr. New York: KTAV, 1968.

Tate, Marvin E., *Psalms 51–100* (WBC 20; Dallas: Word, 1990).

Thackeray, Henry St. John, *The Relation of St. Paul to Contemporary Jewish Thought: An Essay to which was awarded the Kaye Prize for 1899* (London: Macmillan, 1900).

Theissen, Gerd, *Untersuchungen zum Hebräerbrief* (SNT 2; Gütersloh: Mohn, 1969).

Thurston, Robert W., "Midrash and 'Magnet' Words in the New Testament," *EvQ* 51 (1979) 22–39.

———, "Philo and the Epistle to the Hebrews," *EvQ* 58 (1986) 133–43.

Tobin, Thomas H., *The Creation of Man: Philo and the History of Interpretation* (CBQMS 14; Washington, D.C.: Catholic Biblical Association of America, 1983).

Tov, Emanuel, *Textual Criticism of the Hebrew Bible* (Minneapolis: Fortress; Assen/Maastricht: Van Gorcum, 1992).

Treves, Marco, "On the Meaning of the Qumran Testimonia," *RevQ* (1960) 569–71.

Ungern-Sternberg, Arthur Freiherr von, *Der traditionelle alttestamentliche Schriftbeweis "de Christo" und "de Evangelio" in der alten Kirche bis zur Zeit Eusebs von Caesare* (Halle a. S.: Niemeyer, 1913).

Vermes, Geza, *Scripture and Tradition in Judaism: Haggadic Studies* (SPB 4; Leiden: Brill, 1961).

———, *Post-Biblical Jewish Studies* (SJLA 8; Leiden: Brill, 1975).

Vielhauer, Philipp, "Ein Weg zur neutestamentlichen Christologie? Prüfung der Thesen Ferdinand Hahns," *EvT* 25 (1965) 24–72; repr. in idem, *Aufsätze zum Neuen Testament* (TBü 31; Munich: Kaiser, 1965) 141–98.

————, "Paulus und das alte Testament," in L. Abramowski and J.F.G. Goeters, eds., *Studien zur Geschichte und Theologie der Reformation: Festschrift für E. Bizer* (1969) 33–62; repr. in P. Vielhauer, *Oikodome*, 196–228.

————, "Oikodome: Das Bild vom Bau in der christlichen Literatur vom Neuen Testament bis Clemens Alexandrinus," in idem, *Oikodome*, 1–168.

————, *Oikodome: Aufsätze zum Neuen Testament*, vol. 2 (TBü 65; Munich: Kaiser, 1979).

Vollmer, Hans Arthur, *Die alttestamentlichen Citate bei Paulus, textkritisch und biblisch-theologisch gewürdigt nebst einem Anhang über das Verhältnis des Apostles zu Philo* (Freiburg/Leipzig: Mohr-Siebeck, 1895).

Waard, Jan de, *A Comparative Study of the Old Testament in the Dead Sea Scrolls and in the New Testament* (STDJ 4; Leiden: Brill, 1965).

Wansbrough, Henry, ed., *Jesus and the Oral Gospel Tradition* (JSNTSup 64; Sheffield: JSOT, 1991).

Weinfeld, Moshe, "Grace After Meals in Qumran," *JBL* 111 (1992) 427–40.

Weizsäcker, Carl, *Das apostolische Zeitalter der christlichen Kirche* (Freiburg i. B.: Mohr-Siebeck, 1896).

Wengst, Klaus, *Tradition und Theologie des Barnabasbriefes* (Arbeiten zur Kirchengeschichte 42; Berlin/New York: de Gruyter, 1971).

Wenham, David, *The Rediscovery of Jesus' Eschatological Discourse* (Gospel Perspectives 4; Sheffield: JSOT, 1984).

Westcott, Brooke Foss, *The Epistle to the Hebrews: The Greek Text with Notes and Essays* (2d ed.; London/New York: Macmillan, 1892; repr. Grand Rapids: Eerdmans, 1955).

White, Sidnie Ann, "4QDt^n: Biblical Manuscript or Excerpted Text?" in Harold W. Attridge, John J. Collins, and Thomas H. Tobin, eds., *Of Scribes and Scrolls: Studies on the Hebrew Bible, Intertestamental Judaism, and Christian Origins Presented to John Strugnell* (College Theology Society Resources in Religion 5; Lanham, MD/New York/London: University Press of America, 1990) 13–20.

Wilckens, Ulrich, *Der Brief an die Römer (Röm 6–11)* (EKKNT 6/2; Zürich/Einsiedeln/Cologne: Benziger; Neukirchen-Vluyn: Neukirchener, 1980).

Wilcox, Max E., *The Semiticisms of Acts* (Oxford: Clarendon, 1965).

Wilken, Robert L., "The Homeric Cento in Irenaeus, 'Adversus Haereses,' I, 9, 4," *VC* 21 (1967) 25–33.

Williams, A. Lukyn, *Adversus Judaeos: A Bird's Eye View of Christian Apologiae until the Renaissance* (London: Cambridge University Press, 1935).

Wills, Lawrence, "The Form of the Sermon in Hellenistic Judaism and Early Christianity," *HTR* 77 (1984) 277–99.

Wilson, Gerald Henry, *The Editing of the Hebrew Psalter* (SBLDS 76; Chico, CA: Scholars Press, 1984).

Wilson, Robert McL., "Old Testament Exegesis in the Gnostic Exegesis on the Soul," in Martin Krause, ed., *Essays on the Nag Hammadi Texts in Honour of Pahor Labib* (NHS 6; Leiden: Brill, 1975) 217–24.

Wood, H.G., ed., *Amicitiae Corolla: A Volume of Essays Presented to James Rendel Harris D. Litt., on the Occasion of his Eightieth Birthday* (London: University of London Press, 1933).

Wrede, William, *Untersuchungen zum ersten Klemensbriefe* (Göttingen: Vandenhoeck & Ruprecht, 1891).

Wright, Addison G., *The Literary Genre Midrash* (Staten Island, NY: Alba, 1967).

Wright, C. Ernest, *Biblical Archaeology* (rev. ed.; Philadelphia: Westminster; London: Duckworth, 1962).

Wright, N.T., *Christian Origins and the Question of God*, vol. 2: *Jesus and the Victory of God* (Minneapolis: Fortress, 1996).

Wright, R.B., "Introduction" to Psalms of Solomon, in Charlesworth, ed., *Old Testament Pseudepigrapha* 2. 640–41.

Würthwein, Ernst, *The Text of the Old Testament: An Introduction to the Biblia Hebraica* (2d ed.; Grand Rapids: Eerdmans, 1995).

Zeegers-Vander Vorst, Nicole, *Les Citations des Poètes grecs chez les apologistes chrétiens du IIe siècle* (Université de Louvain Recueil de Travaux d'Histoire et de Philologie 4/47; Louvain: Universitaires de Louvain, 1972).

INDICES

Note: Italicized page references signify more detailed treatments.

I. *Index of Modern Authors*

II. *Index of Biblical and Other Ancient Sources*

Divisions:
A. Old Testament
B. New Testament
C. Deuterocanonical References (Apocrypha)
D. Jewish Pseudepigrapha
E. Dead Sea Scrolls, Philo, Josephus, and Rabbinic References
F. Apostolic Fathers
G. Other Early Christian and Gnostic References
H. Greco-Roman References

A. *Old Testament*

Note: OT references follow English translations of the MT; specific LXX references in the text are given in parentheses.

B. *New Testament*

C. *Deuterocanonical References (Apocrypha)*

D. *Jewish Pseudepigrapha*

E. *Dead Sea Scrolls, Philo, Josephus, and Rabbinic References*

H. *Greco-Roman References*

DATE DUE

JUL 12 '00			
		Printed in USA	